# READING ENHANCEMENT AND DEVELOPMENT

·R·E·A·D·

Third Edition

# READING ENHANCEMENT AND DEVELOPMENT

Rhonda Holt Atkinson
Louisiana State University

Debbie Guice Longman
Louisiana State University

**West Publishing Company**
ST. PAUL • NEW YORK • LOS ANGELES • SAN FRANCISCO

| | |
|---|---|
| *Copyediting:* | Mary Byers |
| *Cartoons:* | Richard Longman |
| *Composition:* | Carlisle Communications |
| *Cover Photograph:* | Jim Zietz |
| *Design:* | Paula Schlosser |
| *Index:* | Cindy Dolan |
| *Biographer:* | Jacques Servin |


50 W. Kellogg Boulevard
P.O. Box 64526
St. Paul, MN 55164-1003



Printed in the United States of America

97 96 95 94 93 92 91 90 8 7 6 5 4 3 2 1 0

Library of Congress Cataloging-in-Publication Data

Atkinson, Rhonda Holt.
Reading enhancement and development (READ) / Rhonda Holt Atkinson. Debbie Guice Longman. — 3rd ed.
p. cm.
Rev. ed. of: Reading enhancement and development. 2nd ed. c1988.
Includes bibliographical references.
ISBN 0–314–66785–7
1. Reading (Higher education) 2. Developmental reading. 3. Study, Method of. I. Longman, Debbie Guice. II. Atkinson, Rhonda Holt. Reading enhancement and development. III. Title.
LB2395.3.A85 1990
428.4'07'11—dc20 89–70621
CIP

*To our parents,*
*Edward and Yvonne Holt*
*and*
*Friley and Lillian Guice;*
*to our husbands,*
*Tom Atkinson and Richard Longman;*
*and*
*to our children,*
*Rachel Anne Atkinson and Jacob Guice Longman.*

# CONTENTS

**PREFACE** xv

**1 SQ3R** 2

**SURVEY: LINKING FRAMEWORKS AND TEXTBOOKS** 4
- **Defining Frameworks and Networks** 5
  - ***Using Frameworks to Make Text Predictions*** 7
  - ***Importance of Activating Frameworks While Surveying*** 8
- **Developing Frameworks and Networks** 9
- **Surveying Textbooks** 11
  - ***Organizing Through Outlining*** 11
  - ***Organizing Through Mapping*** 14
  - ***Developing Outlines and Maps with READ*** 14
- **Surveying Supplementary Materials** 15

**THE QUESTIONING STAGE: SETTING GOALS FOR READING** 15

**READ: MARKING AND LABELING TEXT FOR UNDERSTANDING** 26
- **Text Marking: Importance** 26
- **Text Marking: Amount** 27
- **Text Labeling** 27

**RECITE: SUMMARIZING AND CHECKING YOUR UNDERSTANDING** 33
- **Recitation Through Summarization** 34
  - ***The Need for Summarization*** 34
  - ***Constructing a Summary*** 34
- **Checking Your Understanding** 38

**REVIEW: PERMANENCE THROUGH PRACTICE** 39
- **Spaced Study** 39
- **Cramming** 40
- **Study Groups or Partners** 40
- **Overlearning** 41

**CHAPTER SUMMARY** 59
**CHAPTER REVIEW** 59
**REFERENCES** 61

## LISTENING AND NOTETAKING 62

**LISTENING: NOT AS EASY AS IT LOOKS** 64
- **Before the Lecture** 65
  - ***Organization Through Schedule Planning*** 65
  - ***Mental and Physical Preparedness*** 67
- **During the Lecture** 68
  - ***Lack of Attention*** 68
  - ***Inability to Find Main Ideas*** 69
  - ***Inability to Recognize Important Information*** 73
- **After the Lecture** 74

**NOTETAKING: BREAKING BAXTER'S COROLLARY** 75
- **Notetaking: The Act in Active Listening** 75
- **Personalizing Your Notes** 76
- **Lecture Formats** 85
  - ***Text-dependent Lectures*** 85
  - ***Text-independent Lectures*** 86
- **Passive Methods of Notetaking** 86

**IF IT CAN GO WRONG, IT WILL: COMPENSATING FOR INEFFECTIVE LECTURERS** 87
**CHAPTER SUMMARY EXERCISE** 87
**CHAPTER REVIEW** 89
**REFERENCES** 91

## BUILDING GENERAL VOCABULARY 92

**STAGES OF VOCABULARY DEVELOPMENT** 95
**CHAIN OF COMMUNICATION: KINDS OF VOCABULARY** 96
- **Acquiring Vocabulary** 97
  - ***Listening Vocabulary*** 97
  - ***Reading Vocabulary*** 98
- **Remembering New Words** 99
  - ***Vocabulary Techniques*** 100
  - ***Connotation and Denotation*** 101

**HOW WORDS COME TO LIFE: ETYMOLOGY** 105
- **Incoporating Foreign Words** 106
- **Contemporary Additions to Vocabulary** 107
  - ***Words from Technology*** 107
  - ***Words from Products*** 108
  - ***Words from People's Names*** 108
  - ***Words from Letters*** 110
- **Word Histories** 112

WORD APPLICATIONS 114
Common Word Relationships 115
Other Word Relationships 120
Analogies 122
*Definition of Analogy* 122
*Forms of Analogies* 122
*Solving Analogies* 123
CHAPTER SUMMARY EXERCISE 126
CHAPTER REVIEW 127
VOCABULARY ENHANCEMENT EXERCISE 130
REFERENCES 131

4 USING THE CONTEXT 132

USING THE CONTEXT TO IDENTIFY PART OF SPEECH 135
USING TEXT-BASED CONTEXT CLUES 140
Punctuation Text-Based Clues 141
Definition Text-Based Clues 141
Contrast Text-Based Clues 142
Comparison Text-Based Clues 143
Example Text-Based Clues 144
FRAMEWORK-BASED CONTEXT CLUES 148
SPECIALIZED CONTEXTS FOR COLLEGE STUDY 153
CHAPTER SUMMARY EXERCISE 157
CHAPTER REVIEW 158
VOCABULARY ENHANCEMENT EXERCISE 160

5 ANALYZING THROUGH STRUCTURE 162

STRUCTURAL ANALYSIS 165
IDENTIFYING PREFIXES, SUFFIXES, AND ROOTS 166
ASSOCIATING WORD PARTS FOR MEANING 173
LIMITATIONS OF STRUCTURAL ANALYSIS 178
CHAPTER SUMMARY EXERCISE 182
CHAPTER REVIEW 182
VOCABULARY ENHANCEMENT EXERCISE 184

6 FINDING MAIN IDEAS 186

STATED MAIN IDEAS 192
Finding Stated Main Ideas in Paragraphs 192
Locating Topic Sentences 193
Finding Stated Main Ideas in Passages 195

ORGANIZATION IN PARAGRAPHS AND PASSAGES 198
Organizational Patterns 199
*Subject Development* 200
*Enumeratin/Sequence* 200
*Comparison/Contrast* 202
*Cause-Effect* 202
Signal Words That Indicate Text Structure 204
IMPLIED MAIN IDEAS 205
Finding Implied Main Ideas in Paragraphs 206
Finding Implied Main Ideas in Passages 215
SYNTHESIS: MAKING MAIN IDEAS YOUR OWN 217
CHAPTER SUMMARY EXERCISE 234
CHAPTER REVIEW 234
VOCABULARY ENHANCEMENT EXERCISE 236

7 READING CRITICALLY AND DRAWING CONCLUSIONS 238

RIGHTS AND RESPONSIBILITIES OF CRITICAL READERS 241
DIFFERENTIATING BETWEEN FACT AND OPINION 242
Facts: The Truth and Nothing but the Truth 242
Opinions: Quantitative Words 244
Expert Opinion 246
RECOGNIZING PROPAGANDA 248
Image Advertising 248
Bandwagoning 250
Testimonial 250
Plain Folks 251
Name Calling 251
Weasel Words 251
DETERMINING RELEVANCY 252
PURPOSES OR PASSAGES AND AUTHORS' CHOICE OF WORDS 259
Informational Passages 260
Persuasive Passages 260
DRAWING CONCLUSIONS 263
Using Background Knowledge to Make Inferences 264
Making Valid Inferences 268
CHAPTER SUMMARY EXERCISE 282
CHAPTER REVIEW 283
VOCABULARY ENHANCEMENT EXERCISE 285
REFERENCES 286

8 SPEAKING FIGURATIVELY 288

IDENTIFYING IDIOMS 292
RECOGNIZING SIMILES AND METAPHORS 294

**IDENTIFYING SYMBOLS** 301
**GRASPING ALLUSIONS** 305
**RECOGNIZING IRONY** 310
**RECOGNIZING PERSONIFICATION** 318
**DEFINING EUPHEMISM** 323
**CHAPTER SUMMARY EXERCISE** 332
**CHAPTER REVIEW** 333
**VOCABULARY ENHANCEMENT EXERCISE** 336

## 9 READING GRAPHS AND MAPS 338

**THE NEED FOR GRAPHICS** 341
**UNDERSTANDING TABLES** 342
**EXAMINING GRAPHS** 344
- **Bar Graphs** 344
- **Line Graphs** 345
- **Symbol Graphs** 346
- **Circle Graphs** 347

**FOLLOWING FLOWCHARTS** 348
**USING TIMELINES** 349
**READING MAPS** 365
- **Characteristics of Maps** 366
  - ***Features*** 367
  - ***Language*** 367
- **Types of Maps** 368
  - ***Political Maps*** 368
  - ***Physical Maps*** 369
  - ***Special-Purpose Maps*** 369
  - ***Reading Maps*** 371

**CHAPTER SUMMARY EXERCISE** 392
**CHAPTER REVIEW** 393
**VOCABULARY ENHANCEMENT EXERCISE** 395

## 10 READING MATH AND LOGIC WORD PROBLEMS 396

**THE RELATIONSHIP BETWEEN READING AND MATHEMATICS** 399
- **Reading Math Critically** 400
  - ***Drawing Conclusions*** 400
  - ***Determining Direction*** 401
  - ***Marking Relevant Information*** 401
  - ***Varying Rate While Reading*** 401
- **Specialized Language in Mathematics** 402
  - ***Specialized and Technical Vocabulary In Math*** 402
  - ***Using the Context*** 403
  - ***Identifying Mathematical Symbols*** 403

**Thinking About Math Problems** 408
**Steps for Solving Math Problems** 408
**THINKING LOGICALLY** 416
**THE RELATIONSHIP BETWEEN READING AND LOGIC** 417
**Kinds of Logic** 417
***Deductive Logic*** 417
***Inductive Logic*** 420
**That's Illogical: Common Fallacies at Work** 425
***Formal Fallacies*** 425
***Informal Fallacies*** 425
**Steps in Solving Logic Problems** 429
**CHAPTER SUMMARY EXERCISE** 437
**CHAPTER REVIEW** 438
**VOCABULARY ENHANCEMENT EXERCISE** 440
**REFERENCES** 441

**11 ADJUSTING RATE TO PURPOSE: SKIMMING, SCANNING, AND RECREATIONAL READING** 442

**FLEXIBILITY IN READING** 445
**INEFFECTIVE READING HABITS** 448
**Lip Movement and Finger-Pointing** 448
**Lack of Rate Flexibility** 449
**Inefficient Eye Movements** 449
**Disorganization of Information** 450
**VARYING RATE: SKIMMING AND SCANNING** 454
**Skimming: Reading for Main Ideas** 454
***Skimming as a Survey*** 455
***Skimming Text Chapters*** 455
***Skimming Supplementals*** 456
***Steps in Skimming*** 456
**Scanning: Reading for Specific Answers** 464
**RECREATIONAL READING** 469
**Using Recreational Reading to Increase Reading Speed** 470
**Browsing** 470
***Previewing: Personal Predictions*** 470
***Previewing: Text Features*** 473
**CHAPTER SUMMARY EXERCISE** 476
**CHAPTER REVIEW** 477
**VOCABULARY ENHANCEMENT EXERCISE** 479

## 12 TEST TAKING: SAILING THE SEAS OF EXAM PREPARATION 482

**TEST ANXIETY: SEASICKNESS AT ITS WORST** 485
- **Coping with Test Anxiety** 487
  - ***Caring for your Mental and Physical Health*** 487
  - ***Managing Test Anxiety*** 487
- **Making Test Anxiety Work for You** 488

**GETTING SHIPSHAPE: ORGANIZING FOR STUDY** 489
- **Prime Study Time** 489
- **Your Study Environment** 490
- **Getting Organized** 491
- **Memory Techniques** 492
  - ***Mental and Physical Imagery*** 492
  - ***Acronyms and Acrostics*** 493
  - ***Location*** 493
  - ***Word Games*** 494

**WALKING THE PLANK: EXAM TIME** 498
- **Types of Tests** 498
- **Predicting Text Questions** 499
- **Taking Objective Tests** 501
- **Taking Subjective Tests** 505
- **Taking Final Exams** 508
- **Examining Returned Exams** 509
- **Taking Standardized Reading Tests** 511

**CHAPTER SUMMARY EXERCISE** 512

**CHAPTER REVIEW** 513

**VOCABULARY ENHANCEMENT EXERCISE** 515

**REFERENCES** 516

## BIOGRAPHY A-1

## GLOSSARY A-9

## INDEX A-23

# PREFACE

In 1985, we published the first edition of *Reading Enhancement and Development (READ)* to meet the reading needs of post-secondary developmental students. With that goal in mind, we sought to accomplish five objectives: (1) to provide information in a context suitable for post-secondary developmental readers, (2) to explain the mental processes involved in reading, (3) to help post-secondary developmental students become more active readers, (4) to incorporate recent theories and research into post-secondary developmental reading instruction, and (5) to emphasize recreational as well as academic reading at the post-secondary level. While we felt *READ 1E* met these objectives, we realized revisions were needed to meet the changing needs of the students for whom it was written.

The second edition of *READ* in 1988 reflected comments from users and reviewers of the text. These remarks elicited such changes as (1) condensing the text to twelve chapters, (2) adding more content-oriented examples and exercises, (3) revising the math, conclusions, and figurative language chapters to include varied and more difficult exercises, and (4) providing new vocabulary and chapter review exercises.

This third edition of *READ* also represents the wishes of reviewers and users of the text. In an attempt to meet their specifications, we first reorganized the content of the text. While *READ* contains all of its original subject matter, the topics may now reside in different chapters. In addition, several subjects (e.g., text marking and labeling in SQ3R, allusions in figurative language, memory in test-taking) have been introduced. Others have been greatly expanded. For example, new to this edition are single chapters on SQ3R and listening and notetaking. A fourth revision involves the front matter of each chapter. Concerned with meeting the learning styles of all students, we have added concept mapping as a preview strategy to our traditional outlining instruction. We have also increased our emphasis on general vocabulary development by including pre-chapter as well as post-chapter vocabulary exercises. A fifth alteration is the addition of a biographical index of people quoted in the text. It is our hope that, spurred by what a man or woman has to say, students will use this reference to increase their background knowledge and, in so doing, their abilities to learn. Finally, we have continued to emphasize the need to become an academic reader as well as a recreational one. The text now contains two complete content chapters, a myriad of excerpts from textbooks, two short stories, numerous poems, and several newspaper articles. It is our hope that *READ* encourages students to become life-time readers.

A newly-revised teachers' manual accompanies this text as does a computer program. The disk includes the following five programs: (1) HIGHLITE (indicating the importance of previewing and background knowledge), (2) TESTER (reinforcing test-taking strategies), (3) SCANNER (providing realistic practice in varying reading speed), (4) ANALOGY (extending practice of complex word relationships, and (5) HANGMAN (providing practice in determining the meanings of new words, using the context, and deriving meaning through structural analysis).

While *READ* is designed for use in a post-secondary reading course, it can also serve as the principle text for a study skills course or as a resource for English classes or learning assistance centers. It may also be used by the student independently.

The completion of any major project (and, this was one) requires the assistance of many people. We wish first to thank our families who support and assist us in so many ways. Second, we gratefully acknowledge the encouragement given to us by our colleagues in Louisiana State University's Junior Division. Third, our endless gratitude goes to Dr. David Strauss whose sharp wit kept us on our toes. Fourth, we thank the following reviewers whose comments helped shape this edition:

| | |
|---|---|
| Marilyn Bowers | Walters State Community College |
| Vicki Butler | Chemeketa Community College |
| Jennifer Hurd | Arkansas State University-Beebe |
| Elyse M. Kimitzsky | Marian College |
| Barbara L. Miller | Wesley College |
| Jaquelin Hanselman | Hillsborough Community College |
| Martha V. Hartung | Chaminade University of Honolulu |
| Georgia A. Fertig | Coastal Carolina Community College |
| Paul Wolford | Walters State Community College |
| Nancy McKinley | Laramie County Community College |
| Shirley Napier | Walters State Community College |

Finally, we are especially grateful to Clark Baxter whose faith in us never wavers and to Chris Hurney who is the most organized lady we've encountered lately. Without editors like these, authors would perish and word processors rust away.

READING
ENHANCEMENT
AND
DEVELOPMENT

# 1 SQ3R

## TERMS

*Terms appear in the order in which they occur in the chapter.*

SQ3R
surveying
previewing
predict
frameworks
stereotypes
network
overview
outline
heading
subheading
maps
question
text marking
text labeling
recite
summaries
review
spaced study
distributed practice
cramming
study groups
overlearning

## CHAPTER OUTLINE

I. **How does surveying link frameworks and textbooks?**
   A. How are frameworks and networks defined?
      1. *How can frameworks be used to make text predictions?*
      2. *Why is it important to activate frameworks while surveying?*
   B. Why survey textbooks?
      1. *How do you organize through outlining?*
      2. *How do you organize through mapping?*
      3. *How do you use READ to develop outlines and maps?*
   C. Why survey supplementary materials?

II. **How does the questioning stage affect setting goals for reading?**

III. **Why mark and label text while reading?**
   A. Why is text marking important?
   B. How much text should I mark?
   C. How do I label text?

IV. **How do summarizing and checking understanding relate to reciting?**
   A. How do you recite through summarization?
      1. *Why do I need to summarize?*
      2. *How do I construct a summary?*
   B. Why is checking understanding important?

V. **How does review make information permanent?**
   A. What is spaced study?
   B. Is cramming a form of review that makes information permanent?
   C. How do study groups or partners contribute to effective review?
   D. What is overlearning?

## OBJECTIVES

*At the end of this chapter, you should be able to do the following:*

1. Link information in frameworks and textbooks when surveying.
2. Construct questions that set goals for reading.
3. Mark and label text to increase understanding when reading.
4. Evaluate your understanding through recitation.
5. Demonstrate reviewing techniques that increase the permanency of information.

## CHAPTER MAP

*The writer and the reader are two people separated by the same language.*
—*GEORGE BERNARD SHAW*

**W**HEN WRITERS WRITE, they have a plan for what they want to say. Sometimes what they write is clear and easy to understand. Sometimes it is not. Two factors contribute to this difference: you and the text. You may not think of yourself as a source of information. You may think the book is all that's important. If you think this is true, you neglect the part of you that makes sense of the writer's words. On the other hand, the vocabulary, structure, and subject of the text may hinder your understanding of it. You need a plan for reading that incorporates both you and what you read.

This plan is **SQ3R**—*S*urvey, *Q*uestion, *R*ead, *R*ecite, *R*eview. Developed by Francis Robinson in the 1940s, it is one of the oldest and most frequently used study plans. With slight changes, you can use it to read a variety of course materials.

◆

## SURVEY: LINKING FRAMEWORKS AND TEXTBOOKS

**Surveying,** or **previewing,** forms the first step in connecting yourself to the text. It involves examining certain features of the text. In this stage, you accomplish two goals. First, you consider what you already know about the topic. Then, you develop a map to guide you in understanding the chapter.

How does what you already know affect your understanding of new information? Let's say you want to go to a movie. You look in the paper and find two shows you haven't seen. They are *Starfighter* and *The Return of 007*.

How do you choose between the two? By surveying the ads, you **predict** what each movie will be about based on past experiences.

No doubt you have seen movies like *Starfighter* and *The Return of 007*. Although you haven't seen either of these movies, you can predict the general features of the movie.

For example, you predict that *Starfighter* takes place in the future. It may be about warring planets or galaxies. A battle might occur. The props would include some spaceships and space-age weapons. You might also predict that the movie would not be technical in nature.

An exotic setting can be predicted for the *007* movie. Spies from different countries will fight for secrets. Heads of governments will try to seize power. Fast cars and strange characters will be part of the action. You can expect a killing and a mystery or two.

How do you know this?

### Defining Frameworks and Networks

Your mind contains **frameworks** for general types of movies. When you see a movie title, you retrieve the framework for that type of movie. The framework forms a mental organizational structure for holding information. It contains spaces for **stereotypes,** or typical features. The framework also contains your facts and feelings about the information. Thus, frameworks organize everything you know. You consider all these in choosing which movie to see (see Figure 1.1).

A movie or a book title is like an entry word in a reference book. The words help you get the correct framework from your memory. Sometimes reference books give other words to look for on the same topic. In much the same way, the framework you retrieve provides you with a **network** of related information. Using frameworks to build networks is

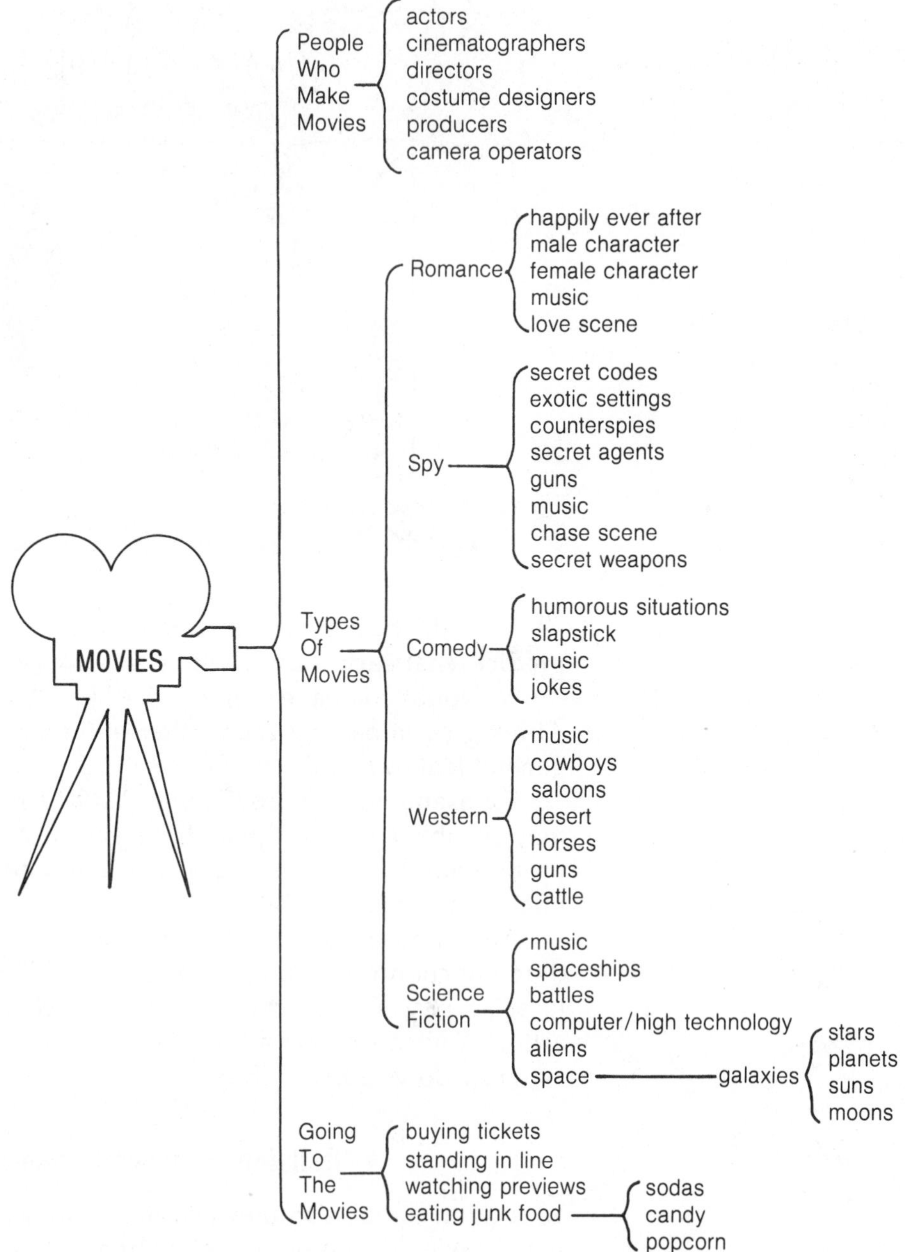


***FIGURE 1.1***
***A Sample Framework for the Movies***

an active process. The network expands as the frameworks grow and are associated with other frameworks. Thus, you have more and more information to use to make predictions.

When you see a movie, your mind fills in the spaces of your general framework with details from the movie you are seeing. Eventually you may forget the details of the movie. But your general movie framework will have been expanded or updated. The next time you retrieve that framework, it will be more complete. Again, you have more information to use in making your next movie prediction.

### *Using Frameworks to Make Text Predictions*

Just as you use your framework to predict what movies are about, you can use your framework to predict what texts are about. You do this by thinking about the facts and concepts you already know about the subject of the text. Then you make predictions about it.

For example, in the space below, write down things you associate with a library.

Now see how many of the concepts you wrote appear in the following passage. Circle the ones you find.

> The college library holds a constantly changing collection. Books in the collection include reference books of both a general and a specific nature. Such books consist of dictionaries, encyclopedias, indexes, yearbooks, handbooks, atlases, gazetteers, and bibliographies. Other books of recreational or supplemental readings are also available. In addition, the library contains current issues and bound volumes of periodicals and newspapers in both English and foreign languages. Pamphlets and clippings pertaining to various subjects are on file as well. Holdings include audiovisual materials such as pictures, films, slides, filmstrips, transparencies, phonograph records, tapes, cassettes, maps, and globes. Many documents are kept on various microforms because of a limited storage space.
>
> Most college libraries file books and documents according to the Dewey decimal system or the Library of Congress system. Students use either paper or computerized versions of a card catalog to locate the items they need.

Librarians perform many functions other than simply checking materials in and out of the library. Their duties include teaching, conducting literature searches, preparing reading lists and bibliographies, helping students, and organizing and maintaining the library collection. A staff of trained student workers help the librarians in their responsibilities.

### *Importance of Activating Frameworks While Surveying*

The next passage is designed to show the value of having a framework in mind as you survey.

> The procedure is actually quite simple. First, you arrange things into different groups. Of course, one pile may be sufficient depending on how much there is to do. If you have to go somewhere else due to lack of facilities that is the next step. Otherwise you are pretty well set. It is important not to overdo things. That is, it is better to do too few things at once than too many. In the short run this may not seem important but complications can easily arise. A mistake can be expensive as well. At first the whole procedure will seem complicated. Soon, however, it will become just another facet of life. It is difficult to foresee any end to the necessity for this task in the immediate future, but then one can never tell. After the procedure is completed one arranges the materials into different groups again. Then they can be put into their appropriate places. Eventually they will be used once more and the whole cycle will then have to be repeated.

*Source:* Bransford, J. D., & Johnson, M. K. "Contextual Prerequisites for Understanding: Some Investigations of Comprehension and Recall." *Journal of Verbal Learning and Verbal Behavior* 2: 6, 1972. Used by permission.

#### *WRITE TO LEARN*

*In a sentence, tell what this passage was about.*

______________________________

______________________________

*Most readers find this passage hard to read. Look at the topic of the passage identified on the last page of this chapter. Reread the passage. On a separate sheet of paper, describe how activating your framework for this topic changes your understanding of the passage.*

Since frameworks often reflect your experiences and general knowledge, they guide understanding. They help you interpret new information and organize information for recall. Now knowing the title of the passage made it hard to understand. Once you knew the title, you retrieved a framework about washing clothes, and the meaning of the passage became clearer. In addition, once you have the framework for washing clothes, you recall ideas more easily. Thus, having a framework aids understanding and recall of information.

## Developing Frameworks and Networks

You possess frameworks for movies, stories, objects, characters, events, and ideas. In fact, you have frameworks for everything. Frameworks consist of anything and everything you know about any subject. Each person's framework for a topic differs since each person's experiences and use of frameworks differs. Some pieces of the framework will, however, be the same.

For example, the framework for *tests* could consist of the following:

| | | | |
|---|---|---|---|
| bonus | essay | #2 pencil | standardized |
| monitor | study | true/false | calculator |
| *A, B, C, D, F* | questions | grades | curve |
| texts | directions | old exams | notes |
| answers | computer sheet | study group | fear |
| oral | blue books | pass/fail | stress |
| final | noncomprehensive | subjective | anxiety |
| paper | coping strategies | objective | midterm |
| points | multiple-choice | reading | handouts |
| pen | instructor | pop quiz | cramming |

These can be organized into smaller frameworks to make a network of related information. Items combine and recombine to form an infinite number of frameworks and networks. A network of related frameworks about tests follows:

| TYPES OF TESTS | PREPARATION | GRADES | FEELINGS |
|---|---|---|---|
| noncomprehensive | study group | bonus | fear |
| multiple-choice | study | points | stress |
| essay | reading | pass/fail | anxiety |
| subjective | answers | *A, B, C, D, F* | coping strategies |
| objective | questions | curve | |
| oral | cramming | | |
| final | | | |
| pop quiz | | | |
| midterm | | | |
| standardized | | | |

| PEOPLE INVOLVED | WHAT TO STUDY | MATERIALS NEEDED |
|---|---|---|
| monitor | texts | blue books |
| instructor | notes | calculator |
| study group | handouts | computer sheet |
| | old exams | #2 pencil |
| | | pen |
| | | paper |

Networking information from old and new frameworks aids the comprehension of the active reader. Analyzing new pieces of information and relating them to past knowledge helps you move from simply recalling facts to synthesizing new concepts. Your ability to retrieve this framework of information helps you to make predictions when surveying new text.

**EXERCISE 1.1**

*Choose one of the following concepts. Write your choice on the line below. Think of things you associate with the concept. List them. Use our framework for tests as an example.*

*Careers* *Transportation* *Campus Activities*

*Title Chosen:* ______________________________

| | | |
|---|---|---|
| **1.** ________ | **11.** ________ | **21.** ________ |
| **2.** ________ | **12.** ________ | **22.** ________ |
| **3.** ________ | **13.** ________ | **23.** ________ |
| **4.** ________ | **14.** ________ | **24.** ________ |
| **5.** ________ | **15.** ________ | **25.** ________ |
| **6.** ________ | **16.** ________ | **26.** ________ |
| **7.** ________ | **17.** ________ | **27.** ________ |
| **8.** ________ | **18.** ________ | **28.** ________ |
| **9.** ________ | **19.** ________ | **29.** ________ |
| **10.** ________ | **20.** ________ | **30.** ________ |

*These words partially make up your framework for the concept you chose. Now organize your framework into a network of information. Use our network for tests as an example. You must think of your own categories.*

## Surveying Textbooks

After considering what you already know about a topic, you need to "case the joint." This gives you a quick **overview** of the chapter. It gives you familiarity with its contents. You know the important ideas in the chapter and where to find them. The steps in this process appear in Table 1.1. Once you've familiarized yourself with the content, you need some direction to help you find your way around the chapter.

> **WRITE TO LEARN**
>
> *On a separate sheet of paper, tell your instructor how to get from this class to your next class.*

The way in which you process information affects the way you organize information. How did you provide directions in the last *Write to Learn* activity? If you made a list of steps or wrote a brief description, you probably learn better when you see information in a traditional outline format. If you drew a sketch to show the way to your next class, you may learn better through a more graphic format such as a map. Outlines and maps help you predict the importance of information while surveying.

### *Organizing Through Outlining*

An **outline** is a collection of ideas that are ranked according to importance. Every idea is subordinate to or summarized by another

**TABLE 1.1** **Steps in Overviewing**

1. *Read the title.* What is the chapter about? Think about what you already know about the topic.
2. *Read the introduction or first paragraph.* The main idea of the chapter is usually found here.
3. *Read the boldface headings throughout the chapter.*
4. *Read the first paragraph or sentence under each heading.* This gives you an overview of each section.
5. *Look at accompanying graphs, charts, and pictures.* Visual aids usually emphasize main points. They also summarize details.
6. *Note any typographical aids (boldface, underlining, italics).* In the body of the text, these aids highlight important terms. When found in the margins, they may outline important facts.
7. *Read the last paragraph or summary.* This often gives the main points or conclusions.
8. *Read the objectives at the beginning of each chapter.* Objectives help you set goals and purposes. Such goals help you determine what you should know or be able to do at the end of each chapter.
9. *Read the vocabulary terms at the beginning or end of each chapter.* You may recognize some of the terms. However, they may have specialized meanings for that topic.

idea. Thus, an outline forms a hierarchical picture of information. You determine importance based on the ways in which ideas fit together. For example, consider these two smaller frameworks from the larger framework *test*.

| GRADES | PREPARATION |
|---|---|
| bonus | study group |
| points | study |
| pass/fail | reading |
| *A, B, C, D, F* | answers |
| *curve* | questions |
| | cramming |

Although *Grades* appeared in the larger framework on page 9, it summarizes the concepts *bonus; points; pass/fail; A, B, C, D, F;* and *curve*. Since no inclusive term in the framework summarized the concepts under *Preparation*, a heading had to be inferred. Because *Grades* and *Preparation* are summary concepts, they are of more importance.

**EXERCISE 1.2**

*The following lists of words are from a general framework. They have been grouped. Label the general framework and each smaller framework. (Hint: Label each smaller framework first. The label for the large framework can be generalized from what the small frameworks have in common.)*

**1.** *General framework:*______________________________

**a.** ____________________

textbooks
clerks
art supplies
notebooks
novels
t-shirts
pens
greeting cards

**b.** ____________________

grants
loans
scholarships
fee exemptions
work/study jobs
vocational rehabilitation

**c.** ____________________

professors
students
deans
secretaries
directors

**d.** ____________________

Sociology
Physics
Art Appreciation
American Literature
Speech

**e.** ____________________

desks
chalkboard
overhead projector
projection screen
bulletin board
podium
wastepaper basket
pencil sharpener

**2.** *General framework:* ______________________

**a.** ______________
operating room
recovery room
emergency room
nursery
nursing station
waiting room

**b.** ______________
heart bypass
cesarean section
hip replacement
face-lift
gall bladder surgery
appendectomy

**c.** ______________
heart-lung machine
dialysis machine
scalpel
wheelchair
gurney
walker

**d.** ______________
osteopath
nurses
occupational therapists
candy striper
obstetrician
surgeons

**e.** ______________
CAT scan
glucose tolerance test
blood test
physical examination
angiogram
X ray

**f.** ______________
cardiac arrhythmia
scraped knee
diabetes
flu
broken arm
ear infection

**3.** *General framework:* ______________________

**a.** ______________
Physical Therapy
Medical Technology
Prepharmacy
Nursing

**b.** ______________
Speech
French
Philosophy
Music
Art

**c.** ______________
Architecture
Landscape Architecture
Interior Design

**d.** ______________
History
Sociology
Economics
Anthropology
Psychology

**e.** ______________
Physics
Botany
Zoology
Geology
Astronomy

One method of organizing information in a chapter is to outline it. The subject of the outline is the same as the subject of your chapter. Each major **heading** in the chapter is a major heading in your outline. Each **subheading** becomes a minor heading. Information found under sub-

**FIGURE 1.2**
**Formal and Informal Outline Formats**

| Formal Outline | Informal Outline with Dashes | Informal Outline with Symbols or Print Style Differences |
|---|---|---|
| I. Personality theorists | Personality theorists | ‡PERSONALITY THEORISTS |
| A. Psychodynamic | —Psychodynamic | *Psychodynamic* |
| 1. Freud | —Freud | Freud |
| 2. Jung | —Jung | Jung |
| 3. Erickson | —Erickson | Erickson |
| B. Behavioral | —Behavioral | *Behavioral* |
| 1. Skinner | —Skinner | Skinner |
| 2. Bandura | —Bandura | Bandura |

headings provides supporting details. You need to reword these headings and subheadings into phrases, sentences, or questions to aid study.

Outlines consist of formal or informal formats (see Figure 1.2). The formal format uses roman numerals (I, II, III, etc.) placed on the left side of the page or margin to note major concepts. You indent ideas that support the major concepts. You indicate these secondary points with capital letters. You show lesser supporting details with indented arabic numerals (1, 2, 3).

Because notes are for your personal use, they need not be formally outlined. The key to an outline is to visually highlight information in some manner. For the sake of consistency, informal outlines retain the indented format of formal outlines. To make informal outlines clearer, you separate major headings and entire sections with a blank line. To construct informal outlines, you use symbols, dashes, various print types, or other means of identifying differing levels of information.

### *Organizing Through Mapping*

**Maps** provide a quick means for you to determine the plan of a chapter. They are pictures that show relationships among concepts. They express patterns of thought. You construct a map by using headings and subheadings in a combination boxed/branching format. You place each major heading in a separate box horizontally (from left to right) in the order in which it appears in the chapter. You then arrange subheadings in a branching formation within the box. For example, see the chapter map for this chapter. For ease in studying, you might reword these headings into phrases, sentences, and questions.

### *Developing Outlines and Maps with READ*

Consider again the directions you gave in the *Write to Learn* on page 11. You found you recalled information better in a written or graphic form. This text gives you the chance to survey by outlining or mapping its chapters. This chapter begins with a complete outline and map. In subsequent chapters, you should complete whichever of the two best suits your learning style. This activity will enhance your recall of information. By the end of the text, you will be able to completely outline or map a chapter by asking questions about its content.

### Surveying Supplementary Materials

Sometimes course readings include supplementary, or additional, materials. They may be articles, portions of other chapters, examples, study guides, or other information the instructor deems important. Some are available for purchase. Instructors place others on reserve (limited circulation) in the library.

Instructors use supplementary readings to tailor courses to fit their needs and the needs of their students. These readings serve three important purposes. First, some reinforce information in a text chapter. These may provide extra information about topics briefly discussed in the chapter. They might simplify complex concepts. Others, such as study guides, help you learn text information more easily. Second, such materials present more current information. This information may provide new or conflicting perspectives on the topic. Finally, supplementary materials may provide general background information. For example, a psychology chapter about personality generally focuses on major personality theories. Supplementary materials might include biographies of the theorists or case studies. Surveying such materials helps you decide how this information relates to the chapter. Then, you verify your prediction when reading.

The format of some supplemental readings is much like that of a text chapter. That is, they contain headings, subheadings, and summaries. You survey these just as you did text chapters (see Table 1.1). On the other hand, sometimes no text features are available to help you locate main points. Here, you use the title and any introductory or summary statements to preview the content. Reading the first sentence of each paragraph also gives you an overview of the material.

◆

## THE QUESTIONING STAGE: SETTING GOALS FOR READING

Any given major requires coursework outside the field. Although you may be keenly interested in the major, your interest in reading about other subjects may lag. Because your goal in reading these subjects is often to finish as fast as you can, you read with little thought. Since understanding rarely results without thought, your lack of interest becomes a problem.

Luckily, that problem is not insurmountable. The **question** step of SQ3R, or the goal-setting stage, forms the solution. When you set goals for reading, you give your reading focus. You create a reason for reading other than getting to the end. You read to meet a goal, or answer a question. Your reading, then, becomes an active, thought-provoking process.

However, asking the right questions isn't always easy. Judge Jacob Braude of the Circuit Court of Cook County, Illinois, often told a story that shows this:

> When his wife left to visit their daughter, a man was left alone at home. To his dismay, another daughter came and left a grandson to stay with him. The next morning the man awakened and prepared oatmeal for breakfast.
>
> "Do you like sugar?" he asked the small boy. His grandson nodded.
>
> "What about butter?" His grandson nodded again.
>
> "Well, how about milk?"
>
> "Sure," the boy said.
>
> When the man placed the steaming bowl of oatmeal with sugar, butter, and milk before him, the boy refused to eat it.
>
> "Why won't you eat it? When I asked, you said you *liked* sugar, butter, and milk?"
>
> "I do," said the boy, "but you didn't ask me if I liked oatmeal."

How can you make sure you ask the right questions while reading? Changing headings and subheadings into questions comprises the easiest way to set goals. This is why questions form outlines and maps in this text. You use certain questioning words to identify main ideas. Others help you locate details. Table 1.2 provides a key to these questioning words.

**TABLE 1.2 Questioning Words for Main Ideas and Details**

| QUESTIONING WORDS FOR MAIN IDEAS | |
|---|---|
| *If You Want to Know . . .* | *Then Ask . . .* |
| a reason | why? |
| a way or method | how? |
| a purpose or definition | what? |
| a fact | what? |
| *QUESTIONING WORDS FOR DETAILS* | |
| *If You Want to Know . . .* | *Then Ask . . .* |
| a person | who? |
| a number or amount | how many/how much? |
| a choice | which? |
| a time | when? |
| a place | where? |

**EXERCISE 1.3**

◆ *For each chapter title below, write an appropriate goal-setting question using words from Table 1.2.*

***Example***

Chapter Title: *The Expansion of Western Civilization*

*person: What groups of people were responsible for the expansion of civilization in the West?*

1. *reason:* __________
2. *method:* __________
3. *time:* __________

Chapter Title: *Self-Handicapping—Smoke Screen for Failure*

4. *definition:* __________
5. *method:* __________

Chapter Title: *Applied Functions: Setting Up Equations*

6. *definition:* __________
7. *time:* __________
8. *choice:* __________

Chapter Title: *Creating New Colonial Empires*

9. *place:* __________
10. *person:* __________
11. *time:* __________

**12.** *method:*________________________________________________

________________________________________________________

**13.** *number:*________________________________________________

________________________________________________________

Chapter Title: *Science, the Zoo, the Computers*

**14.** *fact:*________________________________________________

________________________________________________________

**15.** *time:*________________________________________________

________________________________________________________

## EXERCISE 1.4

*For each paragraph below, write a goal-setting question based on the paragraph's title. Then read the paragraph. Compare your question with the printed one. Put a check by the question that seems most appropriate. If both questions are appropriate, do nothing. If neither is appropriate, change your question into a more appropriate one.*

### Example

*Federal Courts*
*Your question:* *What are federal courts?*________________________

________________________________________________________

Federal courts are either legislative courts or the more familiar constitutional courts. Legislative courts administer a particular body of law and perform legislative as well as judicial tasks. The customs court, the tax court, and the court of military justice are examples of legislative courts. Unlike constitutional courts, legislative courts may issue advisory opinions—that is, they may offer an opinion without having a specific case at hand. Constitutional courts—federal district courts, federal appeals courts, and the U.S. Supreme Court—are the heart of the federal judiciary.



*Goal-setting question:* What comprises federal courts?

*Explanation:* The two questions are equal. A check by either would be a correct answer.

**1.** *Care and Maintenance of Computers*
*Your question:*________________________________________________

________________________________________________________

The key to keeping computers and software in good working order is to use common sense when handling them. Both students and teachers should be able to follow minimal rules for care of the disks and machines before they use the computers. Food, drink, chalk dust, clay, paper clips, and similar materials should be kept away from the equipment; they can cause the keys on the keyboard to jam or, worse, cause the electronic components to malfunction. Dust and dirt can carry electric charges that will break down the flow of current through the microcomputer.

*Source:* Reprinted with permission from *Computers in Education Today* by Mandell and Mandell. 

*Goal-setting question:* What happens when computers are not properly maintained?

**2.** *Social Developments and the Twentieth Century*
*Your question:* ____________________

____________________

The material lives of ordinary human beings during the twentieth century have improved in many ways other than through technological advances. These social developments include a number of changes in the size and distribution of population, medicine and health care, education, and general welfare.

*Source:* Reprinted with permission from *Survey of Western Civilization* by Goff et al. 

*Goal-setting question:* Who developed socially during the twentieth century?

**3.** *The Concept of Abnormal Behavior*
*Your question:* ____________________

____________________

The kinds of problems discussed in this chapter's sections on anxiety and depression disorders often go by the label abnormal behavior. Literally, abnormal behavior is behavior that is "away from the norm," or the usual. This definition implies that there must be some standard of normal behavior; otherwise we would not know when someone's behavior deviated from the norm. There are such standards, but they are not quite as clear as that. In addition, there is some disagreement among psychologists and other mental health professionals as to just what the standard itself should be.

*Source:* Reprinted with permission from *Psychology and Effective Behavior* by Jewell. 

*Goal-setting question:* When was the concept of abnormal behavior derived?

**4.** *Receptiveness to Workers' Ideas*
*Your question:* ____________________

____________________

Another way to motivate employees is to be receptive to the ideas they offer. This, of course, requires the supervisor to have well-developed listening skills. . . . Listening is far more than just hearing. Listening involves *active effort* on the part of the message receiver. It also involves *responding* in appropriate ways to the person who is speaking.

*Source:* Reprinted with permission from *People at Work* by Timm and Peterson. Copyright © 1982 by West Publishing Company. All rights reserved.

*Goal-setting question:* Why should one be responsive to the ideas of workers?

**5.** *Ecology*
*Your question:*____________________________________

________________________________________________

The word *ecology* comes from the Greek word *oikos,* which means "house, home, or place of residence." Ecology, which began as a branch of biology in the 1800's, is the science concerned with the relationships among organisms and their environment. The study of ecology was greatly stimulated by Charles Darwin's (1859) theory that organisms change and evolve in response to their living conditions. Although ecology is still primarily the concern of biologists, social scientists have been interested in the relationship between humans and their environment since the latter part of the nineteenth century. This field, called human ecology, has been part of the American academic scene since the 1920's and has lately attracted considerable attention as the result of recent concern with environmental problems.

*Source:* Reprinted with permission from *Sociology* by Shepard. Copyright © 1984 by West Publishing Company. All rights reserved.

*Goal-setting question:* When did the study of ecology begin?

**6.** *The Industrial Revolution and the Growth of Cities*
*Your question:*____________________________________

________________________________________________

As merchants gained power and wealth during the late medieval period, they often established small industries to give themselves a stable supply of goods. As these industries gradually increased in size, the stage was being set for rapid city growth.

*Source:* Reprinted with permission from *Sociology* by Shepard.

*Goal-setting question:* How did the Industrial Revolution affect the growth of modern cities?

**7.** *Geographic Significance of TV*
*Your question:*____________________________________

________________________________________________

From a geographic viewpoint television plays an important role in enhancing communications and understanding among people in different parts of the world. The airwaves are free: Once a program has been broadcast, it is available to people without regard for cultural barriers. While travel is restricted between East and West Germany, for example, no similar restriction is placed on television programming. East Germans have access to Western programs and vice versa, with schedules for the other country published in the local newspapers for both. Such an arrangement enhances awareness of conditions in other societies. East Germans can see the level of material comfort in the West, and West Germans can view the athletic skill of the Easterners.



*Goal-setting question:* How does television significantly affect geography?

**8.** *Fight or Flight*
*Your question:*________________________________________

____________________________________________________

The sympathetic branch prepares the body for emergency action—for "fighting or fleeing"—by arousing a number of bodily systems and inhibiting others. . . . These changes have a purpose. Sugar is released into the bloodstream for quick energy, the heart beats faster to distribute blood to the muscles, digestion is temporarily inhibited, blood flow in the skin is restricted to reduce bleeding, and so forth. Most sympathetic reactions increase the chances that a person or an animal will survive an emergency.



*Goal-setting question:* Which is better: to fight or to flee?

**9.** *Conditioning Pets*
*Your question:*________________________________________

____________________________________________________

One of the most common mistakes people make with pets (especially dogs) is hitting them it they do not come when called. Calling the animal then becomes a conditioned stimulus for fear and withdrawal. No wonder the pet disobeys when called on future occasions.

*Source:* Reprinted with permission from *Introduction to Psychology* by Coon.

*Goal-setting question:* How can you condition your pet?

**10.** *Sprawl*
*Your question:*________________________________________

____________________________________________________

In the United States suburbs are characterized by sprawl. That is, new areas of housing are developed on land that is not contiguous to the existing built-up area. Private developers, who are responsible for selecting sites for new housing, look for cheap land that can be readily prepared for construction. The new sites are frequently separated from other built-up areas. Because new developments are spread out over a wide area, expensive new roads and water and sewer lines must be built to accommodate them, paid for directly by taxes or installed by the developer and passed on to consumers through higher house prices. Sprawl is also fostered by the desire of families to own large tracts of land.

*Source:* Reprinted with permission from *Cultural Landscape* by Rubenstein and Bacon.

*Goal-setting question:* What causes sprawl?

**EXERCISE 1.5**

*Turn the title and each heading and subheading in the following passage into a goal-setting question. Write these questions on the lines provided following this passage.*

### Exploration: Extrasensory Perception—Do You Believe in Magic?

In a quiet laboratory, Uri Geller, a self-proclaimed "psychic," has agreed to demonstrate his claimed abilities to communicate by mental telepathy, to detect hidden objects, and to predict future events. In the course of testing, Geller was supposedly able to select from a row of 10 film canisters the one that contained an object, correctly guess the number that would come up on a die shaken in a closed box 8 out of 8 times, and reproduce drawings sealed in opaque envelopes.

*Question: Was Geller cheating, or was he using some ability beyond normal perception?*

There is now little doubt that Geller was cheating (Randi, 1980). But how? The answer lies in a discussion of **extrasensory perception (ESP)**— the purported ability to perceive events in ways that cannot be explained by accepted perceptual principles.

#### PARAPSYCHOLOGY

**Parapsychology** is the study of ESP and other **psi** phenomena (*psi* is pronounced like *sigh*), or events that seem to defy accepted scientific laws. Parapsychologists seek answers to the questions raised by three basic forms that ESP could take. These are:

1. **Clairvoyance.** The ability to perceive events or gain information in ways that appear unaffected by distance or normal physical barriers.
2. **Telepathy.** Extrasensory perception of another person's thoughts, or more simply, an ability to read someone else's mind.
3. **Precognition.** The ability to perceive or accurately predict future events. Precognition may take the form of *prophetic dreams* that foretell the future.

   While we are at it, we might as well toss in another purported psi ability:
4. **Psychokinesis.** The ability to exert influence over inanimate objects by willpower ("mind over matter"). (Psychokinesis cannot be classed as a type of perception, extrasensory or otherwise, but it is frequently studied by parapsychologists.)

*Question: Have parapsychologists confirmed the existence of ESP and other psi abilities?*

American psychologists as a group remain skeptical about psi abilities. If you doubt ESP, then you should know that some experiments seem to support its existence. If you are among those who believe in ESP, then you should know why the scientific community doubts many of these experiments!

**Coincidence**

Anyone who has ever had an apparent clairvoyant or telepathic experience may find it hard to question the existence of ESP. Yet, the difficulty of excluding *coincidence* makes natural ESP occurrences less conclusive than they might seem. For example, consider a typical psychic experience. During the middle of the night, a woman away for a weekend visit suddenly had a strong impulse to return home. When she arrived, she found the house on fire with her husband asleep inside (Rhine, 1953).

An experience like this is striking, but it does not confirm the existence of ESP. If, by coincidence, a hunch turns out to be correct, it may be *reinterpreted* as a premonition or case of clairvoyance (Marks & Kammann, 1979). If it is not confirmed, it will simply be forgotten. Most people don't realize it, but such coincidences occur so often that we should *expect* them, not consider them strange or mysterious (Alcock, 1981).

The formal study of psi events owes much to the late J. B. Rhine. Rhine established the first parapsychological laboratory at Duke University and spent the rest of his life trying to document ESP. To avoid problems of coincidence and after-the-fact interpretation of "natural" ESP events, Rhine tried to study ESP more objectively. Many of his experiments made use of the **Zener cards.** In a typical clairvoyance test, subjects tried to guess the symbols on the cards as they were turned up from a shuffled deck. Pure guessing in this test will produce an average score of 5 "hits" out of 25 cards.

Unfortunately, some of Rhine's most dramatic early experiments used badly printed Zener cards that allowed the symbols to show faintly on the back. It is also very easy to cheat, by marking cards with a fingernail or by noting marks on the cards caused by normal use. Even if this were not the case, there is evidence that early experimenters sometimes unconsciously gave subjects cues about the cards with their eyes, facial gestures, or lip movements. In short, none of the early studies in parapsychology were done in a way that eliminated the possibility of fraud (Alcock, 1981).

Modern parapsychologists are now well aware of the need for double-blind experiments, maximum security and accuracy in record keeping, meticulous control, and repeatability of experiments (Rhine, 1974a). In the last 10 years, hundreds of experiments have been reported in parapsychological journals, many of them supporting the existence of psi abilities.

*Question: Then why do most psychologists remain skeptical about psi abilities?* For one thing, fraud continues to plague the field. Walter J. Levy, who was former director of Rhine's laboratory, was caught faking records, as have some others who got positive results. Even honest scientists have been fooled by various frauds and cheats, so there is reason to remain skeptical and on guard.

**Statistics and Chance**

A major criticism of psi research has to do with inconsistency. For every study with positive results, there are others that fail (Hansel, 1980). It is rare—in fact, almost unheard of—for a subject to maintain psi ability over any sustained period of time (Jahn, 1982; Schmeidler, 1977). ESP researchers consider this "decline effect" an indication that parapsychological skills are very fragile and unpredictable (Rhine, 1977). But critics argue that subjects who only temporarily score above chance have just received credit for a **run of luck.** When the run is over, it is not fair to assume that ESP is temporarily gone. We must count *all* attempts.

To understand the run-of-luck criticism, consider an example. Say that you flip a coin 100 times and record the results. You then flip another coin 100 times, again recording the results. The two lists are compared. For any 10 pairs of flips, we would expect heads or tails to match 5 times. Let's say that you go through the list and find a set of 10 pairs where 9 out of 10 matched. This is far above chance expectation. But does it mean that the first coin "knew" what was going to come up on the second coin? The idea is obviously silly.

Now, what if a person guesses 100 times what will come up on a coin. Again, we might find a set of 10 guesses that matches the results of flipping the coin. Does this mean that the person, for a time, had precognition—then lost it? Parapsychologists tend to believe the answer is yes. Skeptics assume that nothing more than random matching occurred, as in the two-coin example.

### RESEARCH METHODS

Unfortunately, many of the most spectacular findings in parapsychology simply cannot be **replicated** (repeated) (Gardner, 1977; Hyman, 1977). More importantly, improved research methods usually result in fewer positive results. Proponents of parapsychology feel that they can point to experiments that meet all possible criticisms. But in virtually every case, the results cannot be repeated by doubters.

Believers in ESP, such as ex-astronaut Edgar Mitchell, claim that other factors explain negative results: "The scientist has to recognize that his own mental processes may influence the phenomenon he's observing. If he's really a total skeptic, the scientist may well turn off the psychic subject." This may sound convincing, but skeptics consider it unfair. With Mitchell's argument in effect, anyone attempting an objective experiment can only get two results: He or she may find evidence of ESP or be accused of having suppressed it. This makes it impossible to disprove ESP to believers, even if it truly does not exist.

Reinterpretation is also a problem in psi experiments. For example, Mitchell claimed he did a successful telepathy experiment from space. Yet, news accounts never mentioned that on some trials Mitchell's "receivers" scored above chance, while on others they scored *below* chance. The second outcome, Mitchell decided, was also a "success" because it represented intentional "psi missing." But as skeptics have noted, if both high scores and low scores count as successes, how can you lose?

#### Stage Esp

Skeptics and serious researchers in ESP both agree on one point. If psychic phenomena do occur, they cannot be controlled well enough to be used by entertainers. Stage ESP (like stage magic) is based on a combination of sleight of hand, deception, and patented gadgets. A case in point is Uri Geller, a former nightclub magician who "astounded" audiences—and some scientists—from coast to coast with apparent telepathy, psychokinesis, and precognition.

Geller's performance on tests was described earlier. Not mentioned is what University of Oregon Professor Ray Hyman calls the "incredible sloppiness" of these tests. One example is Geller's reproductions of sealed drawings. These, it turns out, were done in a room next to the one where the drawings were made. Original reports of Geller's alleged "ability" failed to mention that there was a hole in the wall between the two rooms, through which Geller might have heard discussions of the pictures being drawn. Also unreported was the fact that Geller's friend Shipi Stang was present at every test. Geller's manager has since testified that Stang frequently acted as Geller's accomplice in trickery (Alcock, 1981). Is it a coincidence that when a picture of a rocket ship was drawn, Stang hummed the theme music from the motion picture *2001: A Space Odyssey?* A similar lack of control pervaded every other test. In the "die in the box" tests, for instance, Geller was allowed to hold the box, shake it, and have the honor of opening it (Randi, 1980; Wilhelm, 1976). Why weren't such pertinent details reported?

Sensational and uncritical reporting of apparent paranormal events is widespread. Hundreds of books, articles, and television programs are produced each year by people who have become wealthy promoting unsupported claims. If a person did have psychic powers, he or she would not have to make a living by entertaining, giving demonstrations, or making personal appearances. A quick trip to the gaming tables of Las Vegas would allow the person to retire for life.

**Conclusion**

After close to 130 years of investigation, it is still impossible to say conclusively whether psi events occur. As we have seen, a close look at psi experiments often reveals serious problems of evidence, procedure, and scientific rigor (Alcock, 1981; Hansel, 1980; Marks & Kammann, 1979; Randi, 1980). Yet, being a skeptic does not mean a person is against something. It means that you are unconvinced. The purpose of this discussion, then, has been to counter the *uncritical* acceptance of psi events that is rampant in the media.

*Question: What would it take to scientifically demonstrate the existence of ESP?* Quite simply, a set of instructions that would allow any competent, unbiased observer to produce a psi event under standardized conditions (Moss & Butler, 1978). Undoubtedly, some intrepid researchers will continue their attempts to supply just that. Others remain skeptics, and some consider 130 years of inconclusive efforts reason enough to abandon the concept of ESP (Swets et al., 1988). At the least, it seems essential to be carefully skeptical of evidence reported in the popular press or by researchers who are uncritical "true believers." But then, you already knew I was going to say that, didn't you!

*Source:* Reprinted with permission from *Introduction to Psychology* by Coon. 

1. Exploration: Extrasensory Perception—Do You Believe in Magic?

2. Parapsychology

3. Coincidence

4. Statistics and Chance

5. Research Methods

6. Stage ESP

◆

## READ: MARKING AND LABELING TEXT FOR UNDERSTANDING

In learning it is said that "we hear and we forget; we see and we remember; we do and we understand." Each step of the SQ3R method views reading as an active process. Therefore, reading must entail more than simply sitting and staring at a text. As you read, you need to actively seek the answer to the question you set. This means you look for patterns, or connections, among information. You consider the meanings of terms in their surroundings. You try to summarize main ideas. You draw conclusions. You attend critically to the information in the text. One way to assure that you read actively is to mark your text as you read.

### Text Marking: Importance

**Text marking** sounds simple. You find important information and mark it. You highlight or underline what you want to remember. But, what exactly do you mark? What is really important?

First, what you mark depends on how much you already know about the topic. Consider what might happen if you were studying about the settlement of Salt Lake City. If you're from Salt Lake City, you'd probably mark less. This is because you might already know some of the information. In contrast, if you know little about Salt Lake City, you'll probably mark more. In general, the less you know, the more you mark. The more you know, the less you mark.

Second, if you survey and ask goal-setting questions, what you mark should answer your questions. Thus, you mark the information that highlights terms and main ideas.

Third, you might include other details that support your response. These could consist of the steps in a sequence or other kinds of lists, reasons, conclusions, and so on. Knowing which and what kind of details your inspector deems most important helps you choose what to mark. You generally find this by carefully examining returned tests. Critical evaluation of lecture content also provides this information. Finally, the details you need depend on gaps you might have in your background knowledge.

### Text Marking: Amount

Like Goldilocks and the three bears, your goal should be to mark amounts of information that are "just right." Examine the two examples of text marking found in Figure 1.3. In the first example, the student marked too much information to be useful for study. Remember that the purpose of text marking is to tell the difference between important and unimportant information. Here, there is no difference. Even if you know nothing about a subject, you should be marking half or less of the information.

In the second example, the student marked too little information. This could mean that the student already felt confident about understanding the information. It could also signal a lack of attention, poor understanding, or deficits in understanding what to mark.

### Text Labeling

Imagine that you are on a trip and have gotten lost. When you ask for directions, a friendly citizen gets a map and highlights the route you should take. Thanking your new friend, you start off once more. However, when you look at the map, you find no names for streets, buildings, or other locations. Although you may be able to reach your destination, it will take more effort to get there.

Much the same problem occurs in text marking. Many students read and mark information, just to find themselves somewhat "lost" when they have to study. Only with effort can they reconstruct why they marked their texts as they did.

***FIGURE 1.3***
***Overmarking and Undermarking Text***

## The Problem of Obesity

However you define it, obesity does occur to an alarming extent and is increasing in the developed countries. For example, in the United States some 10 to 25 percent of all teenagers and some 25 to 50 percent of all adults are obese.

Obesity brings many health hazards with it. Insurance companies report that fat people die younger from a host of causes, including heart attacks, strokes, and complications of (type II) diabetes. In fact, among adults, gaining weight often appears to precipitate diabetes. Fat people more often have high blood cholesterol (a risk factor for coronary heart disease), hypertension, complications after surgery, gynecological irregularities, and the toxemia of pregnancy. For men, the risk of cancers of the colon, rectum, and prostate gland rises with obesity; for women, the risk of cancers of the breast, uterus, ovaries, gallbladder, and bile ducts is greater. The burden of extra fat strains the skeletal system, aggravating arthritis—especially in the knees, hips, and lower spine. The muscles that support the belly may give way, resulting in abdominal hernias. When the leg muscles are abnormally fatty, they fail to contract efficiently to help blood return from the leg veins to the heart; blood collects in the leg veins, which swell, harden, and become varicose. Extra fat in and around the chest interferes with breathing, sometimes causing severe respiratory problems. Gout is more common, and even the accident rate is greater for the severely obese.

Beyond all these hazards is the risk incurred by millions of obese people throughout much of their lives— the risk of ill-advised, misguided dieting. Some fad diets are more hazardous to health than obesity itself. One survey of 29,000 claims, treatments, and theories for losing weight found fewer than 6 percent of them effective— and 13 percent dangerous!

Social and economic disadvantages also plague the fat person. Obese people are less often sought after for marriage, pay higher insurance premiums, meet discrimination when applying for college admissions and jobs, can't find attractive clothes so easily, and are limited in their choice of sports. For many, guilt, depression, withdrawal, and self-blame are inevitable psychological accompaniments to obesity.

Although obesity is a severe physical handicap, it is unlike other handicaps in two important ways. First, mortality risk is not linearly related to excess weight. Instead, there is a threshold at which risk dramatically increases. Being

## The Problem of Obesity

However you define it, obesity does occur to an alarming extent and is increasing in the developed countries. For example, in the United States some 10 to 25 percent of all teenagers and some 25 to 50 percent of all adults are obese.

Obesity brings many health hazards with it. Insurance companies report that fat people die younger from a host of causes, including heart attacks, strokes, and complications of (type II) diabetes. In fact, among adults, gaining weight often appears to precipitate diabetes. Fat people more often have high blood cholesterol (a risk factor for coronary heart disease), hypertension, complications after surgery, gynecological irregularities, and the toxemia of pregnancy. For men, the risk of cancers of the colon, rectum, and prostate gland rises with obesity; for women, the risk of cancers of the breast, uterus, ovaries, gallbladder, and bile ducts is greater. The burden of extra fat strains the skeletal system, aggravating arthritis—especially in the knees, hips, and lower spine. The muscles that support the belly may give way, resulting in abdominal hernias. When the leg muscles are abnormally fatty, they fail to contract efficiently to help blood return from the leg veins to the heart; blood collects in the leg veins, which swell, harden, and become varicose. Extra fat in and around the chest interferes with breathing, sometimes causing severe respiratory problems. Gout is more common, and even the accident rate is greater for the severely obese.

Beyond all these hazards is the risk incurred by millions of obese people throughout much of their lives— the risk of ill-advised, misguided dieting. Some fad diets are more hazardous to health than obesity itself. One survey of 29,000 claims, treatments, and theories for losing weight found fewer than 6 percent of them effective— and 13 percent dangerous!

Social and economic disadvantages also plague the fat person. Obese people are less often sought after for marriage, pay higher insurance premiums, meet discrimination when applying for college admissions and jobs, can't find attractive clothes so easily, and are limited in their choice of sports. For many, guilt, depression, withdrawal, and self-blame are inevitable psychological accompaniments to obesity.

Although obesity is a severe physical handicap, it is unlike other handicaps in two important ways. First, mortality risk is not linearly related to excess weight. Instead, there is a threshold at which risk dramatically increases. Being

Consider the marked text in Figure 1.4. Most students would agree that, just by looking, it appears to be appropriately marked. The answer to the question "What is the problem of obesity?" ranges across much of the section. Reviewing for a test several weeks later, you might forget how the information relates. You would need to reread most of what you marked to reconstruct your thoughts.

**Text labeling** helps you identify relationships and summarize information. It does not replace text marking. Instead, you use it in

***FIGURE 1.4***
***Text Marking***

## The Problem of Obesity

However you define it, obesity does occur to an alarming extent and is increasing in the developed countries. For example, in the United States some 10 to 25 percent of all teenagers and some 25 to 50 percent of all adults are obese.

Obesity brings many health hazards with it. Insurance companies report that fat people die younger from a host of causes, including heart attacks, strokes, and complications of (type II) diabetes. In fact, among adults, gaining weight often appears to precipitate diabetes. Fat people more often have high blood cholesterol (a risk factor for coronary heart disease), hypertension, complications after surgery, gynecological irregularities, and the toxemia of pregnancy. For men, the risk of cancers of the colon, rectum, and prostate gland rises with obesity; for women, the risk of cancers of the breast, uterus, ovaries, gallbladder, and bile ducts is greater. The burden of extra fat strains the skeletal system, aggravating arthritis—especially in the knees, hips, and lower spine. The muscles that support the belly may give way, resulting in abdominal hernias. When the leg muscles are abnormally fatty, they fail to contract efficiently to help blood return from the leg veins to the heart; blood collects in the leg veins, which swell, harden, and become varicose. Extra fat in and around the chest interferes with breathing, sometimes causing severe respiratory problems. Gout is more common, and even the accident rate is greater for the severely obese.

Beyond all these hazards is the risk incurred by millions of obese people throughout much of their lives— the risk of ill-advised, misguided dieting. Some fad diets are more hazardous to health than obesity itself. One survey of 29,000 claims, treatments, and theories for losing weight found fewer than 6 percent of them effective— and 13 percent dangerous!

Social and economic disadvantages also plague the fat person. Obese people are less often sought after for marriage, pay higher insurance premiums, meet discrimination when applying for college admissions and jobs, can't find attractive clothes so easily, and are limited in their choice of sports. For many, guilt, depression, withdrawal, and self-blame are inevitable psychological accompaniments to obesity.

Although obesity is a severe physical handicap, it is unlike other handicaps in two important ways. First, mortality risk is not linearly related to excess weight. Instead, there is a threshold at which risk dramatically increases. Being

*Source:* Reprinted by permission from *Understanding Nutrition*, 4th edition by Whitney and Hamilton.

addition to text marking. Text labeling forms a kind of index to help you locate information more quickly. You also use it to write yourself notes for later review.

Text labeling requires several steps. First, you read and mark your text. Then you look for patterns, main ideas, and ways to summarize information. Once you've thought of one or two summary words, you write it in the column next to that information. Finally, you include any notes to yourself about how and what to study (see Figure 1.5).

**FIGURE 1.5**
***Text Labeling***

## The Problem of Obesity

*Rate of obesity– EX-U.S.*

However you define it, obesity does occur to an alarming extent and is increasing in the developed countries. For example, in the United States some 10 to 25 percent of all teenagers and some 25 to 50 percent of all adults are obese.

*Health Hazards*

Obesity brings many health hazards with it. Insurance companies report that fat people (1) die younger from a host of causes, including heart attacks, strokes, and complications of (type II) diabetes. In fact, among adults, gaining weight often appears to (2) precipitate diabetes. Fat people more often have high (3) blood cholesterol (a risk factor for coronary heart disease), (4) hypertension, (5) complications after surgery, (6) gynecological irregularities, and the (7) toxemia of pregnancy. For men, the risk of cancers of the colon, rectum, and prostate gland rises with obesity; for women, the risk of cancers of the breast, uterus, ovaries, gallbladder, and bile ducts is greater. The burden of extra fat (8) strains the skeletal system, aggravating arthritis—especially in the knees, hips, and lower spine. The muscles that support the belly may give way, resulting in (9) abdominal hernias. When the leg muscles are abnormally fatty, they fail to contract efficiently to help blood return from the leg veins to the heart; blood collects in the leg veins, which swell, harden, and become (10) varicose. Extra fat in and around the chest interferes with breathing, sometimes causing (11) severe respiratory problems. Gout is more common, and even the (12) accident rate is greater for the severely obese.

*Risks of Diets*

Beyond all these hazards is the risk incurred by millions of obese people throughout much of their lives— the risk of ill-advised, misguided dieting. Some fad diets are more hazardous to health than obesity itself. One survey of 29,000 claims, treatments, and theories for losing weight found fewer than 6 percent of them effective— and 13 percent dangerous!

*Social, Economic, Psych disadv.*

Social and economic disadvantages also plague the fat person. Obese people are less often sought after for marriage, pay higher insurance premiums, meet discrimination when applying for college admissions and jobs, can't find attractive clothes so easily, and are limited in their choice of sports. For many, guilt, depression, withdrawal, and self-blame are inevitable psychological accompaniments to obesity.

*How unlike other handicaps*

Although obesity is a severe physical handicap, it is unlike other handicaps in two important ways. First, mortality risk is not linearly related to excess weight. Instead, there is a threshold at which risk dramatically increases. Being

*Source:* Reprinted by permission from *Understanding Nutrition*, 4th edition by Whitney and Hamilton.

**TABLE 1.3 Shorthand Symbols for Text Labeling**

| SYMBOL | MEANING |
|---|---|
| Ex | example or experiment |
| FOR | formula |
| Conc | conclusion |
| MI | main idea |
| ! or * | important information |
| → | results, leads to, steps in a sequence |
| (1), (2), (3) | numbered points—then label what the points are |
| 〰〰〰 | important |
| circled word | summarizes process |
| ? | disagree or unclear |
| TERM | important term |
| SUM | summary |
| { | indicates certain pieces of information relate |
| OPIN | author's opinion, rather than fact |

A list of some simple shorthand symbols and their meanings appears in Table 1.3. This list changes depending on your needs and the course you take.

**EXERCISE 1.6**

◆ *Mark and label the passage on ESP in Exercise 1.5. Then answer the goal-setting questions you posed in Exercise 1.5 on the lines below.*

## RECITE: SUMMARIZING AND CHECKING YOUR UNDERSTANDING

After reading you check your understanding. You **recite** the main points that answer your purpose-setting questions. This helps you determine if your understanding is complete.

**8:00 PM** **3 Golden Girls** Sophia cries foul after being hit with a fly ball at the stadium. (R) (In Stereo)

**4 Showbiz Week**

**5 Man Called Hawk** Hawk becomes emotionally involved in the case of two hearing-impaired Gallaudet College students he's hired to protect after they witness a murder. (R) (In Stereo)

**6 Real to Reel**

**9 The Ad Channel** (4 hrs.)

**10 NFL's Greatest Moments** Best Ever Quarterbacks.

**12 George Washington: The Forging of a Nation** During Washington's second term in office, he must face a wave of unpopularity stemming from British and French problems and the Whiskey Rebellion. (Part 2 of 2) (2 hrs.)

**13 Movie *** "The Opposide Sex"** (1956, Comedy) June Allyson, Dolores Gray. A happily married woman leaves for Reno on the advice of her friends. (2hrs., 30 min.)

**15 MacGruder & Loud** When MacGruder shoots an unarmed deaf teen-ager, he must deal with his guilt and the public outcry.

**17 Phenomenal World** Efforts to lessen the impact of earthquakes and predict their occurrence.

**18 Bordertown** When a mysterious lady is stranded in Bordertown due to a flue outbreak, a murder and robbery occurs.

**25 Movie *** "Houseboat"** (1958, Comedy) Cary Grant, Sophia Loren. A wealthy young woman takes a job as a family maid, bringing a widower and his children closer together. (1 hr., 50 min.)

**25 Movietime Previews**

## Recitation Through Summarization

**Summaries** consist of brief paragraphs stating the essential facts of a passage. They are concise in that they tell only basic information. The entries in television guides effectively summarize plots. Like any other summary, they tell main ideas using as few words as possible. Some students think, "The more words, the better." But, an examination of television guide entries proves that a few words can clearly state a complex plot. Summaries, then, condense key concepts.

### *The Need for Summarization*

Summaries written by authors present the key concepts found in a chapter. When found at the beginning of a chapter, they indicate the organization, the main points, and the overall scope of the chapter. At a chapter's end, they provide a condensation of key points for quick review. In the recite stage of SQ3R, your job is to write a summary that provides this information. This job is necessary, even if your text contains a summary. Why?

Writing a summary forces you to note the chapter's main ideas and their supporting details. As a result, you begin to recognize unessential or redundant information. It also aids you in seeing the purpose or intent of the chapter as well as the organizational pattern. Writing a summary enables you to see how information in a chapter is sequenced. Writing a summary is your chance to reconstruct the author's words in your own way and lock this content in your brain. The more personal you make your summary, the better it will be.

This recitation of the main points of a chapter prepares you for the review stage of SQ3R in several ways. First, rereading and locating key points reinforces your preview and initial reading of the chapter. Second, writing a summary involves putting this information in your own words. Third, the process of condensing this information into a concise summary aids memory. The thought and action involved in these processes lock the content in your mind. Furthermore, there is less to remember. Finally, comparing your summary with either that of the text or that of another student helps check your understanding of the chapter. This lets you know if you are ready to move on to review.

### *Constructing a Summary*

Writing a summary entails your being concise and clear. For example, consider the selection below:

#### *Example*

Mammals, backboned animals that feed their young on mother's milk, live almost anywhere. Monkeys and elephants make their homes in warm, tropical regions, and camels and kangaroo rats live in the hot, dry desert. Seals and whales reside in the ocean while Arctic foxes and polar bears live near the North Pole. (52 words)

*Summary: Mammals live almost anywhere including tropical regions, deserts, the ocean, and the North Pole.* (14 words)

To write an effective summary, you follow these steps:

1. *Find the main idea of the chapter.* State this idea in one sentence. This sentence should answer the goal-setting question you posed for the title of the chapter.
2. *Find the main idea of each heading and subheading in the chapter.* State these in one sentence each. These sentences should answer the goal-setting questions you posed for each heading and subheading.
3. *Locate significant supporting details.*
4. *Arrange main ideas in the order of the original chapter with supporting details interspersed as they occurred.*
5. *Rewrite these sentences in your own words.*
6. *Delete any unimportant or redundant information.* This might include definitions, quotations, illustrations, and minor details. Omit any personal opinions or criticism.
7. *If possible, group items or actions together and think of a general term to label them.*
8. *Eliminate unnecessary words.* Make noun and verb sentences. Omit unimportant adjectives and adverbs. Omit expressions like "The chapter says" and "This chapter is about." Use one word instead of two or three. For example, instead of "a large number of people," say "many people."
9. *Use about one third or one fourth as many words as there are in the original.*
10. *Revise your summary until you have the most concise statement of key information possible.*

Summarizing, like reading, is a skill that improves with practice. After this chapter, the summaries in this text will be summary exercises. At first, words and phrases will be deleted from the summary but will be listed at the top of the exercise. You complete the summary by filling in the correct words. Next, the list of deleted words and phrases will be omitted. You supply these by reviewing the chapter. Then, you will be asked to write a summary using key words and phrases. Finally, you will be asked to write a complete summary of the chapter.

**EXERCISE 1.7**

◆ *Summarize each of the paragraphs in Exercise 1.4. Use scratch paper and then write your final revision on the lines below. In addition, determine the number of words in your summary and write that number on the line next to the number of words in the original.*

**1.** ______________________________

______________________________

______________________________

______________________________

______________________________

______________________________

95 words/______ words

**2.** ______________________________

______________________________

______________________________

______________________________

______________________________

______________________________

44 words/______ words

**3.** ______________________________

______________________________

______________________________

______________________________

______________________________

______________________________

94 words/______ words

**4.** ______________________________

______________________________

______________________________

______________________________

______________________________

______________________________

95 words/______ words

5. ______________________________

______________________________

______________________________

______________________________

______________________________

82 words/______ words

6. ______________________________

______________________________

______________________________

______________________________

______________________________

40 words/______ words

7. ______________________________

______________________________

______________________________

______________________________

______________________________

119 words/______ words

8. ______________________________

______________________________

______________________________

______________________________

______________________________

80 words/______ words

9. ______________________________

______________________________

______________________________

______________________________

______________________________

44 words/______ words

**10.** ______________________________

118 words/______ words

**EXERCISE 1.8**

*Use the steps in summarizing to write a summary for the selection in Exercise 1.5 on the lines below.*

## Checking Your Understanding

If, at the end of your reading, you recite correct answers to your purpose-setting questions, then you continue reading.

What if you cannot completely answer your questions? One of two things has happened. Either you have asked the wrong questions, or you have not understood what you read.

You decide where the problem lies by looking at your questions in light of the content of the passage. Does the content answer your questions? If not, you asked the wrong ones. Your skill in developing purpose-setting questions improves with practice.

Recitation becomes easier and more active when you study with someone. This helps you see how others develop questions and find answers. You can also practice by using a tape recorder. First, you record your purpose-setting questions. Then you read and record your answers. When you play your tape, see if your questions were appropriate or if your responses answered the questions correctly. Another way to practice involves writing your questions on index cards. Again after reading, determine if your questions were appropriate. Then, write your answers on the back of the card.

If you find your questions are inappropriate, you form new questions and reread. If your questions appear to be correct but you cannot answer them, you did not understand the text. If you find this to be so, reread carefully paragraph by paragraph. In each paragraph, look for the main idea. Make sure you understand the words as used in the paragraph. Perhaps noting organizational words will help you see relationships that were unclear in the first reading.

Evaluating your text marking also helps you increase your understanding. If you marked too much, you may not be able to separate important from unimportant information. If this is a common problem for you, you need to use a pencil while marking. This allows you the freedom to rethink your notations. If you overmark only on occasion, you can remark text with a contrasting ink or highlighter. If you marked too little, you may not have enough information to comprehend fully. Thus, you need to reexamine the text and make more explicit notations.

Checking your text labels also assists you in evaluating information during recitation. You need to be sure you have labeled all text markings. If you have done so, you can see at a glance where important information lies. If your labels are vague, then reread and relabel your text. Labels should concisely, yet completely, summarize what you've marked.

◆

## REVIEW: PERMANENCE THROUGH PRACTICE

Review takes place through practice. Rather than practice making perfect, it makes information more permanent. Practice assumes many forms. They vary in the amount of time each requires and the depth to which learning occurs. Your purposes for learning and the way you learn best affect your choice of practice activities. No matter which method you choose, each involves repeating information in some way.

### Spaced Study

**Spaced study** consists of alternating short study sessions with breaks. This method is also known as **distributed practice.** You set study goals through time (e.g., 15 minutes) or task limits (e.g., three pages). After reaching these goals, you allow yourself some free time. For example, you could take a walk, have a soft drink, or call a friend.

Spaced study works for many reasons. First, spaced study rewards hard work. The breaks in spaced study serve as your reward for completing a set amount or length of study. Second, knowing you have a certain amount of time or work to study motivates you. Third, because memory has limited capacity, breaks provide time for information to be absorbed. Fourth, when you're studying complex, related information, study breaks keep you from confusing details.

## Cramming

**Cramming** involves frantic, last-minute (and sometimes all night) memorization. In cramming, you "rent" information until a test is over, rather than "owning" it for longer periods of time. Probably the least effective means, cramming lacks permanency.

## Study Groups or Partners

The old saying "Two heads are better than one" describes **study groups** or partners. Their purpose is discussion of information. Therefore, learning becomes a more active process. Group members explain and listen to each other. This allows them to use their auditory, visual, and physical senses. Combining these sensory impressions adds to the active learning. It also makes memory more permanent. Finally, group discussions motivate members. This happens because members make commitments to prepare for and come to study sessions.

Study groups learn different types of information. Group members provide drill in learning definitions, lists, or dates. Discussing complex or confusing information increases the understanding of group members. One note of caution concerns the way in which groups practice. Because most groups discuss information aloud members may neglect practicing their writing. If you have difficulty composing written responses to test items, you also need to practice putting information on paper.

Another factor to consider concerns the composition of the study group. Group members need to be friendly and responsible. Arguing and bad feelings often prevent members from making the most of their study time. A member's lack of preparedness can interrupt the flow of study. Group members must make two commitments. First, they need to arrive on time for all meetings. Second, they need to be prepared to discuss the topic at hand. The group functions best when each member

**TABLE 1.4 Methods of Overlearning**

| METHOD I | METHOD II |
|---|---|
| **1.** List each item separately on note cards.<br>**2.** Learn the first three cards.<br>**3.** Add one card.<br>**4.** Practice all four cards.<br>**5.** Add one card.<br>**6.** Practice all five cards.<br>**7.** Delete the card from the original set that you know the best and add one card.<br>**8.** Practice with all five cards.<br>**9.** Repeat steps 7 and 8 until you know all items. | **1.** Divide the list into manageable units (3 to 5 items per unit, depending on the difficulty of the material).<br>**2.** Learn one set.<br>**3.** Add another set.<br>**4.** Practice all sets.<br>**5.** Repeat steps 3 and 4 until you know all items. |

contributes to the overall learning of the group, and no member uses the group to replace personal learning.

## Overlearning

**Overlearning** (Tenney, 1986) consists of overlapping study. For example, suppose you need to learn a list of 40 terms in history. You can overlearn the list in one of two ways (see Table 1.4). Overlearning reinforces information following initial learning.

**EXERCISE 1.9**

♦ *Use the excerpt on pages 41–57 to complete the following instructions.*

1. Survey the chapter. Underline or highlight everything that you should look at when overviewing a chapter.
2. In this text, major headings are printed in boldface capital letters. Major subheadings are found in boldface flush left on the text column and printed in capital and lowercase letters. Important terms are printed in boldface throughout the text. Make at least one purpose-setting question for the title and for each heading and subheading.
3. Read each section of the text in order to find the answer to your question. If you cannot answer your question, either set a new question or reread.
4. Answer your questions.

**5.** Review your responses to each question to check your accuracy. List below the strategy you would use to review for an exam.

**EXERCISE 1.10**

*Survey chapter two of READ* by underlining or highlighting all information you'd preview as a part of your survey.

## Chapter 1

# Health Information and Behavior

### For Openers . . .

True or false? If false, say what is true.

1. Being well is best defined as being free from disease.
2. Adults catch the most prevalent diseases of today the same way as they caught malaria and smallpox in earlier times.
3. People can make themselves physiologically younger or older by the ways they choose to live.
4. Knowing how to relax can lengthen your life.
5. Women generally live longer than men do.
6. Accidents are among the major causes of death for middle-aged to older adults.
7. If a product label makes the claim "organic" or "natural," this means the product has unusual powers to promote health.
8. A person who wants to change a harmful health habit, and knows how, will do so.
9. Some people fail at making positive behavior changes because they undertake too many changes at one time.
10. You are responsible for changing the harmful health behaviors of the people you care about.

(Answers on page 16.)

## OUTLINE

Health: Your Choice
The Sources of Health Information
Health Behavior and Behavior Change
Other People's Health Behavior
**Spotlight:** The Consumer and Health Fraud

This book is about enjoying life. It challenges you to increase your knowledge, strengths, and skills in many areas—in self-awareness, consumerism, stress management, emotional health, intimate relationships, nutrition, fitness, accident and disease prevention, and many others. Its aim is to enhance your confidence and competence in all these areas.

This is a tall order—especially since everyone already possesses considerable experience and knowledge about all these things. Why read a book about them? Oddly, the experience and knowledge people pick up about life are always somewhat haphazard. Standard schooling, no matter where obtained, ensures that people learn the basics of language and mathematics, but the skills they need to manage their lives are taught only in bits and pieces. This book hopes to fill in some of the gaps for everyone who reads it.

How, then, can people maximally enjoy their lives? By feeling well, confident, and as far as possible, in control of their worlds. And what does it mean to be well? This book defines a well person as one who has not only physical but also mental, emotional, interpersonal, social, and even spiritual, strengths.

Imagine for a moment that you are a magnificently healthy person, with strengths in every one of these realms. The following paragraphs define **health**, using you as an example.

**health:** a range of states; at a minimum, freedom from negative states such as physical disease, physical deterioration, social maladjustment, mental illness, and so on.

At a maximum, a state that some call **wellness**: the achievement of full potential mentally, emotionally, physically, interpersonally, socially, and spiritually.

Ideally, then, as an emotionally healthy person, you have a strong sense of self. You are willing to attempt new learnings and behaviors, and are able to handle setbacks without loss of self-esteem. You have a realistic grasp of current information, and you are sufficiently assertive to resist being victimized by misinformation and fraud. You manage stress with skill and enjoyment, and don't let it become overwhelming. You keep tabs on your emotions, and you manage and express them appropriately. Finally, you know when to seek help. These strengths and how to cultivate them are described in Chapters 2 and 3.

A healthy person cultivates physical health, too. To be physically healthy does *not* mean to be without illness, of course, for illnesses sometimes attack us without our consent or control. But it does mean to manage your food intakes, body weight, physical fitness, and sleep needs so as to support your own health, and it also means to abstain from harmful drug use. Chapters 4, 5, and 6 are devoted to nutrition, weight control, fitness, and sleep; and Chapters 7, 8, and 9 discuss the appropriate uses of medical drugs and to the effects of harmful drugs and the importance of abstinence from them.

A healthy person also has social and spiritual strengths. It is important to be able to develop and maintain intimacy with others and to form successful long-term partnerships. It is important to understand and appreciate your own sexuality, and manage your sexual relationships in a way that enhances the quality of your life. If you are sexually active, you need to understand the principles of contraception, to be able to communicate about it, and to make informed decisions on its use. If you are a woman, then on choosing to bear a child, you need to learn to manage your pregnancy and childbirth with attention to the health of both yourself and your infant. When you become a mother or father, you need to understand human development sufficiently to be able to nurture children or younger people, even if your own parents were not nurturing parents. As you grow older, you will continue learning and facing new challenges; and finally, you will be willing to learn what is required in facing death (your own or someone else's). Chapters 10, 11, 12, and 13 take up these concerns of the human life cycle, and the Spotlight at the end of Chapter 13 is devoted to spiritual health, the part that inspires all the rest.

Since life's events are at times outside an individual's control, you also have to be aware that accidents and infectious diseases (including sexually transmitted diseases) are a real possibility, and take appropriate measures to prevent them. You also know your own familial risk factors for diseases such as heart disease, diabetes, or cancer, and adopt the behaviors that will minimize your risks. Prevention of accidents and diseases is the subject of Chapters 14, 15, 16, and 17. Because you cannot always prevent accidents and diseases, you need to know how to use the health care system to advantage and when to attend to your own medical needs (self-care). Pointers on these important subjects are given in Chapter 18.

Last, and encompassing all of these other health concerns, is your relationship to the larger environment—the earth. You carry your share of the responsibility for this realm. Its importance, and the roles that are rightfully yours in connection with it, are the subjects of Chapter 19.

This long description not only defines health but also implies actions to achieve it. It could be termed a list of **life management skills**. People who have already developed these skills to some extent, and who are actively moving forward toward health goals, are maximizing their chances for enjoyment of life.

**life management skills:** the skills that help a person realize his or her potential to be well and enjoy life; this book's strategies.

## HEALTH: YOUR CHOICE

You change your health by the choices you make every day, whether you mean to or not. The choices you make today will either improve or harm your health, and their effects are compounded by time. Today's choices, repeated for a week, will have seven times the impact. Repeated every day

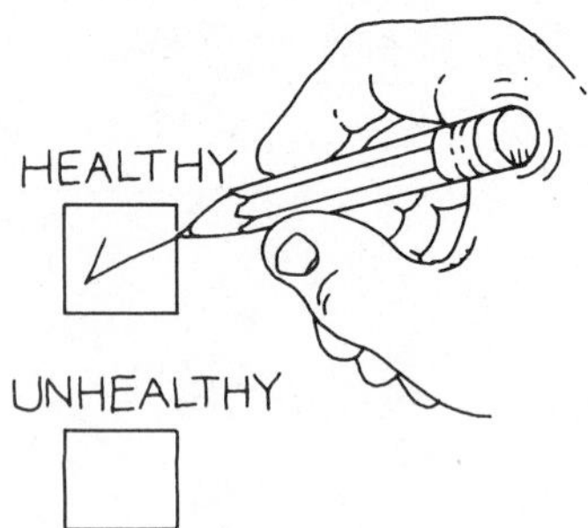


For most people, health through life is largely determined by the choices they make.

for a year, they will have 365 times the impact on your health. Over years, the effects accumulate still further.

With the information available today and presented in this book, you can make choices that will improve the quality of your life and even your statistical life expectancy.

This statement reflects a reality that differs from the reality of the past. People's health has always been influenced by the same factors—their heredity, their environment, and their personal lifestyle choices—but the weights of these factors have changed. Today, personal choices have a much greater influence on health than they had in the past. The reason is that the world we live in is different in many significant ways.

For one thing, far more information is available, thanks to scientific advances. We know more about psychology, physical health, and sexuality than ever before. We know more about the causes of **infectious diseases** and their prevention, and we are beginning to learn enough about the **lifestyle diseases** to have a grasp of what we need to do to prevent those, too. Perhaps only in the spiritual realm can it be said that we are no further advanced than our ancestors; for some age-old truths seem to hold as true today as they ever have, and our task in mastering them is not so much to create new ones as to appreciate the old.

This book uses these terms interchangeably: Infectious disease = communicable disease. Lifestyle disease = degenerative disease. See the glossaries in and at the ends of chapters for all terms that appear in boldface type.

**locus of control:** the location of control inside or outside a person. Before a person will take responsibility and act to acquire health, that person must see that the locus of control of the situation is within. A simpler way to say this is that the person *owns* the responsibility.

Figure 1–1 shows the probable course of a person who invests in learning about health. The investment leads to improved quality of life.

That people have more control over their lives than before means that they have more responsibility. As psychology puts it, the **locus of control**, with respect to many health factors, is inside the individual; people are not the hapless victims of external chance. It is vital to know the difference, because only when people realize that they can change things do they take action. People do not helplessly "catch" the consequences of poor lifestyle choices as they once caught smallpox. A different word is used: they "contract" lifestyle diseases through their own choices.

**FIGURE 1–1 Invest in Learning**

**For the majority of people it pays to learn about health and apply the knowledge.**

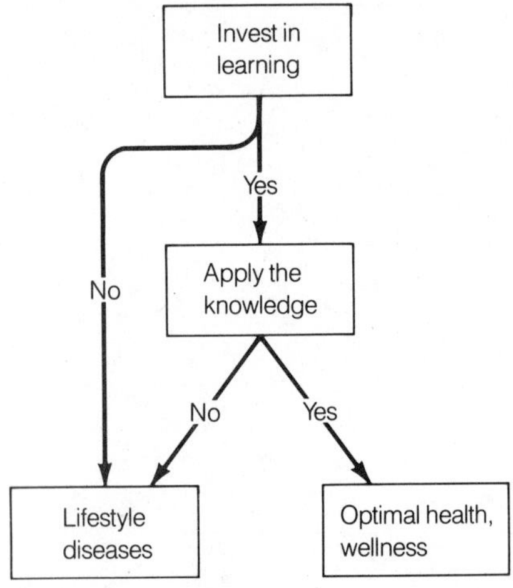


Researchers have given a dramatic demonstration of how personal choices affect health. They studied nearly 7,000 adults in California and noticed that some people seemed young for their age; others, old for their age. To find out what made the difference, the researchers focused on health habits and identified six factors that had maximum impact on **physiological age**: regular, adequate sleep; regularity of meals; regular physical activity; abstinence from smoking; abstinence from, or moderation in, alcohol use; and weight control. The effects of these factors were cumulative. That is, those who followed all six positive practices were in better health, even if older in calendar years, than people who failed to do so. In fact, the physical health of those who reported all positive health practices was consistently about the same as that of people *30 years younger* who followed few or none.[1*] These findings demonstrated that although you cannot alter the year of your birth, you can alter the probable length of your life. In effect, you can make yourself younger or older by the way you choose to live. This chapter's Life Choice Inventory illustrates this point.

Middle-aged to older people served as subjects for the California study just described. For younger people, accidents are a seventh significant cause of loss of life and health. The Life Choice Inventory includes accident

Your age as measured in years from the date of your birth is your **chronological age**. Your age as estimated from your body's health and probable life expectancy is your **physiological age**.

*Reference notes are in Appendix D.

## LIFE CHOICE INVENTORY: HOW LONG WILL YOU LIVE?

prevention as one of the strategies most likely to promote physical health for adults.

This section of the chapter has offered the reasons why it makes sense to study health. The next two sections answer the questions of how to study it and how to apply the information.

## THE SOURCES OF HEALTH INFORMATION

Many sources of information claim that their statements are facts. For example, claims made in advertisements often appear to do this. Actors dressed as scientists or physicians appear on the screen or on the magazine page and make solemn pronouncements to the effect that "research has shown this product to be effective. . . ." But when you look closely, where is the evidence? Not on the screen, and not on the magazine page.

How, then, can the consumer of health information decide whether to believe the claims made by the promoters of health products and services? This section's main purpose is to enhance your skill in distinguishing between valid health information and health **fraud**.

When you encounter a claim for a product or service, you can use a set of basic strategies to help you evaluate it. Ask and find answers to the following questions: Who is making the claim? What are that person's qualifications for making such statements? On what evidence is the claim based? Where was that evidence published? In what language style is it stated?

A simple rule governs the evaluation of claims on the basis of who is making them. If the person or organization making the claim stands to profit by selling you something you would not otherwise buy, discount the claim. It is as simple as that. To get honest, unbiased information on any product or service, find an outside expert who can make an assessment. An example familiar to most people is buying a used car. The salesperson's word alone isn't sufficient, nor is the word of someone who has another car to sell; an independent garage mechanic should be hired to assess the car. The mechanic is not personally involved in the sale and stands to gain most by telling the truth, because the satisfied customer will give a favorable report to other customers.

If the person making the claim does not appear to be motivated by personal gain, then there are some other questions to ask—notably, about the person's education, training, skill, and reputation. A person may be justly famed and admired for one specialty, but that does not indicate qualifications to speak in another specialty area. A noted poet is probably not as well qualified to speak on physical fitness as the trainer of Olympic athletes; a famed heart surgeon may not be knowledgeable about sex therapy; the governor of a state is not an authority on nutrition; and so forth. When an authority makes pronouncements on a given topic, ask yourself whether the person has the education and experience to speak on that topic.

We mentioned four characteristics to look for in sizing up a person's qualifications as an expert. Education is indispensable; there is no substitute for the hundreds of hours of book learning that provide the foundation for a person's expertise. Training is another, for all the book learning in the world is useless until the person has practiced using it in real-life situations. Skill is a third; it normally develops as the result of education and training, but some people do not become skilled even with the best of both. Finally comes reputation: a person earns that by developing the first three assets.

Another thing to notice about a claim is the information source. Health information purveyed by the mass communication media—newspapers, magazines, radio, television—is notoriously unreliable. Books on health written for the public are also so unreliable that most professional organizations maintain committees to combat the misinformation in them. A list of organizations that provide reliable scientific information appears in

### ⊛ STRATEGIES for Evaluating Health Claims

*To evaluate a claim:*

⊛ **Ask who is making the claim. Does that person stand to gain from your believing it?**

⊛ **Ask about the person's education, training, skill, and reputation.**

⊛ **Ask where the claim is published: newspaper, magazine, book written for the public, textbook, journal?**

⊛ **Consult the professional society concerned with the subject matter in question.**

## Credentials of Physicians and Other Health Care Providers

This book uses the term **health care provider** to describe those people to whom you can safely turn for medical care: the physician (M.D., D.O.), the physician's assistant (P.A.), or the nurse practitioner (R.N., R.N.P.). These people can all provide care for ordinary medical problems; all can refer you to specialists for extraordinary problems. The term **client** in place of **patient** is also appropriate. A patient is, literally, a passive person, one who waits, who is dependent on someone else, the physician, for the solution to a medical problem. A client is an active person, one who is in charge of his or her own health and who pays the health care provider for services that person is trained to provide. Sometimes one term, sometimes the other, is used in the chapters that follow, depending on the attitude toward self of the person seeking medical assistance.

Appendix A, and any of them can serve as sources for your own inquiries about the authenticity of scientific information in their areas.*

One way you can gather clues about the validity of health information is to study the language in which a claim is stated. Many buzzwords and phrases can alert you to false or misleading information—among them, the following:

⊛ **Write to the National Council Against Health Fraud.**

⊛ **Be alert to the language in which claims are made.**

- *Organic, health, herbal, natural.* These terms have no legal meaning as used on labels, and although intended to imply unusual power to promote health, they do not.
- *Scientific breakthrough, medical miracle.* Seldom do popular reports prove true when they make statements in defiance of current scientific knowledge—new cure for cancer, a way to lose weight without cutting calories, a tiny pill with enormous power. In advertisements, such claims almost never prove true.
- *Doctors agree, authorities agree.* When the identity of the doctors is not revealed, or when no reference to an authoritative publication is provided, these statements are meaningless. They may mean only that the advertiser persuaded three doctors to agree.

Some false claims are recognizable if you can spot the confused thinking that underlies them. Examples:

- "Tiredness is a symptom of iron-poor blood." This is true. "Therefore, if you are tired, you have iron-poor blood, and you need iron supplements." This is not true because tiredness is also a symptom of other conditions. You need a diagnosis.

⊛ **Don't guess at a diagnosis; be sure.**

*If you have questions about a medical book, product, or service, write to the American Medical Association; about an anticancer book, product, or service, to the American Cancer Society; about a heart disease preventive, to the American Heart Association; about a diet or nutrient supplement, to the American Dietetic Association; and so forth. Many of the professional organizations have also banded together to form the National Council Against Health Fraud (NCAHF), which has branches in many states. The NCAHF monitors radio, television, and other advertising, investigates complaints, and maintains a bimonthly newsletter to keep consumers informed on the latest health misinformation. You can write to the NCAHF at P.O. Box 1276, Loma Linda, CA 92354.

⊛ **Recognize that no food is essential.**

- "People need the essential nutrients or else they'll get sick." This is true. "Therefore, they need food X, which contains nutrients." This is not true, because no food is the unique possessor of any nutrient. Other foods can supply essential nutrients in the amounts needed.

Symptoms especially likely to be used to draw in the unsuspecting consumer are those everybody has—tiredness, aches and pains, occasional insomnia, colds. Another class of such symptoms includes those everyone can see because they involve external parts of the body: the skin, hands, face, hair, scalp, eyes, fingernails.

⊛ **Recognize the child in yourself who frightens easily and delights in magic.**

Some claims are outright tricks that work because we consumers can be like children who frighten easily and delight in magic. The tricks are simple, but they are still attractive. Who hasn't been tempted to buy a product or try a service because it sounds so easy ("no effort"), because it costs so little and produces such a big reward ("something for nothing"), because it will protect you from terrible things (scare tactics), because it will relieve you of some natural characteristic you are being taught to despise, or because it will restore your vitality or youth or beauty or all of these (magical thinking)? Remember: aging is inevitable; so is death. Don't be misled into thinking you can totally prevent them. Learn what is preventable about aging and what isn't. Promote your health in the ways that truly work—they involve your lifestyle choices. None of them is magic.

The first part of this chapter illustrated how health choices affect the quality of life. This middle section has shown how to sort health facts from fads and frauds. Following is information on how to put health facts to work in your own life.

## HEALTH BEHAVIOR AND BEHAVIOR CHANGE

Health knowledge is hardly beneficial if it merely enables people to make A's on tests. It is valuable only if people use it to make informed choices. These choices may require them to change their behavior. The next sections describe this process. They define motivation and itemize the steps to action, explain behavior modification, and, finally, discuss how expectations affect behavior change.

### Motivation

In general, **motives** are forces that move people to act. They may be either instinctive or learned. Instinctive motives, or **drives**, are strongest: hunger and thirst impel you to meet your needs for food and water. Learned motives may also be powerful—consider the desire for possessions, recognition, or achievement. A powerful motive virtually impels a person to act.

A person's **motivation** is modified by three factors: the value of the reward (how big is the reward and what does it cost?), its **latency** (how soon will the reward come or how soon will the price have to be paid?), and its probability (how likely is the reward, how certain the price?).

Contrast these situations:

- Eat ice cream now (immediate reward); notice your weight gain tomorrow (pay later).
- Forgo ice cream now; expect weight loss next week.

- Enjoy a cigarette (a certainty) now; pay with lung disease (a probability) in the future.
- Give up smoking now; enjoy better health in the future.

No wonder it's difficult to motivate people to change their health habits! Nevertheless, if persuaded of the importance, they sometimes do.

The steps that lead to behavior change seem to be these:

- Awareness: "I could choose to change."
- Cognition: "I know how to change."
- Emotion: "I want to change."
- Decision: "I will change."
- Action: "I am changing."

The elements of behavior change.

They don't always appear in the same order, but they always seem to appear.

Being overweight is a problem familiar to many people. (If you can't identify with this problem, substitute some other while reading this.) No doubt you know someone who wants to lose weight. He has taken the first two steps: he is aware of the need, and he knows how—at least, to some extent—yet he still takes no action. Eating fattening foods brings him great pleasure, for one thing. For another, without being aware of it, he may receive some benefits from being fat. (He doesn't have to cope with many sexual advances, for example.) He may *claim* he wants to lose weight, and he may be chronically upset with himself for not getting thinner, yet deep inside he may not really want to change. Many people get stuck at this point.

Wanting is emotional—and when the emotions become positively charged, a rush of energy enables the person to act. Still, even if the wanting is so strong that it brings tears of frustration or anger, emotion is not enough to change behavior. We all can name people who know how to diet and who desperately want to lose weight, and yet who still do nothing. The person has to make a decision—a step in which the **will** is engaged.

Even psychologists don't fully understand how people make decisions. But everyone knows how it feels to arrive at a decision point. One day, your friend who needs to lose weight says, "I'm going to eat wisely from now on," and from that point on, possibly for months, he may not deviate from an unbroken course of restricting calories and losing weight until he seems to have become a completely different person.

In a sense, he is a different person. He has had to let go of his old habits absolutely. He has had to go through a grief experience—the loss of a cherished habit with its rewards. His self-image has had to change. He *was* an overeater; he is now an *ex*-overeater, an abstainer. He *was* a person who avoided facing certain problems by overeating; he is now a person who owns those problems and deals with them constructively. He knows himself better, and he asserts himself more effectively.

The commitment that comes with a firm decision to make a significant life change is profound and transforming. It has been called "the moment of truth," "conversion," "submission," or "total surrender." And total it has to be, for a long road of effort lies ahead.

In case you are reflecting on your own behavior and possible changes, it is as important to know when you are *not* ready as to know when you are. Much needless time and anxiety is wasted struggling with "I should; I ought to; I must" and with shame and guilt over "I can't; I failed again." An important part of arriving at permanent desired behavior change is the awareness that success may require many practice runs. You don't have to succeed totally the first time.

Suppose a person has firmly decided to make a change and is now about to begin. Many changes in individual, small, daily behaviors are going to be necessary. It will help to understand the basic principles of **behavior modification**.

## Behavior Modification

Some psychologists view human behavior as regulated by environmental factors. In simple terms, they see each behavior as sandwiched between two environmental conditions, those that precede it and those that follow it—the **antecedents** and the **consequences**:

$$\text{A (antecedents)} \longrightarrow \text{B (behavior)} \longleftrightarrow \text{C (consequences)}$$

A behavior occurs in response to antecedents (cues or stimuli); the more intense the antecedents are, the more likely the behavior will occur. The behavior leads to consequences, and the more intense these are, the more or less likely the behavior will occur again. Behavior modification involves manipulating these environmental conditions so as to favor the repeated occurrence of a desired behavior and extinguish the occurrence of unwanted behaviors.

Figure 1–2 illustrates strategies to modify antecedents, behaviors, and consequences to cement a desired behavior in place: in this example, studying effectively. Strategies 1 and 2 eliminate or suppress the strength of cues to the unwanted behavior. Strategy 3 increases the strength of cues to the desired behavior. Strategy 4 repeats the wanted behavior itself: the more

**FIGURE 1–2 Behavior Modification Used to Facilitate Effective Studying**

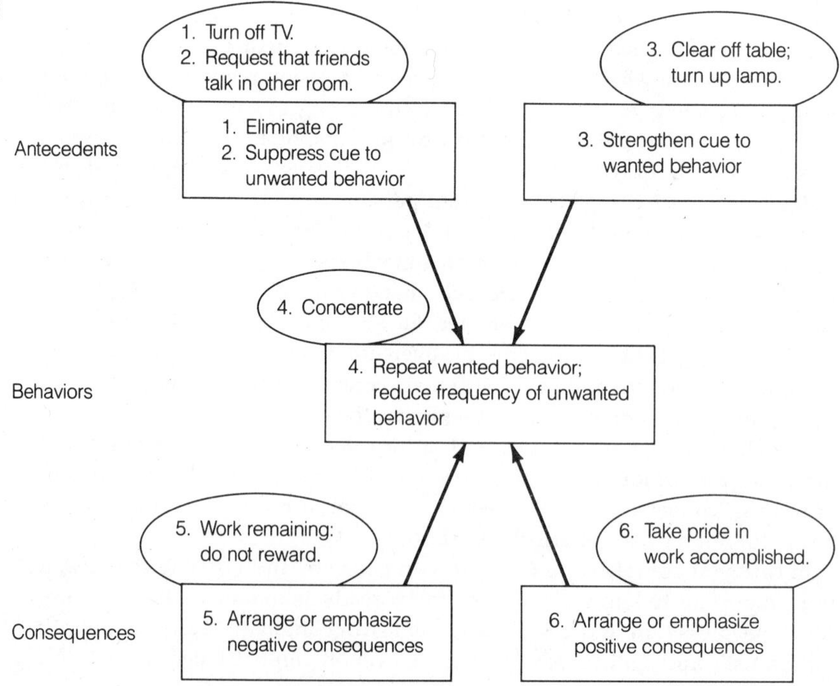

often the desired behavior is repeated, the weaker the tendency to repeat the unwanted behavior. Strategy 5 arranges or emphasizes negative consequences of the unwanted behavior, thus weakening it; and strategy 6 arranges or emphasizes positive consequences of the wanted behavior, thus strengthening it.

The example in the figure illustrates how behavior modification works. Kristin needs to write a paper but lacks enough motivation to get started on it. Conditions are unfavorable: the TV is blaring, two friends have dropped in and are conversing, and there is no inviting place to settle down and work. It is tempting to procrastinate (unwanted behavior). Knowing the principles of behavior modification, though, Kristin modifies the antecedents. Turning off the TV eliminates one cue to procrastination (strategy 1 of Figure 1–2). Requesting that the friends talk in another room suppresses another (strategy 2). Clearing off the table and turning up the lamp provide cues to studying (strategy 3). Once Kristin begins to concentrate, the tendency to procrastinate fades and the work begins to move forward (strategy 4). Self-congratulation is now in order (strategy 6).

A note about emphasizing negative consequences (strategy 5): if Kristin had chosen to procrastinate, the result would have been work left undone—a negative consequence. But to pay much attention to this would be to reward it. Punishment is a form of attention—and attention is a reward. That is why, sometimes, unruly children misbehave more when they are punished. The most effective way to use strategy 5 is to ignore the unwanted behavior, not to call attention to it, and not to punish it.

Behavior modification techniques equip people with a means of effectively changing their behavior if they want to. A particularly attractive feature of these strategies is that they don't involve blaming onself or putting oneself down. The person who understands these techniques can say, "I know how to change— when I'm ready."

## Expectations

Sometimes, even after what seems to be a firm commitment to changed behavior, a person slips back. Why? Once you have instituted a change in your life, you will persist in maintaining that change only if the benefits continue to outweigh the barriers.

Let's switch our attention to a woman who smokes, to examine the broader application of behavior-change principles. She has decided to give up smoking, but after a day without cigarettes, she is a nervous wreck. After two days, she is climbing the walls and driving her friends and lifemate crazy. At this time, the long-distant rewards of eventual respiratory health have receded far into the background in her thinking, and all that she is aware of is her desperate desire for a cigarette. This being the case, it is not surprising that she fails to give up smoking and returns to the habit within one or two days after making the initial effort.

To succeed, this person needs to have realistic expectations and a plan of action. She needs to know from the outset how hard it will be and especially how long it will take before the pain goes away and the rewards begin to come in. It helps, too, to be alert to the immediate rewards—immediate, that is, in terms of days, not years. After a week, she is free of thoughts about cigarettes for several hours at a time, and in climbing stairs, she does not become as winded as before. If she tunes in to these immediate rewards, she may make it through the hard part.

In contrast, the person who returns to the habit may have been unaware that the pain of withdrawal was about to diminish and that rewards were so soon to come. These awarenesses will help to cement the desired behavior change in place.

People need to know, too, that they can't undertake too large a change and expect to succeed. Suppose a person decides to give up cookies and cakes and candies and colas, in fact to avoid all sugar—and not only to do that, but to avoid all fatty foods too—and not only that, but also to give up all alcoholic beverages—and to switch from whole milk to nonfat milk and never to use cream—and to give up salt—and to start jogging a mile every morning and do situps every night—to go to church on Sundays—and to spend at least two added hours each day on homework . . . That person may be in for a rude surprise. All these changes can be made, but not all at once. After only a few days, such a person will be exhausted and will give it all up. We congratulate the person on having identified many worthy goals. Now it's time to plan realistically. New behaviors require energy. They need to be taken up a few at a time—in fact, probably one by one.

This section has not identified all the many steps you can take to ensure that your behavior change efforts will be successful, but it has outlined some of the more important ones. A plan of action that incorporates these steps and others might read like the one in this chapter's Strategies box.

Sometimes people act on a new behavior only for a short time. We don't understand exactly what happens when a person reverts to a negative health habit, but it is clear that at least two things are involved: magical thinking and forgetting. An ex-smoker's magical thinking might sound like this: "I'm a different person now. I can take just one cigarette; I won't get hooked." People sometimes have to make this kind of mistake several times before they finally learn they cannot afford it.

People who have long maintained a new way of life sometimes report episodes in which the old way springs back to consciousness, in dreams or unexpected memories. An ex-drug addict reports that she suddenly felt high again, and it scared her. A dieter dreams that he's been bingeing on chocolate. An ex-alcohol abuser awakens in a cold sweat from a nightmare in which she got drunk. No one seems to know why these episodes occur, but they do serve a useful purpose: they bring back a vivid memory of the old behavior—and its price. Alcohol counselors say, "If you can't remember the last drink, then it wasn't your last." The maintenance of a new behavior sometimes depends on not forgetting that a return to the old behavior would be worse.

Finally, people changing their behavior have to realize that their self-image must change as well. Sometimes the self-image is slow to change, and the behavior slips back. People have to do some psychological work with their physical work to change through and through. A person who gives up smoking has to learn to see herself as a confirmed ex-smoker. A person who takes up swimming every day has to own his new identity: "I am a swimmer."

In summary, the maintenance of changed health-promoting behavior is facilitated by:

- Continued motivation (remembering vividly the price of the old behavior and remaining aware of the benefits of the new).
- A changed self-image.

## STRATEGIES: How to Change Your Behavior

**If you want to change a behavior, try taking the following steps:**

1. Identify the goal, the behaviors that will lead to it, and those that will prevent it. List the advantages and disadvantages of the desired behaviors. Learn what will be involved.
2. Commit to changing. Plan. Dedicate the necessary time and money. Face what you'll have to give up or displace to give high priority to making the change. Mobilize the support of family and friends.
3. Divide the behavior into manageable portions. Set small, achievable goals, and plan periodic rewards.
4. Envision your changed future self. Role-play the new you in your imagination. Buy the equipment you need (owning a pair of jogging shoes gives you a boost toward being a jogger).
5. Pick a time to start, and write it down. Tell others, if that will help reinforce your determination.
6. Plan stepwise progression if suitable. ("The next time, I'll take only one drink on each weekend day.")
7. Try out the plan.
8. Modify the plan in ways that will succeed.
9. Try the modified plan.
10. Evaluate your progress often.
11. Savor your results and value the benefits.

One additional factor helps immensely if behavior change is to succeed, a factor that may be more important than any of those named above:

- Self-esteem.

The person who starts out feeling worthwhile, who cares enough to invest energy and effort in attaining optimal health, is a step ahead of the game from the beginning. The person who begins to succeed in changing behavior gains improved self-esteem from the effort and so wins an advantage for the efforts ahead.

## OTHER PEOPLE'S HEALTH BEHAVIOR

Perhaps you are not resistant to change but are concerned about someone else's behavior: "How can I get my father (mother, friend, child) to change?" These people's choices are *not* your responsibility. You can care about them and you can help them, but you can't change their behavior. No matter how much you may want them to do what you think is best, you cannot make the choice for them. In fact, your best bet is usually to say nothing and let the awareness of what they need to do come upon them from inside. Most importantly, make no negative judgments; these reduce the other person's self-esteem and make change less, not more, likely.

You can, however, facilitate the dawning of awareness. These strategies are especially effective:

- Give straightforward feedback.
- Set an example with your own behavior.
- Offer authenticated information, or make sure it is available.

Here is an example of the first strategy. A student in a health course was earning money by evening babysitting for a young mother who went out to several parties a week. The student observed that the mother usually had two or three drinks before she left home and often came home dangerously drunk. All she dared to say to the woman was, "Gee, every time I see you, you have a drink in your hand."

As it turned out, this was all she needed to say. The woman chose to seek treatment for alcoholism and later thanked the student for her help. "What did I do to help?" the student wanted to know. "You made me aware that I had a problem," the woman replied. "I hadn't realized how far I had gone until I saw myself as you saw me." The student had delivered straightforward feedback, as a mirror does, with no judgment implied.

The second strategy, setting an example, is also effective because it is nonjudgmental. No one likes to be told, "You really ought to quit [behavior A]" or "You really ought to start [behavior B]." In fact, people often do not even like to be reminded of resolutions they themselves have made: "Aren't you going to work out today?" If you change a health habit yourself, however, the person you are concerned about will surely notice and may begin thinking about doing the same thing. When ready, this person may ask you how you did it or ask to join you.

The third strategy, to supply authenticated information, helps increase people's knowledge, so that when they become ready to make a change, they are equipped to do it. The information you offer may be statistics on the effects of a certain health behavior or "how-to" facts such as the meeting time and place for the next smoke-enders class. It is often better not to push such information at people, rather simply to make sure it is available in case they want it.

If you try to influence someone and think you've failed, take comfort in the fact that the "failure" may really be success waiting to happen. Your feedback and information may not tip the scale right now but together with other factors will weigh on the favorable side. It may take years before someone decides to make a lifestyle change for health's sake, but when the change happens, the person may well credit it to something someone said years earlier. Don't hesitate to care. Do what you can, then take satisfaction in having done your best, and let it go.

When someone does make the choice to change to a health-promoting behavior, you then have a further opportunity to help:

- Offer positive reinforcement and support.

Often it is best to keep the verbal praise moderate; some people don't like to have too much attention drawn to their first, tentative efforts. Also, make sure the reinforcement you give is positive, not negative: "I'm glad to see you doing that," not "It's about time you did that" (which takes the credit from your friend). Also: "You look wonderful," not "You look better" (which implies that your friend looked awful before).

Much more could be said about promoting positive choices, but these ideas are enough for a start. Whether it is your own life or other people's that you keep in mind as you read this book, we hope the following chapters will bring you the information you need to make informed health choices.

## STUDY AIDS

1. Identify the areas of life to which the term *health* applies.
2. Itemize life management skills to promote health in the following areas: (a) emotional; (b) physical; (c) interpersonal, social, and spiritual; and (d) life events such as accidents and diseases.
3. Contrast the lifestyle diseases and the infectious diseases. Explain how the nature of the lifestyle diseases makes us responsible to some extent for our own health.
4. Explain the concept of locus of control and how it relates to disease prevention and health promotion.
5. Describe the difference between chronological and physiological age.
6. Identify six factors shown by research to have maximum impact on the physiological age of adults and an additional factor that affects life expectancy in younger adults.
7. List elements a person should consider when evaluating health claims and explain why they are important.
8. Describe ways to recognize false or inflated health claims.
9. List some factors that influence motivation.
10. List and describe the steps that lead to behavior change.
11. Describe six ways in which people can manipulate antecedents, behaviors, and consequences to facilitate behavior change.
12. Identify some requirements for maintaining a changed behavior.
13. Describe a plan of action for ensuring successful behavior change.
14. Describe effective strategies for facilitating desirable health behavior change in other people.

## GLOSSARY

**antecedents:** see *behavior modification.*

**behavior modification:** the changing of behavior by the manipulation of *antecedents* (cues, or environmental factors that trigger behavior), the behavior itself, and *consequences* (the penalties or rewards attached to behavior).

**chronological age:** age as measured in years from date of birth. See also *physiological age.*

*chron* = time

**client:** a person who pays another to perform a service. This term is gradually replacing the term *patient*, as *health care provider* is replacing *physician.* See *health care provider.*

**communicable disease:** see *infectious disease.*

**consequences:** see *behavior modification.*

**degenerative disease:** see *lifestyle disease.*

**disease:** a diagnosable disorder such as heart disease or tuberculosis. Two terms often used to describe disease conditions are *acute* and *chronic.* An acute condition is one that comes on suddenly and may be intense, such as attacks of influenza or heart attacks. A chronic condition is one that progresses and does not go away, such as heart disease, arthritis, or tuberculosis. See also *infectious disease*, *lifestyle disease.*

**drives:** instincts that propel individuals into action, such as hunger, thirst, fear, and needs for sleep and sex. Drives may prompt an individual to act alone or to act in relation to others.

**fraud:** conscious deceit, practiced for profit.

**health:** a range of states with physical, mental, emotional, interpersonal, social, and spiritual components. At a minimum, health means freedom from negative states such as physical disease, physical deterioration, social maladjustment, mental illness, etc. At a maximum, it means the achievement of full potential physically, mentally, emotionally, interpersonally, socially, and spiritually—a state that some call *wellness.*

**health care provider:** a term used in this book to refer to people who are qualified and credentialed to provide safe, expert general medical care—physicians (M.D., D.O.), physician assistants (P.A.), or nurse practitioners (R.N., R.N.P., for registered nurse practitioner). The credentialing of these people is described in Chapter 18.

**infectious disease:** a disease that can be passed from person to person and is caused by a specific disease-carrying agent. Also called *communicable disease.*

**latency:** the time lag between an action and its consequence. (With respect to behavior, latency modifies motivation; that is, the longer the time lag, the weaker the motivation.)

**life management skills:** the skills that help a person to realize his or her potential to be well and enjoy life; this book's strategies.

**lifestyle disease:** a disease characterized by degeneration of body organs due to misuse and neglect. Lifestyle diseases cannot be passed from person to person; they are often influenced by personal lifestyle choices such as eating habits, smoking, alcohol use, and level of physical activity; and they are usually chronic and irreversible. Lifestyle diseases are often called *degenerative diseases.* Examples are heart disease, cancer, and diabetes. See also *disease.*

**locus of control:** the place where responsibility lies. If the locus of control is within a person, then the person is

responsible; if it is outside, then the person may be helpless. When a person perceives correctly that the locus of control is within, then that person is said to *own* the responsibility.
**motivation:** the desire and impulse to act.
**motives:** forces that move people to act. Some motives are instinctive (*drives*); others are learned.
**owning:** being responsible. See *locus of control.*
**patient:** a person who is dependent on a physician or other medical care provider for medical help. See also *client.*
**physiological age:** age as estimated from the body's health and probable life expectancy. See also *chronological age.*
**wellness:** maximal health, the achievement of full potential mentally, emotionally, physically, interpersonally, socially, and spiritually.
**will:** a person's intent, which leads to action.

## QUIZ ANSWERS

1. *False.* The definition of wellness is more ambitious than this. It includes a high level of physical well-being—and emotional, social, and spiritual well-being, too.
2. *False.* The major diseases of adults today are contracted largely as a result of people's lifestyle choices, rather than being "caught."
3. *True.* People can make themselves physiologically younger or older by the ways they choose to live.
4. *True.* Knowing how to relax can lengthen your life.
5. *True.* Women generally live longer than men do.
6. *False.* Accidents are among the major causes of death for younger adults.
7. *False.* "Organic" and "natural" have no legal meaning as used on labels, and although intended to imply unusual power to promote health, they do not.
8. *False.* Wanting and knowing how to change a harmful health habit are not enough; a person also must have the will to change.
9. *True.* Some people fail at making positive health behavior changes because they undertake too many changes at one time.
10. *False.* You are not responsible for the health choices of other people, and you can not change their behavior. You can assist by non-judgmentally enhancing their awareness and providing accurate information to facilitate change when they demonstrate the desire to change.

*Source:* Adapted with permission from *Essential Life Choices* by Whitney and Sizer. 

♦

## CHAPTER SUMMARY

SQ3R consists of five steps—Survey, Question, Read, Recite, and Review. With slight changes, this study plan can be used to read a variety of materials. Surveying, or previewing, involves linking frameworks and networks of background knowledge with information in your textbook. You use these frameworks to predict the content of the text. Surveying also allows you to use outlines or maps to organize this content for study. Finally, surveying is also useful when working with supplementary materials. During the questioning stage of SQ3R, you set goals for reading. The reading step of SQ3R involves an active reading of the text. It also includes text marking and labeling. The fourth stage, reciting, is when you check your understanding of the text. Reviewing, the final step, helps you make information more permanent. You review through spaced study, or distributed practice; cramming; study groups or partners; or overlearning. Of all of these, cramming is least effective.

♦

## CHAPTER REVIEW

*Answer briefly but completely.*

**1.** How does background knowledge affect learning?

______________________________

______________________________

______________________________

______________________________

______________________________

______________________________

**2.** Compare and contrast frameworks and networks.

______________________________

______________________________

______________________________

______________________________

______________________________

______________________________

3. You have been assigned a chapter to read from your biology text. Briefly describe how you will use SQ3R to aid you with this assignment.

4. Contrast an outline and a map.

5. How can you tell the difference between headings and subheadings in this text? Why is this important for any text?

6. Why set goals before reading?

7. Why do you need to label a text you have already marked?

**8.** If in the Recite stage of SQ3R you find you have not asked appropriate questions, what can you do to remedy this?

**9.** Why is cramming the least effective review strategy?

**10.** You decide to set up a study group for your math class. What responsibilities will your group require each member to assume? Why should group members be aware of these responsibilities from the outset? What should happen if group members fail in their duties?

◆

## REFERENCES

Tenney, J. "Keyword Notetaking System." Paper presented at the nineteenth annual meeting of the Western College Reading Association, Los Angeles, Calif. (March, 1986).

### *KEY*

The topic of the passage on page 8 is *washing clothes.*

# 2 Listening and Notetaking

## TERMS

*Terms appear in the order in which they occur in the chapter.*

active listening
syllabus
background knowledge
distractions
self-talk
text structure
terms
curve of forgetting

## CHAPTER OUTLINE EXERCISE

*Complete the following outline by filling in the blanks with the phrases below.*

What are
inability to find main ideas
recognize important information
passive
personalize my notes
before the lecture
What should I do
lecture formats
physically
listening
text-dependent lectures
notetaking
after the lecture
schedule
mentally
act in active listening
lack of attention
ineffective lecturers

I. **Why is ________________ not as easy as it looks?**
   A. What should I do ________________?
      1. *How can I organize through ________________ planning?*
      2. *How can I be ________________ and ________________ prepared?*
   B. ________________ during the lecture?
      1. *How does ________________ affect me during lectures?*
      2. *How does the ________________ affect understanding during lectures?*
      3. *Why is it necessary to ________________?*
   C. What should I do ________________?

II. **How does ________________ break Baxter's corollary?**
   A. Why is note-taking the ________________?
   B. How can I ________________?
   C. What are ________________?
      1. *What are ________________?*
      2. *________________ text-independent lectures?*
   D. What are ________________ methods of notetaking?

III. **How can I compensate for ________________?**

## OBJECTIVES

*At the end of this chapter, you should be able to do the following:*

1. Determine why listening is not as easy as it looks.
2. Take effective notes.
3. Compensate for ineffective lecturers.

## CHAPTER MAP

*Complete the following map by filling in the blanks with phrases from the Chapter Outline Exercise.*

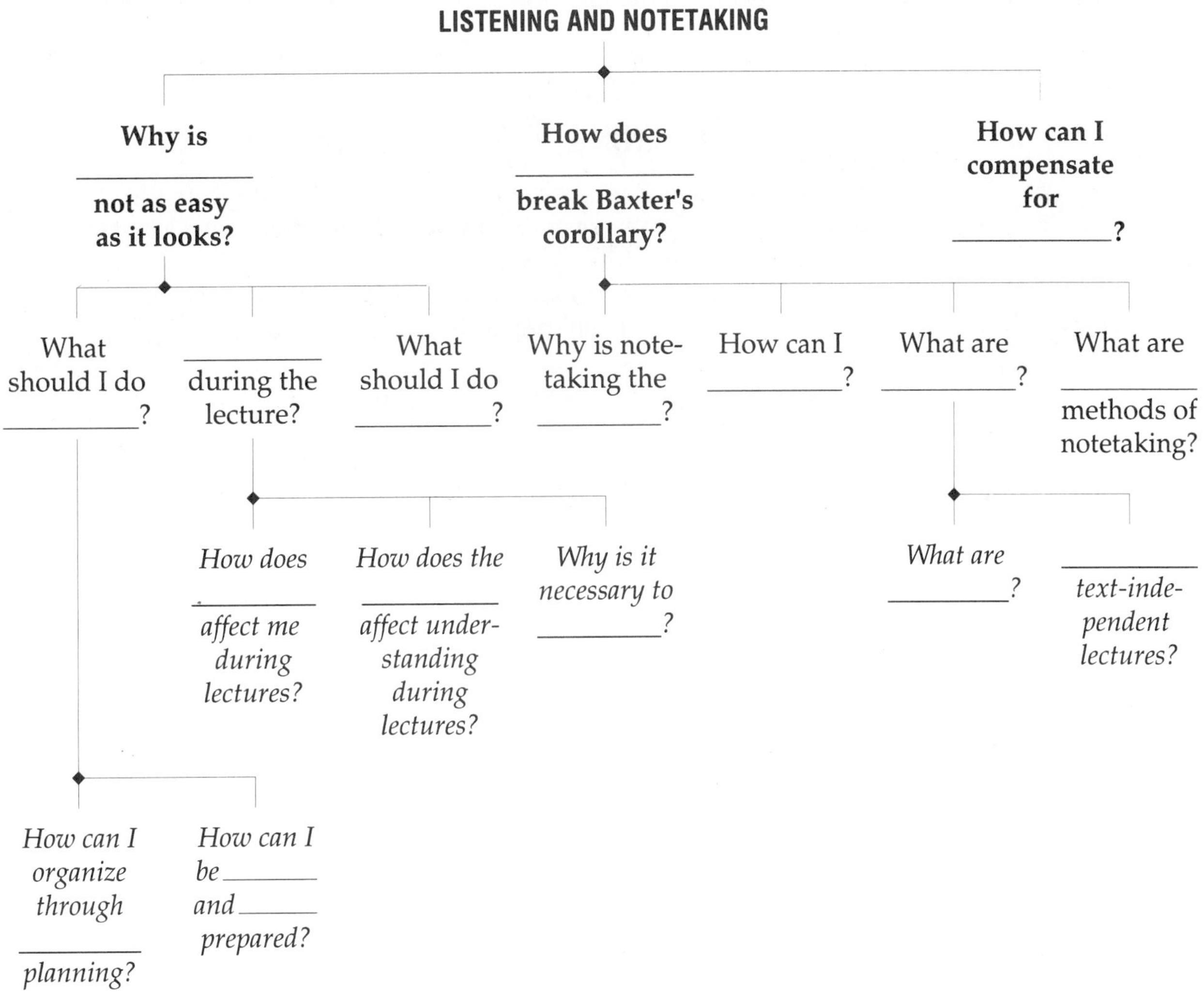

### LISTENING AND NOTETAKING

- **Why is ____________ not as easy as it looks?**
  - What should I do __________?
    - *How can I organize through __________ planning?*
    - *How can I be ________ and ________ prepared?*
  - __________ during the lecture?
    - *How does __________ affect me during lectures?*
    - *How does the __________ affect understanding during lectures?*
    - *Why is it necessary to __________?*
  - What should I do __________?
- **How does ____________ break Baxter's corollary?**
  - Why is notetaking the __________?
  - How can I __________?
  - What are __________?
    - *What are __________?*
    - *__________ text-independent lectures?*
  - What are __________ methods of notetaking?
- **How can I compensate for ____________?**

*HURNEY'S LAW OF HERNIATED HEARING*
*Half of the final exam questions will come from the notes you missed in lectures.*
*BAXTER'S COROLLARY*
*The other half will come from the notes you cannot decipher.*

MURPHY'S LAWS ARE DEFINED as humorous rules that apply to nothing, anything, and everything. The original set consisted of three laws. First, nothing is as easy as it looks. Second, everything takes longer than you think. Third, if anything can go wrong, it will. Since then, people developed their own variations of Murphy's laws. Hurney's law and Baxter's corollary are well known to students everywhere. They are often enforced when students lack listening or notetaking skills.

◆

## LISTENING: NOT AS EASY AS IT LOOKS

Listening appears easy because you've done it all your life. It's hard because few students are ever taught to listen effectively. Most students assume they know how to listen. These listeners often listen passively, or without much effort. Listening, however, is an active process.

How well you listen depends on communication between your instructor, the speaker, and you, the listener. Instructors vary in the way they present information. Some lecture well. Others are average at best. Your ability to distinguish between good and poor lecturers improves with practice. The rating system in Table 2.1 helps you find how effective your instructor is. It also aids you in deciding what you need to do to compensate. The more *A*'s your instructor receives, the more effective that instructor is.

*"Okay, I'll repeat it. I said, 'Students that sit in the back of class and ask questions are woosies!!!' "*

**TABLE 2.1 Rating Checklist for Instructors**

*Indicate how often your instructor does each of the following by marking either A—Always; S—Sometimes; U—Usually; or N—Never.*

| DOES YOUR INSTRUCTOR . . . | A | S | U | N |
|---|---|---|---|---|
| **1.** Explain goals of the lecture? | | | | |
| **2.** Review previous lecture material before beginning new lecture? | | | | |
| **3.** State main ideas in introduction and summary of lecture? | | | | |
| **4.** Provide an outline of the lecture? | | | | |
| **5.** Provide wait time for writing notes? | | | | |
| **6.** Speak clearly and at an appropriate volume? | | | | |
| **7.** Answer questions without sarcasm? | | | | |
| **8.** Stay on topic? | | | | |
| **9.** Refrain from reading directly from the text? | | | | |
| **10.** Emphasize main points? | | | | |
| **11.** Use transition words? | | | | |
| **12.** Give examples to illustrate difficult ideas? | | | | |
| **13.** Write important words, dates, etc., on the board? | | | | |
| **14.** Define important terms? | | | | |
| **15.** Use audiovisual aids to reinforce ideas? | | | | |

**WRITE TO LEARN**

*On a separate sheet of paper, explain why listening is not as easy as it looks.*

## Before the Lecture

**Active listening** is conscious control of the listening act. It takes thought and effort to maintain. Active listening should be considered even before scheduling classes. It is the key to organizing your notes before, during, and after class. Like active reading, it involves preplanned strategies for the listening process.

### *Organization Through Schedule Planning*

You can maximize active listening by the way you schedule your classes. How you organize your school day and your school week plays an important role in how you learn. Careful attention must be paid to your physical and mental states when scheduling classes.

At some colleges, classes meet on alternating days, either two days or three days per week. Avoid scheduling all your classes on just two or three days. You may think this is a way to get free days for "concentrated studying." However, unless you're a very dedicated student, you may find it hard to live up to such a heavy study commitment.

You should schedule your heaviest lecture classes at times when you're most alert. Consider how long you can "take" a course. You may have a choice of twice a week for a longer period of time or three times a week for a shorter period of time. The length of time you can concentrate depends on you. It may be better to take your less interesting classes more often for shorter time periods. Taking less interesting classes right after meals could result in your getting sleepy in them.

Avoid scheduling similar classes, such as sociology and psychology, back-to-back. You could become confused by the similarity in content. Your best bet is to alternate lecture classes with more active classes (math, labs, or P.E.).

**EXERCISE 2.1**

*Fill in the first chart with your schedule for this term. Use the second chart to show how you could rearrange it to maximize your concentration.*

**Current Schedule**

| | SUN | MON | TUES | WED | THUR | FRI | SAT |
|---|---|---|---|---|---|---|---|
| 8-9 AM | | | | | | | |
| 9-10 | | | | | | | |
| 10-11 | | | | | | | |
| 11-12 | | | | | | | |
| 12-1 PM | | | | | | | |
| 1-2 | | | | | | | |
| 2-3 | | | | | | | |
| 3-4 | | | | | | | |
| 4-5 | | | | | | | |
| 5-6 | | | | | | | |
| 6-7 | | | | | | | |
| 7-8 | | | | | | | |
| 8-9 | | | | | | | |
| 9-10 | | | | | | | |
| 10-11 | | | | | | | |

**Rearranged Schedule**

| | SUN | MON | TUES | WED | THUR | FRI | SAT |
|---|---|---|---|---|---|---|---|
| 8-9 AM | | | | | | | |
| 9-10 | | | | | | | |
| 10-11 | | | | | | | |
| 11-12 | | | | | | | |
| 12-1 PM | | | | | | | |
| 1-2 | | | | | | | |
| 2-3 | | | | | | | |
| 3-4 | | | | | | | |
| 4-5 | | | | | | | |
| 5-6 | | | | | | | |
| 6-7 | | | | | | | |
| 7-8 | | | | | | | |
| 8-9 | | | | | | | |
| 9-10 | | | | | | | |
| 10-11 | | | | | | | |

### *Mental and Physical Preparedness*

You need to prepare yourself mentally before going to class. You need to relate new information to what you already know about the topic. In that way you add to old frameworks rather than starting isolated new ones. Therefore, you identify what frameworks you need to retrieve for the class content. You do this by referring to your class **syllabus** (outline of course topics) and by reading the assigned chapters before class. You also need to review your class notes. This helps you build continuity between old and new information.

Your enjoyment and understanding of an activity often depend on your **background knowledge.** For example, most people who know nothing about sports fail to enjoy sporting events. Most people who know nothing about music fail to enjoy classical concerts. The same is true of academic activities. If you know nothing of a subject, you often fail to enjoy and understand that subject. On the other hand, the more background knowledge you have, the more easily you will enjoy and learn from lectures.

One way to increase your background knowledge is to interact with the text. You can acquire background knowledge by completing several activities before a lecture. First, previewing assigned information allows you to get the basics from a chapter. Second, outlining or mapping that information gives you a guide to the chapter's content. Finally, thoroughly reading assigned material fills in details.

Physical preparedness is also necessary for the active listener. You need to be well rested before class. You should be neither too hungry nor too full. You need to dress confortably, but appropriately, for class. Your concentration needs to focus on the content of the lecture, not on the temperature of the room or other distractions. As in reading, to get the best out of your class time, you must be at your best.

Finally, you need to bring everything you need to class. This includes papers, pens or pencils, class notes, your text, and anything else you might need.

You should get to class on time. Being punctual makes a good impression on your instructor. It also gives you time to get your thoughts organized before the lecture begins.

Finally, you need to find a seat near the front of the room. It is also a good idea to sit in the same or nearly the same place each day. Thus, your instructor becomes accustomed to seeing you. If you ever need help outside class, you will be remembered as the active listener who sits in the front of the class.

## During the Lecture

Hurney's law of herniated hearing concerns fractured or broken listening. Such breaks occur during a lecture when you are distracted or miss the key points. While these breaks make listening harder than it seems, preventing them is easier than it seems.

### *Lack of Attention*

**Distractions** draw your attention from the lecture. Some of these factors are beyond your control. Others are not.

Distractions beyond your control are external, or environmental, ones. These include street noises; classroom sounds, like whispering, papers rustling, and people moving; and hall noises. Your instructor's mannerisms pose another distraction you cannot control. Often an instructor's dialect, speech rate, and body language affect your concentration. Since you cannot control these distractions, you must learn to cope with them.

You cope by increasing your interest in the subject. Becoming more interested in what is being said helps you ignore what is bothering you. In 1856, Ralph Waldo Emerson said, "The hearing ear is always found close to the speaking tongue." If you are in a large lecture class, moving closer to the front helps you hear better and focuses your attention.

Distractions within you are internal ones. Physical discomforts, personal concerns, daydreams, and so on keep you from concentrating during lectures. It is difficult to think when you are hungry, tired, or sick. Proper nutrition, rest, and exercise remedy these physical distractions. Worry is another internal distraction. Personal concerns, either large or small, cannot be solved during a class. If your problem is a large one, consulting a counselor or friend helps reduce anxiety. Worry about small problems (getting your laundry done, meeting a friend, running errands, etc.) can be handled by listing them in your notebook. Then forget about them. Your list will remind you of them after class. Daydreaming forms a third common internal distraction. **Self-talk** forces you to pay attention. You interrupt your daydream with a strong internal command like, "STOP! Pay attention now. Think about this later."

**WRITE TO LEARN**

*On a separate sheet of paper, answer the following questions: In which class are you most easily distracted? Why? How can you prevent these distractions from affecting your understanding?*

### *Inability to Find Main Ideas*

Finding main ideas is hard when you have a passage in front of you. This task becomes even more difficult when the information is verbal. In reading, you find the main idea by looking at the **text structure** and supporting details. You use a similar method to find the main ideas of lectures.

Lectures follow the same four patterns texts follow. Instructors either introduce new topics or summarize information or list or rank details. Or, they present two (or more) sides of an issue or identify cause(s) and effect(s) or problem(s) and solution(s). As in textbooks, lecture patterns usually exist in mixed forms. Identifying your instructor's mix and match of patterns helps you predict the direction of the lecture. Table 2.2 provides a description of each of these patterns.

You predict the lecture's pattern and direction by identifying the signals your instructor uses (see Table 2.2). In addition, some words mark the end of a lecture. This is important because instructors often restate main ideas in their summaries. Becoming familiar with these signals helps you organize lecture notes and listen more actively.

**TABLE 2.2 Text-Lecture Patterns and Corresponding Signals**

| *PATTERN* | *DESCRIPTION* | *SIGNAL WORDS* |
|---|---|---|
| Introductory/summary | Identifies main points | Identified by location, either the beginning or end of a discussion of a topic or words such as: in summary, in conclusion, as a review, to summarize, to sum up |
| Enumeration/sequence | Lists or orders main points or presents a problem and steps for its solution | First, second, third . . . first, next, then, finally, in addition, last, and, furthermore, and then, most important, least important |
| Comparison/contrast | Describes ways in which concepts are alike or different or presents two or more sides of an issue | Comparison—similarly, both, as well as, likewise, in like manner<br>Contrast—however, on the other hand, on the contrary, but, instead of, although, yet, nevertheless |
| Cause/effect | Shows the result of action(s) or explains a problem and its solution | Therefore, thus, as a result, because, in turn, then, hence, for this reason, results in, causes, effects |

**EXERCISE 2.2**

◆ *Underline the transition words found in each lecture excerpt. Use the following key and write the lecture type in the space below the excerpt.*

KEY:
I/S introductory/summary
CE cause-effect/problem-solving
E enumeration/sequence
CC comparison/contrast

1. Conquering disease is, and has always been, crucial to the survival of the human race. Disease is not only attributed to physical causes. Many cultural factors also contribute. Immigrants often brought diseases to their new homelands. Domestication of animals such as dogs brought humans in contact with diseases such as rabies more often. In some cultures, religious rituals spread disease because of contaminated conditions. Environmental changes such as deforestation create more open, wet spaces that harbor malaria-carrying mosquitoes. Finally, crowded urban areas are often unsanitary. This draws rats and other disease-carrying vermin. Indeed, humans, to a great degree, are responsible for the diseases that affect themselves and all of mankind.

*Lecture type:* ______________________________

2. Several features distinguish horses of the pre-Cenozoic era from those that evolved during that period of time. Pre-Cenozoic era horses were smaller and had shorter legs and feet. Their evolution resulted in a straightening and stiffening of the back and changes in their teeth. Two of these changes were the widening of the incisor teeth and molarization of the premolars. The face continued to lengthen from that of the pre-Cenozoic time. The brain increased in size and complexity.

   *Lecture type:* ____________________________________

3. The concept of sets is first attributed to Georg Cantor. He was a mathematician of the late seventeenth and early eighteenth centuries. His theory of sets differed greatly from the concept of math at that time and was considered quite controversial. Like many ideas, his theory later found great acceptance. It continues to influence every branch of mathematics today. Venn diagrams help us picture relationships among sets.

   *Lecture type:* ____________________________________

4. Grasses form a family of plants. They have bladelike, opposing leaves connected to a jointed stem. A great number of grass species exist. Many are commercially useful and form the basis of human diet. These include rice, corn, wheat, oats, and barley. In addition, grasses are used as food for animals raised for meat or dairy products. Grasses grow on almost every area of the earth's surface. They are a dominant form of vegetation.

   *Lecture type:* ____________________________________

5. Computers aid writing in many ways. First, a computer helps students acquire the complex thinking and organization skills required in writing. Computers also provide frequent and immediate reinforcement needed when learning a new skill. Third, computers help students see writing as a process that involves many steps. Recognizing revision as one of those steps is facilitated by the computer. This occurs because a computer make revising easy. The final way a computer helps students learn to enjoy writing is in the appearance of the finished product. Since a printer presents a document in neat, typed form, many students feel prouder of their papers. This pride motivates student to keep writing.

   *Lecture type:* ____________________________________

6. Utilization of school computers follows four different patterns. First, schools often develop computer centers or labs. Students come individually or as a group to compute. A second pattern occurs when computers are placed in classes where they have direct application. This includes tutorial programs in special education, business software, and science applications. Third, computers can

be moved from room to room. This provides access, but it also sometimes causes scheduling problems. Finally, computers can be placed in every classroom all the time. Each of these patterns has benefits. Considerations include the resources of the school and the expertise of the users.

*Lecture type:* ______________________________

**7.** Biofeedback training often controls psychosomatic illness. Such illnesses, caused by stress or emotions, are more psychological than physical. To eradicate psychosomatic illness, patients must undergo training. For example, if Juan had headaches and no medical cause were found, he might try biofeedback. First, sensors would be taped to Juan's hands and forehead. Juan would be then trained to redirect bloodflow away from the head. Finally, he would practice these techniques. This would help him stop his headaches before they start.

*Lecture type:* ______________________________

**8.** When looking for a job in advertising, you should acquire and use several key tools. First, you should develop a sample book. This is a collection of your best creative ideas. It shows a prospective employer how you think. Second, you need a portfolio. It consists of samples of the exhibits you've created. Third, you need a resume, or fact sheet that describes yourself. Fourth, a good cover letter serves as your introduction to your employer. These elements are essential to any person going into public relations.

*Lecture type:* ______________________________

**9.** Two kinds of witnesses testify in criminal trials. Lay or nonexpert witnesses testify based on direct evidence. These witnesses provide eyewitness accounts. They may also provide an alibi for the defendant. They cannot give their own opinions or conclusions. Exceptions are made when opinions are based on common experience. The other kind of witnesses are expert witnesses. Unlike lay witnesses, they generally have no first-hand knowledge of the crime. However, they are asked to express their opinions based on their credentials or expertise. Both kinds of witnesses are essential to the case.

*Lecture type:* ______________________________

**10.** Now, let us turn to the topic of Athenian life in the Golden Age. The population consisted of citizens, metics or resident aliens, and slaves. The people led a modest lifestyle. They seemed to care little for material comforts and wealth. Agriculture and trade were the basis of their economy. Religious beliefs changed from belief in many gods to belief in one God. Marriage was an important institution; however, family life declined in general. Political strife began to dominate the people and this ultimately became their downfall.

◆ *Lecture type:* ____________________

### *Inability to Recognize Important Information*

Inability to recognize important information is a third cause of ineffective listening during lectures. This happens because all instructors emphasize main points differently.

SOMETIMES AN INSTRUCTOR . . .

*Writes key information on the chalkboard.* If your instructor writes an outline of the lecture on the board, copying this outline reinforces learning in three ways. First, you learn as you write. Second, copying the outline gives you an idea of the lecture's content. Finally, your outline serves as a guide for study. Instructors also write **terms** (important words) or key points on the board as they lecture.

*Repeats information.* If your instructor says the same information several times, it's probably important to the instructor. Consequently, you might see it on an exam.

*Speaks more slowly.* An instructor speaks slowly to give you time to write down what is said. Hesitations, pauses, and other forms of "wait time" are also clues that information is important.

*Changes tone of voice.* An instructor's voice often gets louder or changes in some other way when stressing an important point. Listen actively for these changes.

*Uses body language.* If an instructor pounds on the desk, moves closer to the class, or makes some other gesture to emphasize a point, it is one he or she feels is essential to your understanding.

*Uses visual aids.* Sometimes your instructor uses films, overhead transparencies, videotapes, or other audiovisual materials to clarify a lecture topic. If an instructor uses such aids, the material is probably important to the instructor.

*Refers to specific text pages.* Information that an instructor knows by page number is probably worth noting and remembering.

*Gives a definition.* Listen for words that indicate a meaning. These include *is, means, are, is called, involves,* and *resembles.*

*Lists a number of major points or steps.* Listen for number words. Your instructor may say, "There are four (or ten, or any other number) steps (or factors, points, reasons) that are important."

*Tells the sequence.* Similar to listing a number of points, your instructor tells the order in which something occurs. Listen for words like *first* (*second, third,* etc.), *then, next, finally,* or *last.*

*Explains why or how things happen.* The instructor gives reasons by using words or phrases such as *because, as a result, thus, therefore,* and *for this reason.*

*Gives many examples.* An instructor gives several examples to help you understand an important concept. The concept is what you should remember. The examples help you remember the concept.

*Refers to information as a test item.* Your instructor might say, "You may see this again," or "This would make a good test question." This is when you should really sit up and take notice.

***EXERCISE 2.3***

*Listen as your instructor reads a prepared lecture. On a separate sheet of paper, write down the points your instructor emphasizes. Following each point, list the cue your instructor used to emphasize the information.*

## After the Lecture

Sometimes a lecture is like a movie that's continued for several nights. Often an instructor doesn't finish discussing a topic during one class. He continues the next class meeting. You need a review, similar to the "scenes from last night's exciting episode." Without this review, you forget what happened in the notes just as you might forget what happened in the movie. In either case, you lose track and, therefore, interest.

Frequent reviews boost your memory. The more often you hear or read something, the easier it is to remember. The "Ebbinghaus curve," or **curve of forgetting** (see Figure 2.1), shows the relationship between recall of information without review and time since presentation. The numbers along the left of the graph indicate amount of material remembered. The numbers along the bottom show the amount of time since the material was presented. Note that on the basis of one exposure, most information is lost within the first twenty-four hours. This curve explains why you are sometimes confused by notes that seemed clear when you took them. Reviewing your notes within twenty-four hours after taking them helps you remember them.

Postlecture reading forms another way to increase your memory following a lecture. After the lecture, you should have seen information on the lecture topic twice. First, you either read or previewed the chapter. Your second exposure was during the lecture. Postlecture reading enables you to focus most on information emphasized in the

***FIGURE 2.1***
***Curve of Forgetting***

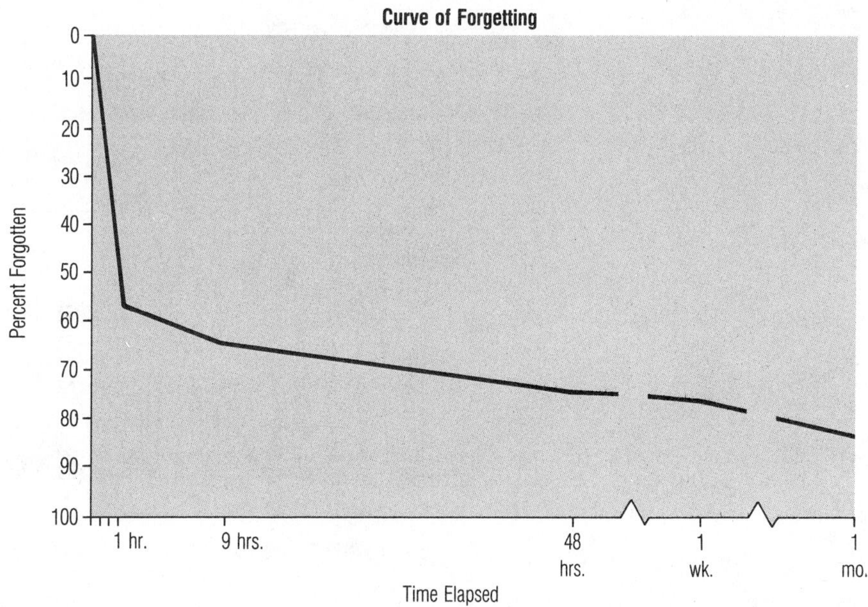


lecture. If you completely read the chapter before the lecture, you focus on the areas that confused you or that were stressed in class. If you previewed the text, this final reading provides information to support the main ideas of the lecture. Postlecture reading fills the gaps in your knowledge.

***EXERCISE 2.4***

*The instructions for this activity will be read once. Follow each instruction carefully. Do not begin until you are told to do so.*

♦

## NOTETAKING: BREAKING BAXTER'S COROLLARY

Baxter's corollary stated that half of a final exam's questions would be from notes you can't decipher. This occurs when you don't have effective notetaking skills. Without a system for determining importance, you might try to write everything. But, you can't write as fast as an instructor speaks. You might get the introduction but miss the conclusions. You might have the first and last steps in a problem and miss the rest. In short, you have gaps which makes your notes confusing.

### Notetaking: The Act in Active Listening

Notetaking aids active listening in several important ways. First, the lecture may be the only source for certain facts. Second, the information

*"Can't read your notes, huh? Well, he can help. He's a graduate student in Archeology who makes money deciphering other students' class notes."*

stressed in a lecture often signals what will be found on exams. Third, class notes serve as a means of external storage. Because you cannot remember everything you hear, notes serve as a form of memory. Specific notetaking strategies help ensure that you write the information correctly (see Table 2.3).

Notes boost your memory of the lecture or the text. Reviewing notes, then, is an important part of note-taking. In general, students who review notes achieve more than those who do not (Kiewra, 1985). If information is in your notes, there is a 34 percent chance of your remembering it (Howe, 1970). There is only a 5 percent chance if you did not record it.

**WRITE TO LEARN**

*On a separate sheet of paper, explain how notetaking is the "act" in active listening.*

### Personalizing Your Notes

As an active note-taker, you must record only important information. What you record is your choice. You decide based on your background knowledge, the topic, and the facts your instructor stresses. As in text marking, the amount you know about a topic affects the amount of

**TABLE 2.3 Guidelines for Taking Notes**

1. *Date each day's notes.* This date serves as a reference point if you need to compare notes with someone or to ask your instructor for clarification. If you are absent, this date identifies which day's notes you need.
2. *Use either an outline or map* (whichever best fits your learning style and course content).
3. *Keep all notes together.* You accomplish this in one of two ways. You can purchase a single spiral notebook or ring binder for each class. Or, you can purchase two large multiple-subject notebooks or loose-leaf binders, one for your classes on Monday-Wednesday-Friday and one for your classes on Tuesday-Thursday. This way you have to carry only one notebook each day. In addition, notebooks with pockets are useful for saving class handouts.
4. *Bring all necessary materials* (notebook, pencils/pens, text, etc.) *to each class.*
5. *Develop a key for your symbols and abbreviations.* Without this, you may be unable to decode your notes and will fall victim to Baxter's corollary.
6. *Try to group and label information to aid recall.*
7. *Write down terms, dates, diagrams, problems, and so forth, written on the board.*
8. *Use white space.* Skip lines to separate important groups of ideas.
9. *Write on only the front of your paper.* This seems wasteful but makes reading your notes easier.
10. *Write legibly.* Notes are worthless if you can't read them. Again, remember Baxter's corollary.
11. *If your instructor refers to specific text pages, turn to those pages and mark the information in your text rather than trying to duplicate information in your notes.* Record in your notes the corresponding numbers of text pages.
12. *Underline or mark important ideas and concepts with a different color ink than the one you used to take notes.*
13. *Compress your notes as you study.* Underline or mark key words and phrases with a different color ink than the one you used to write notes.
14. *Read over notes as soon as possible after class and make corrections and additions.* If you have any gaps, check with another student, your instructor, or the text.
15. *While you wait for class to begin, review notes to set up framework for new material.*

notes you need. More background knowledge requires fewer notes. Less background knowledge calls for more notes.

Notes are unlike other class work. They are not graded. Thus, they need not be grammatically correct. They don't even have to contain complete words. In fact, as a good notetaker, you need to develop your own system of shorthand. In developing your system, you need to limit the number of symbols you use. After you learn a few symbols thoroughly, you can add others. Table 2.4 shows rules for developing your own shorthand system.

**TABLE 2.4 Rules for Developing a Shorthand System**

1. Limit the number of symbols you create.
2. Use the beginning letters of words.

   ***Examples*** assoc associated
   w with
   geog geography
   hist history
   info information
   intro introduction
3. Use standard symbols.

   ***Examples*** & and
   # number
   % percent
   $ money, dollars
   ? question
   + plus
   x times, multiply
   < or > less than or greater than
   ! interesting or surprising
4. Use traditional abbreviations but omit periods.

   ***Examples*** lb pound
   ft foot
   wt weight
   mi mile
   Dec December
   US United States
5. Omit vowels and keep only enough consonants to make the word recognizable.

   ***Examples*** bkgd background
   mxtr mixture
   dvlp develop
6. Drop endings that do not contribute to word meaning.

   ***Examples*** ed
   ing
   ment
   er
7. Add "s" to show plurals.
8. Omit *a, an, the,* and unimportant verbs and adjectives.

   ***Example*** A cause of the Civil War was the issue of slavery.
   Cause of CW = slavery.
9. Write out terms and proper names the first time. Show your abbreviation in parentheses after the term or name. Then, use the abbreviation throughout the rest of your notes.
10. Indicate dates numerically.

    ***Example*** 12/7/41 instead of December 7, 1941
11. Use common misspellings of words.

    ***Examples*** thru through
    nite night
    rite right
12. Express numbers numerically.

    ***Examples*** 1 one
    2 two
    1st first
    2nd second

### EXERCISE 2.5

◆ *Use your personal shorthand system to transcribe the following sentences.*

1. The fat in milk is mostly saturated fat; the cholesterol content is 33 milligrams per cup of whole milk or four milligrams per cup of nonfat milk. Milk is not a high-cholesterol food, certainly, but choosing nonfat in place of whole milk reduces your intakes of both saturated fat and cholesterol.

2. Robberies in an open area include muggings and purse snatching. In cities, this kind of robbery constitutes about sixty percent of reported totals. With this type of crime on the rise, the need for additional police is obvious.

3. According to the May 12, 1988, issue of *Time,* there are some 15,000 lobbyists in Washington, D.C., with a combined budget of two million dollars. There are also 13,000 nonprofit groups in the Capitol. States also have offices in Washington. Because of these groups, almost all Americans are represented in government in ways other than through their national congressmen.

4. Invention is the creation of some new element made by combining two or more already-existing elements. Inventions are governed by new rules. The automobile is an example of an invention of a material nature. An example of inventions of a nonmaterial nature is group marriage.

5. Within the United States, differences exist between northeastern and western dairy farms. Milk is the most common dairy product sold to northeastern cities like New York and Boston, while in western cities, cheese and butter are the most common products. In the northeast, only five percent of milk is made into cheese and butter.

6. In 1982, about ninety-four million people were added to the world's population. Only about eight million lived in Europe and North America. About sixty-three million were Asian and twelve million each were African and Latin American.

7. Neurons come in many sizes and shapes. They often serve unique and specialized functions. On the other hand, all neurons have the same three distinct structural features. The first is the *soma,* or cell body. Second is the *dendrites,* which receive nerve impulses. Third comes the *axon.* It is the mechanism by which the neuron sends its own nerve impulses.

8. The syntax of a language is the rules by which people organize their sentences. Grammar is a broader term than syntax. Grammar includes both syntax and phonetics, the study of how sound form words.

9. The surface of the moon can be divided into two divisions. The *marias,* or "seas," are dark-colored and topographically lower than the *highlands.* The highlands are lighter in color and higher. Because the highlands are the oldest part of the moon, they are heavily cratered. This provides proof of the large numbers of meteors that must have occurred in our solar system four billion years ago.

**10.** Some of the highest mountains in the Cordillera are in the Cascade Range of northern California, Oregon, and Washington. Twice in the twentieth century, Cascade volcanoes have erupted. Mt. Lassen, in northern California, was active from 1914 to 1921. More recently, Mt. St. Helens, in Washington, erupted in May of 1980.

**11.** The three advocates of Stoicism who lived and taught in Rome in the two hundred years following the rule of Augustus were Seneca, who served as an adviser to Nero; Epictetus, who was a slave; and the emperor Marcus Aurelius.

**12.** Mendel was a monk whose original genetics experiments began in the spring of 1856. He divided a garden into seven sections and planted contrasting characteristics next to each other: round seeds next to wrinkled, large next to small, green next to yellow. The other monks called his garden "Mendel's Pea Plantation."

**13.** Desensitization to a phobia involves three steps. First, the client and therapist make a list of fear-provoking situations. Next, the client learns relaxation exercises. Third, once relaxed, the client acts out the least fear-producing situation.

**14.** The history of telecommunications network development is one of decreasing cost and increasing speed and quality. Buffers help avoid message congestion and boost message transit. When buffers are filled, a deadlock occurs.

**15.** A directed graph, also called a diagraph, has the formula G = (V, E). It consists of a nonempty finite set of vertices (V) and a finite set of edges (E) where each edge is an ordered pair of vertices.

**16.** In 1975, Massachusetts enacted a tough gun control law under which a conviction for carrying an illegal gun received a mandatory one-year sentence. Within the next six years, Connecticut and New York also passed laws, but these were even more severe. Persons convicted of a felony who were also armed got an additional five years. Simply carrying an unlicensed gun resulted in a one-year sentence.

**17.** When writing advertising copy, the product you want to sell can be illustrated several ways. First, you could have the product alone. It could be pictured in use, either with or without people. Dramatizations of results or a particular feature can be made. Comparisons or contrasts with other products often sell. An eye-catching cartoon or symbol is often memorable. Charts and diagrams are often impressive. Finally, abstract or symbolic concepts can be related to the product.

**18.** Alzheimer's disease affects five to ten percent of people over age sixty-five. This equals approximately two million people of our current population. By the year 2000, one of every ten adults over age sixty-five is predicted to be a victim of the disease.

**19.** Several evolutionary trends seem to set primates apart from other mammals. These differences are seen in the limbs and means of movement, teeth, diet, sensory capabilities, brain, and behavior.

**20.** To form a kind of paper, papyrus is cut into strips, flattened, and dried. Egyptians wrote on it and rolled it up into scrolls for storage or transport. It was better than clay tablets because it was lighter and easier to use. Papyrus became the writing material of choice for that age.

**EXERCISE 2.6**

*Use your personal shorthand system to transcribe the paragraphs in Exercise 2.2.*

**1.**

**2.**

3.

4.

5.

6.

7.

8. ______________________________

9. ______________________________

10. ______________________________

## Lecture Formats

Lectures follow two general formats. In the first, lecture content mirrors assigned textbook chapters. In the second type, the content of the lecture is not necessarily contained in the text. Rather, the text gives additional information to build your background knowledge. Your response to each type differs.

### *Text-dependent Lectures*

When lectures are text based, your use of the text during the lecture depends on your preclass preparation. If you thoroughly read the chapter before class, you note in your text what the instructor stresses during the lecture. You cross out information your instructor tells you to omit. You write other important information in the margins of the chapter.

If you constructed a note-taking outline or map through text preview, you respond differently. You record class notes and instructions directly on your outline or map. You highlight important sections and cross out sections your instructor tells you to omit. When the instructor refers to specific graphics or quotations, you underline or mark these in your text. Then note them on your outline or map.

### *Text-independent Lectures*

Your responsibility for taking notes increases when instructors cover information not in the text. Because you do not have the text for reference, you need to be an especially active listener. After the lecture, you need to discover the plan of the lecture and outline or map its content. Your class notes and syllabus should aid you in this attempt. Setting study objectives for yourself helps you set goals for learning. This also increases recall. To be sure you understand the content, you either discuss your notes with a classmate or do supplemental reading. Text-independent lectures indicate what your instructor feels is most important about the subject. For this reason, your instructor is a good source for clarifying confusing points. Feel free to ask questions.

## Passive Methods of Notetaking

Napoleon said, "If you want a thing done well, do it yourself." This is especially true of notetaking. Borrowed or bought notes reflect the person who took them. They require no effort or action on your part. Thus, they are not part of active listening. Effective notes reflect you and your personality.

Similarly, using a tape recorder to take notes seems a good solution. After all, a recorder copies every word the instructor says. A recorder doesn't become bored, daydream, or doodle. It appears to be the perfect notetaking solution. On the other hand, using a tape recorder has drawbacks. First, it proves Murphy's second law. That's because listening to and transcribing tapes take longer than you think. Furthermore, transcribing them completely contributes little to understanding the lecture's main ideas. As in underlining too much on a text page, writing each word the lecturer says limits your skill in highlighting important information. Second, because a tape recorder only records what is heard, your notes lack diagrams, terms, and other information the instructor may have placed on the board. Third, technical difficulties sometimes arise. For instance, dead batteries sometimes keep you from getting the notes you need. Fourth, using tape recorders sometimes offends or intimidates instructors. Therefore, if you decide to record notes, you need to get your instructor's permission before class. Fifth, relying on recorders keeps you from learning good notetaking skills. The final and most important drawback is that, as with using borrowed notes, you are a passive listener.

Borrowed or taped notes do have a place, however. When you are ill or absent, having someone else take or tape notes for you is better than not having any. Recording a lecture while you take notes can help you practice good notetaking. Playing the tape allows you to check your notes at a pace you set for yourself. This is also helpful if your instructor speaks too fast.

**WRITE TO LEARN**

*On a separate sheet of paper, answer the following questions: Are you an active listener? How do you know?*

◆

## IF IT CAN GO WRONG, IT WILL: COMPENSATING FOR INEFFECTIVE LECTURERS

Your role in listening depends, in part, on the effectiveness of your instructor. If your instructor is well organized and knows the subject, your job is easier. With an effective instructor, you need only attend to the information that's presented. However, remember Murphy's third law: If it can go wrong, it will. To avoid pitfalls, you need to assume full responsibility for taking good notes. Thus, as your instructor's effectiveness decreases, your need for active listening increases. You cope with ineffective lecturers by compensating for their deficiencies (see Table 2.5).

Whatever the lecture ability or style of your instructor, you need a plan for understanding and remembering what you hear. This plan provides you with the actions necessary to become an active listener. Table 2.6 provides you with such a plan.

◆

## CHAPTER SUMMARY EXERCISE

*Complete the summary by filling in the blanks with the following words:*

| | | |
|---|---|---|
| instructor | passive | external |
| text-dependent | postlecture | ineffective |
| main ideas | text-independent | shorthand |
| mentally | reviews | schedule |

Your ability to actively listen depends on you and your ______. Before the lecture, you plan for listening by organizing your

***TABLE 2.5 Compensating Suggestions for Ineffective Lecturers***

| *IF YOUR INSTRUCTOR FAILS TO . . .* | *THEN YOU . . .* |
|---|---|
| **1.** Explain goals of the lecture | Use your text and syllabus to set objectives |
| **2.** Review previous lecture material before beginning new lecture | Set aside time before each class to review notes |
| **3.** State main ideas in introduction and summary of lecture | Write short summaries of the day's lecture immediately after class |
| **4.** Provide an outline of the lecture | Preview assigned readings before class or outline notes after class |
| **5.** Provide wait time for writing notes | Politely ask instructor to repeat information or speak more slowly |
| **6.** Speak clearly and at appropriate volume | Politely ask instructor to repeat information or speak more loudly |
| **7.** Answer questions without sarcasm | Refrain from taking comments personally |
| **8.** Stay on topic | Discover how the story relates to the topic or use the story as a memory cue |
| **9.** Refrain from reading directly from the text | Mark passages in text instructor reads or summarize or outline these passages in text margin |
| **10.** Emphasize main points | Supplement lectures through text previews and reading |
| **11.** Use transition words | Supplement lectures through text previews and reading |
| **12.** Give examples to illustrate difficult ideas | Ask instructor for clarifying example, discuss idea with other students, create an example for yourself |
| **13.** Write important words, dates, etc., on board | Supplement notes with terms listed in text |
| **14.** Define important terms | Use text glossary or a dictionary |
| **15.** Use audiovisual aids to reinforce ideas | Relate information to what you know about the topic or create a clarifying example for yourself |

_______________ and getting _______________ and physically prepared. During the lecture, you actively listen by avoiding internal and _______________ distractions. You note _______________ and other important information. After the lecture, you lock information into your memory by frequent _______________ and_______________ reading. Taking notes also aids active listening. Creating a personal system of _______________ helps you listen as do strategies for _____ and _______________ lectures. Using a tape recorder or someone else's notes is a _______________ means of notetaking that works only when you can't take notes for yourself. Finally, strategies for coping with _______________ lecturers also increases your ability to listen and take notes effectively.

**TABLE 2.6 Method for Active Listening**

1. Have a purpose for listening.
2. Pay careful attention to the instructor's introductory and summary statements. These usually state main points.
3. Take notes.
4. Sit comfortably erect. Slouching makes you sleepy and indicates to your instructor your disinterest.
5. Look attentive. Show your interest by keeping your eyes on your instructor.
6. Concentrate on what the instructor is saying. Ignore external distractions. Eliminate internal distractions.
7. Think of questions you would like to ask or comments you want to make.
8. Listen for transition words that signal main points.
9. Mark words or references you don't understand. Do not attempt to figure them out now—look them up later.
10. Be flexible—adjust your listening and note-taking to the lecture.
11. If the instructor speaks too quickly or unclearly, then (a) ask the instructor to speak more slowly or to repeat information; (b) leave plenty of white space and fill in missing details immediately after class; (c) exchange copies of notes with classmates; (d) ask the instructor for clarification after class; and (e) be sure to preview lecture topic before class.
12. Avoid being a distraction. (Keep hands still, wait your turn in discussions, avoid whispering, etc.)

◆

## CHAPTER REVIEW

*Answer briefly but completely.*

1. Plan a schedule for next term that maximizes active listening. Justify the way you schedule your classes.

2. Contrast internal and external distractions and methods of coping with each.

**3.** Use the Curve of Forgetting (Figure 2.1) to explain why frequent reviews boost memory.

**4.** List each of your instructors and rank their lecturing abilities on a scale of 1 (poor) to 10 (great). For the instructors who rank below 8, name one way you can compensate for their deficiencies.

**5.** Name three guidelines to note-taking you have started using since reading this chapter.

**6.** Other than those listed in Table 2.4, what three personal shorthand symbols do you use when taking notes?

**7.** Contrast methods of dealing with text-dependent and text-independent lectures.

8. You have an instructor who always reads information directly from the text. What compensating strategies can you use?

9. Why is it important to look attentive during a lecture?

10. What preplanned strategies can you use to ensure active listening?

♦

## REFERENCES

Howe, M. J. "Notetaking Strategy, Review and Long-Term Relationships Between Notetaking Variables and Achievement Measures." *Journal of Educational Research* 63:285 (1970).

Kiewra, K. A. "Investigating Notetaking and Review: A Depth of Processing Alternative." *Educational Psychologist* 20(1):23–32 (1985).

# 3 Building General Vocabulary

## TERMS

*Terms appear in the order in which they occur in the chapter.*

context
connotations
denotations
literal
etymology
acronyms
synonyms
antonyms
homonyms
analogy

*Chapter Outline Phrases*

How can I
etymology
letters
forms of analogies
vocabulary development
techniques
communication
English
define solve
foreign
technology
common
new words
contemporary
word relationships
reading
connotation
denotation
vocabulary
Which words have
apply words
new products
listening
people's names
analogies

## CHAPTER OUTLINE EXERCISE

*Complete the following outline by filling in the blanks with the phrases found below the chapter terms.*

I. **What are the stages of ______________?**
II. **How does the chain of ______________ affect kinds of ______________?**
   A. How can I acquire a better vocabulary?
      1. *What is ______________ vocabulary?*
      2. *What is ______________ vocabulary?*
   B. ______________ remember new words?
      1. *What vocabulary ______________ can I use to remember ______________?*
      2. *What is the difference between ______________ and ______________?*

III. **How do words come to life through ______________?**
   A. How have ______________ words been incorporated into the ______________ language?
   B. What ______________ additions have been made to our vocabulary?
      1. *What words have come from ______________?*
      2. *Which words came from ______________?*
      3. *What words have come from ______________?*
      4. *How do ______________ (abbreviations) form words?*
   C. ______________ interesting histories?

IV. **How can I ______________?**
   A. What are some ______________ word relationships?
   B. What are other ______________?
   C. What are ______________?
      1. *How do I ______________ analogy?*
      2. *What are the ______________?*
      3. *How do I ______________ analogies?*

## OBJECTIVES

*At the end of this chapter, you should be able to do the following:*

1. Identify the stages of vocabulary development.
2. Differentiate among kinds of vocabulary.
3. Describe how words come to life through etymology.
4. Apply words in daily life.

## CHAPTER MAP

*Complete the following map by filling in the blanks with the phrases from the Chapter Outline Exercise.*

**VOCABULARY BUILDING**

**What are the stages of ______?**

**How does the chain of ______ affect kinds of ______?**

- How can I acquire a better vocabulary?
  - *What is ______ vocabulary?*
  - *What is ______ vocabulary?*
- ______ remember new words?
  - *What vocabulary ______ can I use to remember ______?*
  - *What is the difference between ______ and ______?*

**How do words come to life through ______?**

- How have ______ words been incorporated into the ______ language?
- What ______ additions have been made to our vocabulary?
  - *What words have come from ______?*
  - *Which words came from ______?*
  - *What words have come from ______?*
  - *How do ______ (abbreviations) form words?*
- ______ intersting histories?

**How can I ______?**

- What are some ______ word relationships?
- What are other ______?
- What are ______?
  - *How do I ______ analogy?*
  - *What are the ______?*
  - *How do I ______ analogies?*

## VOCABULARY ENHANCEMENT EXERCISE

| | STAGE 0 | STAGE 1 | STAGE 2 | STAGE 3 |
|---|---|---|---|---|
| | *I do not recognize the word.* | *I recognize the word but am un- sure of its meaning and associ- ations.* | *I recognize the word and can make gen- eral associ- ations with it.* | *I recognize the word and can use it in speaking and writing.* |
| **1.** vital | | | | |
| **2.** morsel | | | | |
| **3.** breakthroughs | | | | |
| **4.** collided | | | | |
| **5.** inset | | | | |
| **6.** reputable | | | | |
| **7.** physical | | | | |
| **8.** cast | | | | |
| **9.** documentaries | | | | |
| **10.** scenarios | | | | |

*A word is dead*
*When it is said*
*Some say*
*I say it just*
*Begins to live*
*That day.*
—EMILY DICKINSON

UNTIL A WORD IS communicated, it does not exist. It is only letters. It has no function. When a person uses a word, it is given meaning and use. Thus, words begin to live only when used by people to communicate with one another. This chapter forms an introduction to linguistics—the science of language. As with any science, you need certain tools in order to work with your subject. This chapter gives you the tools for bringing words to life through vocabulary building.

◆

## STAGES OF VOCABULARY DEVELOPMENT

The English writer Samuel Butler said, "Words are like money; there is nothing so useless, unless when in actual use." Words and money do have a lot in common. Both are written on paper. Both consist of symbols. Both require two people to be used. Both must be used to have meaning.

Unlike money, words bombard you from a variety of sources. Some are words you know. Others are unfamiliar. Based on a theory by Edgar Dale (1958), word knowledge exists in progressive stages (see Figure 3.1). This ranges from no knowledge of a word to the ability to use it, to let it live. The stages help you decide what you know about a word. They also tell you what more you need to learn about it. Beginning with this chapter, a vocabulary enhancement exercise will accompany the chapter terms. You will be asked to rate your knowledge of words used in the chapter. At the chapter's end, the words will once again be listed. You will again rate your knowledge of the words. You will also be asked to use them in sentences.

***FIGURE 3.1***
***Continuum of Vocabulary Development***

| | |
|---|---|
| 3 | You know you've seen or heard a word and can use it in speaking and/or writing. |
| 2 | You known you've seen or heard a word and can make general associations about its meaning. |
| 1 | You know you've seen or heard a word before, but you are unsure about its meaning or associations with it. |
| 0 | You see or hear a word you've never seen or heard before and you know it's a new word. |

**WRITE TO LEARN**

*The background experiences people have often affect their points of view. Surroundings, values, family influences, peers, and education color beliefs and opinions. They also determine, in part, how people determine meaning. Part of being a critical reader is learning to understand another person's point of view.*

*On a separate sheet of paper, respond to the following: A friend of yours believes that "when something's over, it's over." What would this friend think about the first two lines in Emily Dickinson's poem ("A word is dead / when it is said"). Do you agree with your friend's point of view, or do you support Dickinson's view? Defend your position in a paragraph.*

## CHAIN OF COMMUNICATION: KINDS OF VOCABULARY

How do people communicate? People communicate by speaking or writing words to one another. Where do these words come from? Where do you learn new words? New words come as a result of listening and reading. They are lodged in your memory for later use as the result of both conscious and unconscious effort on your part. Thus, the reception and expression of words, both new and old, form the chain of communication.

Thus, you possess four kinds of vocabulary (see Figure 3.2). These are listening, speaking, writing, and reading. Two of these—listening and reading—consist of ways you receive verbal information. Speaking and writing are the ways you communicate information.

*"And, if you can't think of a seven-letter word beginning with z that means 'the chemistry of fermentation,' we're not going to win the island cruise giveaway!"*

**FIGURE 3.2**
***The Relationship Between Listening, Reading, Speaking and Writing Vocabularies***

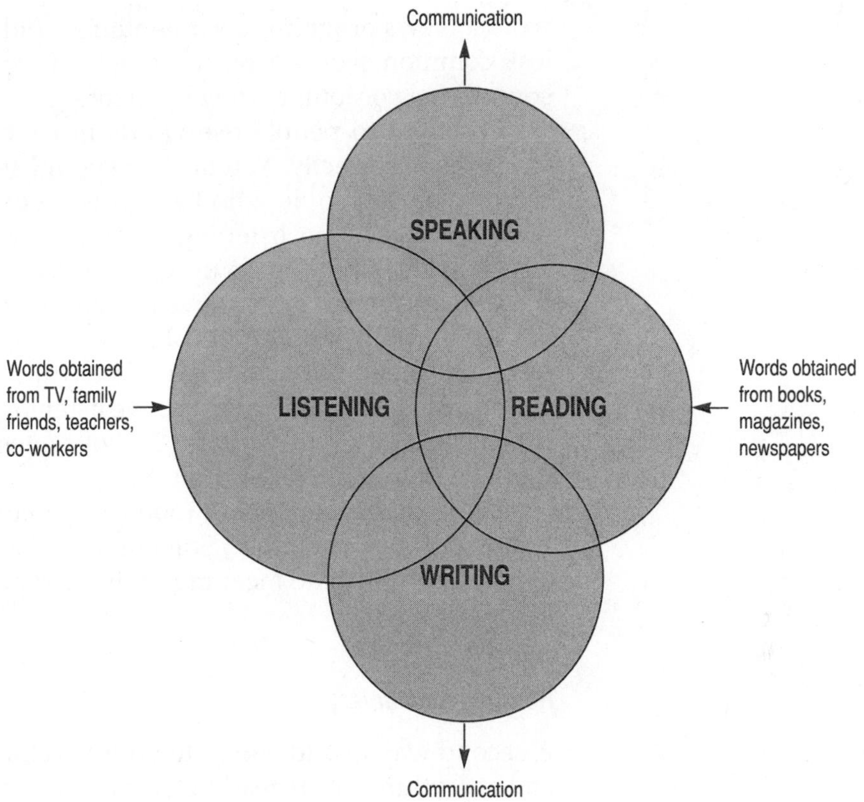


## Acquiring Vocabulary

"Words form the thread on which we string our experiences," said Aldous Huxley in *The Olive Tree* (1937). When we think, we think in words. For example, imagine a large gray animal with a long, trunklike nose and big, floppy ears. What did you imagine? An elephant? Yes. You imagine. You think. You have a word. As a child, you had to experience a concept in order to have a word for it and remember that word. For example, you had to feel the heat of a stove or heater to understand *hot*. As you grew older, the need to experience directly faded. Now, in addition to direct experience, you learn new concepts, new words, through listening and reading.

### *Listening Vocabulary*

Your listening vocabulary is usually the largest. It is also improved with the least amount of effort. Everything heard can be added to this group. But, you must make a conscious effort to understand and recall the new words you hear. Television can be a good source for the development of a listening vocabulary. This depends, however, on the programs you watch. Characters in most situation comedies and dramatic series use common words and phrases. These shows may not contain many new words. News program, documentaries, and even some game shows use less common words from a variety of topics. These are often better sources for vocabulary development.

Listening to people use words in **context** also allows you to hear words used correctly. You improve your listening vocabulary by talking or listening to people who have good vocabularies.

To increase your listening vocabulary you have to do more than be a sponge. A sponge soaks up material without thought. In other words, the human sponge is a passive listener. Instead, make your listening an active learning experience. Listen for context clues. Ask yourself questions about the new word and try to relate it to your own life. This sounds time-consuming, but active listening requires no more time than passive listening (see Chapter 2). Your questions and final understanding take only seconds of thought.

Using the context is not foolproof. Sometimes you won't be able to figure out the meaning. Sometimes you'll simply reach the wrong conclusion about the meaning of the word. If you have any doubts, ask someone.

### *Reading Vocabulary*

A second way to add words to your vocabulary is by reading, anything and everything. Your reading vocabulary and your listening vocabulary share many common words. In other words, most of the words you read will be words that you've already heard. It's important to match the visual form of the word with the right pronunciation. Otherwise, you will see the word in print and not associate it with how it's said. Occasionally you will find that the word you have heard is the same as a word you have been mispronouncing to yourself.

Just as you can use context in listening, you use it in reading. For example, consider this sentence:

> An industry is beginning to *burgeon* in response to the need for daycare.

What does *burgeon* mean? Are there any words or clues to its meaning in the sentence? The words *response* and *need* help you realize that *burgeon* means *grow.* Using surrounding words to figure out a word's meaning is one of the easiest ways to learn new words. This method is called using the context.

Another way to determine the meaning is through *structural analysis.* This means splitting words into definable parts. Consider this sentence:

> The metal pieces were held together by *multilayered* bands.

If you know the prefix *multi* means "many," then *multilayered* means "many layered."

Then, consider this sentence:

> The doctor did not expect the patient to be so *lucid*.

Can you use context clues or word parts to define *lucid?* The structure of the sentence does not give you enough clues to get its meaning. Nor can you divide the word into parts. At this point, you can ask someone who might know the word or—as a last resort—use a dictionary.

You use the dictionary as a last resort for several reasons. First, most words have more than one meaning. If you look at the word in a dictionary, you have no way of knowing which meaning you need. Second, taking time from reading to use a dictionary breaks your concentration. By the time you look up the word, you could forget why you wanted it. This loss of concentration results in a loss of comprehension. Third, using a dictionary takes time and decreases your reading speed. Nonetheless, using the dictionary is sometimes your only alternative for finding meanings of unknown words.

## Remembering New Words

Finding the meaning of a word won't help you unless you remember that word's meaning the next time you see it. In finding ways to make remembering new words easier, you first think about why this new word is important to your vocabulary. Vocabulary development is a little like starting a weight-lifting program. Neither your body nor your speech is changed overnight. Patience and effort help you develop the vocabulary you want. Your vocabulary can and should be a reflection of you. Your vocabulary is you. And like you, your vocabulary should be alive. It should change and grow to meet your needs.

Communication would be a lot easier if you only needed a limited and fixed set of words in a lifetime. Then you could get a list and learn it. However, this would leave you with a very fixed vocabulary. Changes in your life (different jobs, new friends, hobbies, new interests, current events) require changes in your vocabulary. Several strategies help you lock new words into your memory and, thus, change your vocabulary. No matter which of the following strategies you choose to lock new words into your memory, remember these basic suggestions:

STEPS IN VOCABULARY DEVELOPMENT

1. *Limit the number of new words you learn each day.* Your mind can retain only so many.

2. *Be certain you are saying the word correctly.* You do this by checking the pronunciation in a dictionary or by asking someone how to say the

word. Having once learned it wrong, it will be hard for you to change.

3. *Once you know a word, it's yours.* Don't be afraid to use it.

### *Vocabulary Techniques*

Perhaps the first and most important thing to aid memory is writing the new word. As you write it, you need to be sure you say it correctly. This allows you to make visual and oral pictures of the word in your mind. After this step, repetition becomes the key to remembering the word. A word file helps you practice new words.

To create a word file, you use index cards and a small card file box with alphabetical or subject tabs. Word cards usually consist of the word on the front and its meaning on the back. A more effective word card helps you connect personal associations with the word. One way to do this (Carr, 1985) is to write a word you want to know on the card. Then, you draw two connecting lines and one single line below the word (see Figure 3.3). On the first set of lines, you write the word's meaning and synonyms. On the other line, you write your associations with the word. A second way to make word cards more personal (Eeds and Cockrum, 1985) involves dividing each card into four equal spaces (see Figure 3.4). In one space, you write the word and a sentence using it. In the second, you list your associations with the word. The third space contains the word's definition. And the fourth space contains antonyms of the word. Whatever type of word card you prefer, your file can be added to at will and practiced daily. Keeping a collection of word cards and reviewing them helps lock words into your vocabulary.

***FIGURE 3.3***
***Vocabulary Card with Diagram of Pariah***

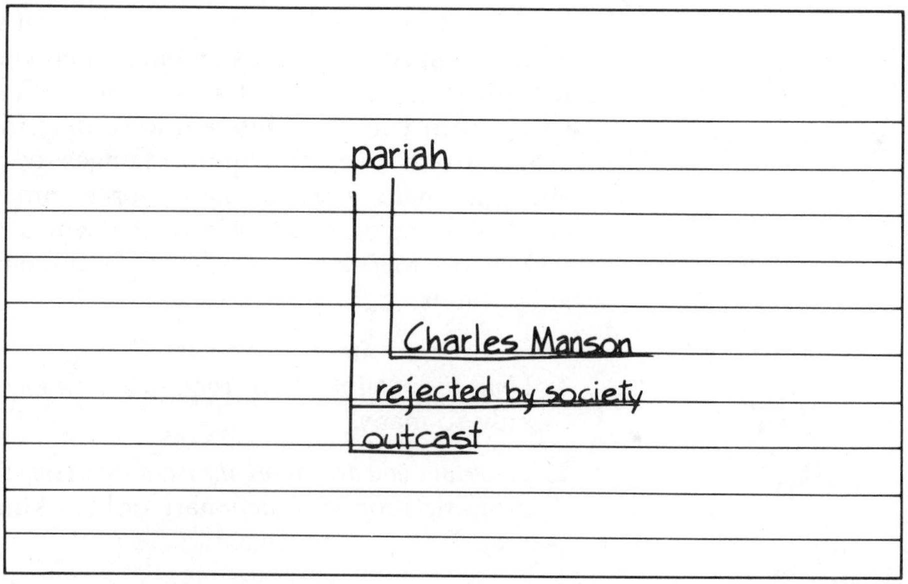

**FIGURE 3.4**
**Vocabulary Card with Boxed Definition of Pariah**

| | |
|---|---|
| pariah<br>The pariah was hated by everyone. | Charles Manson<br>lepers<br>criminals<br>Typhoid Mary |
| Abraham Lincoln<br>Santa Claus | somebody that nobody likes. |

A second way of adding new words to your vocabulary—daily usage—also involves forming personal associations with words. Again, such associations make the word your own. Using the words in your conversation and writing helps the word become a part of you.

By incorporating the word into your speaking and writing vocabularies, you form new associations with it. For example, let's say you want to remember that the word *harried* means *worried or harrassed*. You associate how you feel around final exam time with the word and its meaning. When you use *harried* to describe these feelings to friends, the word is yours.

> **WRITE TO LEARN**
>
> *On a separate sheet of paper respond to the following: Describe how the activities explained in the section "Chain of Communication: Kinds of Vocabulary" form the "thread" of the quote attributed to Aldous Huxley ("Words form the thread on which we string our experiences").*

### Connotation and Denotation

**Connotations** and **denotations** relate to your personal associations with a word. Connotations comprise your understanding of a word. They are the *implied* meanings you derive from hearing, reading, speaking, and writing the word in everyday life. They are synonymous with your associations with the word. On the other hand, denotations are the opposite of your personal associations of a word. Denotations consist of the **literal,** or dictionary, definitions with a word. Your vocabulary includes both denotations and connotations of many words and connotations only of others.

Identifying the connotation of words that are similar in meaning to an unknown word often helps you find a likely meaning for that word. For example, suppose you do not know the meaning of *pamper.* Suppose you associate it with giving into, or spoiling, a small child. Your connotation of *spoiling* helps you define *pamper* as meaning "letting someone have his or her way." Thus, connotations aid you in defining unknown words.

**EXERCISE 3.1**

*Write your connotation for each item in the set of familiar terms. Determine the connotation for the italicized term by comparing the connotations in the set. Then use a dictionary to define the italicized term. Compare your connotation with the denotation. How close were you?*

***Example***

| *Set A Words* | *Connotations* |
|---|---|
| jazz | *the music of New Orleans* |
| rock | *music popular with teenagers* |
| classical | *serious music performed by orchestras* |
| *harmonics* | *music* |
| | *Denotation* |
| *harmonics* | *musical* |

| *Set 1 Words* | *Connotations* |
|---|---|
| tutoring | ______ |
| training | ______ |
| lecturing | ______ |
| *pedagogy* | ______ |
| | *Denotation* |
| *pedagogy* | ______ |

| *Set 2 Words* | *Connotations* |
|---|---|
| problem | ______ |
| mystery | ______ |
| riddle | ______ |
| *enigma* | ______ |

| | Denotation |
|---|---|
| *enigma* | ______________________ |
| Set 3 Words | Connotations |
| error | ______________________ |
| goof | ______________________ |
| blunder | ______________________ |
| *faux pas* | ______________________ |
| | Denotation |
| *faux pas* | ______________________ |
| Set 4 Words | Connotations |
| funny | ______________________ |
| witty | ______________________ |
| comical | ______________________ |
| *droll* | ______________________ |
| | Denotation |
| *droll* | ______________________ |
| Set 5 Words | Connotations |
| scald | ______________________ |
| sear | ______________________ |
| scorch | ______________________ |
| *cauterize* | ______________________ |
| | Denotation |
| *cauterize* | ______________________ |
| Set 6 Words | Connotations |
| bow | ______________________ |
| turn | ______________________ |
| twist | ______________________ |
| *stoop* | ______________________ |
| | Denotation |
| *stoop* | ______________________ |

| *Set 7 Words* | *Connotations* |
|---|---|
| disease | ______________ |
| illness | ______________ |
| ailment | ______________ |
| *malaise* | ______________ |
| | *Denotation* |
| *malaise* | ______________ |
| *Set 8 Words* | *Connotations* |
| probe | ______________ |
| study | ______________ |
| examine | ______________ |
| *inquire* | ______________ |
| | *Denotation* |
| *inquire* | ______________ |
| *Set 9 Words* | *Connotations* |
| schedule | ______________ |
| project | ______________ |
| outline | ______________ |
| *plan* | ______________ |
| | *Denotation* |
| *plan* | ______________ |
| *Set 10 Words* | *Connotations* |
| scan | ______________ |
| examine | ______________ |
| inspect | ______________ |
| *scrutinize* | ______________ |
| | *Denotation* |
| *scrutinize* | ______________ |

### *WRITE TO LEARN*

*On a separate sheet of paper, respond to the following: Imagine you are a spy and have to pass along the secret of* denotation *and* connotation *to your superiors. You cannot give a definition or actually explain the differences between the two. You can, however, identify a word as a denotation and provide several connotations for it. Provide three to five examples of denotations and related connotations so your superiors will be sure to understand what you mean.*

◆

## HOW WORDS COME TO LIFE: ETYMOLOGY

Linguistics is a living science. It changes and grows with the language people use. Learning more about why and how words came to life helps you recall words more easily. Most people use a dictionary entry (see Figure 3.5) to find the correct spelling or meaning of a word. Some people also look at the entry to find pronunciations, parts of speech, singular and plural forms, and sometimes synonyms and antonyms. While a dictionary entry provides such functional information about a word, it tells much more. It often gives the origin, or **etymology,** of the word.

The etymology of a word is its history. Etymologies tell information about the word's evolution, how it was first used, and how it is used now. Etymologies indicate that the English language is living and growing. Although many words have been part of our language for many years, new words are added all the time.

***FIGURE 3.5***
***Sample Dictionary Entry***

**coffee** (kof'e, kof'-), n., adj. — **1** a dark brown drink made from the roasted and ground seeds of a tall, tropical tree or shrub. **2** the seeds from which the drink is made; coffee beans. **3** the plant itself. It belongs to the madder family. See picture under **madder family. 4** the color of coffee; a dark brown, darker than chocolate. **5** a social gathering at which coffee is served. —adj **1** having the flavor of coffee: *coffee ice cream.* **2** having the color of coffee: dark brown. **3** at or in which coffee is served: *a coffee party, a coffee club.* [<Italian *caffe'* < turkish *kahve* < Arabic *qahwah*]

*Source:* Reprinted with permission from the *World Book Dictionary*

**TABLE 3.1 *Foreign Words and Their Countries of Origin***

| abolish, jury, larceny, mackerel, massage, olive | France |
|---|---|
| chino, bonanza, bravado, ranch, spaniel, tomato | Spain |
| whim, reel, shrivel, queer, rift, baffle, scraggy | Scandinavia |
| jilt, nab, bog | Scotland |
| hold, howitzer, toot, yacht, yawl, aardvark, wilt | Holland |
| sauerkraut, strudel | Germany |
| salami, cameo, balcony, macaroni, opera | Italy |
| arsenal, harem, alcohol, algebra | Arabia |
| cocoa, coyote, arroyo, chocolate | Mexico |
| tank, molasses, albino, caste, banana | Portugal |
| tangerine, canary, chimpanzee, zombie | Africa |
| hickory, hammock, tobacco, succotash, raccoon | America (Indian) |

## Incorporating Foreign Words

Do you speak a foreign language? If you speak English, then you probably use words each day that originated in a foreign language. That's because English, in many cases, has been commonly expanded by incorporating foreign words into it. Most of our language has ancient Anglo-Saxon or Latin origins. Words from other languages have also been added to our vocabularies. Table 3.1 shows some foreign words and their sources.

### EXERCISE 3.2

◆ *Match the following words with their languages of origin. This information can be found in a large collegiate dictionary. In the sample dictionary entry, the etymology of the word has been underlined.*

**coffee** (kof'e, kof'-), n., adj. —n **1** a dark-brown drink made from the roasted and ground seeds of a tall, tropical tree or shrub. **2** the seeds from which the drink is made; coffee beans. **3** the plant itself. It belongs to the madder family See picture under **madder family.** **4** the color of coffee; a dark brown, darker than chocolate. **5** a social gathering at which coffee is served. —adj **1** having the flavor of coffee: *coffee ice cream.* **2** having the color of coffee: *dark brown.* **3** at or in which coffee is served: *a coffee party, a coffee club.* [ < Italian *caffé* < /turkish *kahve* < Arabic *qahwah*]

*Source:* Reprinted with permission from the *World Book Dictionary,* 

_______________ **1.** vodka
_______________ **2.** wheeze
_______________ **3.** traffic
_______________ **4.** curd
_______________ **5.** tea
_______________ **6.** iceberg
_______________ **7.** blitz
_______________ **8.** tutti-frutti
_______________ **9.** zen
_______________ **10.** teak
_______________ **11.** paprika
_______________ **12.** squeak
_______________ **13.** yogurt
_______________ **14.** kangaroo
_______________ **15.** fiord

**a.** France
**b.** Norway
**c.** Scandinavia
**d.** Japan
**e.** China
**f.** Denmark
**g.** Germany
**h.** Russia
**i.** Australia
**j.** Portugal
**k.** Italy
**l.** Spain
**m.** Turkey
**n.** Sweden
**o.** Hungary

## Contemporary Additions to Vocabulary

What do you call the screw that holds a lamp shade in place? The whatchamacallit or the *finial?* What is the hinged flap on the wing of an airplane called? The whatchamacallit or the *aileron?* What would you call the fluid in rubber trees? The whatchamacallit or *latex?* Faced with such choices, inventors and others have given names to every product, process, and item they have developed. Because these developments occur every day, our language changes daily with the addition of these words. The value of a vast vocabulary is knowing these names so you can use them to keep the language alive.

### *Words from Technology*

Our words often reflect current interests, trends, and innovations. Technologists in the space and computer industries have been recent contributors to our language. Words from these areas include:

| | | |
|---|---|---|
| astronaut | payload | terminal |
| satellite | space shuttle | output |
| splashdown | monitor | countdown |

| | | |
|---|---|---|
| input | programmer | user-friendly |
| disk | solar cell | byte |
| probe | light-year | compact disk |

### *Words from Products*

Another way new words come into our language is through the development of products. It you invent a new product, you also have to invent a name for it. Many people throughout history have chosen names for products that were so good and that became so well known that all similar products became known by the same name. Look at the following examples:

| | | |
|---|---|---|
| yo-yo | cornflakes | thermos |
| Kleenex | Band-Aid | Sheetrock |
| aspirin | zipper | Xerox |
| Walkman radio | Scotch tape | escalator |
| nylon | trampoline | linoleum |

### *Words from People's Names*

What do the words *macintosh, tawdry,* and *guillotine* have in common? Each of these words came into our language when a person's name became linked to an invention or new concept. *Macintosh* takes its name from Charles Macintosh, a Scottish chemist. He invented a waterproof cape. Today, a macintosh refers to a raincoat. *Tawdry* comes from Saint Audrey, an English queen who died of throat cancer. Her subjects later sold lace neckties as a kind of memorial. Unfortunately, the neckties, called "Saint Audrey's lace," were cheap and gaudy. This was later shortened to "tawdry lace." Today, *tawdry* refers to anything cheap and gaudy. *Guillotine* was derived from the name of Dr. J. I. Guillotin who, in 1789, recommended its use. A guillotine is a instrument of death that beheads its victims. Like many other words whose names come from people, the people associated with *macintosh, tawdry,* and *guillotine* were forgotten. The words live on in our language.

**EXERCISE 3.3**

◆ *Find the people in the histories of the following words. Then define the words. This information can be found in a large collegiate dictionary. In the sample dictionary entry, the history of the word has been underlined.*

> **sideburns** (sīd'bernz'), *n.pl.* whiskers in front of the ears, especially when worn long and when the chin is shaved. [American English, alteration of *burnsides* < Ambrose E. *Burnside,* 1824–1881, a Union general]

▶ **Sideburns—burnsides** are related etymologically but have rarely, if ever, been exactly synonymous. *Burnsides,* now chiefly historical in use, designates relatively long, heavy whiskers, patterned on those worn by General Burnside (1824–1881). *Sideburns,* especially in current use, designates any hairy growth extending downward from a point just in front of the upper base of the ear, with length and closeness of cut being a matter of individual taste.

---



### *Example*

sideburns *General Ambrose Burnside wore full muttonchop whiskers. His distinctive whiskers became known as sideburns. Sideburns are whiskers in front of a person's ears.*

1. lynch ______________________________

2. masochism ______________________________

3. tarmac ______________________________

4. macabre ______________________________

5. malapropism ______________________________

6. ohm ______________________________

**7.** maverick ______________________________

______________________________

______________________________

**8.** saxophone ______________________________

______________________________

______________________________

**9.** leotard ______________________________

______________________________

______________________________

**10.** boycott ______________________________

______________________________

______________________________

### Words from Letters

Sometimes a person—like J. R. Ewing of "Dallas"—uses initials in place of a name. This is usually done when the person's name is long or hard to say. Because the initials are used, they become easier to recall. The person's real name may be forgotten. The same thing can happen with items, concepts, or groups. The initials eventually replace the names. Then, they represent the item, concept, or group. The following are examples of words that have developed from initials:

*PC*—Personal Computer
*TV*—TeleVision
*DWI*—Driving While Intoxicated
*VD*—Venereal Disease

**Acronyms** are another source of new words. These are words formed from the first letters or first few letters of several words. Acronyms sometimes aid your memory. For example, some people remember the order of the colors of the rainbow by thinking *ROY G. BIV*. This phrase stands for red, orange, yellow, green, blue, indigo, and violet. These are the colors of the rainbow in order. Some acronyms have come to replace the words for which they once stood. The following list consists of common acronyms and what they represent:

*SNAFU*—Systems Normal All Fouled Up (in polite terms)
*NABISCO*—NAtional BIScuit COmpany
*M*A*S*H*—Mobile Army Surgical Hospital
*AIDS*—Acquired Immune Deficiency Syndrome

## EXERCISE 3.4

*Identify the words for which the following initials stand. This information can be found in a large collegiate dictionary. There may be a special section for abbreviations. In the sample dictionary entry, the explanation of the initials has been underlined.*

> **LP** (no periods), **1** a long-playing phonograph record: *All five LP versions of the Concerto for Orchestra are excellent* (Atlantic). **2** *Trademark,* a name for a phonograph record of this type.
>
> *Source:* Reprinted with permission from the *World Book Dictionary,* Copyright © 1984, by Doubleday & Company.

***Example***

LP *long-playing record* ______

1. IOU ______
2. GI ______
3. VIP ______
4. IQ ______
5. PTA ______
6. RSVP ______
7. UFO ______
8. TKO ______
9. COD ______
10. ROTC ______

## EXERCISE 3.5

*Write out the words that the following acronyms represent. This information can be found in a large collegiate dictionary. There may be a special section for abbreviations. In the sample dictionary entry, the explanation of the acronym has been underlined.*

> **Zip Code, Zip code, zip code,** or**ZIP Code,** *U.S.* a nine-digit number used to identify a mail-delivery zone in the United States. [<*ZIP,* abbreviation of *Zone Improvement Plan,* the U.S. Postal Service system of coding by zones for faster mail sorting and delivery, introduced in 1963]
>
> *Source:* Reprinted with permission from the *World Book Dictionary,* Copyright © 1984, by Doubleday & Company.

***Example***

ZIP Code *Zone Improvement Plan Code*

1. SONAR ____________________
2. LASER ____________________
3. SCUBA ____________________
4. RADAR ____________________
5. WAVE ____________________
6. AWOL ____________________
7. DJ ____________________
8. WASP ____________________
9. TIP ____________________
10. UNICEF ____________________

## Word Histories

History affects words as well as people. The time, place, and circumstances surrounding an event influence meaning. New words develop to explain or define these events. History continues to change the meanings of these words through use. Sometimes the original meaning of the word differs greatly from a word's current meaning. Although every word has a "past," some are more interesting than others. Like gossip, when you know a juicy piece of information about something or someone, it's hard to forget. This is what makes words, as well as people, memorable.

***EXERCISE 3.6***

*Look up the histories for the following words in a large collegiate dictionary. Then define them. In the sample dictionary entry, the history of the word has been underlined.*

**bon/fire** (bon'fīr'), n. a large fire built outdoors: *The boys made a bonfire of rubbish and driftwood at the beach picnic.* [earlier *bonefire:* a fire to burn bones or, later, corpses]

*Source:* Reprinted with permission from the *World Book* Dictionary, Copyright © 1984, by Doubleday & Company.

***Example***

bonfire *During the Middle Ages, bodies of dead people were burned to ward off disease. They were called bonefires. The less morbid spelling bonfire has a harmless meaning today. A bonfire is a large outdoor fire.*

1. canter__________
2. jingo__________
3. scalawag__________
4. boondocks__________
5. assassin__________
6. bikini__________
7. tarantula__________
8. croquet__________
9. filbert__________

**10.** gerrymander___________________________________________________________________

___________________________________________________________________

___________________________________________________________________

◆

## WORD APPLICATIONS

Think again of the Dickinson poem that appears early in this chapter. It says a word begins to live when it is said, when it is used. After you learn a word, the next step in keeping it alive and growing is to use it.

When you use a word, you build connections between it and other words in your vocabulary. How does this happen? A few years ago a puzzle called a Rubic's Cube was popular. The cube consisted of colored, interlocking pieces. The object of the puzzle was to twist and turn the pieces so that each side of the cube became a solid color. In much the same way, a word consists of many sides and pieces. As you use a word, you twist and turn its meaning until your connotation of it becomes locked in your mind. Once there, your network around the word grows. You link it with other words with similar meanings. You consider words with opposite meanings. You differentiate the word from similar-sounding words, when necessary. Finally, like blocks, you learn to build and manipulate the word and its network. Your connections then comprise all you know about the word and its applications (see Figure 3.6).

**FIGURE 3.6**
***Network of "Weak"***

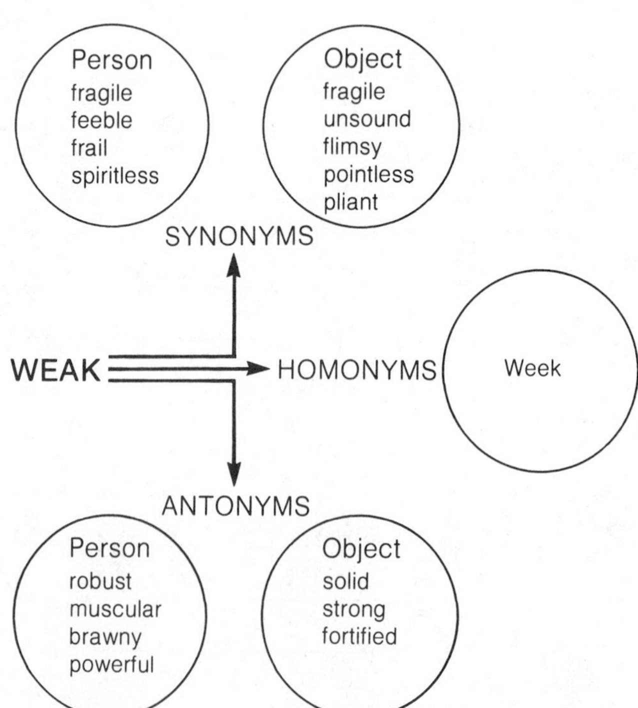

## Common Word Relationships

Three common relationships exist among words. Words that mean the same but look different are called **synonyms.** Synonyms (e.g., pretty/cute) improve your writing and speech by adding variety and flavor. They relieve monotony and make it easier for you to express yourself. **Antonyms** are words that have opposite meanings (e.g., pretty/ugly). They are the opposite of synonyms. **Homonyms** are words that sound alike but have different meanings (e.g., there/their). Since homonyms are words that sound alike, you must consider their definitions or contexts in choosing the correct one to use.

Because these three terms are often confused, here is an easy way to keep them straight:

| Heard alike | Same meaning | An opposite |
|---|---|---|
| O | Y | N |
| M | N | T |
| O | O | O |
| N | N | N |
| Y | Y | Y |
| M | M | M |

Words relate in many other ways as well. When thinking about the associations between two words, you examine those words for ways in which they are different, alike, or related to each other.

**EXERCISE 3.7**

*In each of the groups below, three words are synonyms. Circle the letter of the unrelated word and write the common definition of the three synonyms on the line above the words.*

**Example**

*Common definition:* change

**a.** alter **c.** transform
**b.** modify **(d.)** apply

**1.** *Common definition:* ________________

**a.** core **c.** middle
**b.** heart **d.** exterior

**2.** *Common definition:* ________________

**a.** compose **c.** complete
**b.** design **d.** invent

**3.** *Common definition:* ________________

**a.** box **c.** punch
**b.** drink **d.** knock

**4.** *Common definition:* ________________

**a.** fearful **c.** scary
**b.** anxious **d.** frightened

5. *Common definition:* ______________________
   a. cloth  
   b. garment  
   c. attire  
   d. apparel

6. *Common definition:* ______________________
   a. present  
   b. tip  
   c. bonus  
   d. payment

7. *Common definition:* ______________________
   a. square  
   b. location  
   c. spot  
   d. site

8. *Common definition:* ______________________
   a. crave  
   b. need  
   c. desire  
   d. wish

9. *Common definition:* ______________________
   a. glitter  
   b. gleam  
   c. twinkle  
   d. sprinkle

10. *Common definition:* ______________________
    a. guard  
    b. shield  
    c. honor  
    d. defend

## EXERCISE 3.8

*From the words below, choose two antonyms for each of the words in the exercise.*

***Example***

free  
*imprison*  
*cage*

| | | | |
|---|---|---|---|
| daring | friend | totality | finish |
| avoid | jagged | terminate | weak |
| ally | durable | permanent | brave |
| dirty | sum | powerless | gather |
| congregate | rough | evade | soiled |

1. unstable
   ______________  
   ______________

2. enemy
   ______________  
   ______________

3. begin
   ______________  
   ______________

4. timid
   ______________  
   ______________

5. face
   ______________  
   ______________

6. component
   ______________  
   ______________

7. smooth
______________
______________

8. muscular
______________
______________

9. disband
______________
______________

10. pure
______________
______________

**EXERCISE 3.9**

*Place an **S** beside each word that could be a synonym of the italicized word. Place an **A** beside each word that could be an antonym of the italicized word.*

***Example***

*tame*
_S_ mild
_A_ wild
_S_ docile
_S_ meek
_A_ savage

1. *small*
______ slight
______ ample
______ slender
______ bulky
______ little

2. *fatal*
______ deadly
______ harmless
______ lethal
______ mortal
______ beneficial

3. *student*
______ discipline
______ teacher
______ professor
______ mentor
______ pupil

4. *clumsy*
______ nimble
______ agile
______ spry
______ uncoordinated

5. *shore*
______ sea
______ ocean
______ bank
______ beach
______ coast

6. *show*
______ hide
______ mask
______ display
______ exhibit
______ conceal

7. *shorten*
______ extend
______ enlarge
______ cut
______ abbreviate
______ abridge

8. *noise*
______ racket
______ quiet
______ silence
______ clamor
______ din

9. *frighten*
______ soothe
______ startle
______ terrify
______ scare
______ comfort

10. *consent*
______ contradict
______ approve
______ endorse
______ agree
______ acquiesce

## EXERCISE 3.10

*Circle the correct homonym. Briefly define each.*

**Example**

I will accept (nun, none) of your excuses.
nun: *female member of a religious order*
none: *not any*

1. The wealthy tycoon left her money to her (heir, err).
   heir:__________
   err:__________
2. The diamond ring was 4 (carets, carats).
   carets:__________
   carats:__________
3. The letters *t*, *x*, and *w* are (consonants, consonance).
   consonants:__________
   consonance:__________
4. The committee reached an agreement without (dissent, descent).
   dissent:__________
   descent:__________
5. The (signet, cygnet) swam in the lake near our home.
   signet:__________
   cygnet:__________
6. He used a (philter, filter) to attract his wife.
   philter:__________
   filter:__________
7. The boxer made a (feint, faint) at his opponent.
   feint:__________
   faint:__________
8. The child slept on a (pallet, palate) on the floor.
   pallet:__________
   palate:__________
9. The reception took place in the (knave, nave) of the church.
   knave:__________
   nave:__________
10. The troops faced (intense, intents) opposition in battle.
    intense:__________
    intents:__________

## EXERCISE 3.11

*One of the sentences in each group is wrong. Circle the letter of the sentence in which the italicized word is used incorrectly.*

**Example**

(a) It took all of Sue's *patients* to deal with her little brother. **b.** All of the **patients** had to wait two hours to see the doctor. **c.** The clinic is filled with *patients* on Mondays.
*Explanation:* The incorrect sentence is answer a. The definition of *patients* is "ones who are receiving medical care." The homonym *patience* is needed for this sentence to be correct.

1. **a.** The grain *waved* in the breeze. **b.** The prisoner *waved* his right to an attorney. **c.** The baby *waved* good-bye to his grandparents.

2. **a.** The kitchen faucet has a *leak.* **b.** The stew contained tomatoes and *leaks.* **c.** The oil *leaked* out of the car.

3. **a.** There was an *ordinance* against fireworks within the city limits. **b.** A curfew is an unpopular *ordinance* with young people. **c.** Heavy *ordinance* was used to defeat the enemy of the English people.

4. **a.** The lions roamed the countryside in a *pride.* **b.** We *pride* the door to our cabin open. **c.** She accepted the medal with *pride.*

5. **a.** The *route* to our home is muddy since the last rain. **b.** The game was a *route.* **c.** *The route* to happiness is hard to find.

6. **a.** The bell *wrung* to signal school was beginning. **b.** The ladder was missing several *wrungs.* **c.** The confession was *wrung* from the prisoner.

7. **a.** The knight *sheathed* his sword before entering the castle. **b.** A pillowcase is a sort of *sheathe.* **c.** The darkness *sheathed* the woman as she approached the house.

8. **a.** Congress must approve all *treaties* signed by the United States. **b.** His dissertation was a type of *treaties* on poverty. **c.** The peace *treaties* were broken almost before they were approved.

9. **a.** As is my *want,* I went to bed early. **b.** Small children have many unrealistic *wants.* **c.** What do you *want* from me?

10. **a.** Place the number of your *dependents* on the second line of Form B. **b.** Your sense of *dependents* decreases with age. **c.** Military personnel and their *dependents* are eligible for benefits.

## Other Word Relationships

Many kinds of word relationships are possible (see Table 3.2). Some come from general information and your knowledge of various subjects. Others focus on your understanding of word structure, grammar, and function. Relationships can also reflect order such as cause and effect and sequence. Additional word associations are based on specific features. These include whole and parts, composition, degree, classification, and characterization.

When looking at relationships, the order of the words is important. Changing the order changes the relationship. In word relationships the colon (:) means "is to." For example, instead of "good is to bad," "good : bad" is written. Like all abbreviations, this one saves space and time.

***TABLE 3.2*** ***Word Relationships and Examples***

| *RELATIONSHIP* | *DEFINITION* | *EXAMPLES* |
|---|---|---|
| Synonym | Same or similar in meaning | ancestors : forefathers<br>domain : home<br>monarchy : kingdom<br>__________ |
| Antonym | Opposite in meaning | reality : fantasy<br>active : passive<br>positive : negative<br>__________ |
| Homonyms | Alike in sound | stationary : stationery<br>serf : surf<br>tract : tracked<br>__________ |
| General information | Pieces of common information logically relate to one another | France : Napoleon<br>Florida : Ponce de Leon<br>Airplanes : Earhart<br>__________ |
| Words and word structure | Words relate according to structure, grammar, or function | I : we<br>fight : fought<br>picture : light<br>__________ |
| Part to whole | A piece or portion relates to the total object or concept | jury : trial<br>id : personality<br>planet : solar system<br>__________ |
| Whole to part | The total relates to one of its components | atom : proton<br>cell : chromosome<br>solar system : planets<br>__________ |

**TABLE 3.2 Continued**

| RELATIONSHIP | DEFINITION | EXAMPLES |
|---|---|---|
| Degree (age, time, rank, or size) | A concept relates to a younger/older, larger/smaller, earlier/later or lesser/greater concept. | Stone Age : Atomic Age<br>president : vice-president<br>hill : mountain<br>__________ |
| Person to event, location, or item | Relates a person and his/her corresponding place, time, or deed. | Marie Curie : radium<br>Betsy Ross : American flag<br>Charles Darwin : evolution<br>__________ |
| Object to use | Item relates to its function | blood platelets : clotting<br>test : evaluate<br>food : nourish<br>__________ |
| Source to object | An item's origin and that item | sun : solar energy<br>car emissions : pollution<br>liver : bile<br>__________ |
| Cause and effect | An action relates to its results | learning : knowledge<br>injury : pain<br>flame : heat |
| Characterization | A person or animal relates to a personality trait | fox : sly<br>judge : wise<br>architect : artist<br>__________ |

**EXERCISE 3.12**

◆ *Match the following pairs with their relationships. The relationships may be used more than once.*

***Example***

__*d*__ London : England

| | | |
|---|---|---|
| _____ **1.** tadpole : frog | | **a.** antonym |
| _____ **2.** weigh : way | | **b.** synonym |
| _____ **3.** lion : pride | | **c.** homonym |
| _____ **4.** Memphis : Tennessee | | **d.** part to whole |
| _____ **5.** few : shoe | | **e.** rhyme |
| _____ **6.** painting : artist | | **f.** degree |
| _____ **7.** bank : money | | **g.** object to use |
| _____ **8.** book : tome | | **h.** source to object |
| _____ **9.** chef : kitchen | | **i.** object to source |
| _____ **10.** distress : eustress | | **j.** person to location |

_______**11.** mirage : dream
_______**12.** gills : breath
_______**13.** chief : leaf
_______**14.** cruel : crewel
_______**15.** owl : wise
_______**16.** spill : stain
_______**17.** seek : sought
_______**18.** soldier : brave
_______**19.** Nixon : Watergate
_______**20.** child : adult

**k.** general information
**l.** words and word structure
**m.** cause and effect
**n.** characterization

## Analogies

Intelligence tests often contain questions written in **analogy** form. Thus, analogies seem like strange and difficult concepts. But you probably use them every day.

Suppose you are trying to decide where to eat lunch. You say, "I could go to Burgerland for hamburgers, or I could go to Pizza City for pizza." You would be stating the relationship between places and the kind of food served. When transformed into the analogy form, this statement would be written "Burgerland is to hamburgers as Pizza City is to pizza."

You also use analogies when you decide what to wear. "If it's cold outside, I'll wear a coat. If it's hot, I'll wear shorts." The analogy form would be "cold is to coat as hot is to shorts."

Because analogies require you to identify similar relationships between dissimilar objects, understanding analogies is one of the highest levels of thinking.

### *Definition of Analogy*

An analogy is an implied (unstated) relationship between two pairs of objects. Because the relationship is implied, the first thing you need to decide is what kind of relationship exists between each pair (i.e., synonyms, antonyms, homonyms, part to whole, time, place, age). This relationship can be any type of association.

### *Forms of Analogies*

Analogies are written in one of two ways. Consider again the example of clothing and weather.

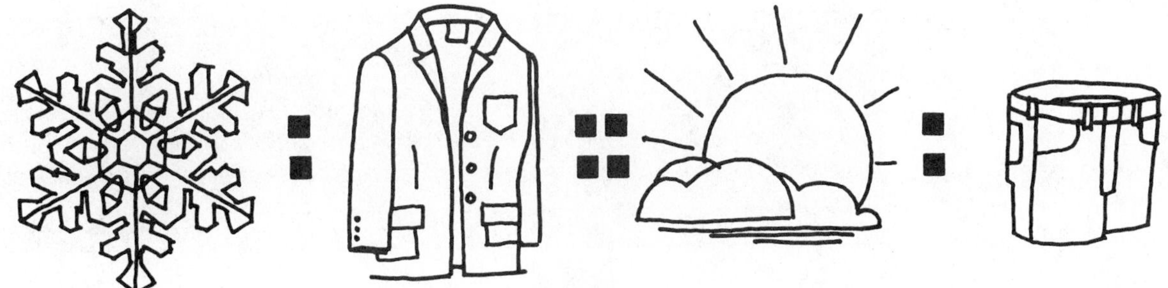

In words, that analogy could be written as follows:

Cold is to coat as hot is to shorts.

or

Cold : coat :: hot : shorts

The colon (:) in the second example means "is to." The pair of colons (::) means "as."

### *Solving Analogies*

An analogy concerns the relationship between two pairs of words. Again, the two pairs are usually dissimilar (not the same), although the relationships between each pair are similar.

For example, look at these analogies.

sour : lemon :: sweet : sugar
*Relationship:* flavor to a food that has that flavor

write : right :: week : weak
*Relationship:* homonyms

April : month :: Friday : day
*Relationship:* specific name to its general time

foot : toe :: hand : finger
*Relationship:* whole to part

STEPS IN SOLVING ANALOGIES

1. Consider the following analogy:

   X : Y :: Z : ?

2. Identify the elements in the first part of the analogy (X, Y).
3. Associate information with each of these elements.
4. Determine how these elements are related.
5. Consider the second pair of elements (Z, ?) in terms of this relationship.
6. Determine the missing element of the second part (?) to complete the analogy.

### WRITE TO LEARN

*On a separate sheet of paper respond to the following: Your ten-year-old brother is going to take a standardized test tomorrow that will contain analogy questions. Keeping his age in mind, explain what an analogy is and give him examples of five different kinds of analogies to solve.*

## EXERCISE 3.13

◆ *Match the following pairs to form a complete analogy.*

**Example**

| | |
|---|---|
| ___*d*___ pretty : cute | **a.** lawyer : courtroom |
| **1.** ______ :: purl : pearl | **b.** stay : leave |
| **2.** ______ :: Disney World : Florida | **c.** scissors : cut |
| **3.** ______ :: ruby : sapphire | **d.** nasty : dirty |
| **4.** ______ :: swim : chair | **e.** play : dance |
| **5.** ______ :: Judas : Jesus | **f.** sticks : styx |
| **6.** ______ :: preacher : church | **g.** Benedict Arnold : USA |
| **7.** ______ :: pollution : disease | **h.** unemployment : poverty |
| **8.** ______ :: pencil : write | **i.** red : blue |
| **9.** ______ :: solemn : happy | **j.** goose : gosling |
| **10.** ______ :: cat : kitten | **k.** Statue of Liberty : New York |

## EXERCISE 3.14

◆ *Complete the analogies below by providing a pair of words that has the same relationship as the given pair. Identify the relationship.*

**Example**

*Relationship: antonyms*

naked : uncovered :: *insult* : *compliment*

1. *Relationship:* ______________________________

   author : inventor :: ______________ : ______________

2. *Relationship:* ______________________________

   entrants : entrance :: ______________ : ______________

3. *Relationship:* ______________________________

   vein : train :: ______________ : ______________

**4.** *Relationship:* ______________________________

strike : bowl :: ______________ : ______________

**5.** *Relationship:* ______________________________

coward : fearful :: ______________ : ______________

**6.** *Relationship:* ______________________________

flammable : inflammable :: ______________ : ______________

**7.** *Relationship:* ______________________________

triangle : pyramid :: ______________ : ______________

**8.** *Relationship:* ______________________________

gallon : gasoline :: ______________ : ______________

**9.** *Relationship:* ______________________________

rain : drought :: ______________ : ______________

**10.** *Relationship:* ______________________________

cat : feline :: ______________ : ______________

**11.** *Relationship:* ______________________________

caterpillar : butterfly :: ______________ : ______________

**12.** *Relationship:* ______________________________

flour : flower :: ______________ : ______________

**13.** *Relationship:* ______________________________

cucumber : pickle :: ______________ : ______________

**14.** *Relationship:* ______________________________

vocal : silent :: ______________ : ______________

**15.** *Relationship:* ______________________________

faith : believe :: ______________ : ______________

## EXERCISE 3.15

*Use the following list of words to fill in the blanks:*

| | | | |
|---|---|---|---|
| item | simple | total | intricate |
| indifference | joy | woe | care |
| barren | common | rich | regal |
| calm | raise | provoke | dip |
| cease | hidden | obvious | persist |

| *SYNONYMS* | *WORD* | *ANTONYMS* |
|---|---|---|
| ***Example*** | | |
| *plump* | stout | *skinny* |
| ______________ | **1.** complicated | ______________ |
| ______________ | **2.** apathy | ______________ |
| ______________ | **3.** fertile | ______________ |
| ______________ | **4.** pacify | ______________ |
| ______________ | **5.** plain | ______________ |
| ______________ | **6.** pause | ______________ |
| ______________ | **7.** plunge | ______________ |
| ______________ | **8.** royal | ______________ |
| ______________ | **9.** misery | ______________ |
| ______________ | **10.** unit | ______________ |

*Use the preceding list to complete the following analogies:*

**1.** defective : faulty :: unit : ______________

**2.** give : withhold :: pacify : ______________

**3.** nook : cavity :: complicated : ______________

**4.** stubborn : pliable :: plain : ______________

**5.** indecent : improper :: misery : ______________

**6.** road : highway :: apathy : ______________

**7.** veracity : dishonesty :: plunge : ______________

**8.** obstacle : bar :: fertile : ______________

**9.** destroy : construct :: pause : ______________

◆ **10.** praise : censure :: royal : ______________

◆

## CHAPTER SUMMARY EXERCISE

*Complete the summary by filling in the blanks with the following words:*

| | | |
|---|---|---|
| histories | word cards | listening |
| denotations | reading | connotations |
| no knowledge | analogies | Etymology |
| continuum | use | |

Words exist through use. You can rank words on a ____________ ranging from ____________ of the word to the ability to ____________ it. Vocabulary development involves remembering the new words you learn through ____________ and ____________. Making ______, forming personal associations, and differentiating between ____________ and ____________ help you recall new words. ____________ concerns the origins of words. Knowing word ____________ also helps you remember words. Developing word relationships and understanding ____________ increase your ability to use words.

◆

## CHAPTER REVIEW

*Answer briefly but completely.*

**1.** Examine the ratings you gave to the vocabulary enhancement words at the beginning of this chapter. For those words you rate as level 3 (You know you've seen or heard a word and can use it in speaking or writing), try to remember the conditions under which you learned them. How can this knowledge improve your future acquisition of words?

____________________________________________

____________________________________________

____________________________________________

____________________________________________

____________________________________________

**2.** Complete the Vocabulary Enhancement Exercise that follows. Examine the ratings you gave to the vocabulary enhancement words at the end of this chapter. Compare and contrast these with your initial ratings. What, if anything, enhanced your understanding of the words? What, if anything, might you do differently to remember the words?

____________________________________________

____________________________________________

____________________________________________

____________________________________________

____________________________________________

____________________________________________

3. Which of the vocabulary techniques discussed in this chapter are you most likely to use and why? Which are you least likely to use and why?

4. Compare and contrast your four kinds of vocabulary: writing, reading, speaking, listening.

5. Your roommate reads very slowly. You suspect that this lack of speed might be the result of his or her using the dictionary rather than using other ways of finding unknown words. Provide at least two reasons why using a dictionary hinders reading speed. Tell your roommate about one other way to find meaning during reading.

6. Compare and contrast denotation and connotation.

**7.** How does understanding etymology increase understanding and recall of a word's meaning?

______________________________________________

______________________________________________

______________________________________________

______________________________________________

______________________________________________

______________________________________________

**8.** The person sitting next to you fell asleep during the lecture on homonyms, synonyms, and antonyms. Explain the differences among these terms and provide an example of each.

______________________________________________

______________________________________________

______________________________________________

______________________________________________

______________________________________________

______________________________________________

**9.** Why do you think intelligence tests contain questions in analogy form? What makes an analogy a challenging kind of question?

______________________________________________

______________________________________________

______________________________________________

______________________________________________

______________________________________________

______________________________________________

**10.** Your math instructor said that solving equations was analogous to solving a murder mystery. The person who sits behind you wants to know the meaning of *analogous*. Since you know *analogous* is a form of the word *analogy*, you volunteer to explain. Record your explanation on the lines below.

______________________________________________

______________________________________________

______________________________________________

______________________________________________

______________________________________________

◆

## VOCABULARY ENHANCEMENT EXERCISE

*Using the scale in Figure 3.1, rate your understanding of the following vocabulary enhancement words to the left of the number. Then write a sentence with each one.*

**1.** bombard

______________________________

______________________________

**2.** continuum

______________________________

______________________________

**3.** comprise

______________________________

______________________________

**4.** vast

______________________________

______________________________

**5.** origin

______________________________

______________________________

**6.** evolution

______________________________

______________________________

**7.** circumstances

______________________________

______________________________

**8.** express

______________________________

______________________________

**9.** entry

______________________________

______________________________

**10.** unconscious

______________________________________________

______________________________________________

◆

## REFERENCES

Carr, E. "The Vocabulary Overview Guide: A Metacognitive Strategy to Improve Vocabulary, Comprehension, and Retention." *Journal of Reading* 28:684–89 (1985).

Dale E. "How to Know More Wonderful Words." *Good Housekeeping* 146:17+ (1958).

Eeds, M., and Cockrum, W. A. "Teaching Word Meanings by Expanding Schemata vs. Dictionary Work vs. Reading in Context." *Journal of Reading* 28:492–97 (1985).

# 4 Using the Context

## TERMS

*Terms appear in the order in which they occur in the chapter.*

context
literal
part of speech
text-based context clues
punctuation text-based clues
definition text-based clues
linking verbs
contrast text-based clues
comparison text-based clues
example text-based clues
framework-based context clues
general vocabulary
specialized vocabulary
technical vocabulary

## CHAPTER OUTLINE EXERCISE

*Complete the following outline by creating goal-setting questions from each heading and subheading in this chapter.*

I. ______________________________

______________________________

II. ______________________________

______________________________

A. ______________________________

______________________________

B. ______________________________

______________________________

C. ______________________________

______________________________

D. ______________________________

______________________________

E. ______________________________

______________________________

III. ______________________________

______________________________

IV. ______________________________

______________________________

## OBJECTIVES

*At the end of this chapter, you should be able to do the following:*

1. Use context to identify part of speech.
2. Determine meaning through text-based context clues.
3. Determine meaning through framework-based context clues.
4. Use specialized context for college study.

## CHAPTER MAP

*Complete the map by creating goal-setting questions from each heading and subheading in this chapter.*

### USING THE CONTEXT

## VOCABULARY ENHANCEMENT EXERCISE

*Rate each of the following words according to your knowledge of them.*

| | STAGE 0 | STAGE 1 | STAGE 2 | STAGE 3 |
|---|---|---|---|---|
| | *I do not recognize the word.* | *I recognize the word but am unsure of its meaning and associations.* | *I recognize the word and can make general associations with it.* | *I recognize the word and can use it in speaking and writing.* |
| **1.** efficient | | | | |
| **2.** similarities | | | | |
| **3.** derive | | | | |
| **4.** relies | | | | |
| **5.** intense | | | | |
| **6.** applied | | | | |
| **7.** encounter | | | | |
| **8.** novel | | | | |
| **9.** metaphoric | | | | |
| **10.** concepts | | | | |

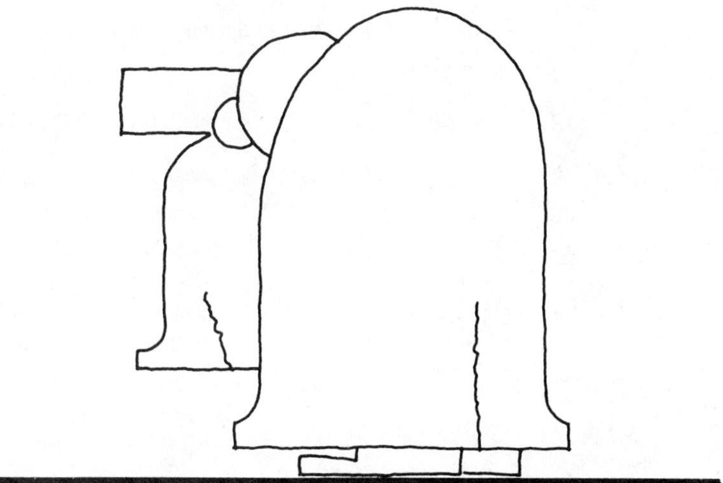

WHAT IS PICTURED HERE? After you've taken a careful look, turn to the last page of this chapter to see if you were correct.

The above cartoon is a droodle, invented by Roger Price in the 1950s. A droodle consists of a little drawing that doesn't look like much of anything until you know its title. Once you know its title, you easily recognize the content of the picture. That's because your mind fills in details. These surroundings give meaning and clarity. Thus, your skill in identifying something depends on your skill in figuring out its connection with its surroundings—its **context.**

Have you ever seen someone somewhere and thought, "That guy really looks familiar. I wonder where I've seen him before?" Suddenly, you remember! He's in your math class. You sit next to him each day. How could you forget him? Easy! He was not in his usual surroundings. He was out of context.

Words and their meanings can also be known by their surroundings—their contexts. Using the context to define unknown words takes practice. But, it is the easiest and most efficient way to identify words. In addition, using the context is the only way to figure out the meaning of the word as it is used in the sentence, passage, or chapter.

Consider the word *bar. Bar* is a common word. But, without surrounding words, you don't know if it describes soap, a place that serves beer, a sand formation, a way to lock the door, or . . . . Readers often miss questions because they identify the **literal** but incorrect meaning of a word when they should identify the way it was used in the passage.

◆

## USING CONTEXT TO IDENTIFY PART OF SPEECH

One consideration in using context is the unknown word's **part of speech.** A word's function in a sentence helps determine its meaning.

**TABLE 4.1 Parts of Speech, Definitions, and Functions**

| PART OF SPEECH | DEFINITION | FUNCTION |
|---|---|---|
| Noun (N.) | Identifies persons, places, or things; collections or groups of persons, places, or things; qualities, actions, conditions, processes, and ideas | Names |
| Pronoun (P.) | Replaces a noun | Names |
| Verb (V.) | Shows action or state of being | States, asks, or commands |
| Adjective (Adj.) | Modifies or limits a noun | Clarifies or describes |
| Adverb (Adv.) | Modifies or limits a verb, adjective, or other adverb | Clarifies or describes |
| Preposition (Prep.) | Connects the noun or pronoun following it to some other word in the sentence | Introduces or shows relationships |
| Conjunction (Conj.) | Joins words or groups of words | Connects |
| Interjection (Intj.) | Expresses strong or sudden feeling | Exclaims |

Consider the following sentences:

I hurt my *back* at work today.
Move *back* three spaces.
The *back* door needs painting.
Can you *back* your car out of the driveway?

The meanings of *back* depend on their uses in each sentence. Although each sentence contains *back,* the word is used as a noun, adverb, adjective, and verb, in that order. Its meaning in the first sentence refers to a part of the body. In the second sentence, *back* indicates the direction in which movement should occur. The third sentence uses *back* to describe which door is to be painted. In the fourth sentence, *back* is an action to be taken by the driver. Thus, the meaning of *back* depends upon its part of speech.

In Lewis Carroll's "The Hunting of the Snark," Carroll writes, "The snark was a boojum." While you may not know what a *snark* or *boojum* is, you do know that both are nouns. Thus, they must be either persons, places, or things. Because part of speech is helpful in determining meaning, Table 4.1 provides a review for you.

## EXERCISE 4.1

*Use context to identify the part of speech of each nonsense word in the sentences below. Then revise the sentence so that it makes sense.*

1. The *ngjkl rrbdes* up a *quiolk* mountain.

   a. *ngjkl* ______________

   b. *rrbdes* ______________

   c. *quiolk* ______________

*Revision:* ______________________________

______________________________

**2.** *Rsipem* in Europe is an exciting *skgope.*

**a.** *Rsipem* ______________

**b.** *skgope* ______________

*Revision:* ______________________________

______________________________

**3.** The *skpzoei* arrived from *skeops* for Juan and *siwe.*

**a.** *skpzoei* ______________

**b.** *skeops* ______________

**c.** *siwe* ______________

*Revision:* ______________________________

______________________________

**4.** *Xdk* and I *sxipedkm* the garage last *xipemen.*

**a.** *Xdk* ______________

**b.** *sxipedkm* ______________

**c.** *xipemen* ______________

*Revision:* ______________________________

______________________________

**5.** The old *kopem* had never gone outside the *xipely simx* town.

**a.** *kopem* ______________

**b.** *xipely* ______________

**c.** *simx* ______________

*Revision:* ______________________________

______________________________

**6.** On *Rsdiu* morning the ferry brings *kiopsk* from as *xsim* away as Alaska.

**a.** *Rsdiu* ______________

**b.** *kiopsk* ______________

**c.** *xsim* ______________

*Revision:* ______________________________

______________________________

**7.** Hearing *imsopin* outside the *uripsm, wersh* rushed to the *prems.*

**a.** *imsopin* ______________

**b.** *uripsm* ______________

**c.** *wersh* ______________

**d.** *prems* ______________

*Revision:* ______________________________________________

______________________________________________

**8.** A sweet potato is a root, *xim* a white potato is a stem.

**a.** *xim* ______________

*Revision:* ______________________________________________

______________________________________________

**9.** The *fjki* magazine cover made my interest in the topic *sipes.*

**a.** *fjki* ______________

**b.** *sipes* ______________

*Revision:* ______________________________________________

______________________________________________

**10.** *Hwmik* has a music *que* that *resip* a theme from a *ximpe* movie.

**a.** *Hwmik* ______________

**b.** *que* ______________

**c.** *resip* ______________

**d.** *ximpe* ______________

*Revision:* ______________________________________________

______________________________________________

## EXERCISE 4.2

*Choose the letter of the correct definition for each sentence below. Use parts of speech to help you find the correct definition.*

***Example***

FLUSH

**a.** filled to overflowing (*adj*)
**b.** in poker, five cards of the same suit not in sequence (*n*)
**c.** having a ruddy, healthy color (*adj*)
**d.** abundant (*adj*)
**e.** arranged edge to edge (*adj*)

__c__ The child's face was flushed from playing outside.

1. ______ The carpenter hammered the nail flush with the board.
2. ______ Jack tried to bluff when he saw the flush in his hand.

ORDER

**a.** members of a religious group (*n*)
**b.** an arrangement or sequence of objects (*n*)
**c.** a rule of law (*n*)
**d.** a written direction to pay money to someone for something (*n*)
**e.** state or condition of functioning or repair (*n*)

3. ______ My telephone was out of order.
4. ______ When I dropped the pages of my paper, they got out of order.
5. ______ The florist got an order for five dozen roses.

POST

**a.** a pole fixed in an upright position (*n*)
**b.** the place or task where a soldier is stationed (*n*)
**c.** to put something up for public notice (*v*)
**d.** to mail (*v*)
**e.** a place of trade (*n*)

6. ______ Carl posted the announcement in the dean's office.
7. ______ Phong posted the letter two days before Jan received it.
8. ______ Kay leaned on a post in the field.

CALL

**a.** to make a brief visit (*v*)
**b.** to speak of or address by a specified name (*v*)
**c.** to shout (*v*)
**d.** to warrant (*v*)
**e.** to suspend (*v*)

9. ______ The ball game was called because of the rain.
10. ______ The situation called for legal action.

### WRITE TO LEARN

*Your roommate overslept and missed class today. On a separate sheet of paper, write your roommate a note explaining how context and part of speech affect each other.*

◆

## USING TEXT-BASED CONTEXT CLUES

**Text-based context clues** consist of written clues to the meanings of unknown words. They are found directly within a sentence, paragraph, passage, or chapter. Knowing the clues helps you define new words in context. Text-based context clues can be words or punctuation marks. You use them to identify unknown words that mean the same or the opposite of words you already know. The clues can also be used to define unknown words that are examples of a group. Table 4.2 shows types and examples of text-based clues.

***TABLE 4.2*** ***Types of Text-Based Context Clues***

| *TEXT-BASED TYPES* | *TEXT-BASED CLUES* | *TEXT-BASED EXAMPLES* |
|---|---|---|
| PUNCTUATION | commas ,,,<br>parentheses ( )<br>dashes —<br>brackets [ ] | The determination of physical characteristics like hair color is the result of polygenic (multiple gene) influence.<br>Aspiration—the act of breathing—was explained in the CPR course. |
| DEFINITION | is, was, are, means, involves, is called, that is, i.e., which means, resembles | Statistics involves using math to make predictions.<br>Mitosis, i.e., the equal division of chromosome material, is a necessary step in cell division. |
| CONTRAST | however, on the contrary, while, but, instead of, on the other hand, although, nevertheless, yet | Random selection is a good method for making choices, but systematic selection is easier to process.<br>ET was an extraterrestrial creature; on the other hand, the children with whom he lived were all from our planet. |
| COMPARISON | similarly, both, as well as, likewise | Many atolls can be found in the Pacific Ocean; similarly, other coral islands are found in the Caribbean Sea.<br>Both the Greek and Roman cultures have contributed much to our current civilization. |
| EXAMPLE | such as, such, like, for example, e.g., other | Unguents, such as first aid cream, Cortaid, Vick-Salve, and Deep Heat, are found in most homes.<br>Psychosomatic disorders, e.g., ulcers and tension headaches, are physical illnesses that result from psychological stress. |

## Punctuation Text-Based Clues

**Punctuation text-based clues** consist of commas, parentheses, brackets, or dashes. The information contained within the punctuation marks usually means the same or nearly the same as the unknown words. Sometimes, however, the unknown word might be separated from its meaning by punctuation marks. Information set off by punctuation may clarify rather than define the word. Thus, finding these clues is not foolproof.

***Example***

The philosopher Descartes helped to establish *dualism* (the separation of mind and body).

*Explanation:* The words within parentheses—the separation of mind and body—define *dualism*.

***EXERCISE 4.3***

*Circle the word (or words) that tells you the meaning of the italicized word.*

***Example***

The owners thought the house was haunted by a *kobold*—a mischievous spirit.

1. User-friendly computer operating systems, often called *transparent systems*, are generally the easiest to use.
2. Major cities use international *icons* (symbols) for traffic, business, and personal applications.
3. *Sociobiology*—a scientific approach to the explanation of behavior—is explained largely in terms of natural selection.
4. *Tectonic* (or earth) movements often follow fault lines.
5. An *inauguration* (installation into office) logically follows an election.

## Definition Text-Based Clues

**Definition text-based clues** join the unknown word with the word(s) that rename it or tell its meaning. The clues precede or follow words that are or act like **linking verbs.** A linking verb shows no action but indicates being. Examples of these clues include *is, was, are, means, i.e.* (that is), *involves, is called, that is,* and *resembles.*

***Example***

The art, science, or profession of teaching is *pedagogy.*

*Explanation:* The linking verb *is* joins *pedagogy* with its meaning—art, science, or profession of teaching.

**EXERCISE 4.4**

*Use definition text-based clues to find the meaning of the italicized word. Circle the meaning.*

**Example**

A *souk* is an open-air marketplace in North America.

1. *Software piracy* consists of illegal copying of copywrited software for commercial or personal use.
2. When a set contains exactly one element, that set becomes a *singleton set*.
3. *Mutation* refers to changes in genetic material of a cell.
4. Medical problems involving the lungs are termed *pulmonary* ailments.
5. A secretion of any of the endocrine glands is called a *hormone*.

## Contrast Text-Based Clues

With **contrast text-based clues,** you use the opposite of known information to determine the meaning of the unknown word. Connecting words like *however, yet, on the other hand, instead of, but, while,* and *although* join the unknown word with another word or phrase that is its opposite in meaning.

**Example**

Some business disputes can be settled out of court; on the other hand, others require *litigation*.

*Explanation:* If *litigation* is the opposite of *out of court* (signaled by "on the other hand"), then *litigation* means *in court*.

**EXERCISE 4.5**

*Circle the meaning of the italicized word by using contrast text-based clues.*

**Example**

Although the patron asked for a solemn poem, the poet wrote *doggerel* verse.

**a.** funny
**b.** sad
**c.** long

1. Dawn follows night; on the other hand, *dusk* follows day.
   **a.** sunrise
   **b.** noon
   **c.** evening

2. On most occasions Abraham Lincoln gave a prepared speech; however, sometimes his remarks were completely *extemporaneous*.
   a. unclear
   b. unrehearsed
   c. understood

3. Although some diseases are *zoonotic*, most diseases are not communicable between humans and other animals.
   a. transmitted between humans and animals
   b. found only in zoos and veterinary clinics
   c. found only in medical hospitals and clinics

4. In the sense that a horse is of unmixed breeding, it is a thoroughbred; however, a mule differs in that it is a *hybrid*.
   a. animal less likely to win a race
   b. the same as a horse
   c. result of breeding a horse and a donkey

5. Ulysses' two eyes made him binocular; on the other hand, the Cyclops was *monocular*.
   a. blind
   b. deaf
   c. one-eyed

## Comparison Text-Based Clues

**Comparison text-based clues** indicate that two or more things are alike. A comparison is possible because the known and unknown words have similarities. Words like *similarly, as well as, both,* and *likewise* show you that comparisons can be made.

***Example***

*Repartee,* as well as other kinds of humorous conversation, kept the talk show from becoming boring.

*Explanation: Repartee* is a kind of humorous conversation.

**EXERCISE 4.6**

*Circle the correct definition for the italicized word by using comparison text-based clues.*

***Example***

The old chair was protected by both handmade *antimacassars* and other coverings.

(a) a decorative protective cloth
b. a stuffed pillow
c. plastic

1. The king and his inner circle were often *cohorts* in crime and they were also companions in more legitimate activities.
   a. on opposite sides
   b. partners
   c. avengers
2. Just as a mother bird sometimes abandons her young, an *apostate* deserts her principles.
   a. enemy
   b. traitor
   c. disciple
3. "From A to Z" is a common expression meaning everything; similarly, the phrase "alpha and omega" is often used.
   a. nothing
   b. something
   c. everything
4. Just as a storm eventually subsides, energy finally *flags*.
   a. ends
   b. flies
   c. clears
5. Vehicles are generally stored in a garage; similarly, airplanes are stored in a *hangar*.
   a. enclosed area
   b. flight plan
   c. runway

## Example Text-Based Clues

**Example text-based clues** tell you that an example of an unknown word follows. You derive the meaning of the unknown word by determining what the examples have in common. Example text-based clues are usually introduced by the following words and phrases: *such as, such, other, for example,* and *like.*

### *Example*

Various means of *conveyance*—for example, cars, subways, and ships—are used around the world.

*Explanation:* Cars, subways, and ships are means of travel. Therefore, *conveyance* must also refer to a form of travel.

**EXERCISE 4.7**

*Identify the meanings of the italicized words in the following sentences based on the example text-based clues.*

***Example***

*Fiduciaries*, like lawyers and bankers, were chosen to manage the young heir's money.

*fiduciaries: persons in charge of trust fund or money*

*Cardinal numbers* like one, two and three differ from *ordinal numbers* such as first, second, and third.

1. *cardinal numbers:* ______________________________

______________________________

2. *ordinal numbers:* ______________________________

______________________________

Planets, globes, and pearls are all *orbs*.

3. *orbs:* ______________________________

______________________________

New, crescent, half, and full describe different *phases* of the moon.

4. *phases:* ______________________________

______________________________

Embezzlement, fraud, and other kinds of *malfeasance* are more common in today's businesses.

5. *malfeasance:* ______________________________

______________________________

**EXERCISE 4.8**

*Determine the meanings of each of the bold-faced words in the passage below. Then identify the type of text-based clue that helped you find the meanings.*

**ADIABATIC PROCESSES AND ATMOSPHERIC STABILITY**

Atmospheric cooling that leads to the formation of clouds and precipitation nearly always results from the rising of air. As a parcel of air rises, it enters areas of reduced atmospheric pressure and consequently expands. The expansion of the rising air requires energy, which is taken from the **kinetic** (or thermal) energy of the air molecules, making the air parcel cooler. When this cooling has reduced the air temperature to the dew point, condensation and cloud formation begin. Clouds are thus the visible tops of rising air currents. The cooling of air resulting from its expansion is termed **adiabatic cooling.** It involves no actual loss of energy, because this energy has not left the air but has merely changed form. As long as the air keeps rising, it continues to cool, causing the condensation or sublimation of additional water vapor. This allows the cloud to grow larger and its constituent water droplets and ice crystals to increase in size, so that eventually they may become large enough to fall as precipitation. Conversely, when the air descends, it undergoes **adiabatic warming** because the surrounding air forces the descending parcel to contract, returning the energy it used in expansion. As the descending air warms, its water vapor holding capacity increases, so that a cloud within a descending airflow will soon evaporate. This is why the descending air associated with high pressure systems produces fair, dry weather.

The concept of atmospheric stability is also important in understanding cloud development. Several different factors can cause air to rise sufficiently to produce clouds and precipitation. If the air is **stable,** however, it has a tendency to resist any lifting influence; if forced to rise, it will return to its original altitude when this becomes possible. **Unstable** air, however, has a tendency to rise; once given an initial lift, it continues to rise on its own. The implications of atmospheric stability on cloud types and precipitation characteristics will be explored shortly.

### DEW AND FROST

Dew and frost both form on the earth's surface. Because they do not fall from the atmosphere, they are not technically considered to be forms of precipitation. **Dew** consists of water droplets that have condensed on surface objects because the overlying air has cooled below the dew point. It nearly always occurs at night and is most likely when the sky is clear, the wind light or calm, and the air moist. Under these conditions, terrestrial radiation often allows land areas to cool rapidly. Conduction with the cold surface then chills the overlying layer of air, forcing the excess atmospheric moisture to condense on available surfaces such as leaves and blades of grass. Dew normally evaporates in the morning as the air is warmed and its water vapor holding capacity increases. It is a relatively minor source of surface moisture, but typically provides land areas in the middle latitudes with from 0.5 to 2.0 inches (12–50 mm) of water per year.

**Frost** forms under nearly identical conditions, but when the dew point is below freezing. Frost is not frozen dew, but instead forms by sublimation directly from water vapor. All products of sublimation have a crystalline structure, and the feathery patterns formed by frost on windowpanes and other surfaces are well known.

### FOG

Dew and frost form when a layer of air just above the surface is cooled below its dew point, and the resulting moisture is deposited on objects at the surface. When a deeper layer of air is cooled, however, condensation or sublimation occurs on atmospheric dust particles. The result is fog. **Fog** is a visible accumulation of minute water droplets or ice crystals suspended in air immediately overlying the surface. It is actually a cloud at ground level.

The most common fog type over land areas is **radiation fog.** It forms under the same clear, calm, moist nighttime conditions that result in the formation of dew and frost. Its presence indicates that conditions for terrestrial radiation favor the cooling of an unusually deep layer of near-surface air, and it is associated with heavy dew or frost. Local **topographic** features often control the distribution of radiation fog. Over flat surfaces, it can form an extensive blanket covering many square miles. In more rugged areas, though, the downhill drainage of air chilled by contact with the cold surface often causes radiation fog to accumulate in valley bottoms, while the surrounding uplands remain clear.

*Source:* Reprinted with permission from *Physical Geography* by Scott. 

**1.** kinetic ______________________________

______________________________

*Type of clue:* ______________________________

**2.** adiabatic cooling ______________________________

______________________________

*Type of clue:* ______________________________

**3.** adiabatic warming ______________________________

______________________________

*Type of clue:* ______________________________

**4.** stable ______________________________

______________________________

*Type of clue:* ______________________________

**5.** unstable ______________________________

______________________________

*Type of clue:* ______________________________

**6.** dew ______________________________

______________________________

*Type of clue:* ______________________________

**7.** frost ______________________________

______________________________

*Type of clue:* ______________________________

**8.** fog ______________________________

______________________________

*Type of clue:* ______________________________

**9.** radiation fog ______________________________

______________________________

*Type of clue:* ______________________________

**10.** topographic ______________________________

______________________________

*Type of clue:* ______________________________

## FRAMEWORK-BASED CONTEXT CLUES

To find meanings from text-based context clues, you look for clues stated in the sentence. A second kind of context does not rely on specific words or punctuation marks to indicate meaning. This kind of context is called **framework-based,** because it relies on your background knowledge and experience.

Framework-based context is more difficult to use than text-based context. Your knowledge of the meanings of surrounding words helps you retrieve relevant frameworks. The background information you find in these frameworks helps you derive the meaning of new words. Common sense and your knowledge of parts of speech also help in defining unknown words. You combine your experience with what the text contains to determine meaning.

*"They expect us to figure out that (1) since cafeterias serve food, and (2) this is a cafeteria, what they're asking us to eat* is *food."*

***Example***

The angry driver shouted *vehemently* during his quarrel with the other driver.

*Explanation:* What does *vehemently* mean? You know what angry means, and you know how people feel when they quarrel. From this, you can figure out that *vehemently* has something to do with strong emotion or intense feeling.

This is an example of using framework-based context to find the meanings of new words. The meaning you find comes from your personal experience.

**EXERCISE 4.9**

◆ *Use framework-based context to decide what the italicized word means. Write your definition beside the word. Then, explain your definition in the lines below it.*

***Example***

Bob, an *introvert,* hates our office parties and never comes to them.

*introvert: someone who doesn't like crowds*

*If someone hates parties and never attends them, he must not like being around groups of people.*

1. Mario's boss was such a *martinet* that employees feared making even the smallest error.

   *martinet:* ______________________________

   ______________________________

   ______________________________

2. After the robbery, the guard was more *vigilant.*

   *vigilant:* ______________________________

   ______________________________

   ______________________________

3. Make your directions *explicit* so there will not be any confusion.

   *explicit:* ______________________________

   ______________________________

   ______________________________

4. The waves *billowed* because a storm was approaching.

   *billowed:* ______________________________

   ______________________________

   ______________________________

**5.** The *nefarious* king killed his enemies and taxed his people unreasonably.

*nefarious:* ______________________________

______________________________

______________________________

**6.** *Scathing* reviews forced the closing of the play after its first performance.

*scathing:* ______________________________

______________________________

______________________________

**7.** Although the fire department responded quickly, the *conflagration* engulfed an entire block.

*conflagration:* ______________________________

______________________________

______________________________

**8.** Although people from all over the country came to the meeting, they *coalesced* into a strong unified force.

*coalesced:* ______________________________

______________________________

______________________________

**9.** People walking in and out of the theater is *obtrusive* during a movie.

*obtrusive:* ______________________________

______________________________

______________________________

**10.** Some politicians have no *compunction* about accepting bribes, although many of their colleagues have been caught doing so.

*compunction:* ______________________________

______________________________

______________________________

**EXERCISE 4.10**

◆ *Define each of the following words. Then read the passage below. After reading, define each of the words again as it is used in context.*

BEFORE READING

1. function ______________________________

2. vague ______________________________

3. clarity ______________________________

4. assembly ______________________________

5. left ______________________________

6. aggravation ______________________________

7. clouded ______________________________

8. obligated ______________________________

9. express ______________________________

10. override ______________________________

In most organizations there are widely differing tasks and activities. The organization itself may exist to fulfill either a clearly specified *function* (to manufacture automobiles) or a *vague* one (to study economic indicators). How the organization goes about its work depends in part on how clearly the tasks are explained to individual workers. A manufacturing operation typically has a fairly high degree of *clarity:* "You will assemble 314 three-wheeled, fiberglass skateboards today." Also, the way the job is to be done is clear: "Insert wheel *assembly* into hole A and attach the freebish fastener." The worker is taught what to do, how to do it, and what he or she will get in exchange for doing it. But it's not always like that.

Climate problems arise when employee behaviors not directly relevant to the work are *left* unclear. An example may be the skateboard assembler who produces the desired number of products (task-relevant behavior) but who insists on playing loud rock music on his radio while working (non-task-relevant behavior) to the eternal *aggravation* of co-workers. Organizational climate becomes *clouded* when workers are unclear about what's appropriate. The employee may be getting conflicting information as to what is acceptable behavior. In the above example, the department manager may think the worker's habits are inappropriate, but the immediate supervisor may disagree. Although the supervisor may be *obligated* to verbally *express* disapproval to the employee, it's entirely possible that a nonverbal message of approval might *override* the words of disapproval and further confuse the employee.

*Source:* Reprinted with permission from *People at Work* by Timm & Peterson. Copyright © 1982 by West Publishing Company. All rights reserved.

AFTER READING

**1.** function ______________________________

______________________________

**2.** vague ______________________________

______________________________

**3.** clarity ______________________________

______________________________

**4.** assembly ______________________________

______________________________

**5.** left ______________________________

______________________________

**6.** aggravation ______________________________

______________________________

**7.** clouded ______________________________

______________________________

**8.** obligated ______________________________

______________________________

**9.** express ______________________________

______________________________

**10.** override ______________________________

______________________________

> **WRITE TO LEARN**
>
> *Tomorrow you will be participating in a debate concerning the value of using the text. Your opponent advocates the use of a dictionary for determining the meaning of unknown words. On a separate sheet of paper, construct an argument for using both text-based and framework-based context instead of the dictionary.*

◆

## SPECIALIZED CONTEXTS FOR COLLEGE STUDY

College courses fall into four major categories: humanities (English, art, music, foreign languages, speech, theater, journalism), social studies (history, political science, sociology, psychology, geography, economics), science and math (astronomy, physics, biology, botany, zoology, geology, computer science), and applied or technical courses (engineering, business, physical education, agriculture, home economics, etc.). Whatever the course, you read assignments, take lecture notes, and complete lab activities. Whatever the task, you will probably encounter unfamiliar words in these specialized contexts.

These words come in three forms. First are **general vocabulary** words. These consist of common words that are not a part of your listening or reading vocabularies. Such words are most likely to be found in humanities courses like literature. Any word in a story or novel that is new to you is an example of this type of vocabulary. Unfamiliar words also occur in the form of **specialized vocabulary.** These words are general vocabulary words that are used in new or unfamiliar ways. Humanities texts use specialized vocabulary when they use symbolic or figurative language. Specialized vocabulary words often appear in social science and science texts also. For example, consider the word *base.* You know the meaning of *base* as it refers to an essential component. Its specialized meaning in science is a nonacidic element. In math it refers to a number system. Such words present problems because the meaning you know may hinder your learning a new meaning. The third type of unfamiliar words you encounter are **technical vocabulary** words. Technical vocabulary words are specific to a content area. They have no meaning outside the context of the course. Such words appear most often in science and applied technology courses. An example of a technical vocabulary word is *ion,* a group of atoms that have a positive or negative charge. Technical vocabulary words may give you trouble in that you need to learn them quickly. This speed is necessary because often you need these words to understand other concepts later on.

**EXERCISE 4.11**

◆ *Below are listed specialized vocabulary terms followed by the subject areas in which they are found. Use a dictionary to define each of them according to the identified subject areas.*

**Example**

base
*chemistry:* *a compound that reacts with an acid to form a salt*
*geometry:* *the line or surface forming the part of a figure that is most nearly horizontal*
*mathematics:* *the number that serves as a starting point for a logarithmic or other numerical system*

1. drift

   *economics:* ______________________________

   *general:* ______________________________

   *geology:* ______________________________

2. core

   *chemistry:* ______________________________

   *general:* ______________________________

   *geology:* ______________________________

   *physics:* ______________________________

3. mode

   *general:* ______________________________

*grammar:* ______________________________

______________________________

*mathematics:* ______________________________

______________________________

*music:* ______________________________

______________________________

*physics:* ______________________________

______________________________

*philosophy:* ______________________________

______________________________

**4.** set

*general:* ______________________________

______________________________

*mathematics:* ______________________________

______________________________

*psychology:* ______________________________

______________________________

**5.** grade

*education:* ______________________________

______________________________

*general:* ______________________________

______________________________

*geology:* ______________________________

______________________________

*zoology:* ______________________________

______________________________

**6.** class

*biology:* ______________________________

______________________________

*general:* ______________________________

______________________________

**7.** plate

*architecture:* ______________________________

______________________________

*art:* ______________________________

______________________________

*general:* ______________________________

______________________________

*geology:* ______________________________

______________________________

*zoology:* ______________________________

______________________________

**8.** bridge

*chemistry:* ______________________________

______________________________

*general:* ______________________________

______________________________

*music:* ______________________________

______________________________

**9.** key

*biology:* ______________________________

______________________________

*figurative:* ______________________________

______________________________

*general:* ______________________________

______________________________

*music:* ______________________________

______________________________

**10.** family

*chemistry:* ______________________________________________

______________________________________________

*general:* ______________________________________________

______________________________________________

*geometry:* ______________________________________________

______________________________________________

*zoology:* ______________________________________________

______________________________________________

◆

**WRITE TO LEARN**

*On a separate sheet of paper, list and categorize the courses in which you are now enrolled as humanities, social studies, science and math, or applied or technical courses. Identify three vocabulary terms associated with each and determine if these terms represent general, specialized, or technical vocabulary.*

◆

## CHAPTER SUMMARY EXERCISE

*Complete the chapter summary by providing the appropriate words to complete the sentences.*

The ______________ of any item is its surroundings. The chapter showed how to use ______________ clues to aid your understanding of new ______________. Knowing the ______________ for a word also helps you identify its meaning. ______________ context clues such as punctuation, ______________, contrast, comparison, and ______ were discussed in the chapter. Text-based clues include commas, brackets, parentheses, and dashes. ______________ text-based clues make use of the opposite of known information. ______________ text-based clues indicate things that are alike. ______________ text-based clues help define words based on what the examples have in common. On the other hand, framework-based context clues are different because the reader must use ______________ or ______________ to help define the words rather than clues from the ______________. ______________ contexts for college study consist of words from various college courses. These words come from either ________ vocabulary, ______________ vocabulary, or ______________ vocabulary terms.

◆

## CHAPTER REVIEW

*Answer briefly but completely.*

1. Other than the examples provided in the chapter, explain how confusions arise when meaning is taken out of context.

2. What is context?

3. Construct one or more sentences and label any five parts of speech.

4. How are adjectives and adverbs alike? How do they differ?

5. How are comparison and contrast text-based context clues alike? How do they differ?

6. In what ways do punctuation text-based context clues differ from other types of text-based context clues?

7. How does framework-based context differ from text-based context?

8. List below the terms found at the beginning of the chapter. Categorize each as specialized, technical, or general.

9. Why can you identify a literal meaning of an unknown word but not find its correct meaning according to its context?

10. Compare and contrast general, specialized, and technical vocabulary.

◆

## VOCABULARY ENHANCEMENT EXERCISE

*Using the scale in Figure 3.1, rate your understanding of the following vocabulary enhancement words to the left of the number. Then write a sentence with each one.*

1. efficient

___

___

2. similarities

___

___

3. derive

___

___

4. relies

___

___

5. intense

___

___

6. applied

___

___

7. encounter

___

___

8. novel

___

___

9. metaphoric

___

___

**10.** concepts

______________________________________________

______________________________________________

## *KEY TO CARTOON*

The item pictured in the droodle at the beginning of this chapter is the Hunchback of Notre Dame examining the Liberty Bell.

# 5 Analyzing Through Structure

## TERMS

*Terms appear in the order in which they occur in the chapter.*

structural analysis
bases
roots
affixes
prefixes
suffixes

## CHAPTER OUTLINE EXERCISE

*Complete the following outline by creating goal-setting questions from each heading in this chapter.*

I. ______________________________

______________________________

II. ______________________________

______________________________

III. ______________________________

______________________________

IV. ______________________________

______________________________

## OBJECTIVES

*At the end of this chapter, you should be able to do the following:*

1. Define and utilize structural analysis.
2. Identify prefixes, suffixes, and roots.
3. Apply word parts to obtain general meaning.
4. Describe the limitations of structural analysis.

## CHAPTER MAP

*Complete the chapter map by creating goal-setting questions from each heading in this chapter.*

**ANALYZING THROUGH STRUCTURE**

## VOCABULARY ENHANCEMENT EXERCISE

*Rate each of the following words according to your knowledge of them.*

| | STAGE 0 | STAGE 1 | STAGE 2 | STAGE 3 |
|---|---|---|---|---|
| | *I do not recognize the word.* | *I recognize the word but am unsure of its meaning and associations* | *I recognize the word and can make general associations with it.* | *I recognize the word and can use it in speaking and writing.* |
| **1.** impulsively | | | | |
| **2.** preceding | | | | |
| **3.** contribute | | | | |
| **4.** wardrobe | | | | |
| **5.** accessories | | | | |
| **6.** gist | | | | |
| **7.** placement | | | | |
| **8.** limitation | | | | |
| **9.** ease | | | | |
| **10.** accurate | | | | |

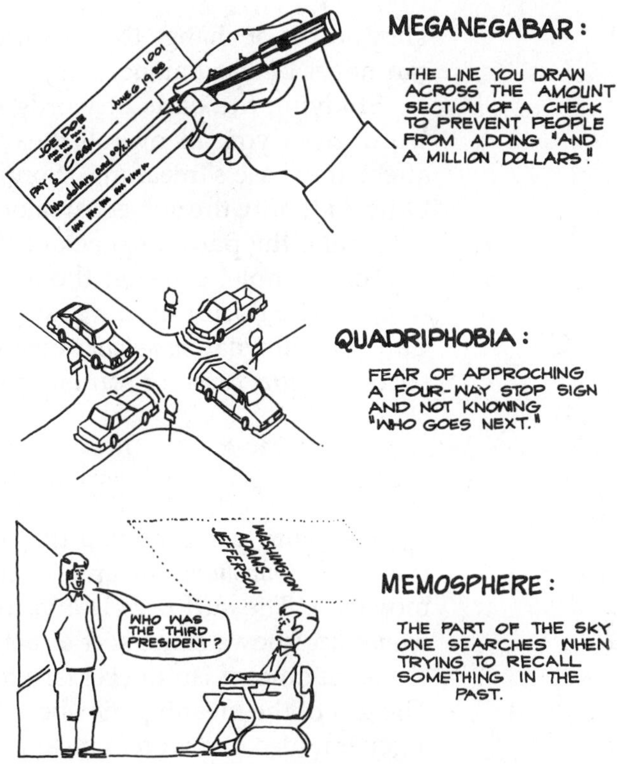


*Source:* Sniglets reprinted with permission of Macmillan Publishing Company. From *Unexplained Sniglets of the Universe* by Rich Hall and Friends. Copyright © 1986 by Not the Network Company, Inc.

A SNIGLET—CREATED BY Rich Hall of Home Box Office's "Not Necessarily the News"—is defined as "any word that doesn't appear in the dictionary, but should." While Hall seems to create sniglets impulsively, he often uses Greek and Latin word parts to construct them. The words in the preceding cartoons show this. *Mega, sphere,* and *phobia* are Greek and Latin word parts. Just as understanding how word parts helps you unlock the meanings of sniglets, they help you unlock the meanings of many words.

◆

## STRUCTURAL ANALYSIS

Although each word part has its own meaning, word parts contribute to the total meaning of a word. Thus, the meaning of an unknown word can often be determined by analyzing its parts. Splitting words into parts to discover the meaning of unknown words is called **structural analysis.**

A word is somewhat like a wardrobe. Parts of words provide the essential meanings. These are called the **bases** or **roots** of the words. The base of a word may be used alone. Others must be used with other bases and/or **affixes.** Affixes **(prefixes** and **suffixes)** are like accessories.

They add to or change the meaning of the base. Like accessories, affixes can never be used alone.

Studying the parts of words tells you many things. The base of a word gives you an overall meaning for the unknown word. Affixes affect the base's meaning. Some affixes provide general meanings. Others identify the subject area of the unknown word. Affixes also help determine the part of speech of the unknown word.

For example, consider the following sentence:

The doctor used a cast to *immobilize* the patient's arm.

Can you tell what *immobilize* means in this sentence? Several meanings, such as *injure, cover,* or *scar* are possible. Look at the parts of this word.

| im | mobil | ize |
|---|---|---|
| not | movable | to make *(verb)* |

The word parts tell you that the arm was "made not movable" by the cast. *Immobilize* means to make something immobile (i.e., not movable). The suffix *ize* is a verb suffix. That tells you that the word *immobilize* shows some sort of action or being.

Sometimes it isn't necessary to determine a word's entire meaning. The gist of the meaning may be all you need to know. The gist gives you a general idea of a word's meaning in context. It also helps you include or exclude answers on tests. Word parts help you determine the gist of a word.

***Example***

Cryptogram means

**a.** a tombstone
**b.** secret writing
**c.** a kind of cookie
**d.** a type of crawling

*Explanation:* If you know that *gram* means writing, you have only one choice. Answer *b* is correct.

◆

## IDENTIFYING PREFIXES, SUFFIXES, AND ROOTS

Prefixes always occur at the beginnings of words. Suffixes are found at the ends of words and indicate the part of speech of a word. Bases or roots come after prefixes, before suffixes, or between prefixes and suffixes. They can also be used alone. If you think you might have trouble recalling where each word part occurs, remember this trick.

Think of the placement of the letters *P, R,* and *S* in the alphabet. They occur there in the same order as in words.

| **P** | **(Q)** | **R** | **S** |
|---|---|---|---|
| R | | O | U |
| E | | O | F |
| F | | T | F |
| I | | | I |
| X | | | X |

Study the lists of prefixes, affixes, and roots in Tables 5.1, 5.2, and 5.3. They are by no means complete. However, they give some of the most common affixes and roots used. They have been grouped for ease in learning.

**TABLE 5.1** ***List of Prefixes***

| *NEGATIVE* | *EXAMPLE* | |
|---|---|---|
| in (not) | incorrect | ____________ |
| il (not) | illegal | ____________ |
| ir (not) | irregular | ____________ |
| un (not) | unknown | ____________ |
| a (not) | asexual | ____________ |
| neg (not) | negation | ____________ |
| anti (against) | antisocial | ____________ |
| contra (against) | contraceptive | ____________ |
| *POSITION* | *EXAMPLE* | |
| en (in) | enroll | ____________ |
| inter (between) | interstate | ____________ |
| pre (before) | precook | ____________ |
| dis/di (apart) | disarm/divide | ____________ |
| de (away/down) | devalue | ____________ |
| trans (across/through) | translucent | ____________ |
| super (above/greater than) | superstar | ____________ |
| sub (under) | submarine | ____________ |
| pro (in front/favor of) | proceed | ____________ |
| re (back/again) | return | ____________ |
| post (after/later than) | postmortem | ____________ |
| circum (around/round) | circumference | ____________ |
| *GENERAL* | *EXAMPLE* | |
| ad (to) | adjourn | ____________ |
| be (by) | beloved | ____________ |
| com (with) | combustion | ____________ |
| con (with) | conjunction | ____________ |
| co (with) | coauthor | ____________ |
| col (with) | collusion | ____________ |
| cor (together) | correlation | ____________ |
| auto (self) | automobile | ____________ |
| homo (same) | homogenized | ____________ |
| hetero (different) | heterosexual | |

**TABLE 5.2 List of Suffixes**

| NOUN | EXAMPLE | |
|---|---|---|
| tion (state of being) | irritation | ______ |
| hood (state of being) | childhood | ______ |
| ship (state of being) | leadership | ______ |
| ance/ence (state of being) | disturbance/ absence | ______ |
| ism (state of being) | patriotism | ______ |
| ness (state of being) | happiness | ______ |
| sion (act of) | confusion | ______ |
| ation (act of) | information | ______ |
| ity/ty (state/condition) | community | ______ |
| ist (one who does) | chemist | ______ |
| or/er (one who) | visitor/sleeper | ______ |
| ment (action or state of) | government | ______ |
| *ADJECTIVE* | *EXAMPLE* | |
| able (able to/capable of being) | desirable | ______ |
| ible (able to) | divisible | ______ |
| ful (full of) | beautiful | ______ |
| ous (having) | courageous | ______ |
| ive (having quality of) | creative | ______ |
| al (pertaining to) | comical | ______ |
| ic (pertaining to) | alcoholic | ______ |
| *VERB* | *EXAMPLE* | |
| en (belonging to/cause to be) | roughen | ______ |
| ize (to become/to make) | minimize | ______ |
| fy (to make) | glorify | ______ |
| *ADVERB* | *EXAMPLE* | |
| ly (in the manner of) | quickly | ______ |

**TABLE 5.3 List of General and Math and Science Roots**

| *GENERAL ROOTS* | | |
|---|---|---|
| *Root* | *Example* | |
| script (write) | manuscript | ______ |
| vert (turn) | extrovert | ______ |
| ject (throw) | interject | ______ |
| port (carry) | transport | ______ |
| vis (see) | vision | ______ |
| rupt (break) | interrupt | ______ |
| dict (say) | dictate | ______ |
| junct (join) | junction | ______ |
| cede (go) | precede | ______ |
| pseudo (false) | pseudonym | ______ |
| mem (mind) | memory | ______ |

**TABLE 5.3 Continued**

*MATH AND SCIENCE AFFIXES AND ROOTS*

| Root or Affix | Example | |
|---|---|---|
| aqua (water) | aquarium | ______ |
| hydro (water) | hydroplane | ______ |
| hemi (half) | hemisphere | ______ |
| semi (half) | semicircle | ______ |
| equi (equal) | equivalent | ______ |
| tele (far off) | telescope | ______ |
| sphere (ball; globe) | atmosphere | ______ |
| quad (four) | quadrangle | ______ |
| geo (earth) | geology | ______ |
| acro (height; top) | acrobat | ______ |
| mega (large) | megaphone | ______ |
| micro (small) | microfilm | ______ |
| onomy (science of) | astronomy | ______ |
| ology (study of) | geology | ______ |
| uni (one) | universe | ______ |
| bi (two) | bicycle | ______ |
| tri (three) | triangle | ______ |
| octa (eight) | octagon | ______ |
| dec (ten) | decade | ______ |
| centi (hundred; hundreth) | centimeter | ______ |
| milli (thousand; thousandth) | millimeter | ______ |
| bio (life) | biology | ______ |
| astro (star) | astronaut | ______ |
| thermo (heat) | thermodynamic | ______ |
| meter (measure) | diameter | ______ |
| ped (foot) | pedestrian | ______ |
| pod (foot) | tripod | ______ |
| kilo (thousand) | kilogram | ______ |
| botan (plant) | botany | ______ |

**EXERCISE 5.1**

◆ *Circle the letter of the correct word. Do not look up the words in a dictionary. Use the prefix meanings in Table 5.1 to find the answer. An example is provided.*

**Example**

Magellan sailed around the world. He ______ the earth.

a. autonavigated
b. conavigated
(c.) circumnaviagated

*Explanation:* The clue is *around*. The only answer with a word part meaning *around* is answer *c*. *Circumnavigated* is the correct response.

1. The events were linked one with another. The events were ______.
   a. contracatenated
   b. concatenated
   c. supercantenated

2. Because of the poor living conditions under which they were forced to exist, the citizens were against the reelection of their president. They had feelings of ______.
   a. sympathy
   b. empathy
   c. antipathy

3. The criminal was a repeat offender, having been convicted again and again. She was a ______.
   a. recidivist
   b. negidivist
   c. autodivist

4. A bird's beak performs the same function as a human's mouth. A beak is ______to a mouth.
   a. homologous
   b. cormologous
   c. contramologous

5. The actions taken by the defendant were not permitted under the current laws. They were ______ activities.
   a. prolicit
   b. illicit
   c. interlicit

6. If an emergency arises, a special news bulletin will air before anything else is shown. It will ______ all other programming.
   a. subempt
   b. circumempt
   c. preempt

7. Chamberlain, the British prime minister in the late 1930s, stepped between the Germans and Czechoslovakians in an attempt to stop World War II. Chamberlain ______ to prevent the war.
   a. interceded
   b. preceded
   c. superceded

8. Sunlight does not reach the deepest part of the ocean. The deepest part of the seas is ______.
   a. antiphotic
   b. aphotic
   c. disphotic

9. The queen found that the morals of the nation were falling down. She described the citizens as ______.
   a. procadent
   b. retrocadent
   c. decadent

10. After about fifty miles, the atmosphere is described as ______. It is composed of several layers, each differing in chemical content from the others.
   a. homospheric
   b. circumspheric
   c. heterospheric

**EXERCISE 5.2**

*Using the suffix clues from Table 5.2, identify the part of the speech for each word. Select from the following responses: noun, adverb, verb, adjective.*

**Example**

*adv* quickly

1. ______ instrumentalist
2. ______ typical
3. ______ altercation
4. ______ soporific
5. ______ contrivance
6. ______ sportive
7. ______ simplify
8. ______ degradation
9. ______ laudable
10. ______ intellectualism
11. ______ reducible
12. ______ scrutinize
13. ______ covetous
14. ______ wakeful
15. ______ hastily

**EXERCISE 5.3**

*Using the suffixes in Table 5.2, supply a word for each of the following definitions.*

| DEFINITION | WORD |
|---|---|
| **Example** | |
| to cause to be soft | *soften* |
| 1. one who writes a newspaper column | ______ |
| 2. having wonder | ______ |

3. a group of neighbors ______________
4. pertaining to metal ______________
5. feeling full of sorrow ______________
6. to turn into a liquid ______________
7. state of being civil ______________
8. one who act ______________
9. state of being refreshed ______________
10. to make sweet ______________

**EXERCISE 5.4**

*Complete the sentence by combining the given definitions of roots and affixes to form words. You may need to rearrange some of the word parts to form the appropriate word. Check the spelling.*

***Example***

Because Abdul's *diction* (say + state of being) is precise and clear, he will make an excellent news reporter.

1. This semester Maria is enrolled in English, history, psychology and ______________ (stars + study of).
2. The solid part of the earth is called the ______________ (earth + globe).
3. ______________ (the act of + seeing + from far away) was first shown at the New York World's Fair.
4. ______________ (pertaining to + life + global) issues concern all people in all countries.
5. ______________ (the act of + breaking + together) often results from the greed for power and money.
6. The author was most famous for her ______________ (study of + three) of the American frontier.
7. Car phones are the most recent evidence of the American need to be ______________ (carry + able to).
8. Washing the windshield increases ______________ (state of being + able to + see).
9. The marriage counselor agreed to ______________ (go + between) the couple.
10. Today's ______________ (heat + measure) are digital.

**EXERCISE 5.5**

*Correct the sentences by providing the correct form of each word in italics.*

**Example**

*Religion* holidays were often connected to important *agriculture* cycles.
*Revision:* *Religious holidays were often connected to important agricultural cycles.*

1. Modern means of *transport* originated in ancient types of *convey.*
   *Revision:* ______

2. The *colony* rejected the *unreason* offer of the British *govern.*
   *Revision:* ______

3. The *emerge* of *nation* peaked during Reagan's term in office.
   *Revision:* ______

4. The *own* of the *corporate* was in dispute.
   *Revision:* ______

5. *History,* the French *revolt* was a *pain* period.
   *Revision:* ______

◆

## ASSOCIATING WORD PARTS FOR MEANING

Like other types of vocabulary, you learn word parts in various ways. One way is to memorize a list of them. However, people sometimes memorize information without really understanding it. That kind of learning is like the purple shirt you bought years ago. It's perfectly good, but you don't know what to wear with it. The information is there, but you don't know what to do with it.

For this reason, you need to relate the word parts with what they mean. Our lists include examples to help you. However, these words may not be ones you use. Exercise 5.6 asks you to find examples that are familiar to you.

Look at these words:

*suicide*
*homocide*
*pesticide*
*genocide*

What do they have in common? They all concern a kind of killing. What part is shared by the words? The common part is *cide*. Therefore, you conclude that *cide* generally means *killing* and *genocide* has to do with killing. Then, you add *genocide* and your idea of its meaning to your vocabulary.

**EXERCISE 5.6**

*For each prefix, suffix, and root in Tables 5.1, 5.2, and 5.3, provide a personal example on the blank lines beside each given example.*

**WRITE TO LEARN**

*The person who sits behind you had a flat tire on the way to class and missed the discussion on structural analysis. On a separate sheet of paper, describe what structural analysis is and how it differs from using the context.*

**EXERCISE 5.7**

*Each set contains three words from the same word part family and the definition of each word. Identify and define the common word part in each set.*

**Example**

xenophobia—fear of foreigners
agoraphobia—fear of open spaces
hydrophobia—fear of water

*Common word part: phobia*

*Definition: fear of*

1. terminal—end of an electric current
   exterminate—to put to an end
   interminable—without end

   *Common word part:* ____________________

   *Definition:* ____________________

2. lobotomy—brain surgery
   dichotomy—cutting something in two
   appendectomy—surgical removal of appendix

   *Common word part:* ____________________

   *Definition:* ____________________

**3.** pronunciation—the voicing of sounds and words
announce—to voice formally or publicly
denounce—to voice strong disapproval

*Common word part:*________________

*Definition:*________________

**4.** synonym—having the same name (meaning the same)
pseudonym—false name
acronym—name formed from the first letter(s) of several words

*Common word part:*________________

*Definition:*________________

**5.** multiply—to increase many times
multiple—having many parts
multilingual—able to speak many languages

*Common word part:*________________

*Definition:*________________

**6.** equality—a condition of being equal
equilateral—a figure with equal sides
equivalent—equal in quality or amount

*Common word part:*________________

*Definition:*________________

**7.** cave—a hollow space
cavernous—describe a large hollow space
excavate—to form by hollowing out

*Common word part:*________________

*Definition:*________________

**8.** traction—the act of drawing or pulling
protract—to drag forward
attract—to pull toward

*Common word part:*________________

*Definition:*________________

**9.** epidermis—the outer protective layer of the skin
hypodermic—relating to under the skin
dermatitis—inflammation of the skin

*Common word part:*________________

*Definition:*________________

10. locus—a place or area
allocation—to place aside for a specific purpose
locality—the place of a specific event

*Common word part:* ______________________

*Definition:* ______________________

**EXERCISE 5.8**

*Circle the response that is unrelated to the others.*

**Example**

a. pedal
b. pedestrian
c. tripod
(d.) pediatrician

*Explanation:* Although *pediatrician* contains the word part *ped,* in this case the word refers to *a doctor specializing in the treatment of children.* The other words all concern the foot.

1. a. hemisphere
b. semicircle
c. earth
d. half moon

2. a. biology
b. astronomy
c. astrology
d. geology

3. a. hydrophobia
b. aquarium
c. hydrology
d. geodesy

4. a. irrelevant
b. irrational
c. irradiate
d. irreparable

5. a. cent
b. century
c. centigrade
d. docent

6. a. geology
b. geomorphology
c. geometry
d. geophysics

7. a. equidistant
b. equipped
c. equilateral
d. equity

8. a. vista
b. envision
c. invisible
d. visualize

9. a. tricycle
b. triad
c. trial
d. trio

10. a. dictate
b. verdict
c. diction
d. dictator

## EXERCISE 5.9

*Complete the following analogies. In analogies, you are tying to determine the relationship among the words. An example illustrates how to read the analogy:*

**Example**

red : stop :: green : ____*go*____

*Explanation:* Read this as "Red is to stop as green is to ." You are to fill in the missing word. In this example, the missing word is *go*.

1. hundredth : centimenter :: thousandth : ____________
2. life : biology :: earth : ____________
3. same : homogeneous :: different : ____________
4. far off : telescope :: small : ____________
5. star : astronaut :: water : ____________
6. sphere : hemisphere :: circle : ____________
7. ten : decameter :: thousand : ____________
8. under : subscript :: above : ____________
9. water : hydrophobia :: height : ____________
10. three : tricycle :: two : ____________

## EXERCISE 5.10

*Circle the best choice that completes each analogy.*

**Example**

biennial : biannual ::______

**(a.)** 2 : 1/2
**b.** 1 : 2
**c.** 2 : 4
**d.** 1 : 2

*Explanation: Biennial* means occurring every two years. *Biannual* means occurring twice a year. The correct response is letter *a*.

1. centennial : bicentennial ::______
   - **a.** 100 : 200
   - **b.** 100 : 50
   - **c.** 10 : 20
   - **d.** 1 : 2

2. ped : pod ::______
   a. onomy : ology
   b. bi : tri
   c. hemi : semi
   d. acro : geo

3. uni : dec ::______
   a. quad : bi
   b. centi : kilo
   c. hemi : uni
   d. octa : milli

4. predecessor : posterity ::______
   a. parents : children
   b. aunts : uncles
   c. brothers : sisters
   d. friends : relatives

5. quadriped : biped ::______
   a. snake : lizard
   b. horse : human
   c. chicken : cat
   d. dog : mouse

◆

## LIMITATIONS OF STRUCTURAL ANALYSIS

Using word parts seems to be an easy and accurate way to define new words. However, this is not always true. For example, the word *colt* comes from a Middle English word. In *colt*, "col" is not a word part.

*island* *isle* *islet* *micro-isle?*

How can you know the difference? Sometimes you find meaning by splitting the word into parts and looking for affixes and/or roots that you can identify. Fortunately, most common affixes and roots are Greek and Latin. Thus, using word parts works most of the time. Your skill in determining when to use structural analysis improves with practice.

**EXERCISE 5.11**

*Each word in the groups below begins with the same letters. Mark each word that contains a prefix meaning* not *or* with.

*un, in, ir il, a:* not

***Example***

_______ under
___√___ unpleasant
___√___ unlock
_______ uncle
_______ union

1. _______ unknown
_______ unconscious
_______ university
_______ unanimous
_______ unfit

2. _______ indirect
_______ indignant
_______ inflexible
_______ industry
_______ insect

3. _______ irony
_______ irregular
_______ irrational
_______ irreversible
_______ irate

4. _______ illiterate
_______ illness
_______ illogical
_______ illustration
_______ illegal

5. _______ amoral
_______ avocation
_______ about
_______ animal
_______ avert

*com, con, co, col, cor:* with

6. _______ combine
_______ comfort
_______ compassion
_______ coma
_______ comic

7. _______ confederate
_______ congratulate
_______ conch
_______ condense
_______ concurrent

8. _______ coagulate
_______ coarse
_______ cocaine
_______ college
_______ cohabitate

9. _______ collaborate
_______ collar
_______ collision
_______ color
_______ collect

10. _______ coral
_______ corduroy
_______ currupt
_______ correspond
_______ correlation

**EXERCISE 5.12**

◆ *Read the following passage on Charles Darwin.*

### Darwin's Life

**Charles Darwin** (1809–1882) was the son of Dr. Robert and Susannah Darwin and grandson of the eminent Dr. Erasmus Darwin. Charles, one of six children, was thought by his family and by himself to be a "very ordinary boy." As an ordinary boy, he did the usual things (collecting shells, stamps, coins) and, at school, he displayed no special inclination for scholarship.

Because he showed little interest in, or aptitude for, anything particular (with the possible exception of science), Dr. Darwin decided that Charles should study medicine at Edinburgh. After two years, Charles conceded medicine was not for him, and instead turned to hunting and fishing, which he thoroughly enjoyed. His father complained that Charles was only interested in "shooting, dogs and cat catching."

For sons who had no discernible academic learnings, parents could, as a last refuge, turn them to the church. Although indifferent to religion, Charles dutifully took up residence at Christ's College, Cambridge, in 1828, at the age of 19. While ostensibly enrolled in theology, Charles became interested in what we today call natural science. He became a constant companion of the Reverend John Stevens Henslow, professor of botany, and often joined his classes in their botanical excursions.

Darwin was graduated in 1831, at the age of 22, not with a distinguished record, but one good enough to satisfy his family, and he could look forward to a serene future as a country cleric. However, that was not to be, for something happened that summer that Darwin referred to as "the most important event of my life."

He received a letter from his friend, Professor Henslow, informing him that he had recommended Darwin as the best-qualified person he knew for the position of naturalist on a scientific expedition that would circle the globe. Darwin was willing, even eager, for this opportunity to combine travel with the pursuit of botany, zoology, and geology, but his father objected and Charles regretfully declined. However, Charles found a champion in his uncle, Josiah Wedgewood, who persuaded Dr. Darwin that the voyage would be desirable. Dr. Darwin reluctantly gave his consent. With mixed feelings of elation and dismay, Charles set sail on board the H.M.S. *Beagle*, December 27, 1831, on a voyage where attacks of seasickness would place him in his hammock for days on end. Having begun the voyage as a clergyman (at least such had been his intent) with hobbies of zoology, botany, and geology, Darwin found, within a short time, that his true calling was natural science. Through his industrious and diligent work of collecting, arranging, and dissecting specimens, Darwin matured from an amateur observer into a professional naturalist.

Darwin went aboard the *Beagle* not as an evolutionist but as a believer in the fixity of species. His observations, however, quickly raised evolutionary suspicions in his mind. As early as 1832, for example, he noted in his diary that a snake with rudimentary hind limbs marked "the passage by which Nature joins the lizards to the snakes." He came across fossils of ancient giant animals that looked, except for size, very much like forms living in the same vicinity, and wondered whether the fossils were the ancestors of those forms. He observed that the Andrean Mountain Range constituted a natural barrier to life and, as might be expected according to geologists, flora and fauna on opposite sides of the range differed.

*Source:* Reprinted with permission from *Introduction to Physical Anthropology* by Nelson and Jarmain. 

*Identify the correct word according to its description. The word is found in the indicated paragraph.*

***Example***

noun meaning "state of being interested" (paragraph 1)
*inclination*

1. noun meaning "state of being learned in school subjects" (paragraph 1)

______________________________

2. verb meaning to go along with (paragraph 2)

______________________________

3. adverb meaning completely (paragraph 2)

______________________________

4. adjective meaning not interested (paragraph 3)

______________________________

5. adverb meaning full of duty (paragraph 3)

______________________________

6. noun meaning study of religion (paragraph 3)

______________________________

7. adjective referring to plants (paragraph 3)

______________________________

8. adjective meaning well known (paragraph 4)

______________________________

9. noun meaning one who does (studies) nature (paragraph 5)

______________________________

10. noun meaning study of the earth (paragraph 5)

______________________________

11. adverb meaning full of sorrow (paragraph 5)

______________________________

12. noun meaning state of being happy (paragraph 5)

______________________________

13. noun meaning state of being ill on an ocean voyage (paragraph 5)

_______________

14. adjective meaning having the quality of industry (paragraph 5)

_______________

15. verb meaning to take apart (paragraph 5)

_______________

◆

## CHAPTER SUMMARY EXERCISE

*Complete the chapter summary by providing the appropriate words to complete the sentences. Words may be used more than once.*

Structural _______________ allows one to determine the _______________ of a word by _______________ the word into its parts. Word parts consist of prefixes, _______________, and _______________. Three ways to learn word parts are: (a) to memorize, (b) to _______________ parts with their meaning, and (c) to draw conclusions based on your _______________ knowledge. Structural analysis doesn't always work, but splitting a word into parts and looking for _______________ and/or roots works most of the time.

◆

## CHAPTER REVIEW

*Answer briefly but completely.*

1. Compare and contrast bases, prefixes, and suffixes.

_______________

_______________

_______________

_______________

2. What information about a word can word parts give you?

_______________

_______________

_______________

_______________

3. Name two times when can knowing the gist of a word is enough.

_______________________________________________

_______________________________________________

_______________________________________________

4. Your reading instructor asks you to learn the word parts in Table 5.2. According to your text, how might you go about doing this?

_______________________________________________

_______________________________________________

_______________________________________________

_______________________________________________

5. Complete the following analogy.
big : large :: base : ____________

6. Describe the limitations of structural analysis.

_______________________________________________

_______________________________________________

_______________________________________________

_______________________________________________

7. From what two languages do most word parts come?

_______________________________________________

_______________________________________________

8. List five suffixes that identify nouns.

_______________________________________________

_______________________________________________

_______________________________________________

_______________________________________________

_______________________________________________

9. Which suffix commonly identifies an adverb? List three times this letter combination does not identify adverbs.

_______________________________________________

_______________________________________________

_______________________________________________

10. What trick helps you remember the order in which word parts occur?

◆

## VOCABULARY EXHANCEMENT EXERCISE

*Using the scale in Figure 3.1, rate your understanding of the following vocabulary enhancement words to the left of the number. Then write a sentence with each one.*

1. impulsively
2. preceding
3. contribute
4. wardrobe
5. accessories
6. gist
7. placement

8. limitation

________________________________________

________________________________________

9. ease

________________________________________

________________________________________

10. accurate

________________________________________

________________________________________

# 6 Finding Main Ideas

## TERMS

*Terms appear in the order in which they occur in the chapter.*

topic
main idea
details
organizational pattern
stated main idea
topic sentence
subject-development pattern
enumeration/sequence pattern
signal words
comparison/contrast pattern
cause-effect pattern
implied main idea
synthesis

## CHAPTER OUTLINE EXERCISE

*Complete the following outline by creating goal-setting questions from each heading and subheading in this chapter.*

I. ____________________________

A. ____________________________

B. ____________________________

C. ____________________________

II. ____________________________

A. ____________________________

1. ____________________________

2. ____________________________

3. ____________________________

4. ____________________________

B. ____________________________

III. ____________________________

A. ____________________________

B. ____________________________

IV. ____________________________

## OBJECTIVES

*At the end of this chapter, you should be able to do the following:*

1. Locate stated main ideas in paragraphs and passages.
2. Identify organizational patterns in paragraphs and passages.
3. Locate implied main ideas in paragraphs and passages.
4. Write main ideas from the synthesis of information from various sources.

## CHAPTER MAP

*Complete the chapter map by creating goal-setting questions from each heading and subheading in this chapter.*

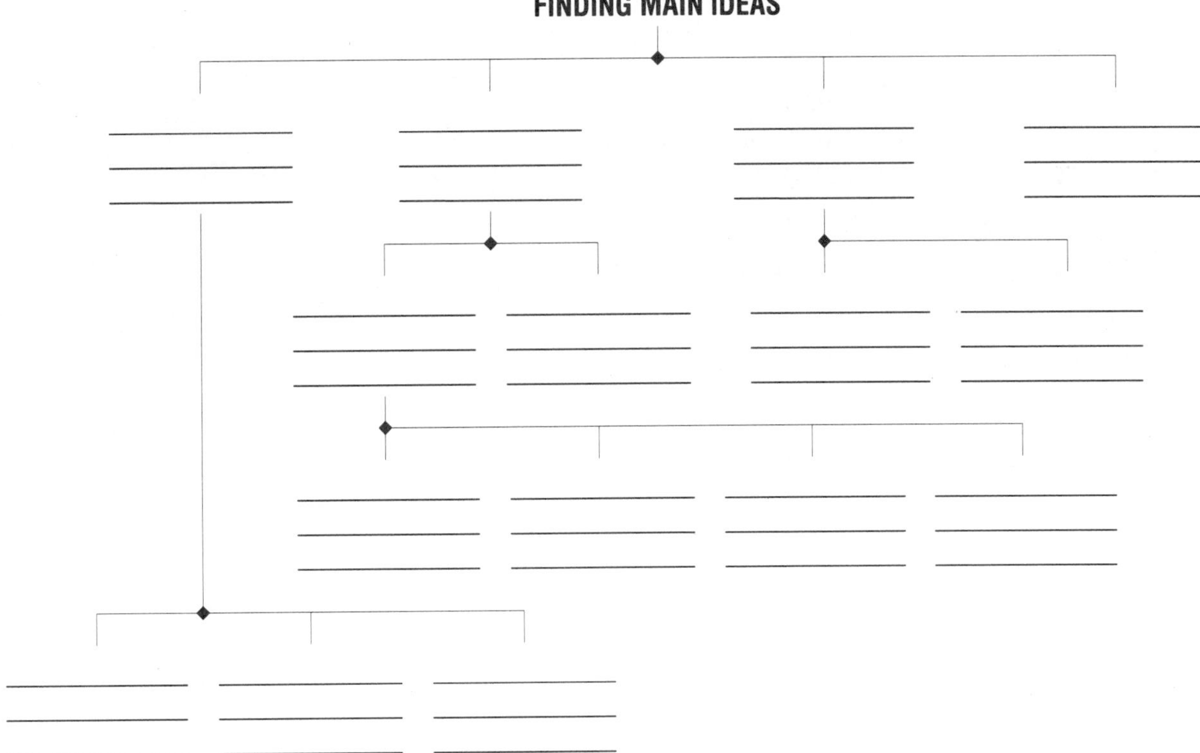

## VOCABULARY ENHANCEMENT EXERCISE

*Rate each of the following words according to your knowledge of them.*

| | STAGE 0 | STAGE 1 | STAGE 2 | STAGE 3 |
|---|---|---|---|---|
| | *I do not recognize the word.* | *I recognize the word but am unsure of its meaning and associations.* | *I recognize the word and can make general associations with it.* | *I recognize the word and can use it in speaking and writing.* |
| **1.** ingredients | | | | |
| **2.** unique | | | | |
| **3.** explicitly | | | | |
| **4.** deck | | | | |
| **5.** coherent | | | | |
| **6.** clarify | | | | |
| **7.** predominant | | | | |
| **8.** initial | | | | |
| **9.** procedure | | | | |
| **10.** consume | | | | |

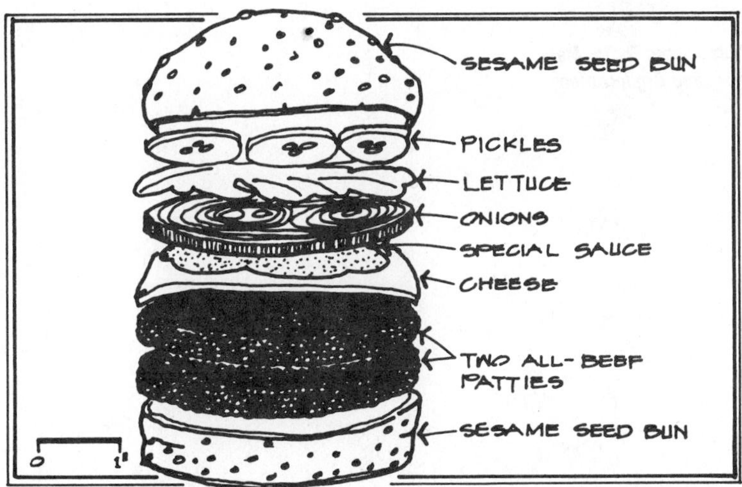


*"Two all-beef patties, special sauce, lettuce, cheese, pickles, onions, on a sesame seed bun."*

—MCDONALDS

CONSIDER THE **TOPIC** *hamburger.* What is a hamburger? Which of the ingredients define its meaning? The meat and bread comprise all that's necessary for a hamburger to exist. They are the **main idea** of the sandwich. They might vary in that some are charcoal-broiled, some are fried. Some buns are whole-wheat, some are white. Individual trimmings make each hamburger unique. They provide the **details** that adapt hamburgers to the taste buds of different people. Some people like their hamburgers plain—bread and meat only. Others like them with "the works." Still others prefer all sorts of detail combinations.

Similarly, a paragraph consists of a topic, main idea, and details. Its topic concerns a broad general subject. Its main idea is the essential element(s) that define the topic. The main idea expresses the key concept. Details limit or describe the main idea. Pictures, conversations, movies, commercials, reading selections, and paragraphs all contain topics, main ideas, and details.

Just as an umbrella must cover all of you to be effective, the main idea must cover all the details within a paragraph to be effective. If either one has any "holes" in it, it's useless. Details support the main idea by telling how, when, how much, how many, why, or what kind. Because details give information about one topic, they relate to each other in some way. This relationship forms the **organizational pattern** of the paragraph. Locating the topic, main idea, details, and organizational pattern helps you understand the speaker or writer's point(s). Finding them increases your understanding. Figure 6.1 shows the relationship of topic, main idea, details, and organization.

**FIGURE 6.1**
***Relationships Among Topic, Main Idea, Details, and Organization***

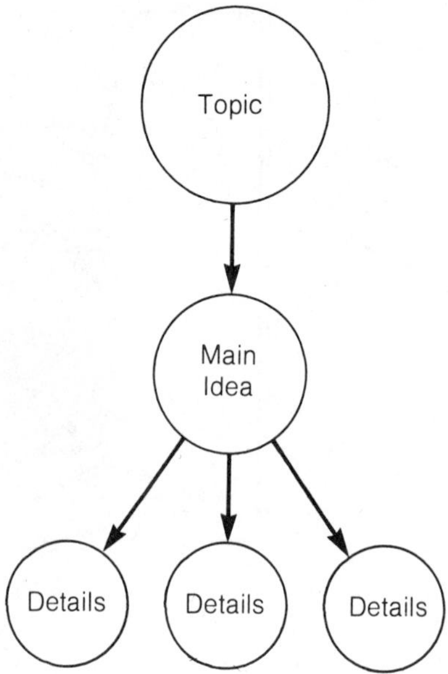


**EXERCISE 6.1**

*The items in each set are related. One of the items is the general topic. Another is the main idea. The rest are details of the topic. Use the outline format to organize the topic, main idea, and details.*

***Example***

| | |
|---|---|
| **a.** Kennedy | **I.** *Great historical leaders* |
| **b.** Lincoln | **A.** *U.S. presidents* |
| **c.** U.S. presidents | **1.** *Kennedy* |
| **d.** Great historical leaders | **2.** *Lincoln* |
| **e.** Washington | **3.** *Washington* |

*Explanation:* The broad general theme (topic) is great historical leaders. The key concept (main idea) is U.S. presidents. The rest are details.

| | |
|---|---|
| **1. a.** "20/20" | **I.** ______________ |
| **b.** TV shows | **A.** ______________ |
| **c.** "60 Minutes" | **1.** ______________ |
| **d.** News shows | **2.** ______________ |
| **e.** "Good Morning, America" | **3.** ______________ |

| | |
|---|---|
| **2. a.** Chemistry | **I.** ______________ |
| **b.** Bunsen burner | **A.** ______________ |
| **c.** Goggles | **1.** ______________ |
| **d.** Beaker | **2.** ______________ |
| **e.** Lab | **3.** ______________ |

| | |
|---|---|
| **3. a.** Intramural sports | **I.** ______________ |
| **b.** Extracurricular groups | **A.** ______________ |

| | |
|---|---|
| c. College organizations | 1. ______ |
| d. Departmental clubs | 2. ______ |
| e. Religious organizations | 3. ______ |

| | |
|---|---|
| 4. a. Physical fitness | I. ______ |
| b. Running shoes | A. ______ |
| c. Aspects of jogging | 1. ______ |
| d. Pulled muscles | 2. ______ |
| e. Walkman-style radios | 3. ______ |

| | |
|---|---|
| 5. a. Nutrition | I. ______ |
| b. Cholesterol | A. ______ |
| c. Animal fats | 1. ______ |
| d. Dairy products | 2. ______ |
| e. Palm and coconut oils | 3. ______ |

| | |
|---|---|
| 6. a. Postsecondary education | I. ______ |
| b. Michigan State University | A. ______ |
| c. Newbury Junior College | 1. ______ |
| d. Junior colleges and universities | 2. ______ |
| e. Coast Community College | 3. ______ |

| | |
|---|---|
| 7. a. Tuition | I. ______ |
| b. Lab fees | A. ______ |
| c. Application fees | 1. ______ |
| d. Campus expenses | 2. ______ |
| e. Fees | 3. ______ |

| | |
|---|---|
| 8. a. English | I. ______ |
| b. Classical | A. ______ |
| c. Literature | 1. ______ |
| d. Puritan | 2. ______ |
| e. Contemporary | 3. ______ |

| | |
|---|---|
| 9. a. Textbooks | I. ______ |
| b. Speech | A. ______ |
| c. Nonfiction | 1. ______ |
| d. Political Science | 2. ______ |
| e. Geography | 3. ______ |

| | |
|---|---|
| 10. a. Paintings | I. ______ |
| b. Sculpture | A. ______ |
| c. Museum | 1. ______ |
| d. Pottery | 2. ______ |
| e. Fine arts | 3. ______ |

**WRITE TO LEARN**

*On a separate sheet of paper, use the words* topic, main ideas, *and* details *to describe a television program.*

◆

# STATED MAIN IDEAS

*If any man wish to write a clear style, let him first be clear in his thoughts . . . .*

—GOETHE

Understanding the main ideas of a text is not always easy. But, when writers clearly state the key concept of a paragraph or passage, reading is made easier. That's because less work is required of you. All you have to do is locate the topic of the paragraph or passage and find a sentence that directly states it.

## Finding Stated Main Ideas in Paragraphs

Every paragraph contains a key concept or main idea. The main idea is usually a complete sentence that tells the central point of the paragraph. To find the main idea, you complete the following process:

STEPS FOR FINDING STATED MAIN IDEAS IN PARAGRAPHS

1. *Read the paragraph.*
2. *Ask yourself what one thing the paragraph covers.* This is the topic.
3. *Look for details that point to or support the idea the paragraph covers.*
4. *Look for a sentence that says this key concept.* This is the **stated main idea.**

***Example***

The jobs that U.S. presidents held before office are varied. Some held more than one job. Over half were lawyers. At least one-fourth were farmers, ranchers, or planters. Six were soldiers. Six were educators. Two worked with newspapers. One was an engineer. Another had been a tailor. One was even a movie star.

*Explanation:* What is this paragraph about? It discusses the work presidents did before their elections. Among these are jobs like working with newspapers, being a lawyer, and acting in movies. Which sentence best states the topic and details? The first, "The jobs that U.S. presidents held before office are varied." This, then, is the stated main idea.

## Locating Topic Sentences

Getting the main idea of paragraphs is crucial to reading. If the main idea were always in the first sentence, you wouldn't need to read the rest of the sentences. The first or last sentence is often the **topic sentence,** but the topic sentence could appear anywhere in a paragraph. It can even be the last sentence. The topic sentence contains the stated main idea.

### EXERCISE 6.2

*For each paragraph below, underline the stated main idea.*

***Example***

Cancer affects one out of every four people. Over one-hundred diseases are called cancer, and each has its own name. Some names reflect the location of the tissue from which they arise. When the suffix *-oma* is added, this means the cancer is a tumor—tissue growing out of control. Immune system cancers are lymphomas. Cancers of the blood-forming organs are leukemias. Cancers of the glands and body linings are carcinomas. Connective tissue cancers are sarcomas.

1. Over twenty-five years ago, Title VII of the 1964 Civil Rights Act was passed. Prior to the act, people might have lost jobs or promotions because they were women, members of minorities, or attended the wrong church. The act guaranteed equal employment opportunities regardless of sex, race, color, religion, or country of national origin. The intent of the law was to prevent unfair discrimination. Such discrimination refers to denial of job access on non-job-related characteristics.

2. Psychologists who view personality in terms of behavior examine it in terms of three factors. First, what is the behavior? Second, what conditions surround the behavior? Third, what results from the behavior? These factors are called behavior, antecedents, and consequences. Since the antecedents occur first, this view is called the A-B-C paradigm.

3. Trees are special kinds of graphs. In the 1800s, Arthur Cayley discovered trees while studying chemical compounds. They represent algebraic expressions, codes, and information chains. Trees are often used in higher mathematics. They are also utilized in computer science, engineering, and genetic research.

4. DNA structure and function directly relate to the study of heredity. Genes consist of DNA secretions responsible for the production of physical traits. A gene is not a separate unit operating in the cell. It is part of the larger DNA molecule. The total of hereditary materials within an individual forms a genotype. While some of the genes may mutate during a person's life, most remain the same.

5. More than any other animal, dinosaurs have captured the public imagination. Unfortunately, the popularization has led to misconceptions about them. Many dinosaurs were large animals. However, some were very small. Indeed, some were the size of chickens. Another common but erroneous perception concerns their ability to adapt. While they did eventually become extinct, they were the major life form for more than 140 million years. Finally, they were not the slow beasts portrayed today. Some were very active and warm-blooded.

6. Sediment layers terminate where eroded, broken by faults, or at the edge of depositional basins. They may also end laterally when rock thins to the point where it is pinched out by other substances. Finally, through lateral gradation, changes in composition or texture may occur until the original substance is no longer recognizable. Sediment layers in rock extend outward in all directions until they terminate.

7. The earth's surface contains many different landforms. These were made by various forces acting on the earth. In the past, it was thought that large land features, such as mountains, were created suddenly as the result of cataclysmic events. Now we believe that most landforms evolved very slowly. As a result, most landscapes contain features of widely varying age produced by forces that are no longer active.

8. The people of the Greek or Hellenic culture were devoted to liberty. They believed in the nobility of human achievement. They refused to submit to tyrants. The spirit of free inquiry was exalted. Knowledge reigned over faith. Among the peoples of the ancient world, they most exemplified the spirit of Western Society. Their culture advanced to the highest stage that the ancient world was destined to reach.

9. Reception and classification centers are recent additions to the correctional system. Such facilities operate on the premise that "a new fish is an unknown fish." Thus, these facilities have more bars, barbed wire, and surveillance devices. They have less activity and personal space. The justification for additional security is that the nature of the residents is unknown, and their stays will be short.

10. In survey research, large numbers of people respond to the same set of questions. Personal interviews, telephone interviews, and paper-and-pencil formats may be used. Surveys are commonly used to gather sociological data. Such data are used to identify trends and incidence of occurrences. Survey research is versatile. It can be used to study attitudes, behaviors, ideals, and values.

## Finding Stated Main Ideas in Passages

Finding the main idea of a passage is similar to finding the main idea of a paragraph, but working with a whole passage is often more difficult. That's because the whole is sometimes equal to more than the sum of its parts. For example, in playing cards, the deck (the whole) is more than just individual cards (the parts). Single cards are not as useful as a deck. It's hard to play a card game when some cards are missing. To find the main idea of a passage, look at each part. Then use the parts to determine the whole (the main idea).

STEPS FOR FINDING STATED MAIN IDEAS IN PASSAGES

1. *Read each paragraph in the passage.*
2. *Find the main idea for each paragraph.*
3. *Identify the topic that all or most of the paragraphs have in common.*
4. *Locate the sentence that says what the paragraphs have in common.* This sentence is often found in the introduction or summary of the passage.

***Example***

Four U.S. presidents were killed while in office. The assassinations shocked the country. Americans mourned the deaths of their leaders.

Abraham Lincoln, sixteenth president of the United States, was the first president to be killed in office. The assassination came five days after the end of the Civil War. He was killed by John Wilkes Booth at

Ford's Theater in Washington, D.C. Several persons were believed to have been involved in the assassination plot.

The second president killed in office was James Garfield. He was the twentieth president of the United States. Garfield was shot by Charles Guiteau only a few months after taking office. Garfield died 80 days after being wounded. Guiteau killed Garfield because the president had refused to name him consul to France.

The twenty-fifth president of the United States, William McKinley, was shot and killed six months into his second term in office. McKinley's assassin, Leon Czolgosz, was an anarchist. Czolgosz confessed to having an urge to kill a great leader.

John Kennedy was the youngest man ever elected president. He was also the youngest to die in office. He was the thirty-fifth president. He was shot while riding in a parade in Dallas, Texas. Lee Harvey Oswald, who had tried to become a Soviet citizen, was arrested and charged with the murder.

*Explanation:* The main idea of the first paragraph is "Four U.S. presidents were killed while in office." The main idea of the second paragraph is found in its first sentence. It says, "Abraham Lincoln, sixteenth president of the United States, was the first president to be killed in office." The third paragraph's main idea states, "The second president to be killed in office was James Garfield." In paragraph four, the first sentence again expresses the main idea. It says, "The twenty-fifth president of the United States, William McKinley, was shot and killed six months into his second term of office." The main idea of the last paragraph is found in the second sentence. It reads, "He was also the youngest to die in office." The main idea of the passage is the same as the main idea of the first paragraph. This is true because all of the other paragraphs provide details about this more general subject.

### EXERCISE 6.3

◆ *Underline the main idea in each paragraph below. Then circle the stated main idea for the entire passage.*

Most earth scientists are committed to the idea of *uniformitarianism*. They define it as "the present is the key to the past." The notion is that natural earth events in the past were produced by the same physical processes that operate now.

On occasion, some landforms appear to defy *uniformitarianism*. Such landforms occur in an area in Washington State. Earth scientists conclude that these features were made by the largest known floods in the earth's history.

This area is in a low elevation, a portion of the Columbia Plateau. It is called the Channelled Scablands because dry river canyons scarred its surface. The dry land varies from flat to hilly. Despite its present dryness, however, there is evidence that large floods occurred. Dry canyons and dry waterfalls exist in this area. There are also large gravel bars and ripple marks showing where water once was. Both soil erosion and deposits also are found here.

Debate on the origins of this area rage. Many scientists first thought it came from melted glaciers. However, the ripple marks could only have resulted from a brief but large flood. The problem was then to decide how and where such floods started. An answer was suggested in 1942. It had been known that much of what is now western Montana was covered by a glacially dammed lake. The lake was called Lake Missoula. J. T. Pardee theorized that the lake was blocked by ice. The melting of this ice allowed for the estimated 300 cubic miles of water to be released within a few hours or days. This flood carved the Channelled Scablands.

**EXERCISE 6.4**

*Underline the main idea of each paragraph.*

**1.** Sacramento is a historic city of the American West. A group of settlers, led by John Sutter, established an early settlement in California. It was located about two miles east of the Sacramento River. Mexico gained control of the settlement for a time. When Sutter pledged loyalty to Mexico, he received 50,000 acres of land. In 1848, gold was discovered at Sutter's sawmill. This brought thousands of settlers to California. Sacramento was settled in 1849 by John Sutter's son near the original settlement.

**2.** Federal agencies employ many workers in Sacramento. The state of California is the city's largest single employer. More than ten local government buildings are open each workday. Indeed, the economy of Sacramento depends greatly on governmental operations.

**3.** Railroad passenger trains and four freight lines serve Sacramento. The city is a crossroads of travel. Four major highways as well as a number of airlines serve the city. One specialized airport is only for business and private airplanes. A deepwater channel links the Port of Sacramento to San Francisco Bay and the Pacific Ocean. Ocean-going ships dock at its port.

**4.** Only about 5 percent of Sacramento's residents were not born in the United States. However, Sacramento's citizens come from varied ethnic groups and religions. Included among these are people from Canada and Japan. Persons of German and Italian ancestry are also part of the city's citizens. Blacks comprise 13 percent of the population while people of Mexican descent make up 15 percent. Roman Catholics form the city's largest religious group. Methodists, Presbyterians, and Baptists are also major denominations.

**5.** Sacramento's public library has five branches. The E. B. Crocker Art Gallery, opened in 1885, contains paintings by European masters. It is the oldest art museum in the West. Ballet and opera are sponsored by cultural groups. The symphony orchestra and theater programs are also popular events. The California State Fair is held in the city every summer. The city has 50 parks. One includes a zoo and a gold course. Eighteen radio and four television stations serve Sacramento. The city has two daily newspapers. Sacramento has many cultural advantages.

**EXERCISE 6.5**

*Referring to the paragraphs in Exercise 6.4, write the number of the paragraph beside the topic it matches.*

______ **a.** Sacramento, the economic aspect

______ **b.** Sacramento, center of transportation

______ **c.** Sacramento, city with a diverse population

______ **d.** Sacramento, a historical perspective

______ **e.** Sacramento, city of refinement.

◆

## ORGANIZATION IN PARAGRAPHS AND PASSAGES

Determining the relationship among the ideas within a paragraph or passage helps you organize them into a coherent whole. This grouping of details helps you understand main ideas. Consider the following paragraph:

> The lipids you eat are in the form of water-insoluble triglycerides, cholesterol, and phospholipids, with the triglycerides predominating (composing about 95 percent of dietary fat). Both of the body's transport systems—lymph and blood—are watery fluids. Clearly, if the lipids were dumped "as is" in the bloodstream, they would clump together to form globs of fat that would clog the arteries.
>
> *Source:* Reprinted with permission from *Understanding Nutrition* 2/e by Whitney and Hamilton. Copyright ©1981 by West Publishing Company. All rights reserved.

Although the last sentence of this paragraph indicates that this procedure is a "clear" one, the process is still hard to understand. The following paragraph shows how the authors compared a common event to a difficult concept to clarify the process:

> The lipids you eat are in the form of water-insoluble triglycerides, cholesterol, and phospholipids, with the triglycerides predominating (composing about 95 percent of dietary fat). Both of the body's transport systems—lymph and blood—are watery fluids. Clearly, if the lipids were

dumped "as is" in the bloodstream, they would clump together to form globs of fat that would clog the arteries. You are familiar with this effect if you have ever carelessly dumped greasy foods down the kitchen sink: the drain became clogged and the grease had to be removed, at great expense to you. The body is smarter with lipids than you may be with your kitchen grease. Although arteries sometimes clog, it is not because pure, unadulterated grease ever travels through them.

*Source:* Reprinted with permission from *Understanding Nutrition* 2/e by Whitney and Hamilton. Copyright ©1981 by West Publishing Company. All rights reserved.

Although the main ideas of the two paragraphs are the same, the second paragraph is easier to understand and recall. Two reasons account for this. First, because you see the association between the common event and the more complex process, you understand it better. Second, because you can visualize the process, it is easier to recall.

## Organizational Patterns

Organizational patterns provide the structure for relating details to the main idea. Knowing the pattern also helps you relate your frameworks for the text more easily. Instead of recalling many separate details, you recall large blocks of information.

Organizational patterns vary according to content, topic, and author's purpose. Identifying this pattern helps you find the main idea and supporting details. Thus, you need to know what types of patterns are possible. You also need to know how to recognize each one.

Four patterns usually appear in textbooks. However, these patterns are seldom pure. This means features of various patterns often appear together. Still, you can often find a predominant pattern that helps you find and recall the main idea.

*"Even a paper on* chaos *mush have some organizational pattern."*

### *Subject Development*

The **subject-development pattern** names the topic. This forms the basis for the collection of details. The details describe and define the topic in various ways. They relate to the topic but may not relate to each other. A biography is an example of subject development. The details (name, age, birthplace, honors) relate to the person being described. Without the topic, the details support but do not relate to each other. In a text chapter, headings and initial sentences often signal this pattern. To use this pattern, you identify (1) the topic and (2) the relationship between the supporting details and the topic.

Figure 6.2 provides an example of this pattern. Here the topic is identified by the heading "Complex." The paragraph defines *complex* (sentence 1) and tells how complexes are used (sentence 2). An example of the complex is identified in sentence 3, and details about the example are given in sentences 4, 5, and 6. The example is used to make the abstract term *complex* more relevant and concrete.

### *Enumeration/Sequence*

The **enumeration/sequence** pattern lists major points in one of two ways. First, in enumerating, or numbering, a list, items appear in a somewhat random order. Thus, all items share equal importance or rank. Grocery lists and New Year's resolutions are common examples of this pattern. Second, if points occur in a specific order, the list is sequenced. Such a step-by-step progression of ideas could show alphabetical placement, rank, direction, size, or time. This structure describes solutions to problems, answers to questions, or proofs of thesis statements. Common examples of the sequence pattern include directions for recipes and descriptions of a route.

**Signal words** often indicate the numerical progression of points or steps. You may or may not be told initially how many points will be discussed. The total number of steps or ranks in the sequence may or may not be given.

To use this pattern, you identify (1) the topic, concept, procedure, or problem, (2) the number of points to be discussed or steps in the

***FIGURE 6.2***
***Subject-Development Pattern***

**Complex**

A culture complex consists of related traits grouped into a pattern. We organize some parts of our lives around culture complexes. An example of such a complex is television-viewing, which is comprised of traits such as the television set as well as the transmitting devices and procedures. The complex also involves related laws, opinions, and jobs. Other traits in this complex include the programs, their scheduling, and their ratings. The television camera is part of this complex, as is the viewing ritual of a family.

*Source:* Reprinted with permission from *Contemporary American Society: An Introduction to the Social Sciences* by Sloshberg and Nessmith. 

sequence, and (3) the signal words that indicate the numerical or sequential order of the points or steps. It is a good idea to count and write numbers beside each point or step. This assures that the number of points or steps you find matches the number said to be in the text. Figures 6.3 and 6.4 provide examples of enumeration and sequence patterns.

In Figure 6.3 the heading "Kinds of Norms: From Manners to Murder" indicates that the topic is types of norms. The abstract idea of a norm is first clarified by several examples (sentences 1 and 2). Sentence 3 indicates there are three types. The first two types—folkways and mores—are identified in sentence 4. The identification of the third type—laws, or formalized norms—is less clear (sentence 5). The last sentence indicates that all three of the types have been identified. If you had difficulty finding all three types, you need to look again between sentences 3 and 6.

The overall concept or procedure being sequenced is identified by the title "Top-down design and testing" in Figure 6.4. The words indicating the progression of the sequence are shown in two ways. In sentences 1 and 2, the order is indicated twice (first and top; next and second), but in the rest of the sentences only numerical steps are given

***FIGURE 6.3***
***Enumeration Pattern***

**Kinds of Norms: From Manners to Murder**

Rules that tell us to say "thank you" are in a different class from those that tell us not to say "You money or your life." Norms range from matters of manners to those of murder. They can be grouped into three major types. William Sumner described two basic kinds: folkways and mores. Supporting these two types are laws, which are formalized norms. These three categories introduce norms for us.

*Source:* Reprinted with permission from *Contemporary American Society: An Introduction to the Social Sciences* by Sloshberg and Nessmith. 

***FIGURE 6.4***
***Sequence Pattern***

**Top-Down Design and Testing**

The hierarchical arrangement of modules inspires us to design and test a program by starting with the top-level module and working downward.

To see how this words, consider how an author might apply the technique to writing a book.

First, the author would decide what the entire book (the top-level module) is to cover. The next step would be to break the material down into chapters (second-level modules). Each chapter would be divided into sections (third-level modules), and as each section was written, the author would deal with paragraphs (fourth-level), sentences (fifth-level), and words (sixth-level modules). (We could consider the characters in words to be a seventh-level, but we won't. Just as we can buy a light bulb at the auto store, we can find the spelling of words in the dictionary.)

*Source:* Reprinted with permission from *The Mind Tool* 3/e by Graham. 

(third, etc.). The last number word is "seventh," which indicates there are seven steps in the procedure. However, a closer look shows the author does not consider the seventh-level stage to be important. The total number of steps in the sequence, therefore, is six.

### *Comparison/Contrast*

The **comparison/contrast pattern** shows relationships between objects or concepts. Comparisons show how the objects or concepts are alike. Contrasts show how they are different. Thus, comparison/contrast patterns discuss likenesses and differences.

These patterns compare details of an object or concept in one of two ways. First, they compare or contrast one detail of an object or concept with a corresponding detail of another object or concept. Or, second, they list all details about one object or concept and compare or contrast that list to a complete listing of corresponding details about another object or concept.

Some paragraphs contain both comparisons and contrasts. However, the structure often consists of only comparisons or only contrasts. Signal words show whether likenesses or differences are being identified.

To use this pattern, you identify (1) the items which are related and (2) the signal words that show comparisons and/or contrasts.

Figure 6.5 provides an example of the comparison/contrast pattern. Here the items to be compared or contrasted in the passage are identified in the heading as "The Upper-Uppers and Lower-Uppers"; however, the meaning of these terms is unclear. The heading is explained in the first sentence. The next five paragraphs describe the upper class.

Although the heading indicated that this section would be about two groups, this appears somewhat unclear. The last paragraph explains the difference. The comparison between these two groups has been implied because they share the same features (paragraph 7, sentence 1). The contrast between them is first mentioned in sentence 2 of paragraph 7. It is not fully identified until sentence 4. The reason for the difference is explained in the rest of the paragraph.

### *Cause-Effect*

The **cause-effect pattern** shows that an action or response had a preceding basis or reason (cause). It describes what happened (effect) and why it happened (cause). To use this pattern, you identify (1) the effect and (2) the cause(s) of the effect.

**FIGURE 6.5**
***Comparison/Contrast Pattern***

**The Upper-Uppers and Lower-Uppers**

Here is a more complete picture of the life-style of the chapter opener's rich man.

The upper classes hold positions, not jobs. Many have reached the point where they can enjoy their life-style without working for it. Their interests are typically in business and finance.

Though they need now worry about jobs, the upper classes still view education as important. Schooling for these people is usually a matter of polish, not job training. A degree from the "right" college is necessary to fit in socially. People from upper-class families are more likely to major in the fine arts than in accounting. And they will attend elite, private schools where they will meet the "right" kind of people.

The upper-class family is more stable than families in any of the other classes. These people marry later, have fewer children, and have a lower divorce rate. In fact, divorce rates are tied directly to class: rates are lowest in the highest classes.

Upper-class people are most likely to attend a Presbyterian, Episcopal, Unitarian, or Congregational church. The religious service is not likely to be emotional in tone. It is more likely to involve a lecture on social ethics than a sermon on the devil and the flames of hell.

Upper-class people are likely to hold conservative economic views but liberal social views. That is, they may resist political change, especially when it involves a redistribution of wealth. They are, however, likely to accept social change, such as in civil rights.

We can easily combine the lower-uppers with the upper-uppers in this section because there is only one major difference between the two. The difference is important enough, however, to make the two classes socially separate. The difference is based on money—not how much one has, but how long one's family has had it. One needs enough wealth to be able to afford the schools, neighborhoods, and resorts of the upper-class life-style. To qualify for the upper-upper class, however, the money must be old. If a family has been rich for only one or two generations, this will probably put them in the lower-upper class. This is true even if the family is more wealthy than some in the upper-upper class. In the United States, many a wealthy family traces its money back to a rough, ruthless businessman, not royalty. Time is needed to soften the image of a family's store of wealth. In time, one's ancestors may even be glorified. Indeed, lineage is something money cannot buy. To be able to boast of a noteworthy ancestor sets one apart from a person who is merely wealthy.

*Source:* Reprinted with permission from *Contemporary American Society: An Introduction to the Social Sciences* by Sloshberg and Nessmith. 

Figure 6.6 provides an example of the cause-effect pattern. As identified by the subheading of the passage, the effect is the power held by interest groups. Paragraph 1 describes that power. The cause of power (politicians believe members of interest groups have longer memories than other citizens) is first identified in sentence 1, paragraph

***FIGURE 6.6***
***Cause-Effect Pattern***

**Why Interest Groups Have Power**

In most cases, the purposes of the interest group are based on the wants and aims of a small segment of the population. If well organized, such a small, activist group can bring to bear a great deal of pressure on politicians. In fact, such small groups can apply much more pressure than much larger numbers of individuals. The strength of interest groups thus helps prevent the "tyranny of the majority" that might be found in a democracy. By joining interest groups, citizens can be heard loud and clear, even if the majority would have them silent.

The politician is likely to believe that members of interest groups are more likely to remember than other citizens. This belief makes possible the success of interest groups. A bloc of written letters from an organized group of activists carries the weight of a bloc vote in the upcoming election. Examples of such groups are the various teachers' associations, the Sierra Club, and the Moral Majority. A typical eastern state teachers' association lists more than 75,000 members. If this number is multiplied by spouses, parents, and voting-age children, a politician is faced with a bloc vote that could decide an election.

Though groups of this nature are small, their bloc voting habits make politicians wary of causing offense. Emotional issues, such as danger to the environment or consumer protection, have created several nationwide groups whose power is out of proportion to the actual numbers of their members. The members, however, are highly vocal and active. Their applied pressures and carefully placed statements in the public media can stir the masses to action, brief as it may be. Since the politician avoids such mass thought and action, the interest group works to influence elected officials by these practices and also by lobbying.

*Source:* Reprinted with permission from *Contemporary American Society: An Introduction to the Social Sciences* by Sloshberg and Nessmith. 

2. Sentence 3 gives a second cause (bloc voting). The rest of paragraph 2 illustrates and describes interest groups. The first three sentences of paragraph 3 indicate a third cause. This cause is identified in sentence 4 as "stirring the masses to action." The last sentence tells how politicians feel about these practices. It also identifies a fourth cause of power (lobbying).

## Signal Words That Indicate Text Structure

You determine each pattern by signal words. They show the direction and organization of the ideas. They also help you draw conclusions and find the main idea. Table 6.1 lists the four patterns, a short description of each, and corresponding signal words.

**TABLE 6.1 Organizational Patterns and Signal Words**

| PATTERN | DESCRIPTION | SIGNAL WORDS |
|---|---|---|
| Subject-development | Names topic and gives numerous facts | (Identified by heading and or combination of heading and initial sentences.) |
| Enumeration/Sequence | Lists main points, orders a list of main points, or presents a problem and steps for its solution | First, second, third, etc.; next, then, finally |
| Comparison/Contrast | Describes ways in which concepts are alike or different | Comparison—similarly, both, as well as, likewise<br>Contrast—however, on the other hand, on the contrary, but, instead of, although, yet |
| Cause-effect | Shows the result(s) of action(s) | Therefore, thus, as a result, because |

**WRITE TO LEARN**

*History books are often organized according to enumeration/sequence and/or cause-effect patterns. On a separate sheet of paper, describe these patterns and explain why this would be so.*

**WRITE TO LEARN**

*On a separate sheet of paper, compare signal words to traffic signs. Be specific in your examples.*

◆

## IMPLIED MAIN IDEAS

*I like to have a thing suggested rather than told in full. When every detail is given, the mind rests satisfied, and the imagination loses the desire to use its own wings.*

—THOMAS BAILEY ALDRICH

Finding implied main ideas allows your mind to work and frees your imagination. It requires more effort than finding stated ones.

Thus, it's difficult and challenging. Finding implied main ideas requires you to find the topic of a paragraph or passage and then infer the key concept.

## Finding Implied Main Ideas in Paragraphs

Sometimes, the main idea of a paragraph may not be stated directly in any sentence. In this case, you read to find the **implied main idea.** Finding the implied main idea is more difficult. However, the same procedure for finding stated main ideas can be followed by changing one step slightly.

STEPS FOR FINDING IMPLIED MAIN IDEAS IN PARAGRAPHS

1. *Read the paragraph.*
2. *Ask yourself what one thing the paragraph covers.* This is the topic.
3. *Look for details that point to or support the one idea the paragraph covers.*
4. *Think of a sentence that states this key concept.* This is the implied main idea.

***Example***

Fluency is one part of creativity. Fluency is the number of ideas a person can devise to solve a problem. Another part of creativity is flexibility. Flexibility is the number of different kinds of ideas a person devises. Originality, whether the ideas are unique or not, is another part of creativity.

*Explanation:* What is this paragraph about? It tells about the different factors that make up creativity. Thus, an implied main idea would be "Creativity comprises several factors."

***EXERCISE 6.6***

◆ *Decide what the implied main idea is for each paragraph. Then compose a sentence stating that main idea. Write it on the lines below the paragraph.*

1. The risks of being overweight are well known. Obesity affects blood pressure and heart disease. It is also implicated in other health issues. These include gout, arthritis, respiratory problems, and diabetes. Overthin people also face health risks. Women need some body fat for normal menstruation. Underweight people are at a disadvantage in a hospital where they may have to go without food to undergo tests or surgery. Low body weight increases risks when fighting life-threatening diseases. These include cancer, respiratory ailments, and infections.

________________________________________

________________________________________

________________________________________

2. The central idea of disengagement theory is that people freely give up social and job roles as they age. This fosters an orderly change from one generation to the next. In addition, it helps older people feel less ashamed when their abilities decline. However, some older people are not ready to give up their roles. They are often discriminated against in the work place. They lose power within society. This makes them feel rejected and depressed. Such feelings could have been avoided if the disengagement theory had been in force.

______________________________________________

______________________________________________

______________________________________________

3. Some ocean currents exist at and near the surface. They result from interactions between the atmosphere and the coast. They greatly affect shipping and ocean travel. The Coriolis effect also modifies ocean currents. The earth's rotation produces this effect. Finally, the arrangement of the ocean basins and continental coasts affects ocean currents. As ocean currents approach land, they are redirected and split into other patterns.

______________________________________________

______________________________________________

______________________________________________

4. Researchers conducted a study in which they gave children IQ tests at the beginning of the school year. They told teachers that some children would show great intellectual gains during the year. Actually, the names of these children were picked at random. There was no real reason to expect they would do better than others. At the end of the year, however, these children did show gains.

______________________________________________

______________________________________________

______________________________________________

5. Fluoride helps bones and teeth grow larger and more perfect. Drinking water is the usual source of fluoride. Fish and tea also supply substantial amounts. Another source is fluoride toothpastes. Some dentists apply fluoride treatment to the surfaces of teeth. Fluoride tablets are also available. Vitamin drops containing fluoride are used for infants.

______________________________________________

______________________________________________

______________________________________________

6. Seventeenth-century Europeans felt lucky if they could grow or earn enough to have one meal a day. Both invading armies and famine scourged their farming lands. The result was malnutrition, illness, and death. Widespread crop failures occurred fairly often. Poor harvests and high prices made food a luxury. Housing was inadequate, and medical treatment nonexistent. Life conditions caused many marriages to be postponed. Birth rates declined.

_______________________________________________

_______________________________________________

_______________________________________________

7. Inside the cell, the most noticeable feature is the nucleus. It is made of DNA and regulates what happens in the cell. Ribosomes are also found in the cell. They are the protein factories of the cell. The endoplasmic reticulum is also involved in protein synthesis. Another cell part, the mitochondria, are double-layered membranes. They are involved in energy production in the cell.

_______________________________________________

_______________________________________________

_______________________________________________

8. Maslow said that humans have physiological needs—needs for food, water, etc. Another need is for safety—feeling safe and secure. Yet another need is to feel that we are loved and important to others. Humans also have needs for esteem—feelings of adequacy and self-respect. Another human need is the need for self-actualization—developing our full abilities and potential.

_______________________________________________

_______________________________________________

_______________________________________________

9. Traditionally, most geographers have worked in postsecondary institutions. However, today geographers are also getting jobs in noneducational settings. The government hires geographers at local, state, and national levels. Geographers are also sought by business and industry.

_______________________________________________

_______________________________________________

_______________________________________________

10. The nuclear family consists of a mother, father, and children. It is a relatively new family structure. An older family type is the extended family. This is composed of two or more adult generations

sharing the same house and money. One of the oldest adults is usually the head of the extended family. A stem extended family consists of three or more generations who live in different houses but share the same financial situation.

______________________________

______________________________

______________________________

**EXERCISE 6.7**

*Read the paragraph and determine the main idea. If the main idea is stated, underline the topic sentence. If the main idea is implied, write a topic sentence for the paragraph in the space provided.*

***Example***

Higher education is costly but can be financed in many ways. Local scholarships are granted by hometown civic clubs, church groups, or other nonprofit groups. State scholarships are available for students who show academic promise. Basic and supplemental educational grants are given by the federal government. Grants do not have to be repaid. Federal loan programs, such as the National Direct Student Loans, must be repaid. Jobs are often available through college work-study and career planning and placement programs.

*Topic sentence:* *main idea stated*

______________________________

1. Creep is the slowest and least noticeable of the slow mass movements of the earth. However, it has the most widespread and important effects. Creep consists of very slow downhill movement of earth material over a period of years. It involves an entire hillside. It probably occurs on any sloping, soil-covered surface. Creep results in the downhill tilting or partial burying of objects such as trees or stones.

   *Topic sentence:* ______________________________

   ______________________________

2. A class system is an ordered set of categories. Karl Marx believed only two classes existed. They might be called the haves and the have-nots. Marx called them the bourgeoisie and the proletariat. Unlike the proletariat, the bourgeoisie own the tools and materials needed for their work. The proletariat, then, supports itself by working for the bourgeoisie. To Marx, class involved a person's relationship to work.

   *Topic sentence:* ______________________________

   ______________________________

3. When the Constitution was ratified in 1788, the founders of the United States dismissed the idea of an official language for the country. The U.S. courts have also rejected the idea. They say everyone has the constitutional right to speak their own language. The Civil Rights Act further protects freedom of language.

   *Topic sentence:*________________________________________

4. Matrices are often used in science. They are essential tools in fields as diverse as economics and physics. They are closely related to systems of linear equations. A matrix is a rectangular array of numbers. The array is enclosed in parentheses or brackets. The numbers in a matrix are called entries or elements. These are arranged in rows and columns. The number of rows and columns determines a matrix's size.

   *Topic sentence:*________________________________________

5. The United States uses two temperature scales. Both have values based on the boiling and freezing points of water. The Fahrenheit scale was developed in 1714. It is less used in other countries. It is, however, the primary scale used in the United States. The metric system scale is Celsius. This scale is also called the centigrade scale. It was devised in 1742.

   *Topic sentence:*________________________________________

6. Different societies assign different roles according to age. At a minimum, cultures distinguish between the young, the adult, and the elderly. In the culture of the United States, critical ages are 6, 16, 18, 21, and 65. These indicate ages when American citizens have different rights and responsibilities. They might also represent times when society treats a person differently. At these ages, a person may go to school, drive, register for the draft, vote, drink alcohol, or retire.

   *Topic sentence:*________________________________________

7. Sarcasm and inducing guilt are verbal forms of manipulation. People use them to control others. Manipulation may also be nonverbal. This includes pouting or sulking. In these cases, a

person tries to affect another without saying what is wrong. Finally, manipulation can be both verbal and nonverbal. While making feeble attempts at cleaning, a person who hates to clean might praise another for doing a good job. Manipulation has many forms but always seeks to control others in an underhanded way.

*Topic sentence:* ________________________________________________

**8.** Some people take an active part in the treatment and recovery of cancer. They are spurred into action, not despair. They encourage family members and friends to cope effectively with their illnesses. In addition, they use the closeness of these relationships to strengthen their determination to fight. These people face each day bravely. Other people with cancer are grief-stricken. They feel each pain is their last. Their sense of impending doom fosters their depression. This hinders the good any medicine might do. These people isolate themselves from family and friends. Their ability to cope with the disease is miniscule.

*Topic sentence:* ________________________________________________

**9.** Many future advertising students worry about their abilities to draw. They feel they need professional help. They think an inability to draw well limits them. However, most company officials are happy with stick figures as long as the idea is clear. As a matter of fact, advertising professionals often hire artists to do sketches for them.

*Topic sentence:* ________________________________________________

**10.** Narcolepsy affects one person in a thousand. This disorder has been misunderstood for years. It is often called "sleep epilepsy." However, it is not a form of epilepsy. Narcolepsy is a sudden onset of sleep during waking hours. Diagnosis is often difficult. It appears to occur as a result of REM sleep during waking hours. In addition, narcolepsy seems to be hereditary. It can be controlled through medication although no known cure exists.

*Topic sentence:* ________________________________________________

**EXERCISE 6.8**

◆ *Identify the organizational type for each of the sections in the following excerpt. Choose from comparison/contrast (CC), subject-development (SD), enumeration/sequence (ES), and cause-effect (CE). Write your choices on the lines provided next to each section.*

### The Nutshell Principle: Key to Success

| Chapter Topics | Key Terms |
|---|---|
| The nutshell principle | Big and brief |
| Billboard viewing | Story-telling situations |
| Demands on creative person | Recognizable symbol |
| Marriage of picture and words | Non-subtle |
| Strip away unessentials | "Teasers" |
| Product as signature | "Capsule medium" |
| Helpful hints | |
| Expanding on poster idea | |
| Good poster ideas adapt | |

The *nutshell principle or poster principle,* which can advance you from being a good copywriter to being a great copywriter, embraces the ability to tell the story in a nutshell. It consists of a selling idea expressed in a strong, dominant visual with a few clever words of copy married to the visual. Although the nutshell or poster principle obviously applies to the medium of outdoor advertising, the billboard, *it can be the key to outstanding advertising in all media.*

#### Peculiarities of Billboard Viewing

An outdoor billboard must be read from a moving vehicle traveling at an average speed of 35 m.p.h. The outdoor billboard may be a few hundred feet away from a viewer who has perhaps five seconds to comprehend your message.

#### Demands on Creative Person

Because of the billboard's fleeting impact, the visual dominates. Your idea must be big and brief, able to be understood at a quick glance. You will need illustrations and symbols that are instantly meaningful and that involve the viewer emotionally. The best illustrations convey a story-telling situation in which the viewer fills in missing gaps of information. One poster based on the copy line "Dean's Milk Grows Giants" showed just one pair of scuffed-up sneakers from which the feet and ankles projected up through the top of the billboard. It had novelty, simplicity, and humor. Most of all, it had universality. People viewing that poster put themselves into the same situation. They understood instantly.

A poster for a utility company showed a single clothespin to represent washday. Even in this age of automatic washers and dryers, the clothespin communicated meaning in a flash. It was an instantly recognizable symbol.

The ideal poster is a perfect marriage of picture and words, with each supporting and explaining the other. The copy line should stem from the illustration; the illustration should expand on the copy line. Example: For the San Diego Zoo the head and neck of a giraffe extended diagonally across the poster with the words: "The world's greatest zoo is in your neck of the woods." Example: For the Fischer Packing Company five hot dogs stuck up from the bottom of the billboard to resemble four fingers and a thumb, with the copy line: "Weiners you can count on." Example: A jar of Mobile #1 synthetic motor oil was shown sitting on top of a snow bank with the words: "Cold remedy."

**Eliminate Unessentials**

In creating a poster use as few elements as possible. As a rule, copy should not exceed five to eight words. In the visual, see what you can take out rather than what you can put in. If, for example, your idea has to do with cooking on a camping trip, you do not have to show a whole forest with a lake and mountains in the distance. *Focus in tightly on the key element.* Show your cooking fire up front, large, with the hint of a tent flap and tree behind it. That's enough to get the story across.

**Product as Signature**

One element of a poster is the product itself, prominently displayed in glorious full color. Thus displayed, perhaps toward a corner of the space, the product or package becomes the signature of the message, eliminating the necessity of including the product name in the copy line. For example, if you show a close-up of a smiling kid with a face full of chocolate and there is a handsome Hershey Bar off to one side, you don't have to say "Hershey Bars are yummy in the tummy." You just say "Yummy in the tummy." That's a corny example but it shows you how to save a couple of those precious few words.

**Helpful Hints for Copywriters**

Tips for creating successful outdoor poster advertising include:

1. Keep your ideas *simple* and *strong.* They must have impact and be understood instantly. Volkswagen showed a motorcycle cop ticketing a chagrined Beetle driver with the copy line: "They Said It Couldn't Be Done."
2. For longest recall, play to the emotions, to which humor can be closely related. Another Volkswagen poster shows the owner inspecting a flat tire, with the copy line: "Nobody's Perfect." British Airways showed a Concorde supersonic plane in flight, with the copy line: "For those who've already arrived."
3. Avoid indirection or subtlety. People don't have time to consider what your message means. One outdoor poster showed the burner on a gas stove with jets of flame leaping up, and the copy line: "No Waiting." Another billboard showed a big Yellow Pages phone directory with the copy line: "Best Seller."
   The exception to avoiding indirection is teaser advertising, where successive parts of the message appear on successive posters. These serve to build expectant interest in a message that will not become clear until the final poster. The most famous example of this type of advertising was done years ago by Byrma Shave. Each successive poster contained a line of a limerick, and only on the final poster did they identify their product.
4. Strive for originality to produce the greatest memorability. One of the most famous posters ever run showed a baby buggy with the copy line: "Only convertible that outsells Ford."

5. If possible, tie your poster to the central advertising or selling theme of your campaign. To a great extent, poster advertising is used as a supporting medium, reinforcing the main selling effort on television, in magazines, or in newspapers.

Posters must contain the story in a nutshell. They look like fun, but they are not all that easy to write. However, if you can develop skill at coming up with sound poster ideas you should automatically be a superior copywriter in all other media, because *a good nutshell idea can almost always be expanded upon.*

**Expanding on Poster Idea**

One of the great poster ads of all time showed a group of nuns entering a VW van, with a copy line that line was sheer genius: "Mass Transit." It portrayed a benefit in a graphic way. It was clean, simple, memorable. It communicated at a glance.

This poster idea might have been easily adapted to other media. It could have been a solid magazine ad as is. Or it could have provided a dramatic illustration at the top of a magazine or newspaper ad with a moderate amount of body copy following.

A television commercial might open with a long shot of the church steeple, then zoom in close as the chimes struck. The camera cuts to a ground-level archway. Out the door come the nuns, perhaps one by one to dramatize the number of them. The Mother Superior might call out each sister's name as it was her turn to load in the bus.

Would that same idea work for radio? We hear church bells. An announcer tells us where the church is. We hear the nuns shuffling out of the church, intoning some kind of chant. We hear the Mother Superior calling out names as they are to load in the van. Perhaps one sister is late arriving. Will there be room for her? You know it—plenty of room! And so on.

**Good Poster Ideas Adapt**

A good, solid poster idea—a nutshell idea—often adapts beautifully to other media. In his book, *The Compleat Copywriter,* Hanley Norins of Young & Rubicam refers to outdoor posters as "the capsule medium." If you can compress a strong selling message into a crisp and colorful capsule, you will almost surely be a successful communicator.

John O'Toole, Chair of the Board of the Foote, Cone & Belding agency said that "an effective poster is two things: it is unexpected and it is relevant. *Unexpected and relevant.* Those two characteristics of an effective poster, it will be noted by those who have heard me talk about advertising before, are the very same attributes I have always said are the essentials of an advertising idea for any medium.

"*That is why I always advise that creative work begin with a poster, no matter what medium the advertising is to eventually appear in.* If it can be expressed as an unexpected and relevant poster, it probably can be turned into a magazine or newspaper ad. And, yes, into a television or radio commercial."

Harken to those words!

**EXERCISE 6.9**

*Read each section of the preceding excerpt and determine the main idea. If the main idea is stated, write the topic sentence in the appropriate blank below. If the main idea is implied, construct a topic sentence and write it in the appropriate blank below. Finally, construct a topic sentence for the entire passage and write it in the appropriate space below.*

THE NUTSHELL PRINCIPLE: KEY TO SUCCESS

(Introduction)________________________________________

____________________________________________________

____________________________________________________

**Peculiarities of Billboard Viewing**________________________

____________________________________________________

____________________________________________________

**Demands on Creative Person**_____________________________

____________________________________________________

**Eliminate Unessentials**__________________________________

____________________________________________________

____________________________________________________

**Product as Signature**___________________________________

____________________________________________________

____________________________________________________

**Helpful Hints for Copywriters**___________________________

____________________________________________________

____________________________________________________

**Expanding on Poster Idea**_______________________________

____________________________________________________

____________________________________________________

**Good Poster Ideas Adapt**________________________________

____________________________________________________

____________________________________________________

## Finding Implied Main Ideas in Passages

Finding an implied main idea of a passage is harder than finding a stated main idea. Because the author does not state the main idea, you rely more heavily on the organizational patterns within and among paragraphs. You examine the parts (details) and infer the whole (main idea). Then, you think of a topic sentence yourself.

STEPS FOR FINDING IMPLIED MAIN IDEAS IN PASSAGES

1. *Read each paragraph in the passage.*
2. *Find the topic for each paragraph.*
3. *Identify the topic that all or most of the paragraphs have in common.*
4. *Think of a sentence that says what the paragraphs have in common.* This sentence will be the implied main idea of the passage.

**EXERCISE 6.10**

*Look back at the paragraphs about Sacramento in Exercise 6.4. Think of a topic sentence for this passage and write it in the space below.*

*Topic sentence:*____________________________________

_______________________________________________

**EXERCISE 6.11**

*Underline the stated main idea in each paragraph. Think of a topic sentence for this passage and write it in the space below.*

*Topic sentence:*____________________________________

_______________________________________________

Two-year colleges have been a rapidly growing and accessible form of postsecondary education. In 1970 over one thousand two-year institutions were enrolling well over a million students. At that time at least one new two-year program was being established every week somewhere in the nation.

Public community colleges are institutions that usually have "open-door" policies for high-school graduates. The largest group of two-year institutions consists of public community colleges. Community colleges are comprehensive in that they provide many course offerings. Excellent guidance and other student service programs are available. Tuition costs are often lower than for other forms of postsecondary programs. The cost of higher education is also decreased because of the accessibility of community colleges.

Extension branches are most often two-year branches of a four-year university. These branches have the accessibility of community colleges. Transfer of credit to the four-year institution is easier. The opportunity for completing advanced programs at the main campus is simplified.

Vocational-technical schools prepare students for specific occupational positions. Admission standards are usually more flexible. However, tuition may be higher than that of other two-year institutions. This is because the cost of vo-tech facilities is usually greater. Also, the ratio of students to teacher is usually lower. Vocational-technical schools are a special type of two-year postsecondary institution.

◆

## SYNTHESIS: MAKING MAIN IDEAS YOUR OWN

*I must create a system, or be enslaved by another man's.*

—WILLIAM BLAKE

One of the more difficult tasks facing students is reading and relating main ideas from various sources. Instructors find some students approach this task much like a mouse eating books. They consume one book after another. What instructors really want is for students to collect numerous details and ideas. Then they want them to keep only what is useful. Instructors want students to consider other opinions before forming their own. They want students to create their own systems for understanding and relating ideas instead of relying on those of others. They want students to synthesize.

**Synthesis** is a way to put together information from various sources. You look for main ideas. You find relationships and associations among different materials. Then you combine independent pieces to form a more complete body of knowledge.

Many college courses require you to write papers. The topic of a paper usually covers a single subject. But, your information may come

*"This synthesis has as many holes as Swiss cheese. Do him a favor. Go hit GLOBAL DELETE."*

from several sources. You synthesize that information to write your paper. Your paper forms your own main idea of the topic.

### *Example*

PASSAGE ONE

Honolulu means "sheltered bay" in Hawaiian. It was a small Polynesian village when discovered by Captain William Brown. Brown, an English seaman, arrived there in the late eighteenth century.

Honolulu, Hawaii, is one of America's fastest-growing areas. It is located on the southeastern coast of the island of Oahu. It is the capital and largest city in Hawaii. Honolulu became the capital of the Kingdom of Hawaii in 1845. It remained the capital when Hawaii became a U.S. territory and later a state.

Honolulu has a mayor-council form of government. These city officials are elected to four-year terms.

The city's largest source of income is military activities. The second largest source of income is tourism. About 500 manufacturing companies are located in Honolulu. The leading industry is food processing. Plastics, oil products, cement, clothing, and glass products are also made in this area.

Honolulu is known as the "Crossroads of the Pacific." It has a port that supports passenger and cargo ships. The airport serves hundreds of planes each day.

Honolulu has a symphony orchestra and community theater. The Honolulu International Center includes an auditorium, arena, and exhibition hall. The city features museums, art galleries, and a Polynesian cultural center. Parks and other recreational facilities are available.

PASSAGE TWO

Phoenix, Arizona, was first settled by pioneers in the 1860s. The settlement was located on the Salt River. One of the pioneers found that an early Indian civilization had existed on the site.

This discovery led to the choice of Phoenix as a name for the settlement. The phoenix was a bird of Greek mythology. It was said to die by fire every 500 years. It then rose from the ashes to live again.

The settlement was true to its name. Pheonix became the largest city in Arizona. It was the capital of the Arizona Territory and is now the state's capital.

The leading economic activity is manufacturing. Chemicals, computers, and electronic equipment are made in the city. Military weapons and processed food are other products of Phoenix. Tourism and military activities also contribute to the city's income.

Air service is provided by the Phoenix Sky Harbor Airport. Passenger and freight trains as well as trucking lines serve the city.

The mayor and six council members are elected for two-year terms. The council hires a city manager as its chief administrator. The mayor, council, and manager form a council-manager type of government.

Phoenix's cultural attractions include three museums and a civic plaza. A civic symphony is enjoyed by the citizens of Pheonix. The city also has a professional basketball team. About 200 parks provide recreation for the area.

PASSAGE THREE

Providence is the second largest city in the New England area. It is the largest city in Rhode Island. Providence is located on Narragansett Bay in the east-central part of the state. Although Providence is the state capital now, other Rhode Island cities have held this honor in the past.

Providence was begun as a settlement for religious freedom. It was founded by Roger Williams in 1636. Williams, an English religious leader, chose the name because he believed God had guided him in choosing a location for the settlement.

Providence and the surrounding areas have over 2,500 manufacturing plants. Much of the world's jewelry is produced there. Silverware, textiles, and nonelectrical machinery are also made in the area.

Providence is a port city. It is served by freight and passenger railroads as well as an airport.

Several museums and art galleries are found in Providence. Many colonial buildings are also preserved. An orchestra and a repertory acting company make their home in this city. The civic center is composed of a sports arena and a convention and exhibition hall.

A mayor-council form of government is used in Providence. The mayor and 26 members of the council are elected to four-year terms.

SYNTHESIS PASSAGE

Although Honolulu, Phoenix, and Providence are in different areas of the country, they have much in common. All are located on bodies of water, and two of them have ports.

These cities are large metropolitan areas. Honolulu and Phoenix are the largest cities in their respective states. Providence is the second largest city in Rhode Island. All of these cities are the capitals of their states. Of the three, only Providence was not the original state capital.

Both Honolulu and Providence use a mayor-council form of city government. Phoenix's city government utilizes a council-manager system.

Manufacturing is an important factor in the economy of all three cities. Military activities and tourism are also important in the economic structure of Honolulu and Phoenix.

Transportation in these cities is varied. All cities are served by airports and trucking lines. Phoenix and Providence have railroads. Providence and Honolulu are ports.

These three cities have many cultural advantages. Symphonies, museums, and civic centers are located in each city. Art galleries, sports arenas, and parks can be found in two of the three cities. Only one city has a theater.

The name of each city has an interesting background. Honolulu, which was discovered by Captain Brown, means "sheltered bay" in Hawaiian. Phoenix, an earlier site of an Indian civilization resettled by pioneers, was named for a mythological bird that died and was reborn every five hundred years. Providence was named because its founder, Roger Williams, believed God had guided him in selecting the location.

Honolulu, Providence, and Phoenix have many similarities.

SYNTHESIS CHART

| | *HONOLULU* | *PHOENIX* | *PROVIDENCE* |
|---|---|---|---|
| *LOCATED?* | southeastern coast of Oahu Island | Salt River | Narragansett Bay |
| *SIZE?* | largest city | largest city | 2nd-largest city |
| *HISTORY?* | | | |
| *ORIGIN OF NAME?* | "sheltered bay" | bird in Greek mythology | religious beliefs |
| *SETTLED BY?* | Capt. Brown | pioneers | Roger Williams |
| *FROM WHAT COUNTRY* | England | | England |
| *STATE CAPITAL?* | | | |
| *Original?* | Yes | Yes | No |
| *Current?* | Yes | Yes | Yes |
| *FORM OF GOVERNMENT?* | mayor-council | council-manager | mayor-council |
| *ECONOMY?* | military<br>tourism<br>manufacturing | manufacturing<br>tourism<br>military | manufacturing |
| *TRANSPORTATION?* | | | |
| *Airports?* | Yes | Yes | Yes |
| *Railroads?* | No | Yes | Yes |
| *Ports?* | Yes | No | Yes |
| *Trucking lines?* | Yes | Yes | Yes |
| *CULTURAL FEATURES?* | | | |
| *Symphony?* | Yes | Yes | Yes |
| *Museums?* | Yes | Yes | Yes |
| *Art galleries?* | Yes | No | Yes |
| *Civic centers?* | Yes | Yes | Yes |
| *Parks?* | Yes | Yes | No |
| *Theater?* | Yes | No | No |
| *Sports?* | No | Yes | Yes |

**EXERCISE 6.12**

◆ *Below are three excerpts concerning the topic of love. Complete the synthesis chart with information from all three passages.*

EXCERPT ONE

### Exploration: Love—Stalking an Elusive Emotion

Love is one of the most intense of all human experiences. Moreover, at one time or another, most people must ask themselves, "Is this love or lust?" "Is it real or infatuation?" "What am I really feeling?" All of which raises the question, What is love? Think, for instance, about the different ways we love our parents, friends, and spouses or lovers.

**Question: How do various kinds of love differ from one another?**

This is the question that recently led psychologist Robert Sternberg to propose his **triangular theory of love.** Although the theory is still preliminary, it may help you think more clearly about your own loving relationships.

## LOVE TRIANGLES

According to Sternberg (1986, 1987), love is made up of **intimacy, passion,** and **commitment.** As you can see in Figure 12–15, each factor can be visualized as one side of a triangle. Notice also that the 3 elements can combine to produce 7 different types of love. We will return to these types in a moment, but first let's briefly explore love's 3 "ingredients."

### Intimacy

A relationship has intimacy, or closeness, if affection, sharing, communication, and support are present. Intimacy grows steadily at first, but in time it levels off. After it does, people in long-term relationships may gradually lose sight of the fact that they are still very close and mutually dependent.

### Passion

Passion refers mainly to *physiological arousal.* This arousal may be sexual, but it includes other sources too. As discussed earlier in this chapter, arousal, no matter what its cause, may be interpreted as passion in a romantic relationship (Bersheid & Walster, 1974b). This is probably why passionate love often occurs against a backdrop of danger, adversity, or frustration—especially in soap operas and romance novels! Passion is the primary source of love's *intensity.* It's not surprising, then, that romance inspires the strongest feelings of love. In contrast, love for siblings is least intense (Sternberg & Grajeck, 1984).

### Commitment

The third side of the love triangle consists of your decision to love another person and your degree of long-term commitment to them. Commitment starts at zero before you meet a person and it grows steadily as you get acquainted. Like intimacy, commitment tends to level off. However, it may waver up and down with a relationship's good times and bad times. Commitment drops rapidly when a relationship is in serious trouble.

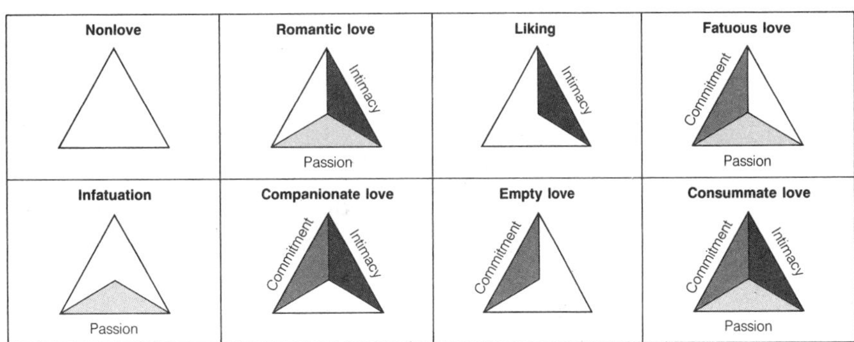


***FIGURE 12–15***
***Sternberg's Triangular Theory of Love***

## SEVEN FLAVORS OF LOVE

The presence or absence of intimacy, passion, and/or commitment produces 8 triangles. The first defines **nonlove,** a total absence of all three elements.

In **liking,** you feel close to a person and communicate well with her or him. However, you do not feel any passion or deep commitment to the person. A likeable classmate might fall into this category.

**Romantic love** mixes intimacy (closeness and sharing) with passion (often in the form of physical attraction). Despite its intensity, romantic love does not involves much commitment at first. Think, for example, of a summer romance that ends in a relatively easy parting of ways.

**Fatuous love** describes commitments made rapidly on the basis of physical attraction (passion), but without much emotional intimacy. Fatuous love is of the boy-meets-girl-and-they-get-married-a-month-later type. Relationships started this way risk failure because lovers make a commitment before they really get to know each other well.

**Infatuation** is an even more superficial form of love. In this case, a person is inflamed with passion, but shares no intimacy or commitment with the beloved. In time, of course, infatuation may lead to more lasting kinds of love.

**Companionate love** refers to affection and deep attachment that is built on respect, shared interests, and firm friendship. Companionate love is lower-key emotionally. However, it is steady and long-term and tends to grow in time. Companionate love is the "kind of affection we feel for those with whom our lives are deeply intertwined" (Walster & Walster, 1978).

Couples sometimes reach a point where there is little passion or intimacy left in their relationship. If they stay together merely out of commitment or habit, they experience **empty love.**

**Consummate love** occurs when two people are passionate, committed to one another, and emotionally close. Complete, balanced love of this kind occurs only in very special relationships.

#### How Do I Love Thee?

The categories described here are certainly not the last word on love. Undoubtedly, other kinds of love also exist. In addition, Sternberg's theory may place too much emphasis on passion. In most relationships, intimacy and commitment are a bigger part of love than passion is (Clark & Reis, 1988).

Our culture also tends to place much emphasis on passion as the main basis for "falling" in love. However, this overlooks the fact that the passionate, breathless stage of love typically lasts only about 6 to 30 months (Walster & Walster, 1978). What happens when this period ends? Quite often, people separate.

There is a degree of danger in expecting to live forever on a romantic cloud. People who are primarily caught up in passionate love may neglect to build a more lasting relationship. Rather than downplaying companionate love, it is helpful to realize that lovers must also be friends. In fact, consummate love is basically a blending of romantic love and companionate love.

You may be tempted to match the love triangles with your own relationships. If you do apply the theory, remember that relationships vary greatly and that few are perfect (Trotter, 1986). In another study, Sternberg and Michael Barnes (1986) found that relationships are generally satisfying if you think the other person feels about you the way you would *like* for her or him to feel about you.

In the 1970s, some politicians belittled the study of love as "unscientific." But in a world often wracked by violence, hatred, and despair, what could be more important than understanding the elusive state we call love?

*Source:* Reprinted with permission from *Introduction to Psychology: Exploration and Application* 5/e by Coon. 

EXCERPT TWO

## A Triangular Theory of Love

Sternberg and his colleagues began by trying to identify the nature of love. Is it a single, indivisible entity, or can it be understood better in terms of a set of separate aspects? After analyzing data from people who answered questions about love on special questionnaires, they concluded that the second explanation is more accurate. The following are among the many aspects of love that they identified.

- Having high regard for the loved one
- Valuing the loved one in one's life
- Promoting the welfare of the loved one
- Experiencing happiness with the loved one
- Giving emotional support to the loved one
- Communicating intimately with the loved one
- Receiving emotional support from the loved one
- Sharing oneself and one's things with the loved one
- Being able to count on the loved one in times of need

You can see that these aspects of love are not limited to romantic love. They fit any kind of love relationship, yet clearly not all such relationships are alike. The researchers went on, therefore, to investigate kinds of love. What makes romantic love different from infatuation or companionate love or the love of a child for a parent or the love of a parent for a child? These investigations led to what Sternberg calls a triangular theory of love.

The three sides of the triangle in the **triangular theory of love** are passion, commitment, and intimacy. Passion is the *motivational* component; it is characterized by physical arousal and an intense desire to be with the loved one. Commitment is the *cognitive* component. Sternberg describes it as both a short-term decision to love another person and a long-term commitment to maintain love. The *emotional* component is intimacy, which includes communication, support, and sharing.

Passion, commitment, and intimacy are the basic dimensions under which the various aspects of love, such as those just listed, can be grouped. Different love relationships may be visualized as triangles of different shapes, depending upon which of the three components are the most important in the relationship. In Figure 8–1, you see triangles representing three possible love relationships. Of Sternberg's three components, commitment is the most important in the love between a parent and a child, so this side of triangle *a* is the longest. Intimacy gets a significant, but shorter, side; and passion is missing, as shown by the dotted line for this component.

In a reverse of the parent-child relationship, intimacy is the strongest component of the best-friend love triangle *b*, with commitment making a shorter side. Passion again is absent. By contrast, passion is the dominating component in triangle *c*, which represents an infatuation relationship. Intimacy is moderate, but commitment is missing.

All in all, there are eight possible kinds of love relationships that can be described using Sternberg's three components. Trotter (1986) presents a detailed explanation with some interesting illustrations, or you may want to try out this method for yourself by drawing triangles of the important love relationships in your life.

Sternberg and his colleagues believe that their three-sided theory of love has potential for helping them understand love relationships, particularly romantic love relationships, more fully. One of the ways they have been using this concept in research is to examine how the perceptions that members of a couple have of their own triangles affect satisfaction with the relationship.

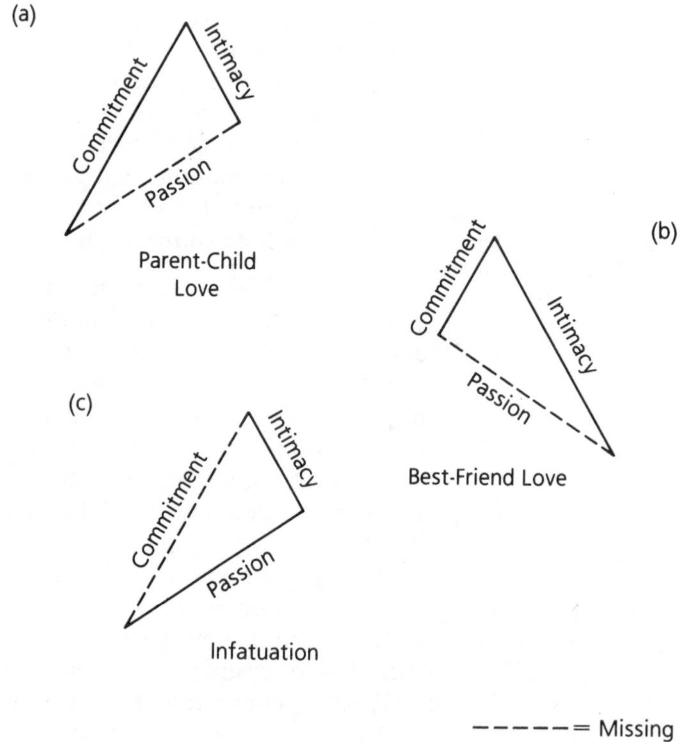


***FIGURE 8–1***
***The Triangles of Love: Some Examples***

One of the most interesting aspects of this research concerns the comparison of (1) the way each half of a couple believes the other *actually* feels about him or her with (2) the way he or she would *like* the other person to feel (Sternberg & Barnes, 1985). What the investigators found was that a *match* between these perceptions is critical to satisfaction with a romantic relationship. If the triangle you would draw to describe the way you believe your partner in a romantic relationship *really feels* is not quite similar to the one you would draw to describe the way you *want* him or her to feel, you are likely to be dissatisfied with the relationship.

In this comparison, what is important is the way you *believe* your partner feels. This may or may not be the same as your partner would say he or she feels. Thus, this research points up yet again the importance of communication to relationships. If one partner is unable to express his or her feelings sufficiently well for the other to believe there is equal love, a potentially good relationship may be destroyed.

The work of Sternberg and his colleagues owes much to earlier investigators who developed and tested questionnaires to measure liking and love (e.g., Rubin, 1970). The particular contribution of the three-sided theory lies in its ability to generate specific research questions about love that may be tested in a scientific manner. For example, are romantic love relationships characterized by a triangle with three equal sides (equal measures of passion, commitment, and intimacy) the relationships that last? Do the triangles change in predictable ways as good relationships age? Answers to these and many other questions not only might enable counselors and therapists to find better ways to help couples with troubled relationships but also increase our understanding of the nature of love.

*Source:* Reprinted with permission from *Psychology and Effective Behavior* by Jewell. 

EXCERPT THREE

## Love and Intimacy

To say that we love another is, perhaps, to give him or her the most positive evaluation of which we are capable. We talk a great deal about love, but researchers cannot always agree on what we mean by the word. In one sense this is a semantic problem. Love can refer both to the heart-pounding excitement of a first sexual encounter and to the gentle affection between two elderly brothers.

Many people would just as soon not know why couples fall in love. Senator William Proxmire once ridiculed two psychologists who were studying love and had requested an $84,000 federal grant. Proxmire stated, emphatically, "Right at the top of the things we don't want to know is why a man falls in love with a woman." At the same time, however, scientists are finding that, if anything, passionate love and interest in romantic feelings are growing. In the 1960s when college students were asked whether they would marry someone who met all of their needs but whom they didn't love, 24 percent of the women and 60 percent of the men said that they wouldn't. When asked again in 1979, 80 percent of the women and 86 percent of the men said that they wouldn't. Love has apparently become more important than ever. The *New York Times* columnist James Reston, responding to Senator Proxmire's statement, provided a rationale for continuing to study love:

> If the sociologists and psychologists can get even a suggestion of the answer in our patterns of romantic love, marriage, dissolution, divorce—and the children left behind—it could be the best invest-

ment of federal money since Mr. Jefferson made the Louisiana Purchase. (Reston, 1975)

Kelley (Kelley, 1983, p. 274) has outlined the behaviors of love as follows:

1. Verbal expression of affection.
2. Self-disclosure: revealing intimate facts.
3. Nonmaterial evidence of love: giving emotional and moral support, showing interest in another's activities and respect for his or her opinions.
4. Feelings not expressed verbally: feeling happier, more secure, more relaxed when other is around.
5. Material evidence of love: giving gifts, performing physical chores.
6. Physical expression of love: hugging and kissing.
7. Willingness to tolerate less pleasant aspects of other: tolerating demands in order to maintain the relationship.

Love can be divided into two classifications: passionate love, which is a temporary but intense reaction to another, and conjugal love, which is a long-term relationship based on friendship and mutual respect.

### PASSIONATE LOVE

**Passionate love** is an intense emotional reaction. An individual experiencing it thinks constantly about the person he wants to be with, and thinks of that person in the context of love. Passionate love generally leads to an unrealistic evaluation of the love object.

Researchers have argued that three criteria must be met before passionate love can occur (Berscheid & Walster, 1974). First, the person must be exposed by her culture to the idea of passionate love. In many cultures the idea of love at first sight or passionate love is uncommon. Instead, marriages often are arranged, and love is viewed as something that may develop after many years of companionship. In modern Western culture the idea of passionate love not only is common but also is considered something to be expected. It is heralded in our writings, songs, theater, and television programs. Because of this, a person in our culture not only thinks more about spontaneous and passionate love but also expects to fall in love, even suddenly.

Second, for passionate love to occur, an appropriate person must be present. For most people the person must be an attractive member of the opposite sex. Passionate love and sexual attraction are well associated with each other.

The third important criterion is an emotional arousal that the individual interprets as love. This reaction may take the form of sexual arousal or even of anxiety at meeting the other person.

The onset of passionate love is relatively swift and sudden (Berscheid, 1983). Interestingly, a mild feeling such as liking, especially if it has continued over a long time, does not usually become something as intense as passionate love. This supports the idea that liking and passionate love are not simply different points along a single continuum of attraction, but rather are qualitatively different phenomena with different antecedents (Berscheid, 1983). Ironically, passionate love also is quite fragile, compared to something as stable as liking. Passionate love rarely lasts for long, and it is generally replaced by either a loss of interest or a more enduring conjugal love.

Unfortunately, a cultural expectation, an attractive person, and physical arousal don't give us much to go on if we plan to build a long-term relationship, such as a marriage. Countless couples have fallen in love and have married quickly, only to find later that they were not well suited to each other. A survey of over 200 college couples who were dating, and who stated that they were in love, found that, by the end of 2 years, one-half of the couples had broken up. At the beginning of their love affairs, they had felt a strong physical attraction for each other and had believed that their futures would be shared. But, by the time 2 years had passed, one-half of them stated that they were either bored with the relationship or had found that they did not share similar interests (Hill, Rubin, & Peplau, 1976).

These findings may indicate that liking and loving are two different things (Sternberg, 1987). Consider the following, both of which are true stories, although the names have been changed to protect confidentiality.

> Tom sat right behind Jane in biology class. For Tom, it was love at first sight. From the very first day he saw Jane, he could think of little else: Thoughts of her preoccupied him constantly. Tom was therefore crushed when Jane found herself a boyfriend, Peter. Prior to that time, Tom had never really gotten to know Jane. His interactions with her all took place in his mind. Finally, Tom started having conversations with her and discovered that although he was still madly in love with her, he did not like her a whole lot.
>
> Mike and Louise had been dating for about 3 months. Both of them seemed happy in the relationship, but their friends saw trouble. Louise just seemed a whole lot more involved than Mike. One night, Louise confessed her love and let on to her plans for their future together. Mike was dumbfounded. He had not made any plans and did not want them. Mike told Louise that he liked her but did not love her and did not think he ever could. Mike broke off the relationship the next day. (Sternberg, 1987, p. 331)

Perhaps the strongest relationships are the ones in which the two partners *both* like and love each other.

### CONJUGAL LOVE

After we fall passionately in love with and are aroused by someone, our passion generally doesn't last long—at least not at the same level—even if we continue to love and stay with that person. Our diminishing emotional passion may be supplanted by a **conjugal love** relationship. People who have romantic expectations that their sexual passion will remain at a high level usually face disappointment. Psychologist Ellen Berscheid interviewed a large number of undergraduates and asked what their reaction would be if their passion disappeared from their marriage. More than one-half said that they would want a divorce (Berscheid, 1983). Yet psychologists have found that disappearance of passion is generally what happens. This may explain, at least to some degree, the high divorce rate in the United States.

Yet conjugal love often becomes deeper and more powerful than the initial passionate love was. Researchers have found that the most stressful experience the average person will ever face is the death of a spouse (Holmes & Rahe, 1967). Perhaps, more than any other factor, sharing experiences with each other develops conjugal love, or, as it is sometimes called, *companionate love.* Another aspect of conjugal love is the willingness to make sacrifices for each other.

*Source:* Reprinted with permission from *Psychology by Dworetzky. Coyright © 1988 by West Publishing Company.* 

SYNTHESIS CHART

| *COMPONENTS OF THEORIES* | *AUTHORS* | | |
|---|---|---|---|
| | *Coon* | *Jewell* | *Dworetzky* |
| *DEFINITION* | | | |
| *ASPECTS* | | | |
| *TYPES AND DESCRIPTION* | | | |
| *THEORY* | | | |

## EXERCISE 6.13

◆ *Using the synthesis chart you created in Exercise 6.12, write a short passage comparing and contrasting the triangular theory of love discussed in the Coon and Jewell excerpts.*

____________________________________________

____________________________________________

____________________________________________

____________________________________________

**EXERCISE 6.14**

*Using the synthesis chart you created in Exercise 6.12, write a short passage contrasting the types of love discussed in all three excerpts.*

**EXERCISE 6.15**

*Using the synthesis chart you created in Exercise 6.12, write a short passage developing a definition of love.*

**EXERCISE 6.16**

*Using the synthesis chart you created in Exercise 6.12, write a short cause-effect passage based on five of the descriptions of the types of love in the theory of love triangles.*

**EXERCISE 6.17**

*Using the synthesis chart you created in Exercise 6.12, write a short enumeration/sequence passage based on the aspects or behaviors of love.*

◆

## CHAPTER SUMMARY EXERCISE

*Complete the chapter summary by providing the appropriate words to complete the sentences.*

Every paragraph or passage has a topic, a main idea, and details. The ______________ is the general ______________ of the paragraph. The ______________ is the key concept. ______________ provide additional information. Stated main ideas are found in ______________ sentences. These are located at the ______________, middle, or ______________ of paragraphs or passages. The ______________ of paragraphs and passages helps in finding main ideas. Four types of text organization are ______________, ______________, ______________, and ______________. In addition to being stated, main ideas can also be ______________. This means you must decide for yourself what the ______________ of a paragraph or passage is. Finally, ________ is a way you interweave main ideas from many ______________ into a ______________ of your own.

◆

## CHAPTER REVIEW

*Answer briefly but completely.*

**1.** Your text compares a main idea to an umbrella. It says if either has holes, they are useless. How can a main idea have holes in it?

______________________________________________

______________________________________________

______________________________________________

______________________________________________

**2.** Compare stated and implied main ideas to denotation and connotation.

______________________________________________

______________________________________________

______________________________________________

______________________________________________

**3.** What is the importance of a topic sentence? Where does it commonly appear?

______________________________________________

______________________________________________

4. Explain the phrase "the whole is equal to more than the sum of its parts." How does this relate to main ideas?

5. How does knowing the organizational pattern of a text help you find and understand main ideas?

6. How is the section entitled "Organizational Patterns" (pages 199–204) organized: subject-development, enumeration/sequence, comparison/contrast, or cause-effect? Defend your answer.

7. Reread Figure 6.4. List the signal words that indicate the type of text structure it exemplifies.

8. Explain the term *implied main idea.* What does *implied* mean? List three synonyms for the word *implied* that could be used in this context.

9. Name two occasions when synthesis is important in college study.

______________________________________________

______________________________________________

______________________________________________

______________________________________________

10. Complete the following analogy.
plagiarism : copy :: synthesis : ______________ .

◆

## VOCABULARY ENHANCEMENT EXERCISE

*Using the scale in Figure 3.1, rate your understanding of the following vocabulary enhancement words to the left of the number. Then write a sentence with each one.*

1. ingredients

______________________________________________

______________________________________________

2. unique

______________________________________________

______________________________________________

3. explicitly

______________________________________________

______________________________________________

4. deck

______________________________________________

______________________________________________

5. coherent

______________________________________________

______________________________________________

6. clarify

______________________________________________

______________________________________________

**7.** predominant

______________________________________________

______________________________________________

**8.** initial

______________________________________________

______________________________________________

**9.** procedure

______________________________________________

______________________________________________

**10.** consume

______________________________________________

______________________________________________

# 7 Reading Critically and Drawing Conclusions

## TERMS

*Terms appear in the order in which they occur in the chapter.*

critical reading
fact
opinion
propaganda
inferring
primary sources
secondary sources
connotation
qualitative
expert opinions
bias
image advertising
bandwagoning
testimonial
plain folks
name calling
weasel words
relevancy
conclusions
implied
literal
details
inferences
implications
background knowledge
logical inference
assumption
non sequitur

## CHAPTER OUTLINE EXERCISE

*Complete the chapter outline by putting the following goal-setting questions in the correct format:*

Why do facts represent the truth, and nothing but the truth?
How do you differentiate between fact and opinion?
What is a testimonial?
How do authors' choice of words affect the purposes of passages?
How do you use background knowledge to make inferences?
How do you make valid inferences?
What are weasel words?
How do you determine relevancy?
What is an expert opinion?
What are the rights and responsibilities of critical readers?
What is bandwagoning?
What are informational passages?
How do you draw conclusions?
What is image advertising?
What makes opinions qualitative words?
How do you recognize propaganda?
What is plain folks?
What is name calling?
What are persuasive passages?

## OBJECTIVES

*At the end of this chapter, you should be able to do the following:*

1. Identify the rights and responsibilities of critical readers.
2. Differentiate between fact and opinion.
3. Recognize propaganda.
4. Determine relevancy.
5. Distinguish among purposes of passages and authors' choice of words.
6. Draw conclusions.

## CHAPTER MAP

*Complete a chapter map by putting the goal-setting questions found in the Chapter Outline Exercise in the correct mapping format.*

## VOCABULARY ENCHANCEMENT EXERCISE

*Rate each of the following words according to your knowledge of them.*

| | STAGE 0 | STAGE 1 | STAGE 2 | STAGE 3 |
|---|---|---|---|---|
| | *I do not recognize the word.* | *I recognize the word but am unsure of its meaning and associations.* | *I recognize the word and can make general associations with it.* | *I recognize the word and can use it in speaking and writing.* |
| **1.** strive | | | | |
| **2.** deception | | | | |
| **3.** absolutes | | | | |
| **4.** validity | | | | |
| **5.** sublime | | | | |
| **6.** pathetic | | | | |
| **7.** suppressed | | | | |
| **8.** evasive | | | | |
| **9.** conveyed | | | | |
| **10.** vicariously | | | | |

♦

## RIGHTS AND RESPONSIBILITIES OF CRITICAL READERS

Samuel Taylor Coleridge once identified four kinds of readers. He described the first as being like an hourglass. Their reading, like sand, runs in and out and leaves nothing behind. Coleridge said the second kind was like a sponge. These readers soak up everything. Then they release it in nearly the same state, only a little less clean. The third type is like a strainer. All that is good flows through it. The refuse remains. The final kind of reader is like the slaves in the diamond mines of India. These readers throw away what is worthless. They keep the purest gems.

As a skilled reader, you strive to be like the fourth type Coleridge describes. You realize that not all that is written is true and correct. Everything you read, you read critically. You accept your responsibility to separate what is valuable and useful from what is not.

Table 7.1, "The Bill of Rights and Responsibilities for Critical Readers," contains a framework for evaluating what you read.

**Critical reading** is a decision-making process. It requires wisdom, thought, and logic. Since you must carefully evaluate what you read, many advanced thinking skills are involved in critical reading. Three of the skills used in critical reading are telling the difference between **fact** and **opinion,** identifying **propaganda,** and **inferring** information.

**TABLE 7.1** ***The Bill of Rights and Responsibilities for Critical Readers***

*RESPONSIBILITIES*

1. You have the responsibility of getting all of the facts, and getting them straight.
2. You are responsible for separating facts that you can confirm from opinion when you read.
3. You are responsible for resisting misleading lines of reasoning and propaganda.
4. Your are responsible for deciding what is relevant and irrelevant when you read.
5. You have the responsibility to entertain the author's point of view objectively. Negativism and criticism are not the same thing.
6. For better or for worse, you are responsible for the conclusions you draw when reading, even if the author provides you with false or misleading information.

*RIGHTS*

1. You have a right to all of the facts, though you may have to root them out for yourself.
2. You have a right to be exposed to contrasting points of view.
3. You have a right to ask questions, even if it annoys the instructor.
4. You have a right to your own opinion, even if it contradicts recognized authority.

*Source:* Reprinted with permission of R. Scott Baldwin and John Readence: International Reading Association.

**WRITE TO LEARN**

*On a separate sheet of paper, answer the following question: Which of the responsibilities delineated in Table 7.1 do you consider the most important in critical reading? Why?*

◆

## DIFFERENTIATING BETWEEN FACT AND OPINION

*Thank God, except at its one moment there's never any such thing as a bare fact. Ten minutes later, half an hour later, one's begun to gloze over the fact with a deposit of some sort.*

—ELIZABETH BOWEN

Is everything you read true? Can you trust experts? Do you accept as fact everything you see? Should you believe everything you hear?

P. T. Barnum is often thought to have said, "There's a sucker born every minute." Barnum owned a circus he described as "The Greatest Show on Earth." He often used exaggeration and deception to create interest in his show. Logically he might have thought a sucker is born every minute. Thus, many people accept this as his spoken opinion. However, no record exists of Barnum making this statement. Indeed, the word *sucker* was not commonly used in this context in Barnum's day.

In a free country like ours, almost anything anyone thinks can be printed or said somewhere. Whether those thoughts begin as fact or not, distortions, or deposits, occur. You are responsible for determining if information is fact or opinion. You control whether you exist as a critical judge of information or just another sucker.

### Facts: The Truth, and Nothing but the Truth

Witnesses sworn in during trials promise to tell all the facts they know about a crime. Their opinions are immaterial, or not important. What the judge wants to hear are facts. Witnesses tell what they know to be true. They describe what they actually saw or heard. They cannot add to, subtract from, or change the facts in any way. It is the judge's job to determine how closely the witness sticks to the bare facts.

What is a bare fact? A fact is a statement of reality. For example, there are seven days in a week. That's a fact. Canada is north of the United States. That's also a fact. Facts also exist in the form of events

*"Of course, I swear to tell the truth. I'm as honest as a giraffe is long."*

known to have occurred. For instance, Columbus discovered America in 1492. The bombing of Pearl Harbor occurred on December 7, 1941. These are facts. Facts are truth.

When evaluating what you read, you act as a judge. You decide if what you read is fact. Facts are based on direct evidence or on actual observation or experience. They are called **primary sources.** These consist of original documents or first-person accounts of an event.

**Secondary sources** also provide facts. They interpret, evaluate, describe, or otherwise restate the work of primary sources. Because information may be lost in translation, primary sources are preferred.

Words telling about facts are descriptive. They give details but are not judgmental. They express absolutes. They represent concepts that can be generally agreed upon. Words like *dead, freezing,* and *wet* are examples of such words. Other words limit a statement of fact. They show the possibility of other options. Look at the difference between these two statements: "I make good grades." "At times, I make good grades." The words *at times* limit the truth of the first sentence. Words like *frequently, occasionally,* and *seldom* are examples of such words.

### WRITE TO LEARN

*On a separate sheet of paper, respond to the following: According to Elizabeth Bowen, facts last only one moment. What causes facts to be distorted? Give a practical example of this.*

**EXERCISE 7.1**

*Name ten words that describe but do not judge. Do not use any examples used in this chapter.*

**Example**

dead, dry, pregnant

1. ______________________ 6. ______________________

2. ______________________ 7. ______________________

3. ______________________ 8. ______________________

4. ______________________ 9. ______________________

5. ______________________ 10. ______________________

## Opinions: Qualitative Words

Like facts, opinions are also a form of truth. The difference between the two lies in whose reality is represented. Facts belong to all people. They are universally held. An opinion belongs to one person, you.

An opinion is what you think about a subject. It is a viewpoint, belief, or judgment. Opinions reflect attitudes or feelings. Words describing opinions are interpretive.

Remember **connotation?** That's your opinion of what a word means. Consider the word *pretty.* One person may think that a dress is pretty. Someone else might think it is not pretty. It depends on what you think—your opinion.

Objectivity refers to an authors' skill in reporting facts without including personal opinions, feelings, or beliefs. Inclusion of biased material undermines the validity and value of what you read.

Words expressing opinions are **qualitative.** They tell about the value of something. For example, a three-year-old child might think that 500 pennies (five dollars) is a large amount. That would be his opinion. However, to a millionaire, 500 pennies is small change. That would be her opinion.

Some examples of qualitative words are *cute, bad,* and *sour.* Some phrases indicate an opinion is forthcoming. These help you recognize opinion for what it is. Examples of such phrases are *in my opinion, I believe,* and *I think.*

**EXERCISE 7.2**

*Name ten words that express quality. Do not use any examples used in this chapter.*

**Example**

ugly, fat, difficult

1. ______________________ 2. ______________________

3. ______________________ 7. ______________________

4. ______________________ 8. ______________________

5. ______________________ 9. ______________________

6. ______________________ 10. ______________________

**EXERCISE 7.3**

*Distinguish between fact and opinion by placing an F before each phrase that is a fact and an O before each phrase that is an opinion.*

***Example***

__*F*__ the largest college in the state
__*O*__ a large campus

_______ **1.** a drab room

_______ **2.** cold weather

_______ **3.** 60 cycles per second

_______ **4.** the most popular candidate

_______ **5.** an overripe banana

_______ **6.** the best agency for the job

_______ **7.** 100 armed soldiers

_______ **8.** a liter of $H_2O$

_______ **9.** a sour taste

_______ **10.** the hottest day on record

_______ **11.** a foot-long hotdog

_______ **12.** black type on white paper

_______ **13.** 0° C

_______ **14.** a light copy

_______ **15.** a terrible smell

**EXERCISE 7.4**

*Read the following excerpt. Underline the facts and circle the opinions your find. Some sentences may contain both facts and opinions. As an example, the first two have been done for you.*

Even the (richest and most protected people on earth) are now feeling the effects of the population's growth. <u>This growth is taking place even in the United States and Canada,</u> where people have been acting responsibly and limiting family size. Immigrants escaping from overcrowding in their own countries account for at least half of the growth of our population. People feel the impact of population growth as stress from lack of space, more noise, more cars, more toxins, more crime, more illness, and simultaneously less peace, less quiet, less greenery, less oxygen, less clean air and water. They also experience the effects of population growth indirectly, in the scarcity of resources that once were common. The more people crowd into cities, the more land outside the cities is needed to produce for those people, but as the suburbs advance, less land is available—hence the rising costs of food, water, fuel, and other resources.

People in industrial societies often fear that to stop population growth would be to stop progress. This view assumes that growth and progress are the same thing, but they are not. Growth means only greater numbers; progress is intentional movement toward a goal. Further increases in population will drain the economy, not foster its growth, because rising numbers of people mean more people living in poverty. Progress toward meeting the basic needs of our present population could take place better without growth. People who must scramble for food and water have no energy to strive for higher purposes. In fact, growth must stop for real progress to continue; people must limit their numbers.

*Source:* Reprinted with permission from *Essential Life Choices* by Whitney and Sizer. 

## Expert Opinion

The background of the person giving an opinion affects the value of the opinion. Anyone can give an opinion, but some are **expert opinions.** Your dentist might say, "This is a good car." An auto mechanic might say, "This is a good car." Which person would you trust to know more about cars?

An expert opinion depends on many factors. In reading, you judge an author's educational and professional backgrounds. Often an author's background affects point of view, what is said about a topic, and the way in which facts are reported. You find background information about an author in the preliminary or concluding statements of an article or a book. A biographical dictionary or an encyclopedia also contains such information. You also gain this knowledge through discussions with others in the field. You judge where the author works and the reputation of that institution.

You also judge the reputation of the author. However, this works both as an advantage and a disadvantage. Sometimes authors who are well-known authorities in one field write below their standards in another. As a critical reader, you need to know the difference.

Sometimes information about the author's credentials is missing. You then need another way to judge the information. For example, suppose an article in *Today's Science* compares the incidence of cancer in America with that of France. The author, who is unknown to you, concludes that the air in France is cleaner than that in America, and that this keeps the French in better health. Since you have no information about the author's background, you cannot evaluate the author's qualifications or bias. In this case, you judge the standards and credibility of the journal containing the article.

### WRITE TO LEARN

*On a separate sheet of paper, respond to the following: In your American history class, a graduate student in history guest lectures. She asserts that Grover Cleveland was America's most effective president. Do you consider hers an expert opinion? Justify your answer.*

### EXERCISE 7.5

*Distinguish among facts, opinions, and expert opinions using the following key: F—facts, O—opinions, and X—expert opinions.*

**Example**

__*F*__ According to registration figures, more students have enrolled part-time than ever before.

_______ **1.** According to last term's grades, more people failed Dr. Jimenez's class than any other person in the department.

_______ **2.** According to a periodic table of the elements, carbon has an atomic weight greater than that of hydrogen.

_______ **3.** According to last year's quarterback in the Superbowl game, the sport of football has its ups and downs.

_______ **4.** According to the person who sits behind me in English, our instructor is the best poet on campus.

_______ **5.** According to my major professor, four courses in physical education are required for graduation.

_______ **6.** According to our state senator, athletics have no place in higher education.

_______ **7.** According to an editorial in our campus newspaper, most students fail to study adequately.

_______ **8.** According to the dean of our department, campus orientation activities are better than ever.

_______ **9.** According to six English majors, English 2031 is the easiest course in the program.

_______ **10.** According to the doctors at the student health clinic, I have the flu.

◆

# RECOGNIZING PROPAGANDA

*Advertisements are now so numerous that they are very negligently perused, and it is therefore become necessary to gain attention by magnificence of promises, and by eloquences sometimes sublime and sometimes pathetic.*

—SAMUEL JOHNSON (1758)

Advertisements have been around a long time. The magnificent promises and sublime and pathetic words they use to sway our minds are called propaganda. Propaganda is a form of persuasion. It is used to change or sway opinions. Propaganda is one-sided, telling only one side of an issue to make you believe that side is the right one. It is used to try to make you think a certain way or believe or desire a certain thing.

Politicians often use propaganda to convince voters. Advertisers also use propaganda to try to convince you to buy their products. Authors slant the meaning of text, or **bias** it, through propaganda. This leads you to form opinions that conform to those held by the author.

Bias is hard to identify in a text unless you know the subject or the author's background. For example, suppose an author who has published several books on psychology states, "Freud was the greatest psychologist of modern times. Everyone knows about him. A student's greatest learning experience is reading about Freud." Clearly, the statement contains bias, the author's beliefs about the subject. While this author is qualified to discuss Freud, the information provided about Freud is biased.

You can be wary of the effect of propaganda by knowing what it is. Common types of propaganda include **image advertising, bandwagoning, testimonial, plain folks, name calling,** and **weasel words** (see Figure 7.1). Because propaganda is more obvious in advertising, it is easier to recognize it there. However, once you know what to look for, you also can find propaganda fairly easily in written work.

## Image Advertising

In image advertising, a person, product, or concept is associated with certain people, places, sounds, activities, or symbols. This association creates a mental picture. The new concept is tied to feelings about the old concept. The people who sell the product are actors. They are paid to endorse a product. However, their opinions are not expert ones.

**FIGURE 7.1**
**Examples of Propaganda**

Image Advertising

***Examples***

Fine wines and rich people; cars and western or outdoor settings; politicians and American symbols
Your examples:

___

___

___

Bandwagoning

***Examples***

Soft drink advertisements; generalizations, such as, "*Everybody* in college is a genius"
Your examples:

___

___

___

Testimonial

***Examples***

Bill Cosby and pudding; Jerry Lewis and muscular dystrophy
Your examples:

___

___

___

Plain Folks

***Examples***

Politicians shaking hands and kissing babies; a young woman advertising wart remover;
Your examples:

___

___

___

***FIGURE 7.1***
***Continued***

Name Calling

***Examples***

One soft drink challenging another in a taste test; aspirin or cold remedies (eight of these, four of these, or one of ours); competitions between hamburger chains
Your examples:

______________________________

______________________________

______________________________

Weasel Words

***Examples***

"Leave dishes *virtually* spotless"; Cleans your teeth as white as *they* can be"; politicians promise not to ask for *unneeded* taxes; *almost* no poisons were found in the water supply
Your examples:

______________________________

______________________________

______________________________

## Bandwagoning

In bandwagoning, the theme is "join the crowd." If you, as a child, said, "Everyone buys hightop tennis shoes. I want some, too," then you used this technique to convince your parents to let you buy what you wanted. You, like others who use bandwagoning, implied that you would be left out by not being like everyone else. Bandwagoning is a form of peer pressure. Because you conform to the wishes or beliefs of the group, bandwagoning tends to suppress individualism.

## Testimonial

In a testimonial, a famous person or authority on the subject says a product, person, or idea is good. A testimonial suggests that if a famous person likes it, you should too. You rarely see famous people selling soap or mouthwash. Because they are famous, you don't really think they need those kinds of things. Besides, it might be bad for their images. Celebrities also give testimonials for good causes, such as campaigns against drug abuse and for medical research.

### Plain Folks

When plain folks is used in advertising, people seem to be average and ordinary. The idea is to make you feel like a friend or neighbor endorses a product. This is almost the opposite of testimonial. This ad wants you to trust the judgment of an average person. This type is also used to show a person in authority is really "one of the gang."

### Name Calling

An old English proverb goes, "Sticks and stones will break my bones, but names will never hurt me." Unfortunately, this is not true in advertising. **Name calling** is a form of propaganda that forms unfair comparisions.

In name calling, a product or cause is made to appear better in relation to a competing product or cause. This is accomplished by the use of unpopular or unflattering language about the competition. You are led to believe that one product or cause is superior to another. Name calling can be either obvious or subtle. Often, advertisers use obvious name-calling techniques while politicians use these techniques more indirectly. As a knowledgeable person, you need to recognize both.

### Weasel Words

Weasels are animals with keen sight and smell that are known for their quickness and slyness. Because of these characteristics, one form of propaganda involves the use of weasel words. These are evasive words that lack exact meanings. Their meanings cannot be pinned down. Implications are made but promises are not assured. Like the animal they are named for, weasel words leave the speaker with a quick and sly way out. As Theodore Roosevelt said, "When a weasel sucks eggs, the meat is sucked out of the egg. If you use a 'weasel word' after another there is nothing left over."

**EXERCISE 7.6**

*Reread the excerpt in exercise 7.4 and look for examples of bias. Then answer the following questions.*

1. What two views do the authors express about people living in the United States and Canada?

______________________________

______________________________

______________________________

2. In contrast, how do you think the authors feel about people living in other countries?

3. What kind of picture do the authors paint of city life?

4. What words and phrases do the authors use that lead you to think of life as a "rat race"?

5. What do the authors lead you to believe about parents who choose to have large families?

**WRITE TO LEARN**

*On a separate sheet of paper, respond to the following: You are the advertising manager of a company that manufactures a new kind of school notebook. Devise a television advertising campaign for your product. Justify the type of propaganda technique you decide to use.*

## DETERMINING RELEVANCY

**Relevancy** means separating what is important from what is unimportant. Relevancy, like opinion, is in the eye of the beholder. What is relevant to one person may or may not be relevant to another. In addition, what is relevant in one situation may or may not be relevant in another.

*"No, Albert, Physics is* not *relative to Geography."*

Anderson and Pichert (1978) conducted a research study in which they examined the effect of point of view on recall. Subjects read a passage about what two boys did at one boy's home while playing hooky from school. Some readers were asked to read as if they were burglars. Others were asked to read as if they were home buyers. A third group read from no particular viewpoint. Researchers found that the reader's point of view affected what was relevant and later recalled. For example, those readers who read as burglars were more likely to recall where money was kept. That's what was relevant to them. Readers who read as home buyers recalled more about the house's landscape. That's what was relevant to them. Relevancy, then, depends on your point of view or your purpose for reading.

## EXERCISE 7.7

♦ *Mark the relevant facts for each statement.*

***Example***

Choosing a career involves many factors

_______**a.** business stationery

_______**b.** your interests

_______**c.** the pay scale

_______**d.** education required

_______**e.** experience required

1. Various factors should be thought of when choosing a course.

_______a. prerequisite courses

_______b. your curriculum

_______c. your interests

_______d. time of the class

_______e. place of birth

2. Buying a house is an important decision.

_______a. cost

_______b. color of house

_______c. size of house

_______d. location of house

_______e. size of fireplace

3. Voting for a political candidate must be considered carefully.

_______a. economic policy of candidate

_______b. sex of candidate

_______c. the candidate's personal finances

_______d. candidate's ability

_______e. candidate's integrity

4. Medical care is important.

_______a. personality of receptionist

_______b. qualified doctors

_______c. low office rent

_______d. hospital facilities

_______e. use of new techniques

5. It's often hard to choose safe toys for small children.

_______a. breakability

_______b. color

_______c. buttons that come off

_______d. use of electricity

_______e. washability

6. Choosing a spouse requires careful thought.

_______ a. compatibility

_______ b. same interests

_______ c. height

_______ d. eye color

_______ e. commitment to one another

7. Selection of the right pet is difficult.

_______ a. allergies

_______ b. size

_______ c. sex

_______ d. care required by pet

_______ e. license fees

8. Passing a course is hard work.

_______ a. studying

_______ b. attending intramural games

_______ c. taking notes

_______ d. reading the text

_______ e. using the right color of ink

9. Buying a car involves careful consideration.

_______ a. color

_______ b. gas mileage

_______ c. cost

_______ d. financing

_______ e. license plate

10. Reckless driving is hazardous.

_______ a. speeding tickets

_______ b. insurance rates

_______ c. jail

_______ d. speedometer limits

_______ e. accidents

**EXERCISE 7.8**

*List three relevant factors for each of the following perspectives.*

TOPIC: SELECTING A COLLEGE

**1.** Parents of a student

**a.** ________________________________________

**b.** ________________________________________

**c.** ________________________________________

**2.** College athlete

**a.** ________________________________________

**b.** ________________________________________

**c.** ________________________________________

**3.** Handicapped student

**a.** ________________________________________

**b.** ________________________________________

**c.** ________________________________________

**4.** Honors student

**a.** ________________________________________

**b.** ________________________________________

**c.** ________________________________________

**5.** Returning adult student

**a.** ________________________________________

**b.** ________________________________________

**c.** ________________________________________

**EXERCISE 7.9**

*After reading this passage, respond to the following statements.*

Houston was founded following the Texas battle for independence from Mexico in 1836. Two brothers from New York purchased 2,000 acres hoping to make Houston as great a city as New Orleans. It incorporated and became a town the following year. Houston takes its name from Sam Houston, a hero in the Battle of San Jacinto. Sam Houston was also the republic's first elected president. Houston served as the capital of the Republic of Texas for the next two years.

One hundred and fifty years passed. Houston grew from a pioneer town to become the largest city in Texas. It is also our country's fourth largest city. More than 1.5 million people make it their home. The Houston metropolitan area covers over 7,000 square miles. Houston is located in Harris County in the southeast part of the state. It is the county seat of Harris County.

Houston's climate is a mild one. The average winter temperature is about 55 degrees. The average summer temperature is about 85 degrees. Houston receives almost fifty inches of rain each year.

Oil was found in southeast Texas at Spindletop in 1901. Houston connects with the Gulf of Mexico through the Houston Ship Channel. The ship canal was completed in 1914. The canal was opened by President Woodrow Wilson. The discovery of oil combined with the opening of the shop canal stimulated industrial growth.

Today, over 200 industries—oil, chemical, steel, and others—line the canal. More than 6,000 ships dock along the canal each year. Indeed, Houston is the third largest port in terms of total tonnage. It ranks second in its handling of foreign tonnage. As a result, many foreign banks have representative offices in Houston. Many nations also maintain consular offices there.

NASA's Lyndon B. Johnson Space Center makes its home in Houston. Thus, Houston serves as one of America's premier space-age headquarters. The Space Center has been the headquarters for astronaut training, equipment testing, and flight control for Skylab and space shuttle missions.

Houston's Texas Medical Center is a major health complex. It serves the needs of the city, state, and region. It houses many medical research groups as well as providing health care. During the 1970s numerous earth and physical scientists, as well as professionals in the life sciences, relocated in Houston.

Houston's benefits attract both tourists and hometown residents. The Astros baseball team and the Oilers football team are located there. Numerous high schools and universities also provide avenues of entertainment. Houston is home to a symphony orchestra, opera company, and many other musical groups. Museums, art galleries, and parks complete Houston's cultural atmosphere. The Astrodome, Astroworld, and the battleship *Texas* provide both amusement and education for all.

**1.** You are a historian interested in writing about Texas history before 1900. List three relevant facts you could include in your account.

**a.** ______________________________

**b.** ______________________________

**c.** ______________________________

**2.** You are retired and planning to move. List three relevant facts that might encourage you to locate in Houston and the rationale for including each one.

**a.** ______________________________

**b.** ______________________________

**c.** ______________________________

3. You have just graduated with a degree in engineering. List three relevant facts that might encourage you to apply for jobs in Houston.

   a. ______________________________

   b. ______________________________

   c. ______________________________

4. You are planning a vacation to Houston. List three attractions you might visit or activities you might pursue.

   a. ______________________________

   b. ______________________________

   c. ______________________________

5. You are a native of Spain and are interested in opening a branch of your company in Houston. What relevant facts might encourage you to pursue this endeavor?

   a. ______________________________

   b. ______________________________

   c. ______________________________

6. You like small towns and wide-open spaces. What relevant facts might discourage you from moving to Houston?

   a. ______________________________

   b. ______________________________

   c. ______________________________

7. You are studying pollution and its effects on the environment. List three relevant facts about Houston that are indicators of possible pollution problems.

   a. ______________________________

   b. ______________________________

   c. ______________________________

8. You have just received a degree in medical technology. List three factors that might encourage you to apply for a job in Houston.

   a. ______________________________

   b. ______________________________

   c. ______________________________

9. You enjoy sports. What relevant facts about Houston would help you pursue this hobby?

   a. ______________________________

   b. ______________________________

   c. ______________________________

10. You are a music major with a minor in theater. What three relevant facts about Houston might encourage you in this pursuit?

   a. ______________________________

   b. ______________________________

   c. ______________________________

◆

## PURPOSES OF PASSAGES AND AUTHORS' CHOICE OF WORDS

Every semester college instructors ask the routine question: "Why did you come to college? Traditionally, the answers are almost as clichéd as the question. But, once a student answered, "I came to be went with—but I ain't yet." Everyone has a purpose, a goal they mean to achieve. Authors are not different. They, too, write with an objective in mind. They are unlike poets, artists, or composers who create for the joy of it. Instead, authors write to influence your understanding, emotions, beliefs, or actions.

Because writing is purposeful, the author seeks to obtain a desired response from you. For example, if an author writes to inform, then you learn information you have not known before. If an author writes to persuade, then your belief sways in that direction. If an author writes to entertain, you, after reading, feel amused or interested. These, then, comprise the three purposes authors have when writing. They are informing, persuading, and entertaining.

With the purpose foremost in mind, an author sometimes mixes the three. For example, an author might add humor to informative writing. Or, an author might support a persuasive paper with information. Because texts usually contain humorous passages to capture your interest, only the persuasive and informative types will be discussed in this section.

Whatever the goal, an author choose words carefully. This choice is critical because words form the means by which a message is conveyed. Choosing a wrong word can end in a reader's being confused or alienated. This holds true particularly when you realize words have more than one meaning. For example, consider the following sentence, "Thomas Edison was a *religious* worker." Does this mean he worked hard? Or, does it mean he was a church worker? Examine the same sentence using either *diligent* or *devout*. With the choice of one of these words, meaning is clearer. When misunderstandings are lessened, an author's purpose is more likely to be achieved.

## Informational Passages

Informational passages seek to educate. Usually, an author tries to present material in a way that readers will easily understand. Such writing often consists of explanations, analyses, descriptions, demonstrations, and definitions. It also includes examples, statistics, comparisons, contrasts, and expert opinions. Although it is most often found in textbooks, newspapers and magazines also include informative writing.

## Persuasive Passages

An author writes a persuasive passage to bring about a change in either your opinion(s) or your behavior(s). Authors change your opinion by convincing you to agree with what they think. Such writing seeks to make you believe their points of view. No action is required on your part. For example, an author might try to convince you that conserving resources is necessary for survival. Authors try to change your behavior in two ways. First, they change your beliefs. Then, they ask for a promise of action on your part. For example, an author might convince you that conservation is necessary. Then, you'd be asked to recycle waste products in order to conserve resources.

Persuasive writing is found in educational, cultural, or historical documents. Like informative writing, it includes examples, statistics, comparisons, contrasts, and expert opinions.

### EXERCISE 7.10

*Decide whether the purpose of the passage is to inform (I)* or persuade *(P)*. Write the letter of your response on the blank next to the paragraph. Be ready to justify your choice.

**Example**

___P___ Employee education is the responsibility of the employee, not of the organization. An employee needs to take special education classes, graduate from high school and college, and have a variety of learning experiences that will help him or her to be able to deal more effectively with the organization or life generally. Today, the general attitude seems to be shifting from job training to employee education. Nadler feels we will see a shift from training people in specific skills to training them to be prepared for a general place in an organization that is different from their present position. As the employee gains wider experience, more maturity and understanding, and better appreciation for life and people, she/he has greater opportunities for advancement. To become educated, as well as trained, should be a goal for every member of society.



**1.** _______ To truly create a motivational climate, there must be openness between managers and subordinates. Each must have a clear understanding of both the organization's goals and, to the degree possible, the individual employee's goals. The manager must be flexible, creative, and receptive to new ideas from his or her subordinates. The only way this can be conveyed is through effective communication and positive interpersonal relationships.

**2.** _______ One possible response to a blocked need is simply to cope with it. Coping means that people struggle or contend with the problem, often by trial and error, until they achieve some degree of satisfaction. During the recent turbulent years of monetary inflation, all of have learned to cope to some extent with rapidly increasing prices. Many of us have switched to lower-cost meats, returned to heating with firewood, and reduced our consumption of gasoline. Although these changes are often less enjoyable than our preinflation lifestyle, we are responding to a blockage caused by a loss of purchasing power by coping.

**3.** _______ Organizations exist for the purpose of accomplishing things that cannot be done by individuals working alone. From the day that the earliest cave dweller discovered that he or she could not move a large boulder alone but needed to enlist the help of others, people have organized efforts. As the tasks at hand became more and more complicated, the organization structure, too, became more complex. Today, with enormous tasks such as building elaborate missile systems, huge nuclear power generators, expansive water conservation systems, and ambitious space exploration programs, the need for sophisticated organizations is greater than ever.

**4.** _______ Is there an ideal way to build an organization? The search for that elusive butterfly, "the one best way," has been going on for some time. Nevertheless, it continues to be elusive and will probably never be found. Organizational complexity and differences in organization goals, tasks, member characteristics, and the like make any pat formula suspect. A more appropriate question may be "What can a manager do to understand the positive and negative characteristics of organizational design?"

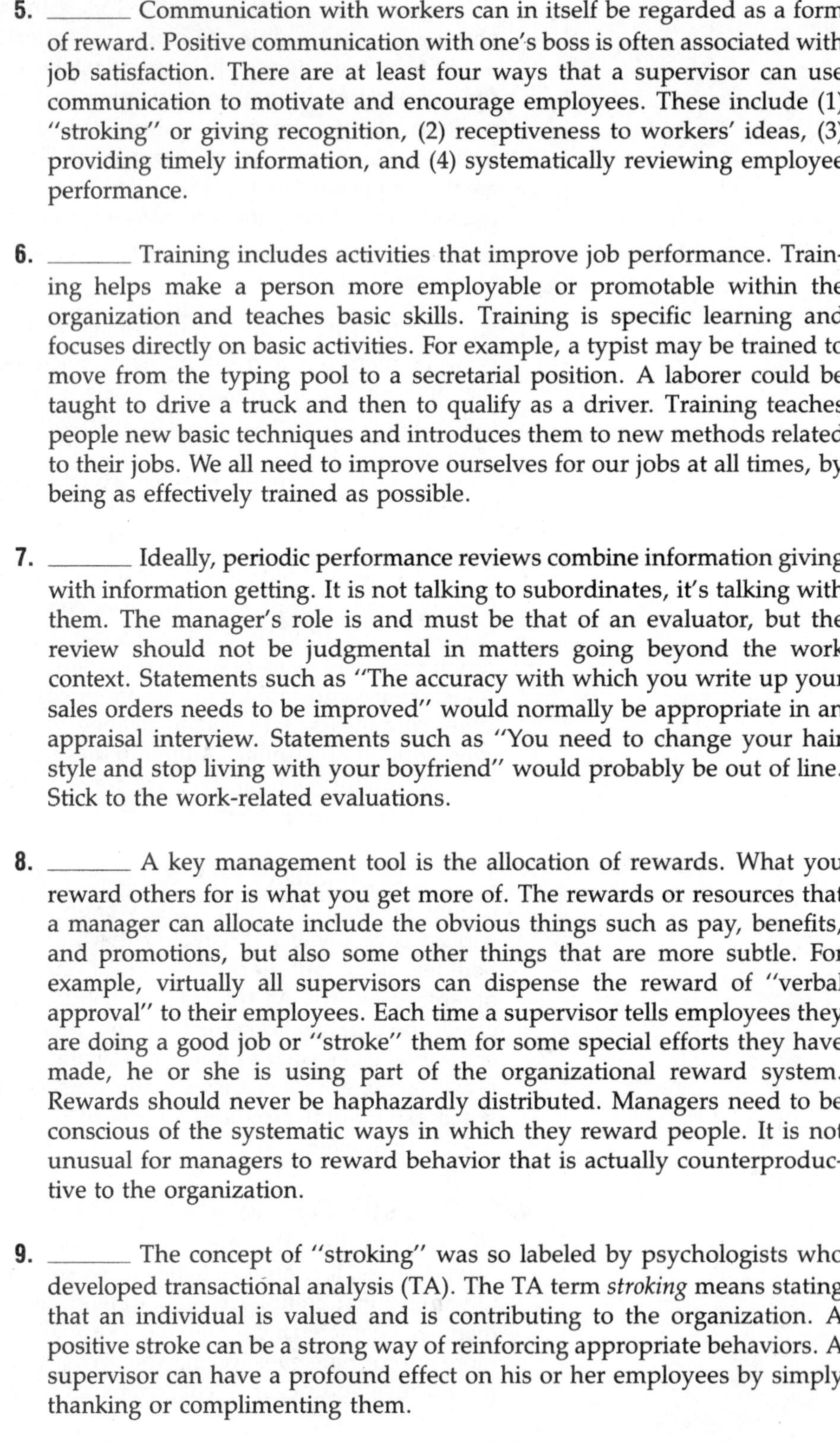

5. ______ Communication with workers can in itself be regarded as a form of reward. Positive communication with one's boss is often associated with job satisfaction. There are at least four ways that a supervisor can use communication to motivate and encourage employees. These include (1) "stroking" or giving recognition, (2) receptiveness to workers' ideas, (3) providing timely information, and (4) systematically reviewing employee performance.

6. ______ Training includes activities that improve job performance. Training helps make a person more employable or promotable within the organization and teaches basic skills. Training is specific learning and focuses directly on basic activities. For example, a typist may be trained to move from the typing pool to a secretarial position. A laborer could be taught to drive a truck and then to qualify as a driver. Training teaches people new basic techniques and introduces them to new methods related to their jobs. We all need to improve ourselves for our jobs at all times, by being as effectively trained as possible.

7. ______ Ideally, periodic performance reviews combine information giving with information getting. It is not talking to subordinates, it's talking with them. The manager's role is and must be that of an evaluator, but the review should not be judgmental in matters going beyond the work context. Statements such as "The accuracy with which you write up your sales orders needs to be improved" would normally be appropriate in an appraisal interview. Statements such as "You need to change your hair style and stop living with your boyfriend" would probably be out of line. Stick to the work-related evaluations.

8. ______ A key management tool is the allocation of rewards. What you reward others for is what you get more of. The rewards or resources that a manager can allocate include the obvious things such as pay, benefits, and promotions, but also some other things that are more subtle. For example, virtually all supervisors can dispense the reward of "verbal approval" to their employees. Each time a supervisor tells employees they are doing a good job or "stroke" them for some special efforts they have made, he or she is using part of the organizational reward system. Rewards should never be haphazardly distributed. Managers need to be conscious of the systematic ways in which they reward people. It is not unusual for managers to reward behavior that is actually counterproductive to the organization.

9. ______ The concept of "stroking" was so labeled by psychologists who developed transactional analysis (TA). The TA term *stroking* means stating that an individual is valued and is contributing to the organization. A positive stroke can be a strong way of reinforcing appropriate behaviors. A supervisor can have a profound effect on his or her employees by simply thanking or complimenting them.

**10.** _______ Various individuals within organizations are affected by the stresses of corporate life. Corporate mismanagement principally concerns people who serve in key positions and who must make decisions. As they make ineffective decisions, they use ineffective management techniques, they waste time, or they see income falling or new products failing, they tend to be filled with stress. Everyone fears for his or her credibility and position. No one wants to fail. The level of stress tends to increase as employees progress up the organizational ladder.



◆

## DRAWING CONCLUSIONS

This bizarre story was first told to me by a retired Chicago broadcasting executive, who now lives on Washington Island in Wisconsin.

He said: "I was having dinner with this friend of mine named Lee, who has a vacation home up here.

"Lee is an avid fisherman and he likes to go out on Lake Michigan and catch those big salmon.

"When he goes back to Chicago, he takes one of the salmon with him, and he has a chef at his country club fix it up real nice, with all the trimmings, and he has some friends over for dinner.

"Well the last time he did this, he had about 18 people over to his home.

"While the guests were gathering in the living room, Lee's wife went into the kitchen and was horrified to see that the cat was up on the table nibbling on the fish.

"She grabbed the cat and threw him out the back door. Then she went and got Lee and showed him what the cat had done.

"Lee said there was no problem, because the cat had only nibbled a little bit of it. An inch or two.

"He just flipped the fish over, rearranged the vegetable garnish, and went on with the dinner.

"Well, at about 9 o'clock, one of the guests had to leave, so Lee went out to move a car in the driveway.

"But when he went outside, what does he find but his cat, lying there dead as a doornail.

"Lee took one look at the dead and cat and he went to the phone and called his doctor and told him what had happened, about the cat eating the salmon.

"The doctor told him: 'Get all your guests—and I mean all of them—over to the hospital in 20 minutes and I'll pump out all their stomachs.'

"So they all went to the hospital. You can imagine how some of them reacted. They were pretty mad.

"And they were even madder after they got their stomachs pumped out. That's not a pleasant experience.

"After it was done, Lee went home. He was feeling pretty low, having all those friends mad at him.

"Just as he was getting out of his car, his neighbor walked up to him and said: 'Lee, I've been trying to reach you to tell you how sorry I am.'

"Lee said: 'Sorry for what?'

"The neighbor said: 'For killing your cat. It was me. I accidentally backed my car over your cat earlier this evening and I'm afraid it's dead.'

"So the salmon wasn't tainted at all. And isn't that the darndest story you ever heard."

*Source:* Mike Royko, "Fisherman Uses a Whopper as Bait." Reprinted by permission of Tribune Media Services.

For better or for worse, your last responsibility as a critical reader is for the **conclusions** you draw, even if the author provides you with false, incomplete, or misleading information. The preceding story helps you realize it's not always easy to draw the right conclusion. Conclusions are based on both **implied** (hinted) and **literal** (stated) information.

Much of the reading you do is based on literal information or specific facts. The answer to a literal question is found in the text. You can physically point to the word or phrase that answers that question. Answers to literal questions are the stated **details** of a text.

Inferred information is not found directly in the text. You must make mental connections to determine the meaning implied by the author. The word, phrase, or sentence that answers the question cannot be found. This answer may be a detail or a main idea. (See Chapter 6 for more information about implied main ideas.) **Inferences** and **implications** relate to drawing conclusions. A reader or listener makes inferences based on information implied by a speaker or author.

## Using Background Knowledge to Make Inferences

You may not understand the above cartoon unless you know Descartes' philosophy of life. It states "I think, therefore I am." In the cartoon, since Descartes "thinks not," he no longer exists. Without this connection, the cartoon loses meaning. Such connections form the basis of understanding. As Robert Frost said, "All thought is a feat of association: having what's in front of you bring up something in your mind that you almost didn't know you knew." The more associations you make, the easier you draw conclusions.

In writing, an author assumes you have a certain amount of **background knowledge.** This is what you know about the world, your

"And, the magic words are, 'I think not.' "

personal store of information. It is part of your framework for a given topic.

You develop background knowledge through learning. However, it is much more than the knowledge you gain from formal schooling. It is the information you learn from living. You gain background knowledge by having various experiences.

However, there are many things you will never be able to experience. Probably you will never go to the moon, be president, or live in another country. There are things you might never want to experience. These might include fighting a war, wrecking a car, or losing an election. All these experiences can be had vicariously. That means you don't actually have the experiences, but you learn about them as if you had.

You learn vicariously in many ways. You see movies or look at pictures. You talk to people who have actually had the experiences. You read about the experiences. All of these ways help you increase your own background knowledge

### WRITE TO LEARN

*On a separate sheet of paper, respond to the following: One of your classmates missed yesterday's lecture. Explain how people acquire information vicariously. Then provide several examples to clarify your explanation.*

**EXERCISE 7.11**

*Cartoons require you to use background knowledge to draw conclusions. For each of the following cartoons, answer the accompanying questions.*

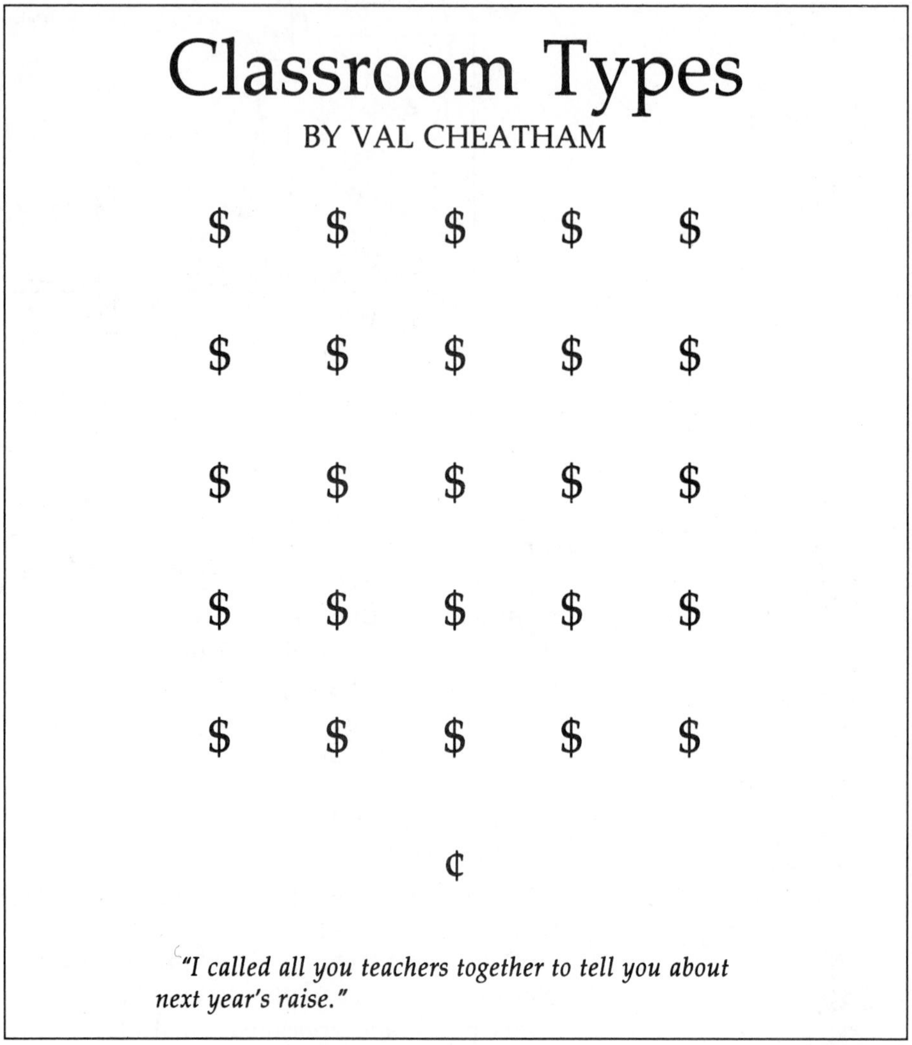

*Source:* Reprinted by permission of Val R. Cheatham.

**1.** What is happening? ______________________________

______________________________

**2.** How do you know? ______________________________

______________________________

**3.** Who is speaking? How do you know? ______________________________

______________________________

4. What are $? Why was that symbol used?

5. Who is ¢? Why was that symbol used?

6. Where do you think this meeting takes place? Why?

*Source:* Reprinted by permission of George Abbott.

1. What is happening?

2. How do you know?

3. Who are the characters? How do you know?

4. If you could create dialogue for the characters, what would they say? Why?

**5.** Where does this scene take place? How do you know?__________

________________________________________

**6.** What do you think happened before this meeting?__________

________________________________________

## Making Valid Inferences

Sometime the right conclusion will be easy to make. Sometimes it will be hard. Sometimes, like Lee in the fish story, you will consider all the facts, both stated and hinted, and still reach the wrong conclusion. Drawing conclusions improves with practice. Using the knowledge you have and thinking actively helps you draw valid conclusions. Three types of conclusions are possible. They include **logical inferences, assumptions,** and **non sequiturs.**

A logical inference is a conclusion that cannot be avoided. Once you consider the stated facts, you can infer nothing else. This inference is somewhat like a theory in geometry that says, "If $a = b$ and $b = c$, then $a = c$."

A second type of inference is an assumption. This conclusion is based on given facts and your background knowledge. It is the most common type of conclusion. Such an inference probably will be true, but it also could be false.

Non sequiturs are the third type of conclusion. Non sequiturs are not supported by fact or do not follow from the given evidence. Indeed, they are inferences that make no sense.

**EXERCISE 7.12**

◆ *Use the following information to make logical inferences.*

***Example***

All dogs have four legs. Fido is a dog. Fido has four legs.

*Fido: has four legs.*

1. Ted is taller than Joe. Joe is taller than Larry, Bill, and Calvin. Calvin is shorter than both Larry and Bill. Albert is taller than Joe and Ted.

   *Albert:* ____________________

2. The sum of the three angles in a triangle is 180 degrees. Angle *A* is 90 degrees and angle C is 30 degrees.

   *Angle B:* ____________________

3. Kaylene is older than Dora, who is older than Alice. Alice and Carey are twins. Alice was born at 6:00 a.m. and Carey was born at 6:08 a.m.

   *Carey:* ____________________

4. John is Tony's cousin. Tony is Hank's nephew. How are Hank and John related?

   *Hank:* ____________________

5. Jim wants to go to the movie. He catches the "B" line bus which is scheduled to arrive 10 minutes before the movie is to start. The bus gets caught in a traffic jam for one-quarter hour.

   *Jim:* ____________________

6. Roger has more programming experience than Raylene, who has more experience than Lars. Will has the same amount of experience as Chuck and Raylene. Larry has less experience than Lars.

   *Lars:* ____________________

7. Widget worms eat only citrus fruits. Ms. Hjelmer bought apples, oranges, grapes, and bananas at the grocery store to make a fruit salad for dinner. The widget worms devoured the citrus fruit while she was at her afternoon neighborhood meeting.

   *The fruit salad:* ____________________

8. Ellis is a better Scrabble player than Ivy. Ivy is not quite as good as Holly and Sherry, who play equally well, and both are not as good as Ellis. Kathy is just slightly better than Ivy.

   *Ivy:* ______________________________

9. Joe is facing east and speaking with Enrico, who is directly facing Joe. Enrico is squinting because the sun is shining directly in his eyes. What time of day is it?

   *The time:* ______________________________

10. Jenny is slower than Katrina but faster than Rachel. Katrina is slower than Joy but faster than Jenny.

   *Joy:* ______________________________

### EXERCISE 7.13

*Read each paragraph and answer the questions below.*

1. To help a person who is choking, first ask this critical question: "Can you make any sound at all?" If the victim makes a sound, relax. You have time to continue with your questioning to see what you can do to help; you are not going to have to make a quick decision. But whatever you do; don't hit him on the back. If you do, the particle may become lodged more firmly in his air passage.

   *Source:* Reprinted with permission from *Understanding Nutrition* 2/E by Whitney and Hamilton. 

   a. Why can you relax if a choking victim can make a sound? ______

   ______________________________

2. Some people believe there are two kinds of body fat: regular fat and "cellulite." Cellulite is supposed to be a hard and lumpy fat that yields to being "bunked up" only if it is first broken up by methods like the massage or the machine typical of the health spa. The notion that there is such a thing as cellulite received wide publicity with the publication of a book by a certain Madam R of Paris, which sold widely during the 1970s. The American Medical Association reviewed the evidence on cellulite (there was none) and concluded that cellulite was a hoax.

   *Source:* Reprinted with permission from *Understanding Nutrition* 2/E by Whitney and Hamilton. 

   a. How many kinds of body fat are there?______________________________

   ______________________________

   b. Why is the first mention of cellulite in quotation marks?______

   ______________________________

**c.** What is the difference between regular fat and cellulite?______

______

**d.** What is the writer's opinion of Madam R?______

______

**3.** As with murder, a society may also have different attitudes about sex at different times. Kissing and intercourse before marriage were viewed differently during the colonial era than today. Kissing in public was considered unacceptable behavior. One historian recorded the event of a Captain Kemble who, returning from a long sea voyage, kissed his lady as he stepped on shore. As a result, he "was promptly closed in the stocks."

*Source:* Reprinted with with permission from *Human Sexuality: The Search for Understanding* by Knox. 

**a.** What is the purpose of stocks?______

______

**b.** How have society's views toward murder changed?______

______

**4.** Some doctors prescribe amphetamines ("speed") to help with weight loss (the best known are dexedrine and benzedrine). These reduce appetite—but only temporarily. Typically the appetite returns to normal after a week or two, the lost weight is regained, and the user has the problem of trying to off the drug without gaining more weight.

*Source:* Reprinted with permission from *Understanding Nutrition* 2/E by Whitney and Hamilton. 

**a.** Other than reducing appetite, how do amphetamines affect the human body?______

______

**5.** Food can lodge so securely in the trachea that all air is cut off. No sound can be made because the larynx is in the traceha and makes sounds only when air is pushed across it. This has happened often enough so that the event has been given a name—cafe coronary.

*Source:* Reprinted with permission from *Understanding Nutrition* 2/E by Whitney and Hamilton. 

**a.** Why is the event called *cafe coronary?*______

______

**b.** What is the common name for this event?______

______

6. People have varying needs to be recognized and valued by others and by themselves. We all like to receive "strokes" which say to us, "Your efforts are recognized, and you are regarded as a person of value." Work in organizations can often provide such esteem needs through the dispensing of organizational rewards. Even subtle rewards such as private offices, carpeting on the floor, or a more desirable location in the workroom can convey this recognition and sense of worth to an individual employee.

*Source:* Reprinted with permission from *Supervision* by Timm and Peterson. 

a. What are *strokes?* ____________________

____________________

7. The United States is moving away from sexual straightjackets, which assumed woman's natural place was at home while man's was out seeking fame and glory, to a broader participation of both parties. Today, more than half the American labor force is women. And a larger percentage of those women also function as mothers and homemakers in addition to their job responsibilities. The trend seems to be increasing, especially when economic difficulties make the two-paycheck family the norm rather than the exception.

*Source:* Reprinted with permission from *Supervision* by Timm and Peterson. 

a. What is meant by *sexual straightjackets?* ____________________

____________________

b. How did the term get its name? ____________________

____________________

c. What proportion of today's American labor force is male? ________

____________________

d. In today's society, are there more one-paycheck or two-paycheck families? ____________________

____________________

e. What are some ways in which men can participate more broadly in the family? ____________________

____________________

8. Paralanguage is the study of *how* something is said (not what is said) by the words that are used. Sarcasm is a good example of paralanguage. The young quarterback who is confronted by his coach after

he had tossed a pass to the opposite team that resulted in an interception and a touchdown could hear words such as "Way to go, Bill. That was the most beautiful pass I have ever seen anyone throw!"

*Source:* Reprinted with permission from *People at Work* by Timm and Peterson. 

**a.** How does the coach really feel about Bill's pass?______________

______________________________________________

**b.** How does Bill fee about his pass?______________________

______________________________________________

**9.** Americans recognize that we are a diverse culture. This awareness is evident in our entertainment (which, many contend, reflects our self-perception as a nation). A few years ago it would have been considered the "kiss of death" to use minority actors in many television programs, but today many top-rated programs regularly bring people of different races and backgrounds into our living rooms. It's becoming easier to recognize common *human* similarities. And to reduce unrealistic and unproductive stereotypes.

*Source:* Reprinted with permission from *People at Work* by Timm and Peterson. 

**a.** What is a *"kiss of death?"*______________________________

______________________________________________

**b.** Where do you think this term originated?_________________

______________________________________________

**c.** In sentence 1, to whom does *we* refer?____________________

______________________________________________

**10.** What messages do the physical attractiveness and body shape of others send to you? Study your own physical appearance and body shape, and analyze what you might be saying to others. Many aspects of physical attractiveness and body share are not covered in this section, such as body odor, freckles, moles, and beauty marks. All these have a major impact on one's effectiveness as a communicator.

*Source:* Reprinted with permission from *People at Work* by Timm and Peterson. 

**a.** How do freckles and beauty marks affect one's effectiveness as a communicator?______________________________

______________________________________________

**EXERCISE 7.14**

*Read each of the following passages. Place an X beside those conclusions that make sense. On the line after each statement, explain why you consider the statement to be a valid conclusion.*

***Example***

To pass Mr. Horn's course, a student must pass the final. Mark attended class every day. He did his homework regularly. He made a B at midterm. On his final paper he made an A. Mark failed the final exam.

**a.** ______ Mark is a poor student.______

**b.** __X__ Mark did not pass the course. *To pass the course, one must pass the final. Mark failed the final.*

**c.** __X__ Mark is a diligent student. *Went to class, did homework, made As & Bs.*

**d.** ______ Mr. Horn doesn't like Mark.______

**e.** ______ Mark is lazy.______

**1.** What a day! The slick streets had almost caused Katrina to have an accident. She had forgotten to bring an umbrella. Then Katrina dropped her books in a puddle. When she got back to her car, she found her lights had been on all day. The car battery was dead.

**a.** ______ Katrina's car wouldn't start.______

______

**b.** ______ Katrina was late for class.______

______

**c.** ______ Katrina left her books in the puddle.______

______

**d.** ______ It rained that day.______

______

**e.** ______ She wrecked the car.______

______

**2.** Kareem was enrolled in a freshman physics class last term. On the first test, 67% of the students passed. Kareem failed the exam.

**a.** ______ Kareem dropped the course.______

______

**b.** ______ Kareem was in the lower 33%.______

______

**c.** ______ Kareem made an F on the exam.______

______

**d.** ______ Kareem hates physics.______________________________

______________________________

**e.** ______ Kareem is a freshman.______________________________

______________________________

**3.** Fran looked in the mirror. She had planned to wear her black dress to the dance. Now it was too tight. It was also too late to buy another dress. Fran couldn't understand what happened. The dress had fit her last year. Maybe she could borrow something from Megan.

**a.** ______ Megan is Fran's sister.______________________________

______________________________

**b.** ______ The dress is new.______________________________

______________________________

**c.** ______ Fran has gained weight.______________________________

______________________________

**d.** ______ The dress is out of style.______________________________

______________________________

**e.** ______ Fran and Megan are about the same size.______________

______________________________

**4.** Jill missed her speech class for the first time today. She went to Student Center before class. She ended up staying there longer than she had planned. But, a full house in poker doesn't come along every day.

**a.** ______ Jill is a compulsive gambler.______________________________

______________________________

**b.** ______ Jill has played cards before.______________________________

______________________________

**c.** ______ Jill hates speech class.______________________________

______________________________

**d.** ______ Jill won money in the card game.______________________________

______________________________

**e.** ______ It is not against the rules to play cards in the Student Center.______________________________

______________________________

______________________________

5. Manny had not felt well for several days. He had lunch at the restaurant. The meal consisted of ham, salad, peas, and a roll. Manny drank milk. After lunch, he felt ill. His head and stomach hurt. Manny went back to the doctor.

   a. ______ Manny is a hypochondriac.______

   b. ______ Manny is allergic to milk.______

   c. ______ Manny had had medical attention before.______

   d. ______ Manny had the flu.______

   e. ______ The ham was spoiled.______

6. Debouch State University has selective admissions. A student must have a high school grade point average of at least 3.0. DSU has an outstanding art department. My sister, Jen, is a student there.

   a. ______ Jen is an art major.______

   b. ______ Jen met all of DSU's admission requirements.______

   c. ______ Jen is the first in her family to go to college.______

   d. ______ Jen was the valedictorian of her high school class.______

   e. ______ Jen had a 3.0 or higher grade point average in high school.______

7. Anita met a guy at a bar last week. His name was Ted. They talked for several hours. Before the bar closed, Ted left. He told Anita he'd call her the next day. It's been five days since then. She hasn't heard from him yet. Anita has almost given up hope.

   a. ______ Ted will never call Anita.______

**b.** ______ Anita has bad breath. ______

**c.** ______ Anita still thinks Ted might call. ______

**d.** ______ Anita enjoyed talking to Ted. ______

**e.** ______ Anita left after Ted. ______

**8.** Juanita turned in a paper on the Civil War last term. She got an A on it. Now Jay, her boyfriend, is in a history class. He asked to see her paper. Jay made an A on his paper, too.

**a.** ______ Jay copied Juanita's paper. ______

**b.** ______ Jay and Juanita wrote papers on the same topic. ______

**c.** ______ Jay is taking the same class that Juanita took. ______

**d.** ______ Both Juanita and Jay appear to be good writers. ______

**e.** ______ Juanita and Jay have the same major. ______

**9.** Todd had a party last weekend. His friends came and stayed until 2:00 A.M. They played music and danced. Around midnight, the police came. Neighbors had complained about the noise.

**a.** ______ It was Todd's birthday. ______

**b.** ______ The music and the conversation at the party were loud. ______

**c.** ______ Todd's friends were rowdy. ______

**d.** ______ Todd's friends stayed until morning. ______

**e.** ______ Todd was arrested.________________________

________________________________________

**10.** Joe and his steady girlfriend Kai went out Friday night. Around 9:00 P.M., Kai said she had a headache. She asked Joe to take her home. When Joe left, Kai called Tom. "Come on over. Joe's gone," she said.

**a.** ______ Kai is two-timing Joe.________________________

________________________________________

**b.** ______ Kai was really ill.________________________

________________________________________

**c.** ______ Tom knows about Joe.________________________

________________________________________

**d.** ______ Kai's headache was a fake.________________________

________________________________________

**e.** ______ Joe knows about Tom.________________________

________________________________________

**EXERCISE 7.15**

*Read the passage below. Then answer the questions that follow it by drawing valid conclusions.*

### Fetal Therapy

As indicated in this chapter, many inborn errors influence fetal development. These errors can result in the death of the fetus or in serious lifelong handicaps. Many errors in human development are inherited. Others, such as fetal alcohol syndrome, are environmentally induced. In past decades, the pregnant woman had no way of knowing that her fetus was abnormal. However, during the last decade, it has become possible to monitor the development of the fetus by amniocentesis, X-rays, and ultrasound. These new techniques determine everything from vitamin deficiencies to serious anatomical deformities such as spina bifida.

When life-threatening defects are detected, the parents are given the option of abortion. Until recently, parents had only two choices: raise a deformed or mentally retarded child or abort it. In the next decade, some parents will have a third choice: fetal therapy to correct the defect so the child will be normal. It is estimated that about 3 percent of all children in the United States are born with birth defects. Fetal therapy should drastically reduce this percentage.

The idea of such therapy is not new. Many obstetricians and pediatricians have wanted to treat children before birth. The first fetus to be successfully treated while still in its mother's womb had an inherited form of vitamin $B_{12}$ deficiency. Once the defect was detected, massive injections of vitamin $B_{12}$ were given to the mother. The vitamin passed through the placenta and cured the deficiency in the fetus. The next incident was similar: an inherited deficiency in biotin (another vitamin) metabolism. Again, the mother was given the vitamin, which reached the fetus via the placenta.

In the next decade, many chemical errors, ranging from enzyme to nutrient to hormone deficiencies, will probably be corrected in this fashion. Drugs as well as vitamins may be administered to treat fetuses suffering from infections and other diseases. If the need is for compounds that do not cross the placenta barrier, then injection could be made through the mother's abdominal wall into the amniotic fluid. The fetus could then absorb or even swallow the substances.

The first surgical procedure done on a fetus involved the removal of a block in the urethra. This condition is usually fatal shortly after birth because the blockage is not normally detected in newborns. This particular fetus was a male twin. Surgeons inserted a small tube (catheter) through the abdomen of the mother and into the opening of the blocked urethra at the tip of the penis. They then pushed the catheter to the bladder, opening the blockage. The urine drained through the catheter into the amniotic fluid until the birth.

Recently, a fetus was moved part way out of its mother's womb so surgeons could correct a kidney problem. After the therapy, the fetus was placed back in the womb.

The fetal therapies mentioned here are pioneering efforts to correct problems of development before it is too late. Many experiments are being conducted with animals to determine the limits of surgical manipulation of fetuses. For example, experiments demonstrated that it was possible to insert a valve in the brain of a monekey fetus while the fetus was still in the mother's womb. This was first done on a human fetus in 1981. The fetus suffered from hydrocephalus (water on the brain). In the United States, nearly five thousand human infants are born each year with hydrocephalus. Cavities within the brain accumulate fluid. As this fluid increases, the brain often swells to enormous proportions. Normal development of brain cells is inhibited, and the child either dies or is mentally retarded. This condition can also cause blindness, paralysis, and many other disorders of the nervous system.

We will hear much more about fetal therapy in the next decade. Surgeons are already proposing to correct fetal hernias of the diaphragm. If such hernias are left untreated, the abdominal organs compress the lungs and the child dies. Ruptures in fetal membranes may also be surgically corrected. If they are left unrepaired, they can strangle the fetus or cause its premature expulsion from the uterus. Many other repairs, including those to a variety of other hernias, perforations, and malformed organs, will be possible in the coming decade.

Yet, before fetal therapy can become a common practice, many ethical and philosophical issues will have to be settled. One of the most important is that of the risk of fetal therapy to the mother. There are also risks for the fetus. Some have proposed that it might be easier to induce premature birth in the third trimester and surgically correct fetal defects outside the womb. However, this would bring greater risks for the fetus in both premature birth and therapy.

Another problem is that of telling parents that the fetus might be treatable while allowing abortion as an alternative. How will these decisions be made? Who will make them? Some specialists have suggested that an ethical review board will have to screen cases proposed for fetal therapy and will have to set guidelines for human fetal research to minimize risks as much as possible.

Fetal therapy is a proven technique. In the next decade, the procedures will become far more sophisticated than they are today. The limits of this therapy can hardly be imagined. Even though there will be ethical questions concerning the procedures, the advances should reduce the probability of stillbirths and of mental and physical birth defects.

*Source:* Reprinted with permission from *Biology: Today and Tomorrow* by Ward and Hetzel. 

1. What is the environment that produces fetal alcohol syndrome?

2. How would pro-choice advocates feel about fetal therapy?

3. How would anti-abortionists feel about fetal therapy?

4. Can a fetus live outside the womb? How? Justify your answer.

5. In the fifth paragraph of this excerpt, what was the condition of the other twin?

6. In the seventh paragraph of this excerpt, to what does the word *cavities* refer?

7. What is meant by "stillbirth?"

8. What is the third trimester?

9. What are some of the risks to the mother in fetal therapy?

**10.** Other than those discussed in this excerpt, what are some of the ethical and philosophical questions to be considered in fetal therapy?

_______________

_______________

_______________

_______________

_______________

### *WRITE TO LEARN*

*On a separate sheet of paper, respond to the following: Explain the cartoon on page 268. What inferences did you make in finding its meaning?*

◆

## CHAPTER SUMMARY EXERCISE

*Use the following key concepts to write a summary of this chapter:*

| | |
|---|---|
| critical reading | fact |
| opinion | propaganda |
| expert opinions | bias |
| image advertising | bandwagoning |
| testimonial | plain folks |
| name calling | weasel words |
| relevancy | conclusions/inferences |
| background knowledge | logical inference |
| assumption | non sequitur |

_______________

_______________

_______________

_______________

_______________

_______________

_______________

_______________

_______________

◆

## CHAPTER REVIEW

*Answer briefly but completely.*

1. Contrast primary and secondary sources.

2. Complete the following analogy.
   qualitative : opinion :: ______________ : fact

3. Complete the following analogy.
   bandwagoning : peer pressure :: ______________ : a famous person

4 Why would an author use weasel words?

5. Explain the idea that relevancy is "in the eye of the beholder."

**6.** Which of the two purposes do the authors of *READ* have? Justify your answer.

______________________________________________

______________________________________________

______________________________________________

______________________________________________

**7.** Provide two meanings for the italicized word in each of the following sentences. Then choose new words and rewrite the sentences to make their meanings more explicit.

**a.** The Chief Justice has *retired*.

*1st meaning:*______________________________

*2nd meaning:*______________________________

*Revision 1:*______________________________

______________________________________________

*Revision 2:*______________________________

______________________________________________

**b.** The labor leader has a new *secretary*.

*1st meaning:*______________________________

*2nd meaning:*______________________________

*Revision 1:*______________________________

______________________________________________

*Revision 2:*______________________________

______________________________________________

**c.** Jose is a *poor* student.

*1st meaning:*______________________________

*2nd meaning:*______________________________

*Revision 1:*______________________________

______________________________________________

*Revision 2:*______________________________

______________________________________________

**8.** Complete the following analogy.
implied : hinted :: literal : ______________

9. What role does background knowledge play in inferencing?

10. List and define three types of conclusions. Which are often valid, sometimes valid, and usually invalid?

◆

## VOCABULARY ENHANCEMENT EXERCISE

*Using the scale in Figure 3.1, rate your understanding of the following vocabulary enhancement words to the left of the number. Then write a sentence with each one.*

1. strive

2. deception

3. absolutes

4. validity

5. sublime

**6.** pathetic

______________________________

______________________________

**7.** suppressed

______________________________

______________________________

**8.** evasive

______________________________

______________________________

**9.** conveyed

______________________________

______________________________

**10.** vicariously

______________________________

______________________________

◆

## REFERENCES

Anderson, R. C., and Pichert, J. W. (1978). Recall of previously unrecallable information following a shift in perspective. *Journal of Verbal Learning and Verbal Behavior,* 17, 1-12.

# 8 Speaking Figuratively

## TERMS

*Terms appear in the order in which they occur in the chapter.*

figurative language
figures of speech
literal
background knowledge
imagery
idiom
similes
metaphors
clichés
symbols
allusions
cross-reference
context
irony
sarcasm
understatement
hyperbole
structural irony
tone
personification
inanimate
euphemism

## CHAPTER OUTLINE EXERCISE

*Complete the chapter outline by putting the following goal-setting questions in the correct format:*

How do you grasp allusions?
How do you recognize personification?
How do you define euphemism?
How do you identify idioms?
How do you recognize irony?
How do you recognize similes and metaphors?
How do you identify symbols?

## OBJECTIVES

*At the end of this chapter, you should be able to do the following:*

1. Identify idioms.
2. Compare and contrast similes and metaphors.
3. Identify symbols.
4. Trace allusions.
5. Recognize irony.
6. Identify personification.
7. Define euphemism.

## CHAPTER MAP

*Complete a chapter map by putting the goal-setting questions found in the Chapter Outline Exercise in the correct mapping format.*

# VOCABULARY ENHANCEMENT EXERCISE

*Rate each of the following words according to your knowledge of them.*

| | STAGE 0 | STAGE 1 | STAGE 2 | STAGE 3 |
|---|---|---|---|---|
| | *I do not recognize the word.* | *I recognize the word but am unsure of its meaning and associations.* | *I recognize the word and can make general associations with it.* | *I recognize the word and can use it in speaking and writing.* |
| **1.** beacon | | | | |
| **2.** jest | | | | |
| **3.** aptly | | | | |
| **4.** mythology | | | | |
| **5.** discrepancy | | | | |
| **6.** revision | | | | |
| **7.** respectability | | | | |
| **8.** regions | | | | |
| **9.** swastika | | | | |
| **10.** culture | | | | |

FIGURATIVE LANGUAGE conveys information and emotion. It appears in everyday speech. TV and radio commercials contain **figures of speech.** So do movies, billboards, box tops, and greeting cards. Figurative language is perhaps most commonly found in literature, especially poetry.

Figurative words make language more brief, forceful, vivid, or precise. They also make language more entertaining. For example, consider the following sentence:

Her smile showed her happiness.

Now, consider the same idea expressed figuratively:

Like a shining half-moon, a smile lit her face.
Her smile was a glowing beacon of happiness.
Happiness pushed her lips toward heaven.

These statements express the idea of happiness more vividly. They push **literal** meaning to an imaginary level. Thus, figurative language provides an image for your mind's eye.

When you read, then, images should form in your mind. This helps you picture a person, feeling, or situation more clearly. As images connect with **background knowledge,** you more easily recall what's been said. The use of such figurative language is called **imagery.** Authors create images to appeal to your five senses—smell, taste, hearing, sight, and touch.

As a reader, your role is like that of a movie director. You cast the characters. You play and replay scenes. However, your effectiveness as a director depends in part on the author. Both the types and numbers of figures of speech an author uses affect your understanding. Somewhat like Goldilock's porridge, figurative language can be overdone, underdone, or just right.

## EXERCISE 8.1

*Rewrite the following sentences using figures of speech.*

***Example***

The stars shone in the sky.
*The stars twinkled like Christmas lights in the sky.*

**1.** Sue had oval-shaped eyes.

______________________________

______________________________

**2.** The book was an old favorite that I had often read.

______________________________

______________________________

3. The music was terribly loud.

4. The dress was too tight to wear.

5. It was too hot to think.

6. The path was worn by the travelers.

7. The man ran quickly down the alley.

8. The gymnast was agile as he exercised on the mat.

9. The convict was trapped in the house.

10. The clouds almost blocked the sun.

## IDENTIFYING IDIOMS

*Slang is a poor-man's poetry.*

—JOHN MOORE

An **idiom** is a kind of figurative speech most commonly found in conversations. It is also found in informal writing. The word *idiom* comes from the Greek word *idios,* which means "one's own." Idioms, then, can be described as the "figurative language of the people," or slang.

Idioms are generally specific to geographical regions, time periods, or cultures. Their meanings are usually not literal. While people in a particular time or region understand the phrase, outsiders may be confused by the same phrase. This makes idioms difficult to learn. Idioms are often learned by speaking with and listening to people in the area.

Idioms are often found in recreational reading. Authors use them to set the scene or make the settings of their stories more realistic. Understanding idioms from other places and times aids your comprehension.

### *Examples*

REGIONAL, CULTURAL

soda, pop, Coke, soft drink (names of nonalcoholic beverages in parts of the United States)

hoagie, po' boy, submarine, hero (names of sandwiches in parts of the United States)

TIME

hippie (1960s–1970s)
Victory Garden (World War II)
totally awesome (1980s)
far out (1960s–1970s)
peachy-keen (1950s)
streak (1970s)
yuppies (current)
dinks (current)

## EXERCISE 8.2

◆ *Match the following idioms with their literal meanings:*

### *Example*

___o___ carrot top

______ **1.** once in a blue moon

______ **2.** beat the rap

______ **3.** between a rock and a hard place

______ **4.** Russian roulette

______ **5.** brainstorm

______ **6.** bury the hatchet

______ **7.** have a chip on your shoulder

**a.** hindsight

**b.** no-win situation

**c.** ready for a fight

**d.** very rarely

**e.** in a predicament

**f.** needing a shave

**g.** prestigious North Eastern colleges

_____ **8.** Ivy League
_____ **9.** 5 o'clock shadow
_____ **10.** Catch 22
_____ **11.** It's Greek to me.
_____ **12.** hair of the dog that bit you
_____ **13.** by hook or by crook
_____ **14.** lame duck
_____ **15.** Monday-morning quarterback

**h.** without authority
**i.** incomprehensible
**j.** cure equals cause
**k.** suicide game
**l.** to make peace
**m.** group exchange
**n.** by any means
**o.** red hair
**p.** escape the consequences

**EXERCISE 8.3**

*Match the following idioms according to their meanings:*

***Example***

__*e*__ idiot box

**1.** _____ get the short end of the stick
**2.** _____ bite the bullet
**3.** _____ off the wall
**4.** _____ paint the town red
**5.** _____ stuck-up
**6.** _____ hung over
**7.** _____ brown-noser
**8.** _____ eat humble pie
**9.** _____ Mr. Clean
**10.** _____ bunk

**a.** eat crow
**b.** boot-licker
**c.** harebrained
**d.** Goody Two-shoes
**e.** boob tube
**f.** left holding the bag
**g.** humbug
**h.** on a high horse
**i.** hang tough
**j.** party hardy
**k.** three sheets to the wind

## RECOGNIZING SIMILES AND METAPHORS

Two kinds of figures of speech that involve making comparisons are **similes** and **metaphors.** Similes and metaphors compare two unlike ideas. At first glance, the two ideas seem totally different. They appear to have nothing in common. However, a closer look reveals a basic relationship between them. The words *like* or *as* signal that a simile is being used. In a metaphor, one idea is described as if it were another,

*"As ashes through the hour glass so are the days of our lives."*

without the use of *like* or *as*. Sometimes it is difficult to remember that similes, not metaphors, are cued by *like* or *as*. Remember this trick:

**A**
**SimiLe**
**I**
**K**
**E**

Consider again the example from the beginning of this chapter:

Her smile showed her happiness.

The first two revisions are examples of a simile and a metaphor.

Like a shining half-moon, a smile lit her face. (simile)
Her smile was a glowing beacon of happiness. (metaphor)

Some similes and metaphors are used so often they lose their freshness. When this happens, they no longer add vividness to language. Thus, they become ineffective. Such similes and metaphors are called **clichés.**

**EXERCISE 8.4**

◆ *Label each of the following quotations as either a simile (S)* or a metaphor *(M).* Then identify the two things being compared and name one feature the two have in common.

***Example***

*M* "There is a case for keeping wrinkles. They are the long-service stripes earned in the hard campaign of life."
—*London Daily Mail* editorial

*Compares* *wrinkles* *and* *service stripes*

*Trait in common: parallel lines, work to earn*

_____ **1.** "An iron curtain has descended across the continent." —Sir Winston Churchill

*Compares* _______________ *and* _______________

*Trait in common:* _______________________________________

_____ **2.** "Religion . . . is the opium of the people." —Karl Marx

*Compares* _______________ *and* _______________

*Trait in common:* _______________________________________

_____ **3.** "Books take their place according to their specific gravity as surely as potatoes in a tub." —Ralph Waldo Emerson

*Compares* _______________ *and* _______________

*Trait in common:* _______________________________________

_____ **4.** "The cares that infest the day, / Shall fold their tents, like the Arabs, / And as silently steal away." —Henry Wadsworth Longfellow

*Compares* _______________ *and* _______________

*Trait in common:* _______________________________________

_____ **5.** "Heaven has no rage like love to hatred turned, nor hell a fury like a woman scorned." —William Congreve

*Compares* _______________ *and* _______________

*Trait in common:* _______________________________________

_____ **6.** "Our words have wings, but fly not where we would." —George Eliot

*Compares* _______________ *and* _______________

*Trait in common:* _______________________________________

_____ **7.** "Men are like trees: each one must put forth the leaf that is created in him." —Henry Ward Beecher

*Compares* _______________ *and* _______________

*Trait in common:* _______________________________________

_____ **8.** "a word fitly spoken is like apples of gold in pictures of silver." —Proverbs 25:11

*Compares* _______________ *and* _______________

*Trait in common:* _______________________________________

_____ **9.** "Ships that pass in the night, and speak to each other in passing; / Only a signal shown and a distant voice in the darkness; / So on the ocean of life we pass and speak on another, / Only a look and a voice; then darkness again and a silence." —Henry Wadsworth Longfellow

*Compares* ______________ *and* ______________

*Trait in common:* ______________________________

### WRITE TO LEARN

*On a separate sheet of paper, compare and contrast the similes in the following quotations. How do the differences between them affect the overall meaning and tone of the quotation?*

*I think that I shall never see*
*A poem as lovely as a tree.*
*—Joyce Kilmer*

*I think that I shall never see*
*A billboard as lovely as a tree.*
*Indeed, unless the billboards fall,*
*I shall never see a tree at all.*
*—Ogden Nash*

## EXERCISE 8.5

*Answer briefly but completely.*

**Example**

"The law is a jealous mistress and a stern mistress." —Erskine Sanford in Orson Welles's *The Magnificent Ambersons*

**a.** *Type:* *M* *Compares* *law* *and* *mistress*

**b.** What sex is the law portrayed as?

*female*

**c.** How is law like a mistress?

*It is jealous and stern.*

**1.** "Life with Mary was like being in a phone booth with an open umbrella. No matter which way you turned, you got it in the eye." —Barry Nelson in Mervyn LeRoy's *Mary, Mary*

**a.** *Type:* ______ *Compares* ______________ *and* ______________

**b.** What kind of person was Mary?

______________________________

______________________________

**c.** What kind of person was the speaker? Justify your response.

______________________________________________

______________________________________________

**2.** "A golf course is nothing but a poolroom moved outdoors." —Barry Fitzgerald in Leo McCarey's *Going My Way*

**a.** *Type:* ______ *Compares* ________________ *and* ________________

**b.** Identify three ways in which a poolroom is like a golf course.

______________________________________________

______________________________________________

______________________________________________

**c.** What is Fitzgerald's opinion of both golf and pool?

______________________________________________

______________________________________________

**3.** "I think you must have an adding machine for a heart." —Bette Davis in Archie Mayo's *Bordertown*

**a.** *Type:* ______ *Compares* ________________ *and* ________________

**b.** What kind of person has "an adding machine for a heart"?

______________________________________________

______________________________________________

**c.** Describe a situation that would indicate a person has "an adding machine for a heart."

______________________________________________

______________________________________________

**4.** "You're the most beautiful plank in your husband's platform." —Adolphe Menjou in Frank Capra's *State of the Union*

**a.** *Type:* ______ *Compares* ________________ *and* ________________

**b.** What was the husband's profession?

______________________________________________

______________________________________________

**c.** What does "plank" mean in this context?

______________________________________________

______________________________________________

**5.** "Champagne's funny stuff. I'm used to whiskey. Whiskey is a slap on the back, and champagne's heavy mist before my eyes." —James Stewart in George Cukor's *The Philadelphia Story*

**a.** *Type:* ______ *Compares* ________________ *and* ________________

**b.** What does *funny* mean in this context?

______________________________________________

______________________________________________

**c.** How is whiskey like a slap on the back?

______________________________________________

______________________________________________

**6.** "Not a beautiful face, but a good face. She's got a face like a Sunday School picnic." —Dick Powell in Edward Dmytryk's *Murder, My Sweet*

**a.** *Type:* ______ *Compares* ________________ *and* ________________

**b.** What's the difference between a beautiful face and a good face?

______________________________________________

______________________________________________

**c.** What kind of personality might a person with "a face like a Sunday School picnic" have?

______________________________________________

______________________________________________

**7.** "Don't bother to read the note, I'll tell you what it says: 'Eleven roses, and the twelfth is you.' " —Gail Patrick in Gregory La Cava's *Stage Door*

**a.** *Type:* ______ *Compares* ________________ *and* ________________

**b.** What kind of person wrote the note?

______________________________________________

______________________________________________

**c.** What was the person like who received the roses?

______________________________________________

______________________________________________

**8.** "Look, when I came here, my eyes were big blue question marks. Now they're big green dollar marks." —Jean Arthur in Frank Capra's *Mr. Smith Goes to Washington*

a. *Type:* ______ *Compares* ______________ *and* ______________

b. What was the speaker like when she arrived?

______________________________________

______________________________________

c. What might have happened to change the speaker?

______________________________________

______________________________________

9. "Jonathan is more than a man. He's an experience—and he's habit-forming. If they could ever bottle him, he'd outsell gingerale." —Barry Sullivan in Vincente Minnelli's *The Bad and the Beautiful*

a. *Type:* ______ *Compares* ______________ *and* ______________

b. How does the speaker feel about Jonathan?

______________________________________

______________________________________

c. To what other substance could you compare Jonathan?

______________________________________

______________________________________

### WRITE TO LEARN

*The guy who sits next to you missed the lecture on similes and metaphors. On a separate sheet of paper, identify the metaphors in the following quotations and then explain to him how they could be made into similes.*

*"Architecture in general is frozen music." —Friedrich von Schelling*
*"A house is a machine for living in." —C. E. Jeanneret Le Corbusier*

## EXERCISE 8.6

*Match the word with the phrase to complete the cliché.*

**Example**

___*e*___ pretty as a ______________

______ 1. white as ______________

______ 2. cute as a ______________

______ 3. black as ______________

______ 4. cried like a ______________

a. button
b. baby
c. coal
d. snow
e. picture
f. grass
g. rock

| | | |
|---|---|---|
| ______ **5.** hard as a ______________ | | **h.** mouse |
| ______ **6.** soft as ______________ | | **i.** ice |
| ______ **7.** fat as a ______________ | | **j.** pig |
| ______ **8.** cold as ______________ | | **k.** silk |
| ______ **9.** quiet as a ______________ | | |
| ______ **10.** green as ______________ | | |

**EXERCISE 8.7**

*Rewrite the clichés in Exercise 8.6. The new similes should use comparisons that are original and unique.*

***Example***

*pretty as a girl going to her first dance*

**1.** ______________________________

**2.** ______________________________

**3.** ______________________________

**4.** ______________________________

**5.** ______________________________

**6.** ______________________________

**7.** ______________________________

**8.** ______________________________

**9.** ______________________________

**10.** ______________________________

◆

## IDENTIFYING SYMBOLS

**Symbols** are like metaphors and similes with one major difference. Similes and metaphors name both ideas being compared. Symbolism is harder because only one of the ideas is given. You must infer the other. For example, the sentence "Peace is like a dove in the hand of a nation" would be a simile. "Peace is a dove" is a metaphor. A dove alone symbolizes peace.

Justice Robert Jackson once said, "A person gets from a symbol the meaning he puts into it. And, what is one man's comfort and inspiration is another's jest and scorn."

Symbols are based on your own background knowledge and experiences. In general, symbols are universally understood. This is due to years of association between the symbol and the object it represents.

Some symbols mean different things in different cultures. For example, in Western countries, white is a symbol of purity. In Eastern cultures, such as Japan or India, white is a symbol of death or mourning.

Other symbols have no strong meaning for a specific culture. Think of how you feel about the flag of another country. You may recognize the flag of England when you see it. However, it does not fill you with the same sense of patriotism as the American flag. In the United States, the American flag (or the colors red, white, and blue) symbolizes our country. It evokes a patriotic feeling.

The meaning of the symbol depends on the context. It also depends on the time and place in which it is used. For instance, the swastika was originally an ancient Greek religious sign. It was also used by Orientals and American Indians. Its meaning changed when Hitler adopted it as a symbol. It become one of the most hated symbols in history. It stood for the evil associated with Nazi Germany.

Table 8.1 lists common symbols. Their meanings are in parentheses. Symbols can be used alone or as parts of other figurative language. The symbol lends its meaning to the overall image as shown in the examples below.

***TABLE 8.1*** ***Common Symbols and Their Meanings***

| | |
|---|---|
| *COLOR* | *OBJECTS* |
| yellow (fear) | heart (love, soul) |
| green (jealousy, money, growth) | rose (love) |
| purple (royalty) | cross (Christianity) |
| red (anger, danger) | red cross (first aid) |
| blue (sadness) | skull and crossbones (danger, poison, piracy) |
| white (innocence, purity, death) | four-leaf clover (good luck) |
| black (death) | horseshoe (good luck) |
| *ANIMALS* | Uncle Sam (United States) |
| bear (Soviet Union) | white hats (good guys) |
| owl (wisdom) | black hats (bad guys) |
| fox (cunning, trickery) | flag (patriotism) |
| lion (strength, bravery) | tree (life) |
| hawk (war) | rainbow (promise) |
| dove (peace) | cloud (trouble) |
| stork (babies) | olive branch (peace) |
| elephant (memory; Republican party) | laurel wreath (victory) |
| turkey (stupid or inept person) | light, light bulb (thought, knowledge) |
| black cat (bad luck) | winter (old age, death) |
| donkey (Democratic party) | spring (youth) |
| crow/buzzard/vulture (death) | |

**Examples**

green-eyed monster (someone who is jealous)
a yellow streak down his back (someone who is a coward)
spring chicken (someone young)
broken heart (a failed romance)
resting on his laurels (relying on earlier victories or successes)

**EXERCISE 8.8**

*Match each of the following symbols with its synonym or antonym.*

**Example**

___*k*___ crow

_______ **1.** donkey
_______ **2.** hawk
_______ **3.** bear
_______ **4.** heart
_______ **5.** turkey
_______ **6.** horseshoe
_______ **7.** black
_______ **8.** lion
_______ **9.** red
_______ **10.** white hats

**a.** Soviet Union
**b.** rose
**c.** yellow
**d.** four-leaf clover
**e.** owl
**f.** elephant
**g.** winter
**h.** skull and crossbones
**i.** black hats
**j.** dove
**k.** death

**EXERCISE 8.9**

*Identify the symbols in each of the following quotations. Then indicate what they represent.*

**Example**

"A university should be a place of light, of liberty, and of learning." —Disraeli

*Symbol(s): light*

*Represent(s): open-mindedness, freedom*

**1.** "Mister, the stork that brought you must have been a vulture." —Ann Sheridan in William Keighley's *Torrid Zone*

*Symbol(s):* _______________

*Represent(s):* _______________

2. "I always gagged on that silver spoon." —Orson Welles in Welles's *Citizen Kane*

*Symbol(s):*____________________

*Represent(s):*____________________

3. "My salad days / When I was green in judgment, cold in blood / To say as I said then." —William Shakespeare

*Symbol(s):*____________________

*Represent(s):*____________________

4. "They got a little blue chair for little boys and a little pink chair for little girls." —Henry Jones in Mervyn LeRoy's *The Bad Seed*

*Symbol(s):*____________________

*Represent(s):*____________________

5. "I'm an elephant, Miss Jones. A veritable elephant. I never forget a good deed done me or an ill one. I consider myself a kind of divine justice. Other people in this world have to forget things. I do not." —Charles Coburn in Sam Wood's *The Devil and Miss Jones*

*Symbol(s):*____________________

*Represent(s):*____________________

6. "Good Friday . . . in a way . . . is not Good Friday at all. It is Black Friday—a very Black Friday. It is Good Friday only in the sense that we know Easter will follow." —J. Edward Lantz

*Symbol(s):*____________________

*Represent(s):*____________________

7. "When a dove begins to associate with crows, its feathers remain white but its heart grows black." —German proverb

*Symbol(s)*____________________

*Represent(s):*____________________

8. "Well, spring isn't everything, is it, Essie? There's a lot to be said for autumn. That has beauty, too. And winter—if you're together. —Lionel Barrymore in Clarence Brown's *Ah, Wilderness!*

*Symbol(s):*____________________

*Represent(s):*____________________

9. "Jealousy's eyes are green." —Percy Shelley

*Symbol(s):*____________________

*Represent(s):*____________________

**10.** "Nowhere are prejudices more mistaken for truth, passion for reason, and invective for documentation than in politics. That is a realm, peopled only by villians or heroes, in which everything is black or white and gray is a forbidden color." —Mason Brown

*Symbol(s):*________________________________________

*Represent(s):*________________________________________

◆

## GRASPING ALLUSIONS

**Allusions** are somewhat like symbols. Both express ideas in a shortened form. Both require background knowledge for understanding. Both use commonly known information to be understood. Symbols draw from similes and metaphors that have become well known over time. On the other hand, allusions refer to works of literature, history, and the arts. Thus, allusions are aptly named. They *allude* (refer) to some character, writing, event, music, etc.

Consider a **cross-reference** in a dictionary or an encyclopedia. It tells you where to get more information. Allusions comprise a kind of cross-reference that does not tell you where to go for more facts. Instead, when authors use allusions they ask you to connect the allusion to its source from memory. Grasping allusions, then, requires vast amounts of background information.

Authors, as well as speakers, often allude to characters, phrases, terms, or places. These come from mythology (Pandora's box, Herculean strength, a Siren song) and history (honest as George Washington, as beautiful as Helen of Troy, Benedict Arnold). The Bible (Garden of Eden, patience of Job, wise as Solomon) and other works of literature (grinning like a Cheshire Cat, "I'll think about that tomorrow," a Scrooge) also provide allusions. Finally, allusions come from media sources like television ("Beam me up, Scotty"; "Where's the beef?") and movies ("You dirty rat!"; "Play it again, Sam"; "Here's looking at you, kid!").

If you do not recognize an allusion at once, there is hope. First, you look carefully at the **context.** This provides clues to the allusion's meaning. Then you search your memory for possible links with other information. If nothing comes to mind, you can attempt to look it up. Dictionaries of all sorts and books of quotations provide the sources of some allusions.

**EXERCISE 8.10**

*Provide the specific source and meaning of each of the following italicized allusions.*

**Example**

The reporter opened *Pandora's box* with that question.

*Source: Mythology*

*Meaning: a box that held all the world's problems; when Pandora opened the box, they escaped, leaving only hope.*

1. The workers attacked the task with *Herculean* strength.

   *Source:*____________________

   *Meaning:*____________________

2. The ruler led his people with *Machiavellian* fervor.

   *Source:*____________________

   *Meaning:*____________________

3. A bank president needs to be as honest as *George Washington.*

   *Source:*____________________

   *Meaning:*____________________

4. The bride was as beautiful as *Helen of Troy.*

   *Source:*____________________

   *Meaning:*____________________

5. Every office has its *Benedict Arnold.*

   *Source:*____________________

   *Meaning:*____________________

6. Hawaii is a *Garden of Eden.*

   *Source:*____________________

   *Meaning:*____________________

**7.** New mothers need the patience of *Job.*

*Source:*________________________________________

*Meaning:*_______________________________________

________________________________________________

**8.** New mothers need to be as wise as *Solomon.*

*Source:*________________________________________

*Meaning:*_______________________________________

________________________________________________

**9.** Grinning like a *a Cheshire cat,* the winner of the lottery accepted her check.

*Source:*________________________________________

*Meaning:*_______________________________________

________________________________________________

**10.** *"I'll think about that tomorrow"* is a procrastinator's slogan.

*Source:*________________________________________

*Meaning:*_______________________________________

________________________________________________

**11.** Few parents are *Scrooges* when it comes to buying toys for their children.

*Source:*________________________________________

*Meaning:*_______________________________________

________________________________________________

**12.** Many motorists wish they could say, *"Beam me up, Scotty."*

*Source:*________________________________________

*Meaning:*_______________________________________

________________________________________________

**13.** *"Where's the beef?"* was often heard during the presidential campaign.

*Source:*________________________________________

*Meaning:*_______________________________________

________________________________________________

**14.** The master of ceremonies toasted his guest speaker with the words, *"Here's looking at you, kid!"*

*Source:* ______________________________

*Meaning:* ______________________________

______________________________

**EXERCISE 8.11**

*Identify the source and meaning of each italicized allusion found in the following quotations.*

**Example**

"I fear the *Greeks,* even when they *bring gifts.*" —Virgil

*Source: story of Trojan Horse*

*Meaning: Some gifts have hidden meanings.*

**1.** A million million spermatozoa / All of them alive: / Out of their catacylsm but one poor *Noah* / Dare hope to survive. —Aldous Huxley

*Source:* ______________________________

*Meaning:* ______________________________

______________________________

**2.** [on smoking] A custom loathsome to the eye, hateful to the nose, harmful to the brain, dangerous to the lungs, and in the black, stinking fume thereof, nearest resembling the horrible *Stygian* [adjective form of *Styx*] smoke of the pit that is bottomless. —King James I

*Source:* ______________________________

*Meaning:* ______________________________

______________________________

**3.** "Every man meets his *Waterloo* at last." —Wendell Phillips

*Source:* ______________________________

*Meaning:* ______________________________

______________________________

**4.** "I would rather sleep in the southern corner in a little country churchyard, than in the tombs of the *Capulets.*" —Burke

*Source:* ______________________________

*Meaning:* ______________________________

______________________________

5. "Cast a cold eye / On life, on death. / *Horseman,* pass by!" —W. B. Yeats

*Source:* ____________________

*Meaning:* ____________________

____________________

6. "All I said was that our son—the apple of our three eyes, Martha being a *cyclops*—our son is a beanbag." —Edward Albee

*Source:* ____________________

*Meaning:* ____________________

____________________

7. "What is equally maddening about the visit of your child to some distant home is the call you get from the mother or father there telling you how lovely and helpful your child has been. . . . At moments like these, you truly feel that you have *fallen down the rabbit hole.*" —Bill Cosby

*Source:* ____________________

*Meaning:* ____________________

____________________

8. "Every great man nowadays has his disciples, and it is always *Judas* who writes the biography." —Oscar Wilde

*Source:* ____________________

*Meaning:* ____________________

____________________

9. "*Aunt Jemima and Uncle Tom* are dead, their places taken by a group of amazingly well-adjusted young men and women, almost as dark, but ferociously literate, well-dressed and scrubbed, who are never laughed at." —James Baldwin

*Source:* ____________________

*Meaning:* ____________________

____________________

10. "I don't believe in God because I don't believe in *Mother Goose.*" —Clarence Darrow

*Source:* ____________________

*Meaning:* ____________________

____________________

◆

## RECOGNIZING IRONY

**Irony** involves saying one thing and meaning the opposite. Ironic situations, when things work out to be completely different from what is expected, also occur. Irony often shows humor or sarcasm. **Sarcasm** is irony used to hurt the feelings of others. Sarcasm occurs when the opposite of literal words or phases is intended.

It's often difficult to determine how irony is used. The writer's or speaker's tone or manner helps you decide. If the rest of the passage or speech is basically humorous, then the phrase is meant to be humorous. If the writer or speaker wants to hurt the reader/listener or show anger, then sarcasm is being used.

Irony comes in several forms. The first is **understatement.** This occurs when the size, degree, or seriousness of something is shown as less than it really is. The second form of irony is **hyperbole.** Hyperbole is the opposite of understatement. It happens when something is described as better than it really is. **Structural irony** implies a discrepancy between what a character expects to get and gets, between what a character thinks and the reader knows, and between what a character deserves and gets. All types of irony occur in everyday life.

How can you tell if an author is being ironic? First, the context of the phrase helps. Second, the **tone** of the passage aids your decision. If the figure of speech has generally the same tone as the rest of the passage, the author does not intend irony. For example, if the rest of the passage is basically humorous, then the figure of speech is meant to be humorous.

## EXERCISE 8.12

◆ *Explain the irony in each of the following situations:*

**Example**

"Bachelor's wives and old maids' children are always perfect." —Sebastian-Roch Nicolas Chamfort

*Since bachelors have no wives nor old maid children, whatever advice they give has to be somewhat short-sighted. They require their nonexistent wives and children to behave perfectly.*

1. "The happiest days are when babies come." —in *Gone with the Wind,* Melanie rejoicing in an event that means her death

2. "We're not quarreling! We're in complete agreement! We hate each other!" —wife yelling at her husband in *The Band Wagon*

3. "I've come to the conclusion that the world would be a healthier place if more people were sick." —patient praising his nurse in *The Hasty Heart*

4. "It's a nice building. You get a better class of cockroaches." —James Earl Jones showing his apartment to Diahann Carroll in *Claudine*

5. "I wanted to marry her when I saw the moonlight shining on the barrel of her father's shotgun." —Eddie Albert explaining his sudden matrimonial desires in *Oklahoma!*

6. "You know, Sherry, you have one great advantage over everyone else in the world. You've never had to meet Sheridan Whiteside." —Bette Davis indicating the importance of being Sheridan Whiteside to Sheridan Whiteside (Sherry) in *The Man Who Came to Dinner*

7. "If you nurse as good as your sense of humor, I won't make it to Thursday." —Walter Matthau in *The Sunshine Boys*

**8.** "Anybody who wants to get out of combat isn't really crazy, so I can't ground him." —Jack Gilford explaining why he can't excuse a soldier from combat in *Catch 22*

**9.** "Sure we're speaking, Jedediah. You're fired." —Orson Welles in Welles's *Citizen Kane*

**10.** "If God ever wanted to be a fish, He'd be a whale. Believe that. He'd be a whale." —Harry Andrews offering bar-side religion in *Moby-Dick*

**11.** "In spite of everything, I still believe that people are really good at heart." —last line of *The Diary of Anne Frank,* an autobiography found after its author had died in a Nazi concentration camp

**12.** "Goodness, what beautiful diamonds!" "Goodness had nothing to do with it, dearie." —Mae West in *Night after Night*

**13.** "Nice speech, Eve. But I wouldn't worry too much about your heart. You can always put that award where your heart ought to be." —Bette Davis "congratulating" Anne Baxter in *All about Eve*

**14.** "I'm more or less particular about whom my wife marries." —Cary Grant in *His Girl Friday*

**15.** "Your husband has a great deal to be modest about." —Clifton Webb about Robert Young's well-founded humility in *Sitting Pretty*

**EXERCISE 8.13**

*Circle the letter of the response that best shows irony.*

**Example**

Megan was walking to class. Her arms were loaded with books. As she got near the class, she saw Ted. He was in front of her. He opened the door, walked into the room, and closed the door. Megan was left standing outside the room. She said,

**a.** "Ted, open the door."
**(b.)** "Thanks a lot, Ted."
**c.** "Ted, my arms are full of books."

1. Giordana looked at the letter. She had been fired again. She said,
   - **a.** "This is my lucky day."
   - **b.** "Unemployment here I come."
   - **c.** "R and R—just what the doctor ordered."
2. Ray failed English for the third time. He said,
   - **a.** "Who needs English anyway?"
   - **b.** "I've got to stop studying so hard!"
   - **c.** "What an idiot I am!"
3. Your best friend borrows your car. She goes to a party and has too much to drink. On the way home, she totals your car when she hits a police car head-on. Which response to your friend would show irony?
   - **a.** "The early bird gets the worm."
   - **b.** "With friends like you, who needs enemies?"
   - **c.** "How could you do this to me? I'm your best friend!"
4. Herbert never finishes a project on time. When he promised his boss he'd meet the next deadline, his boss said,
   - **a.** "I won't hold my breath."
   - **b.** "It will be the first time."
   - **c.** "There's no hurry!"
5. Joe was badly hurt in the first half of the game. Indeed, a rival player had fouled him on purpose. As Joe was taken off the court, his teammates yelled, "Don't worry, Joe. We'll show them!" Ironically,
   - **a.** Joe's team won by 75 points.
   - **b.** Joe's team tied the game.
   - **c.** Joe's team lost the game by 75 points.

**EXERCISE 8.14**

*Read the following passage. Then answer the questions below.*

## The Next Decade

### The Cells of Henrietta Lacks

Biologists have learned much about cell structure and function by studying cells and fragments of tissue removed from multicellular organisms. They nurture and maintain these cells and tissues in special culture chambers under carefully controlled conditions. The first truly successful cell cultures were established in 1912 from heart muscle and fibroblast cells taken from chicken embryos. They grew and reproduced for thirty-four years before they were allowed to die. Today many human cell lines have been cultured continuously through thousands of cell generations.

The most famous of the human cell lines is that of HeLa cells, established in 1951 after a young black woman had been admitted to Baltimore's Johns Hopkins Hospital with suspected cervical cancer. As an essential part of the diagnosis, a small sample of living tissue was removed from her cervix. Some of this tissue was given to Dr. George Gey, a researcher at the hospital who was trying to culture various kinds of cancer cells. Until then, no one had been successful in culturing cells from human malignancies, but this time the cells flourished. They reproduced a new generation of cells as often as once a day. Because of this great breakthrough, research on these and similar cells began in earnest. HeLa cells were eventually sent to laboratories throughout the world, where they became the basic cell line for many kinds of cellular research.

What happened to the young woman whose cells were distributed to laboratories all over the world? Unfortunately, she died shortly after the diagnosis of cervical cancer was made, and she was soon forgotten. For many years even her name was a mystery. Many thought it was Helen Lane, others Helen Larson. HeLa is an acronym for her name. Today we know that her name was Henrietta Lacks, and although she is dead, her cells provide her with a unique type of immortality.

When carefully cultured, HeLa cells cling tenaciously to life. They have served as culture systems for numerous types of viruses, including the polio virus. If not for HeLa cells cultures, the development of the polio vaccine might have been long delayed. HeLa cells have been subjected to detailed chemical analyses and careful studies of nutritional requirements. They have been used to test the potential effects of radiation on human cells. They have been recipients of foreign nuclei, such as mouse nuclei, in studies of nuclear control of cell function. (In the latter instance, HeLa cells synthesized mouse proteins.) Recently, biologists around the world have found many human cell cultures contaminated and taken over by the highly competitive HeLa cells.

The use of HeLa cells for experimental purposes continues to increase, and special facilities have been established to grow them in large numbers. The National Science Foundation supports two such major centers, one at the University of Alabama in Birmingham, the other at the Massachusetts Institute of Technology in Cambridge. Both institutions have received unbelievable numbers of requests for HeLa cells.

The University of Alabama Center has received and filled single orders for as many as a trillion HeLa cells (approximately 1.5 kilograms). The Massachusetts Institute of Technology receives weekly orders for 2 billion cells from one scientist alone.

As cellular research continues to expand, during the next decade, additional culture centers may need to be established, and the cells of the young black woman will continue to be used in research on cancer, viral infections, developmental biology, and genetics. Few, if any, scientists expect to ever clone humans. But if they do succeed, maybe the first clone will be Henrietta Lacks.

*Source:* Reprinted with permission from *Biology: Today and Tomorrow* by Ward and Hetzel. 

**1.** How does Henrietta's last name reflect irony?

**2.** How is the sentence "When carefully cultured, HeLa cells cling tenaciously to life" ironic in light of what happened to Henrietta?

**3.** Consider the following sentence: "Recently, biologists around the world have found many cell cultures contaminated and taken over by the highly competitive HeLa cells." What is ironic about this statement?

**4.** Reread the last paragraph of the excerpt. What is ironic about Henrietta's cells being used in cancer research?

5. The 1950s were a time of great racial prejudice in the United States. Consider the following quote from Roger Bacon: "There are four chief obstacles in grasping truth, which hinder every man . . . namely, submission to faulty and unworthy authority, influence of custom, popular prejudice, and concealment of ignorance accompanied by . . . a display of our knowledge." In light of these two pieces of information, how did the use of Henrietta's cells show irony?

______________________________________________

______________________________________________

______________________________________________

______________________________________________

______________________________________________

**WRITE TO LEARN**

*Read the following poem by Dorothy Parker. Then on a separate sheet of paper, explain why this poem is ironic in nature.*

RESUME

Razors pain you;
Rivers are damp;
Acids stain you;
And drugs cause cramp.
Guns aren't lawful;
Nooses give;
Gas smells awful;
You might as well live.



◆

## RECOGNIZING PERSONIFICATION

**Personification** is used when **inanimate** objects are given traits or abilities of living things. A thing or concept is represented as a person. A writer or speaker uses personification to create a more vivid image. Because you know about people, an author uses human qualities and traits to describe unfamiliar situations, feelings, or objects. Consider once again the factual statement at the beginning of this chapter:

Her smile showed her happiness.

The final revision uses personification to make a more vivid picture in your mind:

Happiness pushed her lips toward heaven.

This sentence uses personification in that happiness is an emotion. It does not have life. It cannot *push*. Because you are human, you know the force that pushing takes. Thus, you are better able to realize the strength of the girl's happiness. This idea is not as effectively shown in the first, literal statement.

## EXERCISE 8.15

◆ *Answer briefly but completely.*

**1.** "I am not yet so lost in lexicography, as to forget that words are the daughters of the earth, and that things are the sons of heaven." —Samuel Johnson

**a.** What is the definition of *lexicography?* ____________________

____________________

**b.** Identify two examples of personification in this quotation.

____________________

____________________

**c.** How do these examples of personification relate to the meaning of *lexicography?* ____________________

____________________

____________________

**2.** "The eyes have one language everywhere." —George Herbert

**a.** What does it mean for eyes to have one language?

____________________

____________________

**b.** Give three examples of how eyes can express language.

____________________

____________________

**c.** Identify three emotions a person can express with only the eyes.

____________________

____________________

**3.** "Trees and fields tell me nothing: men are my teachers." —Plato

**a.** Provide three examples of things "trees and fields" tell you.

______________________________

______________________________

______________________________

**b.** Provide three examples of things "trees and fields" could *not* tell you.

______________________________

______________________________

______________________________

**4.** "Malice often takes the garb of truth." —William Hazlitt

**a.** What is the definition of *malice?*______________________________

______________________________

**b.** What example of personification is found in this quotation?

______________________________

______________________________

**c.** Provide an example of malice robed in the garb of truth.

______________________________

______________________________

**5.** "Golden slumbers kiss your eyes, smiles awake you when you rise." —Thomas Dekker

**a.** Locate one example of personification.______________________________

______________________________

______________________________

**b.** What happens when "golden slumbers kiss your eyes"?__________

______________________________

______________________________

**6.** "Slowly, silently, now the moon / Walks the night in her silver shoon." —Walter De la Mare

**a.** Identify one example of personification.______________________________

______________________________

**b.** How else might you personify the moon?__________

**7.** "Drink to me only with thine eyes / And I will pledge with mine; / Or leave a kiss but in the cup, / And I'll not look for wine." —Ben Jonson

**a.** Identify one example of personification.__________

**b.** How does Jonson feel about the person to whom this is written?

**8.** "An army marches on its stomach." —attributed to Napoleon Bonoparte

**a.** Identify the personification used in this quotation.__________

**b.** What does the quotation mean?__________

**9.** "I met Murder on the way— / He had a mask like Castlereagh." —Percy Bysshe Shelley

**a.** Identify the personification used in this quotation.__________

**b.** How can a person meet Murder?__________

**10.** "Insanity runs in my family. It practically gallops." —Joseph Kesserling

**a.** Identify the personification used in this quotation.__________

**b.** What does Kesserling think about his relatives?__________

**EXERCISE 8.16**

*Read the following poem by Emily Dickinson. Then answer the questions below it.*

The clouds their backs together laid,
The north began to push,
The forests galloped till they fell,
The lightning skipped like mice;
The thunder crumbled like a stuff—
How good to be safe in tombs,
Where nature's temper cannot reach,
Nor vengeance ever comes!

1. What is "nature's temper"?

2. Identify the two lines that contain examples of both personification and similes. Explain the similes by indicating what they compare.

3. Where does Dickinson find a safe haven? What does this symbolize?

4. List the two examples of personification you consider to be the best ones in this poem. Justify your response by explaining these examples and why you chose them.

5. List two reasons a person might be safe in a "tomb."

◆

## DEFINING EUPHEMISM

*Any euphemism ceases to be euphemistic after a time and the true meaning begins to show through. It's a losing game, but we keep on trying.*

—JOSEPH WOOD KRUTCH

The word **euphemism** comes from two Greek word parts—*eu,* which means good, and *pheme,* which means voice. It translates literally into "good voice." Euphemisms are used when "good" or pleasant phrases are substituted for "bad" or unpleasant phrases. They make things sound better than they really are. You use them when you don't want someone to know the truth. Or, you use them to soften the reality of negative statements.

Some euphemisms are more commonly used than others. You have probably heard or used many of them yourself. These phrases improve a situation or lend it an air of respectability.

### EXERCISE 8.17

*Match the following euphemisms with their actual meanings.*

**Example**

__*f*__ embezzler

_____ **1.** exotic dancer

_____ **2.** nice personality

_____ **3.** lingerie

_____ **4.** different

_____ **5.** assertive

_____ **6.** strategic movement to the rear

_____ **7.** memorial garden

_____ **8.** intoxicated

_____ **9.** file 13

_____ **10.** landfill

**a.** underwear
**b.** pushy
**c.** stripper
**d.** ugly
**e.** strange
**f.** thief
**g.** cemetery
**h.** trash
**i.** drunk
**j.** dump
**k.** retreat

### EXERCISE 8.18

*List three euphemisms for each of the following:*

**Example**

fired
*quit*
*let go*
*laid off*

1. restroom

______________________________

______________________________

______________________________

2. death or dying

______________________________

______________________________

______________________________

3. overweight

______________________________

______________________________

______________________________

4. underweight

______________________________

______________________________

______________________________

5. nagging

______________________________

______________________________

______________________________

**EXERCISE 8.19**

*Rank from 1 (best) to 4 (worst) each of the following words and their euphemisms:*

***Example***

__2__ buried
__*1*__ interred
__*4*__ planted
__*3*__ deep-sixed

| 1. | | 2. | |
|---|---|---|---|
| ______ | stealing | ______ | spy |
| ______ | five-finger discount | ______ | tattle-tale |
| ______ | shoplifting | ______ | informer |
| ______ | misappropriate | ______ | secret agent |

3. ______ white lie
______ fib
______ stretching the truth
______ verbal fabrication

4. ______ pregnant
______ one in the oven
______ in a family way
______ knocked-up

5. ______ retiree
______ senior citizen
______ old folks
______ Gray Panther

6. ______ assistant
______ lackey
______ gopher
______ Girl (or Boy) Friday

7. ______ mixed breed
______ Heinz 57
______ mutt
______ mongrel

8. ______ vagrant
______ loiterer
______ hobo
______ adventurer

9. ______ shy
______ tied to the apron strings
______ wallflower
______ backward

10. ______ single
______ available
______ unattached
______ unwed

**EXERCISE 8.20**

*Read the following short story. Then answer the questions below.*

**THE CHASER**
**John Collier**

Alan Austen, as nervous as a kitten, went up certain dark and creaky stairs in the neighborhood of Pell Street, and peered about for a long time on the dim landing before he found the name he wanted written obscurely on one of the doors.

He pushed open this door, as he had been told to do, and found himself in a tiny room, which contained no furniture but a plain kitchen table, a rocking-chair, and an ordinary chair. On one of the dirty buff-colored walls were a couple of shelves, containing in all perhaps a dozen bottles and jars.

An old man sat in the rocking-chair, reading a newspaper. Alan, without a word, handed him the card he had been given. "Sit down, Mr. Austen," said the old man very politely. "I am glad to make your acquaintance."

"Is it true," asked Alan, "that you have a certain mixture that has—er—quite extraordinary effects?"

"My dear sir," replied the old man, "my stock in trade is not very large—I don't deal in laxatives and teething mixtures—but such as it is, it is varied. I think nothing I sell has effects which could be precisely described as ordinary."

"Well, the fact is—" began Alan.

"Here, for example," interrupted the old man, reaching for a bottle from the shelf. "Here is a liquid as colorless as water, almost tasteless, quite imperceptible in coffee, milk, wine, or any other beverage. It is also quite imperceptible to any known method of autopsy."

"Do you mean it is a poison?" cried Alan, very much horrified.

"Call it a glove-cleaner if you like," said the old man indifferently. "Maybe it will clean gloves. I have never tried. One might call it a life-cleaner. Lives need cleaning sometimes."

"I want nothing of that sort," said Alan.

"Probably it is just as well," said the old man. "Do you know the price of this? For one teasponful, which is sufficient, I ask five thousand dollars. Never less. Not a penny less."

"I hope all your mixtures are not as expensive," said Alan apprehensively.

"Oh dear, no," said the old man. "It would be no good charging that sort of price for a love potion, for example. Young people who need a love potion very seldom have five thousand dollars. Otherwise they would not need a love potion."

"I am glad to hear that," said Alan.

"I look at it like this," said the old man. "Please a customer with one article, and he will come back when he needs another. Even if it *is* more costly. He will save up for it, if necessary."

"So," said Alan, "you really do sell love potions?"

"If I did not sell love potions," said the old man, reaching for another bottle, "I should not have mentioned the other matter to you. It is only when one is in a position to oblige that one can afford to be so confidential."

"And these potions," said Alan. "They are not just—just—er———"

"Oh, no," said the old man. "Their effects are permanent, and extend far beyond casual impulse. But they include it. Bountifully, insistently. Everlastingly."

"Dear me!" said Alan, attempting a look of scientific detachment. "How very interesting!"

"But consider the spiritual side," said the old man.

"I do, indeed," said Alan.

"For indifferernce," said the old man, "they substitute devotion. For scorn, adoration. Give one tiny measure of this to the young lady—its flavor is imperceptible in orange juice, soup, or cocktails—and however gay and giddy she is, she will change altogether. She will want nothing but solitude, and you."

"I can hardly believe it," said Alan. "She is so fond of parties."

"She will not like them any more," said the old man. "She will be afraid of the pretty girls you may meet."

"She will actually be jealous?" cried Alan in a rapture. "Of me?"

"Yes, she will want to be everything to you."

"She is, already. Only she doesn't care about it."

"She will, when she has taken this. She will care intensely. You will be her sole interest in life."

"Wonderful!" cried Alan.

"She will want to know all you do," said the old man. "All that has happened to you during the day. Every word of it. She will want to know what you are thinking about, why you smile suddenly, why you are looking sad."

"That is love!" cried Alan.

"Yes," said the old man. "How carefully she will look after you! She will never allow you to be tired, to sit in a draught, to neglect your food. If you are an hour late, she will be terrified. She will think you are killed, or that some siren has caught you."

"I can hardly imagine Diana like that!" cried Alan, overwhelmed with joy.

"You will not have to use your imagination," said the old man. "And, by the way, since there are always sirens, if by any chance you *should*, later on, slip a little, you need not worry. She will forgive you, in the end. She will be terribly hurt, of course, but she will forgive you—in the end."

"That will not happen," said Alan fervently.

"Of course not," said the old man. "But, if it did, you need not worry. She would never divorce you. Oh, no! And, of course, she herself will never give you the least, the very least, grounds for—uneasiness."

"And how much," said Alan, "is this wonderful mixture?"

"It is not as dear," said the old man, "as the glove-cleaner, or life-cleaner, as I sometimes call it. No. That is five thousand dollars, never a penny less. One has to be older than you are, to indulge in that sort of thing. One has to save up for it."

"But the love potion?" said Alan.

"Oh, that," said the old man, opening the drawer in the kitchen table, and taking out a tiny, rather dirty-looking phial. "That is just a dollar."

"I can't tell you how grateful I am," said Alan, watching him fill it.

"I like to oblige," said the old man. "Then customers come back, later in life, when they are rather better off, and want more expensive things. Here you are. You will find it very effective."

"Thank you again," said Alan. "Good-by"

"*Au revoir,*" said the old man.

*Source:* Originally from *The New Yorker.* Copyright 1940 by John Collier.

**1.** List three examples of similes and metaphors from the story. Explain them literally.

**2.** Identify the allusion used in the story. What is its meaning? From what source does it come?

**3.** What does the old man sell?

**4.** What is Alan looking to buy?

**5.** Explain the irony in the old man's saying "*Au revoir*" as Alan leaves.

**6.** Define the following in context.

**a.** (p. 325, line 3) *obscurely:*

**b.** (p. 325, line 16) *precisely:*

**c.** (p. 326, line 4) *imperceptible:*

**d.** (p. 326, line 40), *solitude:* ______________________________

______________________________

**e.** (p. 327, line 28) *phial:* ______________________________

______________________________

**7.** Explain the metaphor "a look of scientific detachment" (p. 326, line 33).

______________________________

**8.** Why does the old man call his more expensive potion a "life-cleaner"?

______________________________

**9.** From what source might Alan have gotten the old man's address?

______________________________

**10.** Explain the significance of the title of this story.

______________________________

**EXERCISE 8.21**

*Read the following excerpt. Then answer the questions that follow it.*

### The Cult of George Washington

In 1776, when the American colonies declared independence, many considered democracy a radical and frightening experiment. It was feared that without the tradition of aristocracy and monarchy, government might deteriorate into mob rule and domination by popular tyrants. The Founding Fathers were deeply afraid of investing power in any man, for they believed that power was incompatible with liberty. Yet, if they wanted to fight a war, they needed a general.

Into this situation came George Washington. Washington was *not* a charismatic leader. In fact, he was something of a cold fish. He was stern and distant, not warm in his affections. Nor was he particularly bright. Thomas Jefferson said of him that his mind was not "of the very first order . . . It was slow in operation, being little aided by invention or imagination, but sure in conclusion." Today, we might call him a plodder. Nor did he have any previous military experience. His major qualification for office was that he didn't want the job. When it was forced on him, he said, "Lest some unlucky event should happen, I beg it may be remembered by every gentleman in this room, that I, this day, declare with utmost sincerity, I do not think myself equal to the command I am honored with." His humility turned out to be appropriate, for his generalship was not brilliant and his armies met with many defeats.

Still, within weeks of his appointment as commander of the Continental Army, Washington began to be an object of near worship. George III's pictures were taken down and George Washington's put in their place. The music to "God Save the King" was retained, but the words were changed to "God Save Great Washington." In the end, many would have been glad to give him voluntarily the kingship they had feared he would demand.

Why did the cult of Washington develop? There appear to be three reasons. One is the colonists' strong belief that God was on their side. If God was on their side, then Washington must be God's agent on earth; he was widely proclaimed to be the American Moses. Ministers told their congregants that it would be a sin not to support the war. Second, Washington was a symbol for a union that did not yet exist. The Articles of Confederation had little authority. No structure or institution represented the United States—only Washington symbolized the fledgling nation's unity. Finally, in an atmosphere of near paranoia about the abuse of power, Washington's indifference to power, the relief with which he relinquished his command and his presidency, made him a hero.

By the time of his death, Washington was virtually deified. One of his eulogists said,

Did he, like Caesar, after vanquishing his countrymen's foes, turn his conquering armies against that country? Far, far otherwise. Before the great Council of our Nation, the PATRIOT-HERO appeared, and in the presence of numerous, admiring spectators, resigned his victorious sword into the hands of those who gave it.

AUGUST Spectacle! Glorious Example! For my own part, I Never contemplate it but each fiber vibrates with rapture, and the vital current trembles through every artery of my frame.

The cult of Washington is a home-grown example of Durkheim's theory about the functions of religion. By worshipping Washington, the colonists were worshipping themselves—their nation and the virtues they believed it embodied.

*Source:* Reprinted with permission from *Sociology* 21E by Brinkenhoff and White. 

**1.** Reread the second paragraph. Explain the metaphor "cold fish."

______________________________________________

______________________________________________

**2.** Reread the second paragraph and the first two sentences in the third paragraph. Explain the irony in this section.

______________________________________________

______________________________________________

**3.** Refer to the second paragraph and describe a person who would be characterized by the idiom *plodder.*

______________________________________________

______________________________________________

**4.** Reread the fourth paragraph. Explain the allusion found here. What is its source? How would Washington resemble this figure?

______________________________________________

______________________________________________

______________________________________________

______________________________________________

**5.** Refer to the fourth paragraph again. How could Washington symbolize the United States? Does he do so today? Justify your answer.

______________________________________________

______________________________________________

______________________________________________

______________________________________________

**6.** Consider how most people become heroes. What is ironic about the way Washington became a hero?

______________________________________________

______________________________________________

______________________________________________

7. Explain the allusion to Caesar in the first eulogy? What is its source?

8. What is ironic about Washington being compared to Caesar here?

9. Explain the metaphor *homegrown* located in the last paragraph.

10. Explain the metaphor *fledgling* located in the fourth paragraph.

◆

## CHAPTER SUMMARY EXERCISE

*Use the following key concepts to write a summary of this chapter:*

figurative language
background knowledge
idioms
metaphors
allusions
personification
figures of speech
imagery
similes
symbols
irony
euphemism

◆

## CHAPTER REVIEW

*Answer briefly but completely.*

1. Explain the following statement from your text: "Figurative language is most commonly found in literature, especially poetry."

2. Why are authors concerned with creating images that appeal to your five senses?

3. What is the role of idioms in a country's culture? What is their value?

4. How does a simile or metaphor become a cliché?

5. Compare and contrast similes, metaphors, and symbols.

6. What happens to understanding if you cannot make a connection between an allusion and its source?

7. Contrast the three types of irony.

**8.** Why is *personification* aptly named?

**9.** Name a profession that would use euphemisms every day. Provide an exemplary scene.

**10.** Consider the following sentence:

The letter made the man cry.

Choosing from the following types of figures of speech, revise this sentence five times.

**a.** a simile

**b.** a metaphor

**c.** irony

**d.** personification

**e.** an allusion

**f.** an euphemism

**g.** a symbol

◆

## VOCABULARY ENHANCEMENT EXERCISE

*Using the scale in Figure 3.1, rate your understanding of the following vocabulary enhancement words to the left of the number. Then write a sentence with each one.*

1. beacon

2. jest

3. aptly

4. mythology

5. discrepancy

6. revision

7. respectability

8. regions

9. swastika

10. culture

# 9 Reading Graphs and Maps

## CHAPTER TERMS

*Terms appear in the order in which they occur in the chapter.*

tables
graphs
flowcharts
maps
timelines
row
column
headings
labels
trends
bar graphs
histograms
line graphs
symbol graphs
pictorial graphs
circle graphs
key
legend
symbols
scale of distance
latitudes
longitudes
meridians
equator
Northern Hemisphere
Southern Hemisphere
degrees
Greenwich meridian
prime meridian
political map
boundaries
physical map
topography
elevation
altitude
sea level
special-purpose map

## CHAPTER OUTLINE EXERCISE

*Create an outline for this chapter on the following lines.*

______________________________________________
______________________________________________
______________________________________________
______________________________________________
______________________________________________
______________________________________________
______________________________________________
______________________________________________
______________________________________________
______________________________________________
______________________________________________
______________________________________________
______________________________________________
______________________________________________
______________________________________________
______________________________________________
______________________________________________
______________________________________________
______________________________________________
______________________________________________
______________________________________________
______________________________________________

## OBJECTIVES

*At the end of this chapter, you should be able to do the following:*

1. Describe the need for graphics.
2. List and apply the eight steps in reading tables.
3. Describe and apply the eight steps in reading graphs.
4. Explain flowcharts.
5. Locate information on timelines.
6. Describe the three most common kinds of maps and apply rules for reading them.

## CHAPTER MAP

*Create a map for this chapter in the space below.*

## VOCABULARY ENHANCEMENT EXERCISE

*Rate each of the following words according to your knowledge of them.*

| | *STAGE 0* | *STAGE 1* | *STAGE 2* | *STAGE 3* |
|---|---|---|---|---|
| | *I do not recognize the word.* | *I recognize the word but am unsure of its meaning and associations.* | *I recognize the word and can make general associations with it.* | *I recognize the word and can use it in speaking and writing.* |
| **1.** continuum | | | | |
| **2.** phenomena | | | | |
| **3.** clarify | | | | |
| **4.** suffices | | | | |
| **5.** discern | | | | |
| **6.** decipher | | | | |
| **7.** obsolete | | | | |
| **8.** mandate | | | | |
| **9.** vegetation | | | | |
| **10.** glaciers | | | | |

◆

## THE NEED FOR GRAPHICS

Each term, you register for your college classes. Perhaps you see a counselor to choose your courses. Your counselor may say:

> "Your English course meets on Mondays, Wednesdays, and Fridays at eight o'clock. You'll have a two-hour break after English class on Wednesdays when you have your biology lab. Math will be after your biology lab on Wednesdays. It will be after your two-hour break on the days that you have English but not biology lab. You'll probably want to eat lunch during that two hours, except on Wednesdays. Then you won't be able to eat until after your math class.
>
> "On Tuesdays and Thursdays your first class will be biology. It will start at nine and finish at ten-thirty. Then, you'll have a break for an hour-and-a-half on Tuesdays. Of course, you won't have a break on Thursdays. You have your ROTC lab from ten-thirty until noon then. Your history class will meet right after your ROTC lab on Thursdays. It will meet after lunch on Tuesdays.
>
> "If you're planning to work, you'll have plenty of time in the afternoons.
>
> "You look confused. Let me make a sketch of your schedule. Seeing it on paper may make it easier to understand." (See Figure 9.1.)

***FIGURE 9.1***
***Schedule Chart***

| | SUN | MON | TUES | WED | THURS | FRI | SAT |
|---|---|---|---|---|---|---|---|
| 8-9 | | English | | English | | English | |
| 9-10 | | | Biology | Biology | Biology | | |
| 10-11 | | | | Lab | | | |
| 11-12 | | Math | | Math | ROTC lab | Math | |
| 12-1 | | | History | | History | | |
| 1-2 | | | | | | | |
| 2-3 | | | | | | | |
| 3-4 | | | | | | | |
| 4-5 | | | | | | | |
| 5-6 | | | | | | | |
| 6-7 | | | | | | | |
| 7-8 | | | | | | | |
| 8-9 | | | | | | | |
| 9-10 | | | | | | | |
| 10-11 | | | | | | | |

Which of these is easier for you to follow? The chart provides a graphic plan of where and when you are in class. It organizes the information your counselor gave you. This makes the schedule easier to understand and follow.

Often a sketch of information is more understandable than text. **Tables, graphs, flowcharts, maps,** and **timelines** organize information graphically.

What do you usually do when a chapter includes a graph or table? Many students skip graphics. They do this because they think it takes too long to understand them. However, reading graphics takes less time and effort than reading the same information in text.

Graphics organize and relate information. They also explain or make written information clearer. In some cases, graphics provide information that would be hard to explain without their use.

◆

## UNDERSTANDING TABLES

Tables show how information is related. They organize information into rows and columns. A **row** runs horizontally across the page (left to right). A **column** runs vertically down the page (top to bottom). **Headings** or **labels** identify rows or columns.

One way a table is organized is by identifying the presence or absence of common features for specific items. If an item possesses the feature, a mark is made in the box or space where the item and feature meet. If the item does not possess that feature, the box or space remains blank.

For example, in Table 9.1 students (items being analyzed) are organized by the English courses they have completed.

This kind of table helps you associate details with students. It shows you which courses they have completed. You can draw several conclusions about the data in the table. You can also identify which courses need to be taken. The probable number of terms a student has been enrolled in college also could be calculated. In addition, you can use the

***TABLE 9.1 English Courses Completed at Taylor College***

| | ENGL 101 | ENGL 102 | ENGL 201 | ENGL ELECTIVE |
|---|---|---|---|---|
| GAINES, L. | X | X | | |
| GALVEZ, K. | X | X | X | |
| LING, V. | X | X | | |
| MONROE, R. | X | | | |
| MOORE, G. | X | | | |
| SMITH, B. | X | X | X | |
| WELLS, S. | X | X | X | X |

table to summarize information. For example, all students have completed English 101. Only one student has completed the English elective.

Your instructor probably keeps at least two kinds of tabular records for your class. The first kind often resides in a gradebook. It shows presence or absence of the students in class. A second kind shows the amount or quality of the item being compared. In a gradebook, this kind of information would be each student's grades.

Table 9.2 provides much useful information. From it, you can identify the details or the grades for each student. You can make inferences about how well each student is doing in the class. You can find **trends** (directions in which features change). For example, look at

***TABLE 9.2*** **Gradebook Chart**

| | DATE | 10/7 | 10/14 | 10/21 | 10/28 | 11/4 | | | |
|---|---|---|---|---|---|---|---|---|---|
| NAME | | Test 1 | Test 2 | Test 3 | Test 4 | Test 5 | | | |
| Gaines, L. | 1 | 0 | 61 | 75 | 81 | 71 | | | |
| Galvez, R. | 2 | 98 | 87 | 80 | 72 | 65 | | | |
| Long, V. | 3 | 90 | 85 | 93 | 60 | 0 | | | |
| Monroe, R. | 4 | 70 | 74 | 81 | 86 | 93 | | | |
| Moore, G. | 5 | 48 | 0 | 59 | 73 | 68 | | | |
| Smith, B. | 6 | 88 | 70 | 81 | 79 | 0 | | | |
| Wells, S. | 7 | 65 | 64 | 81 | 79 | 70 | | | |
| | 8 | | | | | | | | |
| | 9 | | | | | | | | |
| | 10 | | | | | | | | |
| | 11 | | | | | | | | |
| | 12 | | | | | | | | |
| | 13 | | | | | | | | |
| | 14 | | | | | | | | |
| | 15 | | | | | | | | |
| | 16 | | | | | | | | |
| | 17 | | | | | | | | |
| | 18 | | | | | | | | |
| | 19 | | | | | | | | |
| | 20 | | | | | | | | |

the grades for Galvez, K., and Monroe, R. Galvez's grades begin high but worsen with each test. Monroe's test scores show an opposite trend. Monroe's scores improve with each test.

STEPS IN READING TABLES

1. *Read the title.* This tells you the subject or general content of the table.
2. *Identify the type of table.* This helps you to determine the kind(s) of information given. A table tells you the presence or absence of a feature, or it tells you the quantity or quality of a feature.
3. *Look at the labels or headings on the table.* These tell you the items being compared and the features used to compare them. You need to keep the items and features in mind in order to know when and how the relationships change.
4. *Note any general trends.*
5. *If you are looking at a table as part of the surveying step of SQ3R, stop your examination.* Continue previewing the chapter.
6. *When you read the section of the text that refers to the table, identify the text's purpose before turning to the table.* Does the author want you to note specific facts, generalizations, or trends?
7. *Use the purpose set by the text to look at specific areas of the table.*
8. *Reread the section of the text that referred to the table.* Make sure you understand the points and relationships noted by the author.

◆

## EXAMINING GRAPHS

Graphs symbolically represent information. They often show concepts better than words. This is because they show large amounts of data in small amounts of space. Graphs show quantitative comparisons between two or more kinds of information. The most common types include **bar graphs** or **histograms, line graphs, symbol** or **pictorial graphs,** and **circle graphs.**

### Bar Graphs

Bar graphs compare and contrast quantitative values. They show the amount or quantity an item possesses. Although the units in which the items are measured must be equal, they can be of any size and can start at any value. If the units are large, the bar graph indicates an approximate rather than an exact amount. Bar graphs are sometimes called histograms. Figure 9.2 is an example of a bar graph.

**FIGURE 9.2**
**Central State College Student Enrollment**

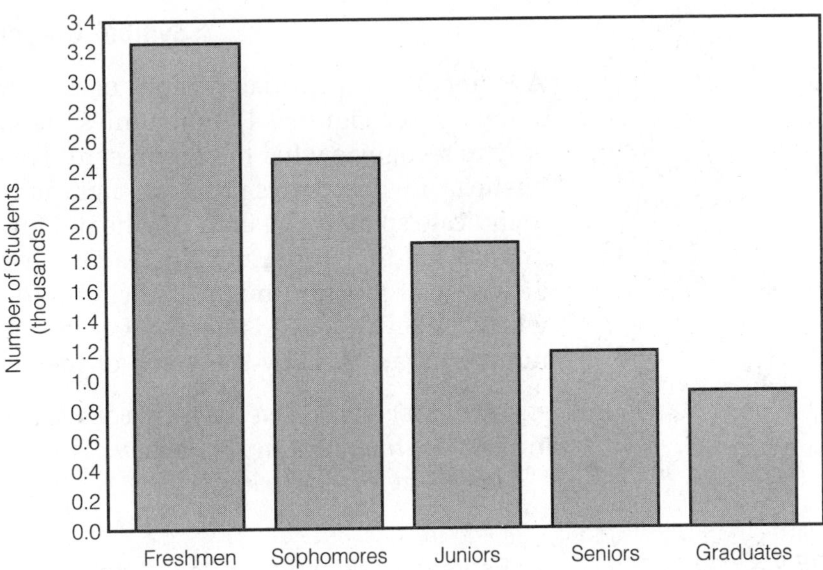


## Line Graphs

A line graph shows quantitative trends for an item over time (see Figure 9.3). Each line on the graph represents one item. A **key** or **legend** tells if more than one item is shown. The trends show directions of change that can increase, decrease, or stay the same. Line graphs are often considered to be more accurate than bar graphs. However, accuracy depends on the size of the units used.

**FIGURE 9.3**
**Central State College Student Enrollment**

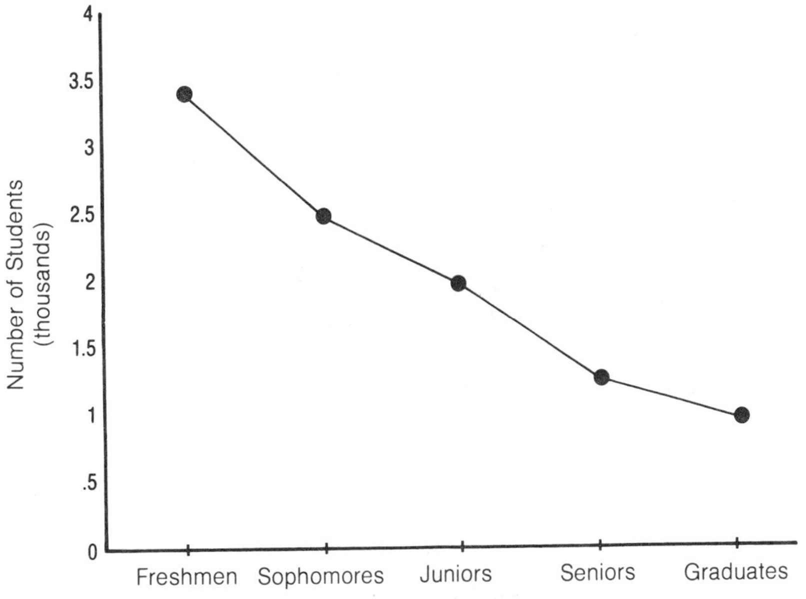

## Symbol Graphs

A symbol, or pictorial, graph uses **symbols** to show quantitative amounts (see Figure 9.4). Sometimes the symbols are drawn so that it is easy to recognize what they represent. For example, to show how many bushels of wheat states produce, a graph may use a small bushel basket to indicate so many bushels of wheat. However, symbols do not always imply what they represent. Instead of a small bushel basket, the graph of wheat production might use circles to indicate so many bushels of wheat. A key or legend tells what each symbol equals. You multiply the number of symbols by the value of the symbol to determine totals.

STEPS IN READING BAR, LINE, AND SYMBOL GRAPHS

1. *Read the title, heading, or caption.* This identifies the general group of objects being compared.

***FIGURE 9.4***
***Retention Rates in U.S. Schools (1972 to 1984)***

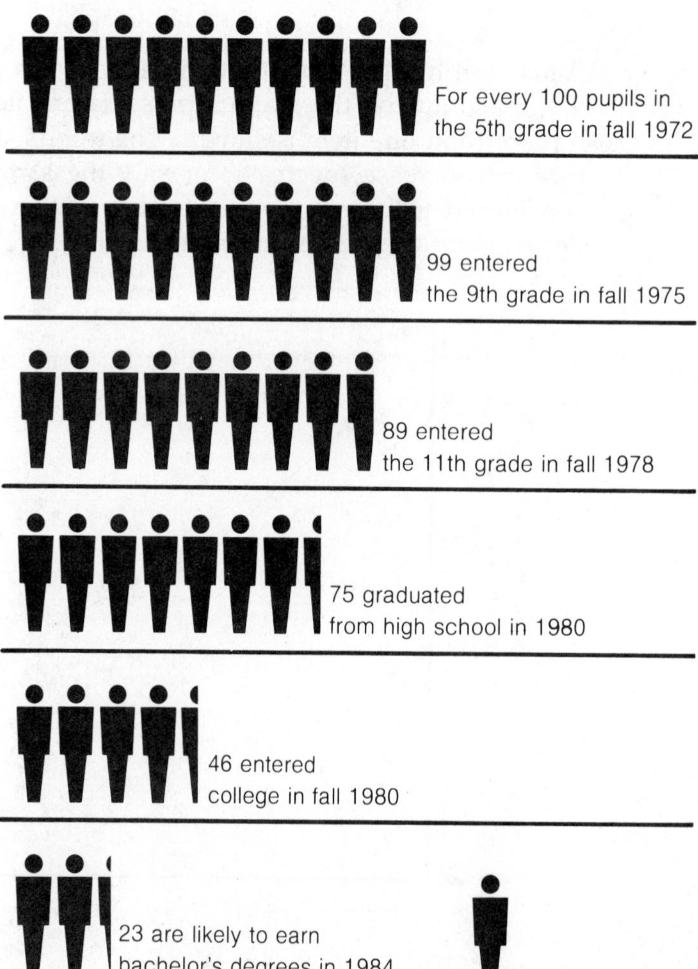

2. *Look at the labels or headings for each item or unit.* Identify the specific objects being compared or contrasted.
3. *Identify the units used to measure the items in a bar or line graph or the number that each symbol represents in a symbol graph.*
4. *Note any general trends.*
5. *If you are looking at a graph as part of the surveying step of SQ3R, stop your examination.* Continue previewing the chapter.
6. *When you read the section of the text that refers to the graph, identify the text's purpose before turning to the graph.* Does the author want you to note specific facts, generalizations, or trends?
7. *Use the purpose set by the text to look at specific areas of the graph.*
8. *Reread the section of the text that referred to the graph.* Make sure you understand the points and relationships noted by the author.

**WRITE TO LEARN**

*Estimate the average number of hours you spend daily in each of the following activities:*

*________ time spent in class*
*________ time spent at work*
*________ time spent at home/personal activities*
*________ time spent sleeping*
*________ time spent relaxing*
*________ time spent studying*

*On a separate sheet of paper, construct a bar, line, or symbol graph to display this data.*

## Circle Graphs

A circle graph shows how a whole unit is divided into parts (see Figure 9.5). Because a circle graph focuses on the relationships within a single

**FIGURE 9.5**
***Central State College Student Enrollment***

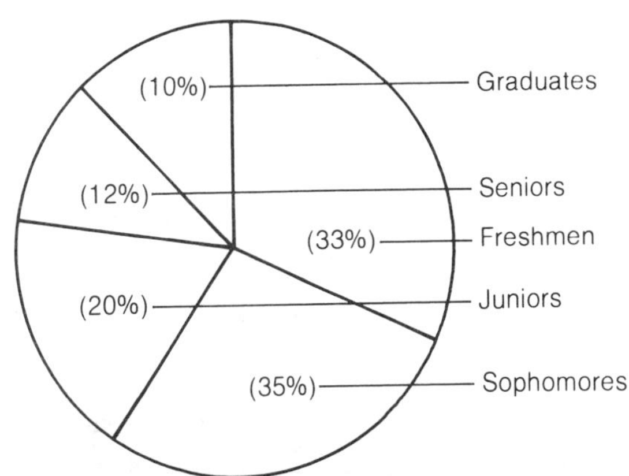

unit, a single circle graph represents a single unit. The parts of a circle graph are expressed as percentages and/or fractions. This is because all of the parts equal the whole unit or 100% of the unit.

Because circle graphs deal with fractions instead of units on a continuum, reading circle graphs differs from reading other graphs.

**WRITE TO LEARN**

*On a separate sheet of paper, use the data in the previous Write to Learn to construct a circle graph.*

◆

## FOLLOWING FLOWCHARTS

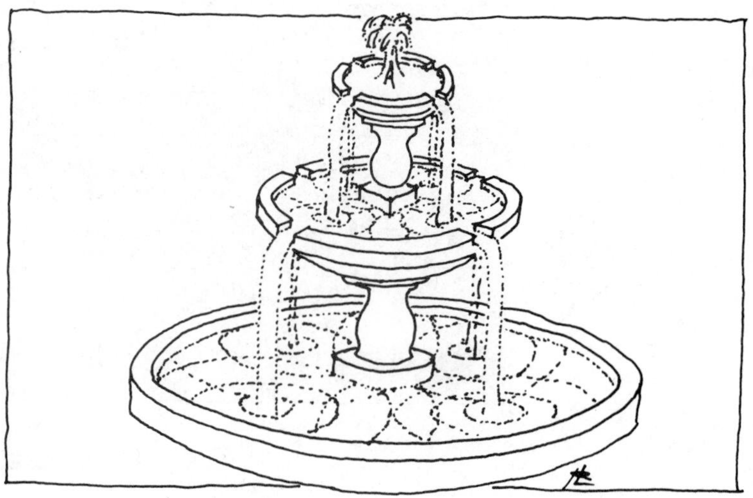

If you've ever watched a fountain, you know it directs the path of water in specific ways. Whatever's in the fountain "goes with the flow." Likewise, authors often want you to "go with their flow" when the concept they're explaining is difficult. To simplify the process, they create flowcharts (see Figure 9.6).

Flowcharts also indicate arrangement. These show degrees of relationships. Such flowcharts often depict chains of command within organizations. Thus, the information forms a hierarchy rather than steps in a process.

Flowcharts are generally clearer than written text. Arrows show the direction of the steps. Circles, boxes, or other shapes depict what should be done at each level.

**FIGURE 9.6**
**Registration Flowchart**

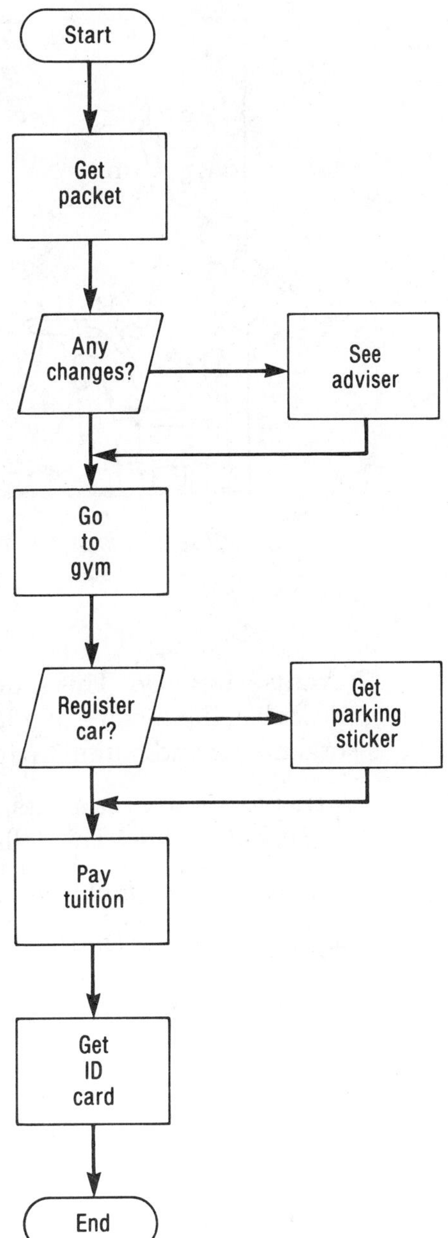


## USING TIMELINES

According to Thomas Mann, "Time has no divisions to mark its passing. There is never a thunderstorm to announce the beginning of a month or a year." While nature has no mechanism for marking special events, authors do. They use timelines to show you the order in which

"To put it into perspective, this is your life in relation to recorded time."

events happened. This sequence, or chronology, graphically outlines or describes the history of a topic (see Figure 9.7). It provides a means of organizing and summarizing important dates or events.

STEPS IN FOLLOWING TIMELINES

1. *Look at the title.* This tells you what time period is being covered.
2. *Look at the beginning and ending times on the line.*
3. *Notice any trends.*

**FIGURE 9.7**
***South Central Junior College Academic Calendar Summer Term***

| | |
|---|---|
| June 1 | Dorms open |
| 3 | Orientation for new students |
| 4 | Registration |
| 5 | Classes begin |
| 12 | Final day to add class for credit or to change sections |
| 24 | Last day to drop course without getting a W grade |
| 30–31 | Preregistration for fall term |
| July 4 | Independence Day holiday |
| 5–7 | Midterm exam period |
| 8 | Midterm grades due in Records Office |
| 22 | Last date to resign from the college |
| 29 | Last day of class |
| 30–31 | Final exam period |
| Aug. 6 | Summer commencement |

4. *Notice any breaks in trends.* If the data seem to change abruptly or if there is a long gap between events, this may be significant and worth your attention.
5. *Make inferences.*
6. *If you are looking at a timeline as part of the surveying step of SQ3R, stop your examination.* Continue previewing the chapter.
7. *When you read the section of the text that refers to the timeline, identify the text's purpose before turning to the timeline.* Does the author want to note specific facts, generalization, or trends?
8. *Use the purpose set by the text to look at specific areas of the graphic.*
9. *Reread the section of the text that referred to the timeline.* Make sure you understand the points and relationships noted by the author.

**WRITE TO LEARN**

*On a separate sheet of paper, construct a timeline chronicling ten of the most important events in your life.*

**EXERCISE 9.1** ◆ *Examine the following quality table and answer the questions below.*

**TABLE The Orders of Fossil and Living Mammals and Their Geologic Ranges**

| CLASSIFICATION | LIVING SPECIES | COMMON NAMES | TRIASSIC | JURASSIC | CRETACEOUS | PALEOCENE | EOCENE | OLIGOCENE | MIOCENE | PLIOCENE | PLEISTOCENE | RECENT |
|---|---|---|---|---|---|---|---|---|---|---|---|---|
| CLASS MAMMALIA | | | | | | | | | | | | |
| Subclass Prototheria | | | | | | | | | | | | |
| *Order Docodonta* | | | X | X | | | | | | | | |
| *Order Triconodonta* | | | X | | | | | | | | | |
| *Order Monotremata* | 3 | Spiny anteater, platypus | | | X | X | X | X | X | X | X | X |
| Subclass Allotheria | | | | | | | | | | | | |
| *Order Multituberculata* | | | | X | X | X | X | | | | | |
| Subclass Theria | | | | | | | | | | | | |
| *Order Symmetrodonta* | | | | X | X | | | | | | | |
| *Order Pantotheria* | | | | X | X | | | | | | | |
| *Order Credonta* | | | | | X | X | | | | | | |
| *Order Condylartha* | | | | | X | X | X | X | | | | |
| *Order Marsupialia* | 242 | Opossum, kangaroo, koala | | | X | X | X | X | X | X | X | X |
| *Order Insectivora* | 406 | Shrew, mole, hedgehog | | | X | X | X | X | X | X | X | |
| *Order Xenungulata* | | | | | | X | | | | | | |
| *Order Taeniodonta* | | | | | | X | X | | | | | |
| *Order Tillodontia* | | | | | | X | X | | | | | |
| *Order Dinocerata* | | | | | | X | X | | | | | |

**TABLE** ***Continued***

| CLASSIFICATION | LIVING SPECIES | COMMON NAMES | TRIASSIC | JURASSIC | CRETACEOUS | PALEOCENE | EOCENE | OLIGOCENE | MIOCENE | PLIOCENE | PLEISTOCENE | RECENT |
|---|---|---|---|---|---|---|---|---|---|---|---|---|
| CLASS MAMMALIA | | | | | | | | | | | | |
| *Order Pantodonta* | | | | | | X | X | | | | | |
| *Order Astraptheria* | | | | | | X | X | X | | | | |
| *Order Notoungulata* | | | | | | X | X | X | X | X | X | |
| *Order Litopterna* | | | | | | X | X | X | X | X | X | X |
| *Order Rodentia* | 1687 | Beaver, squirrel, mouse, rat, porcupine, gopher | | | | | | | | | | |
| Subclass Theria | | | | | | | | | | | | |
| *Order Lagomorpha* | 63 | Pika, rabbit, hare | | | | X | X | X | X | X | X | X |
| *Order Primates* | 166 | Lemur, tarsier, loris, monkey, human | | | | X | X | X | X | X | X | X |
| *Order Edentata* | 31 | Anteater, sloth, armadillo | | | | X | X | X | X | X | X | X |
| *Order Carnivora* | 284 | Dog, cat, bear, skunk, seal, weasel, hyena, raccoon, panda | | | | X | X | X | X | X | X | X |
| *Order Pyrotheria* | | | | | | | X | X | | | | |
| *Order Chiroptera* | 853 | Bats | | | | | X | X | X | X | X | X |
| *Order Dermoptera* | 2 | Flying lemurs | | | | | X | X | X | X | X | X |
| *Order Cetacea* | 84 | Whale, dolphin, porpoise | | | | | X | X | X | X | X | X |
| *Order Tubulidentata* | 1 | Aardvark | | | | | X | X | X | X | X | X |
| *Order Perissodactyla* | 16 | Horse, rhinoceros, tapir | | | | | X | X | X | X | X | X |
| *Order Artiodactyla* | 171 | Pig, hippo, camel, deer, elk, bison, cattle, sheep, antelope | | | | | X | X | X | X | X | X |
| *Order Proboscidea* | 2 | Elephant | | | | | X | X | X | X | X | X |
| *Order Sirenia* | 5 | Dugong, sea cow, manatee | | | | | X | X | X | X | X | X |
| *Order Embrithopoda* | | | | | | | | X | | | | |
| *Order Desmostyla* | | | | | | | | X | X | | | |
| *Order Hyracoidea* | 11 | Hyrax | | | | | | X | X | X | X | X |
| *Order Pholidota* | 8 | Scaly anteater | | | | | | X | X | X | X | X |

*Source:* Reprinted with permission from *Historical Geology,* by Wicander and Monroe. 

**1.** Identify the common names of mammals in three different orders who have geologic ranges of eight periods.

______________________________

______________________________

______________________________

______________________________

**2.** Identify three orders of mammals that are no longer in existence.

______________________________

______________________________

3. Which order has the most living species?

4. Which order has the fewest living species?

5. How do mammals in order Cetacea differ from mammals in most other orders?

**EXERCISE 9.2** ◆ *Examine the following quantity table and answer the questions below.*

**TABLE Vitamins**

| *VITAMIN* | *SOURCE* | *FUNCTION* | *RESULT OF DEFICIENCY* |
|---|---|---|---|
| *WATER-SOLUBLE VITAMINS (cannot be stored)* | | | |
| $B_1$ (thiamine) | Whole-grain cereals, nuts, pork, liver, eggs | Coenzyme in oxidation of carbohydrates and synthesis of ribose | Beriberi, which causes paralysis of smooth muscles |
| $B_2$ (riboflavin) | Beef, veal, lamb, eggs, many vegetables | Coenzyme in oxidation of glucose and fatty acids | Dermatitis |
| Niacin (nicotinic acid) | Meats, breads, cereals, peas, beans, nuts, many vegetables | Part of NAD and FAD | Pellagra, dermatitis, diarrhea |
| $B_6$ (composed of three compounds) | Spinach, corn, tomatoes, yogurt, cereals, liver, meats | Coenzyme in synthesis of proteins and nucleic acids | Slow growth, dermatitis, convulsions |
| $B_{12}$ | Milk, eggs, cheese, most meats | Coenzyme for synthesis of DNA; red blood cell production | Pernicious anemia |
| Pantothenic acid* | Green vegetables, cereals, liver | Component of coenzyme A in Krebs cycle | Not known |
| Folic acid (folacin)* | Leafy green vegetables, liver | Coenzyme in synthesis of DNA; hemoglobin production | Megaloblastic anemia |

**TABLE** ***Continued***

| VITAMIN | SOURCE | FUNCTION | RESULT OF DEFICIENCY |
|---|---|---|---|
| *WATER-SOLUBLE VITAMINS (cannot be stored)* | | | |
| Biotin* | Eggs, liver, yeast | Coenzyme in synthesis of nucleic acids and metabolism of amino acids | Dermatitis, fatigue, depression |
| C (ascorbic acid) | Citrus fruits, juices, leafy green vegetables, tomatoes | Involvement in synthesis of protein; collagen of bone and cartilage; promotion of iron absorption | Anemia, scurvy |
| *FAT-SOLUBLE VITAMINS (can be stored)* | | | |
| A | Yellow and green vegetables, fish, milk, butter | Synthesis of visual pigments; maintenance of epithelial tissues | Nightblindness; increased susceptibility to infection |
| D | Fish, egg yolk, milk, exposure of skin to ultraviolet light | Promotion of calcium and phosphorus absorption | Rickets |
| E | Nuts, wheat germ, green vegetables | Prevention of oxidation of vitamin A; possible help in maintaining stability of cell membranes | Sterility, kidney problems |
| K* | Spinach, cauliflower, liver | Blood-clotting factor | Delayed blood clotting |

**Also produced by the bacteria in the intestinal tract.*

*Source: Reprinted with permission from* Biology Today and Tomorrow *by Ward and Hetzel.* 

**1.** What would you need to eat if you were deficient in both riboflavin and vitamin D?

______________________________

**2.** Identify any three vitamins you need to avoid dermatitis.

______________________________

**3.** Identify two vitamins that are coenzymes for synthesis of DNA.

______________________________

**4.** What vitamins are also produced by bacteria in the digestive tract?

______________________________

______________________________

**5.** What is the result of a deficiency in pantothenic acid?

______________________________

______________________________

**6.** What vitamins did Popeye get from eating spinach?

______________________________

______________________________

7. What vitamins would you get from eating liver?

_______________________________________________

_______________________________________________

8. Children are often told to eat their carrots. What vitamin would they get from carrots? What is its function and what is a result of this vitamin deficiency?

_______________________________________________

_______________________________________________

9. What foods might you eat to combat depression?

_______________________________________________

_______________________________________________

10. What is the main difference between water-soluble and fat-soluble vitamins?

_______________________________________________

_______________________________________________

## EXERCISE 9.3

◆ *Examine the following bar graph and answer the questions below.*

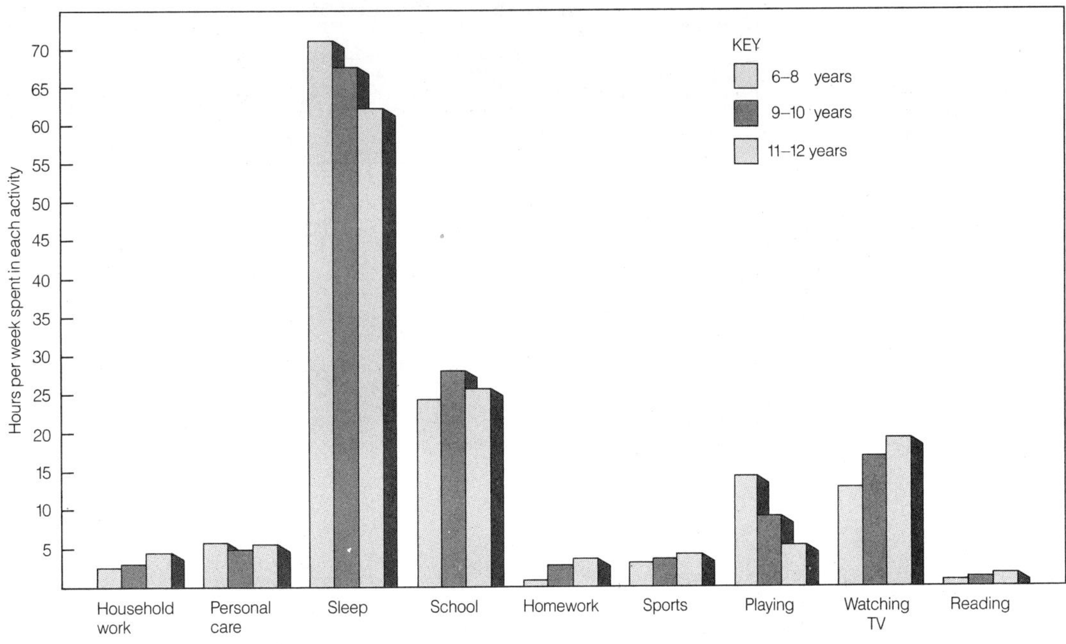


***Amount of time per week spent by school-aged children in various tasks.***

*Source:* Reprinted with permission from *Psychology* by Dworetzky. 

1. What three groups are being compared?

2. What does the graph tell you about the reading habits of all three groups?

3. Compare the 11–12-year-old group with the 6–8-year-old group in each of the following areas:
   a. playing

   b. personal care

   c. watching TV

4. Which of the three groups spends the most time sleeping? How do you account for this?

_______________

_______________

_______________

_______________

_______________

5. Which of the three groups spends the least time doing homework? How do you account for this?

_______________

_______________

_______________

_______________

_______________

**EXERCISE 9.4**

*Examine the following line graph and answer the questions below.*

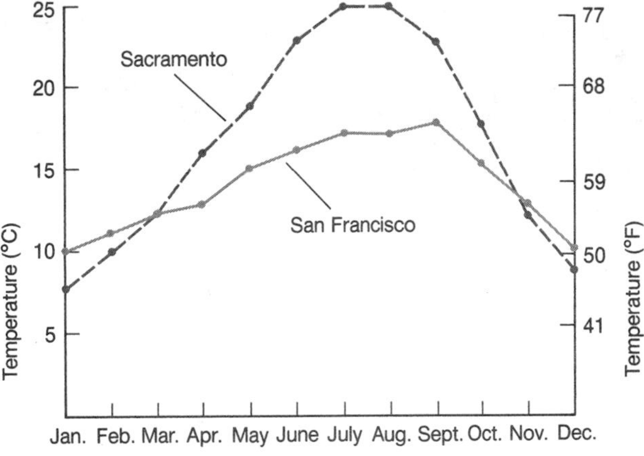


*Source:* Reprinted with permission from *Physical Geography* by Scott. 

1. What two items are being compared on this graph?

_______________

_______________

_______________

_______________

_______________

2. In what month is the highest temperature in Sacramento? San Francisco? What is this temperature for each?

3. In what month is the lowest temperature in Sacramento? San Francisco? What is this temperature for each?

4. In what months are the temperatures of the two cities the same? What are these temperatures?

5. In what month is the greatest temperature difference between the two cities? Approximately how much is the difference?

**EXERCISE 9.5**

♦ *Examine this symbol graph and answer the following questions.*

Students in School

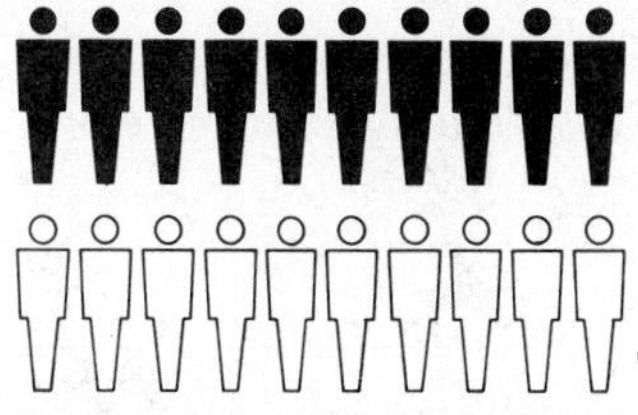

End of 1st grade

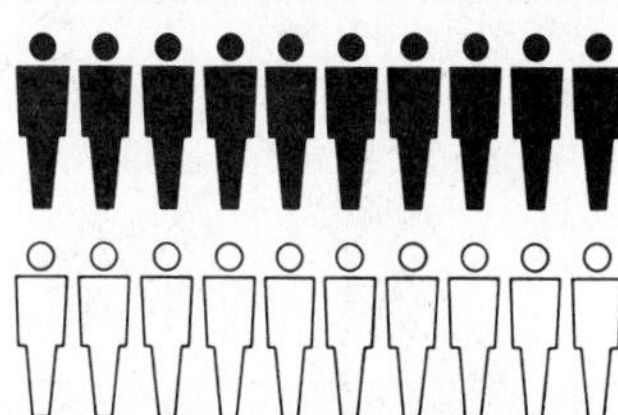

End of 4th grade

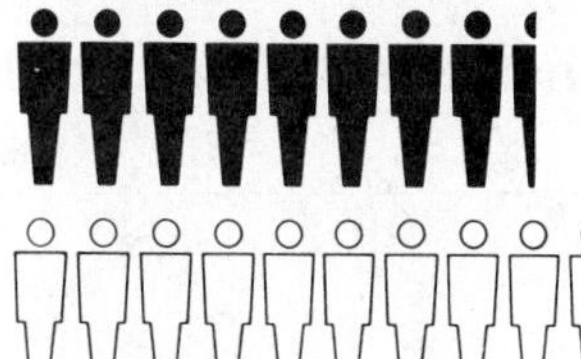

End of 8th grade

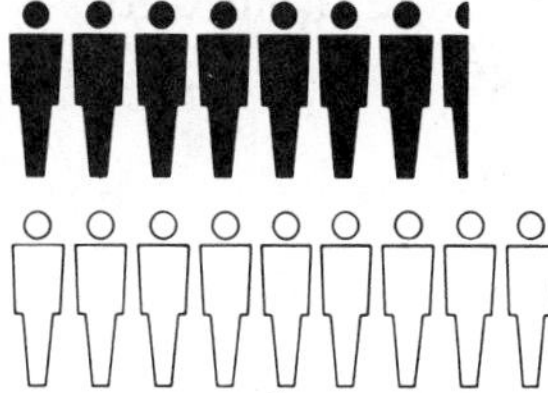

End of 12th grade

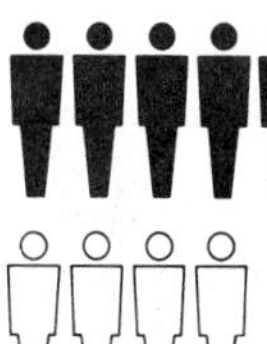

Enter college

Get bachelor's degree

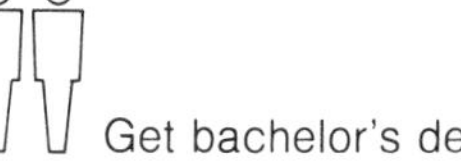

= 10 Males

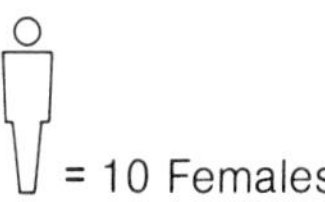

= 10 Females

1. What is the subject of the graph?

2. What does each symbol represent?

3. What trend is found between male and female students in elementary and high school?

4. What trends exist between male and female students in college?

5. What percentage of students out of the original number completing first grade get a bachelor's degree?

**EXERCISE 9.6**

*On separate sheets of paper, construct a bar graph, a line graph, and a symbol graph using the data below.*

**TABLE Imports and Exports for Five Nations**

| | TOTAL DOLLAR AMOUNTS (IN MILLIONS) | |
|---|---|---|
| *Country* | *Imports* | *Exports* |
| *PLATLAND* | 400 | 900 |
| *ORANGE REPUBLIC* | 100 | 50 |
| *BENGAL STATES* | 200 | 550 |
| *SOUTH DOMINION* | 400 | 400 |
| *MADISONLAND* | 300 | 200 |

## EXERCISE 9.7

*Examine the following circle graphs and answer the questions below.*

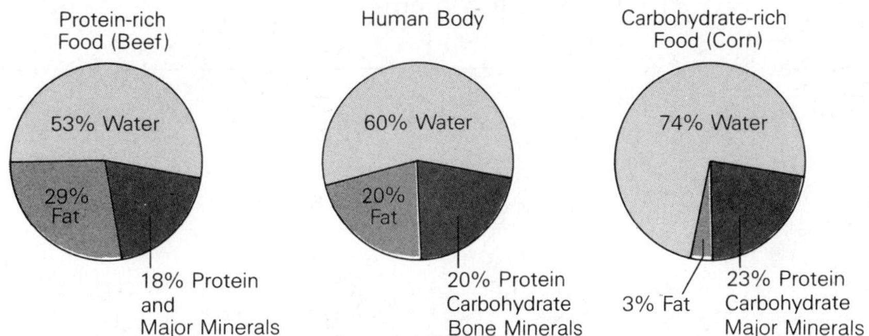


***Foods and the human body are made of the same classes of chemicals. (Vitamins and other constituents are not shown, because the amounts are too small to be seen on a graph this size.)***

*Source:* Reprinted with permission from *Understanding Nutrition* 4/e by Whitney and Hamilton. Copyright © 1987 by West Publishing Company. All rights reserved.

**1.** What is the subject of the three circle graphs?

**2.** Which of the three contain the most protein and minerals? How much does each contain?

**3.** If a 200-pound person's body contains 120 pounds of water and 40 pounds of protein, carbohydrates, and minerals, how much fat does it contain?

**4.** According to the information in the title of these graphs, vitamins and other constituents are not shown because the amounts are too small to be seen on such a graph. Examine each graph carefully. Vitamins and other constituents comprise less than what percent of either protein-rich food, the human body, or carbohydrates? How do you know this?

**5.** What two foods are compared in the first and last graphs? Which contains the most fat? Why do the percentages represented in the first graph more closely resemble those in the second than those in the third?

**EXERCISE 9.8** ◆ *Examine the following flowchart and answer the questions below.*

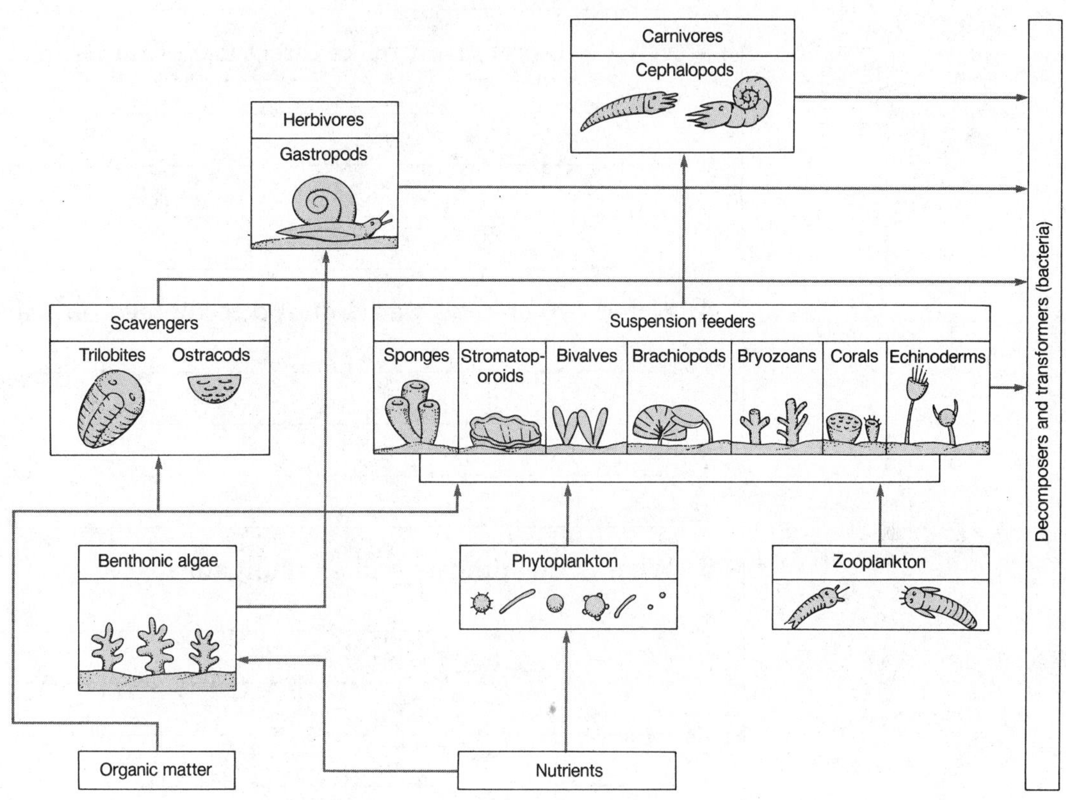


***Tropic analysis of an Ordovician reef community showing the relationship between the various organisms of the community. The phytoplankton and benthonic algae are primary producers, occupying the lowest trophic level. The primary consumers are the suspension feeders, making up the majority of the community. The highest trophic level is occupied by the carnivores, which in this community are the cephalopods.***

*Source:* Reprinted with permission from *Historical Geology* by Wicander and Monroe. 

**1.** On what do gastropods feed? On what do cephalopods feed?

______________________________________________

______________________________________________

______________________________________________

______________________________________________

**2.** Why are the suspension feeders the primary consumers of the community?

______________________________________________

______________________________________________

3. What two organisms make direct use of nutrients?

4. Name two animals that do not directly feed on scavengers.

5. What is the ultimate end of all organisms?

**EXERCISE 9.9**

*Examine the following timeline and answer the questions below.*

**TABLE** ***Major Influences on Curriculum***

| TIME | INFLUENCE |
|---|---|
| 1635–1770 | Religion; schools expected to promulgate the religious beliefs in the country. |
| 1770–1860 | Political; schools should educate the public to ensure the preservation of democracy. |
| 1860–1920 | Economic; schools should educate people to fill new jobs in a rapidly expanding economy. |
| 1920–present | Mass Education; schools should provide equal educational opportunity to all citizens. |
| 1957–present | Excellence in Education; schools should do a better job in educating American youth. This movement resulted from the discovery in World War II that many graduates were very weak in mathematics and science. Sputnik also was a major influence. |

1. For how many years was religion a major influence on curriculum?

2. Examine each of the ranges of time. Which influence has affected curriculum the longest amount of time?

3. Examine each of the ranges of time. Which influence has affected curriculum the shortest amount of time?

4. During what years did the U.S. economy grow most rapidly?

5. During the American Revolution from 1776–1783, what was the focus of political influences on the curriculum?

◆

## READING MAPS

Across the Yegua River a sign pointed south to Dime Box. Over broad hills, over the green expansion spreading under cedars and live oaks, on into a valley where I found Dime Box, essentially a three-street town. Vegetable gardens and flowerbeds lay to the side, behind, and in front of the houses. Perpendicular to the highway, two streets ran east and west:

> one of worn brick buildings facing the Southern Pacific tracks, the other a double row of false front stores and wooden sidewalks. Disregarding a jarring new bank, Dime Box could have been an M-G-M backlot set for a Western.

William Least Heat Moon wrote this description of the town of Dime Box in *Blue Highways: A Journey into America* (Little, Brown and Co., 1983). Had Mr. Least Heat Moon been a cartographer (a person who makes maps), he could have drawn a graphic illustration of Dime Box.

Every place has a specific location. Each location in the world, including Dime Box, has specific and special characteristics. These locations and characteristics are placed on globes or maps. Locations are shown on globes in three-dimensional form. Maps, on the other hand, are two-dimensional graphics of specific locations.

Maps comprise the only practical way to show large amounts of space. Because maps show much information, they are more effective than written accounts. Such text would be lengthy and confusing, at best. Thus, maps perform two jobs. First, they reduce an area to a size that can be shown on one sheet. Second, they show only those phenomena of interest.

Maps are most commonly found in geography or history texts, although they may also be included in science, math, or literature texts and recreational reading books. Maps help you clarify the text. Thus, map-reading skills aid your understanding.

## Characteristics of Maps

Maps show many different types of information. To understand this data, you need to identify this information. You do this by examining the features and language the map uses.

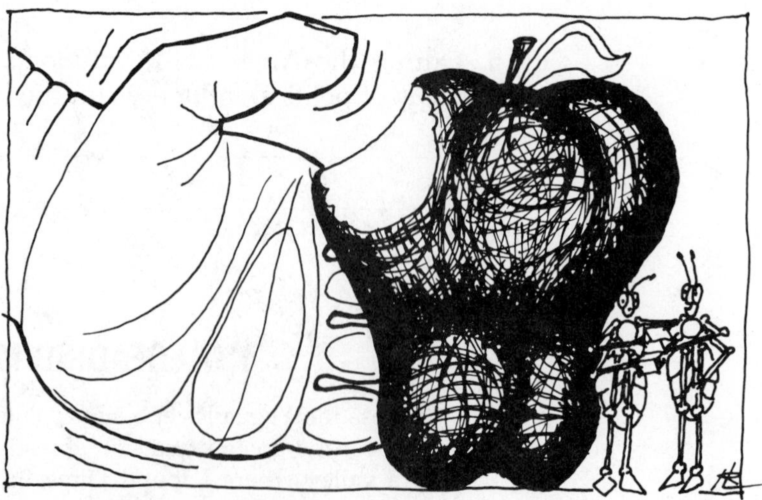

*"Let's see that map again. I was sure that apple was on the other side of the pie."*

### *Features*

Among the most basic types of map information are the title, date, location, **scale of distance,** and legend, or key.

The map title indicates the purpose of the map. It provides you with a chance to connect the map with information you know or have read. Referring to the title in your notes serves as a way of summarizing the data a map contains.

The date of a map indicates its accuracy. This is true because older maps sometimes contain obsolete information. In most cases, knowing the year of the map suffices.

Many maps indicate location by referring to **latitudes** and **longitudes** (or **meridians**). Others show location by placing a small inset showing the area of the map within its larger geographical setting. This allows you to recognize areas that might have otherwise been hard to discern.

To draw a map the actual size of the area it represents would be impossible. So, maps show areas that are reduced in size. A scale of distance shows the relationship between the distance of a place located on a map and this distance in real life. Scales can be shown in the following three ways:

Fraction 1″ : 100 miles
Written Statement 1 inch equals 100 miles

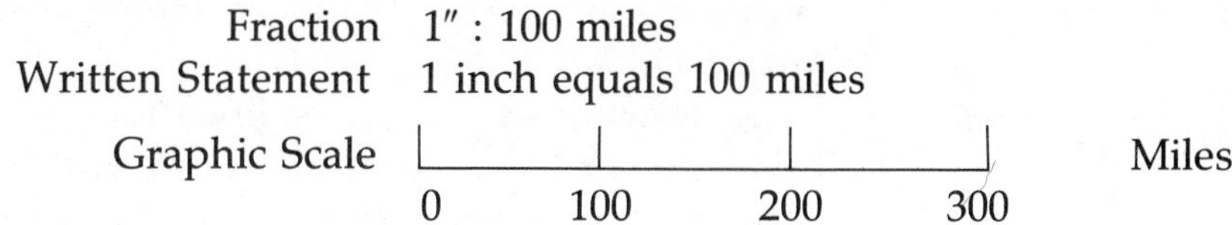


Symbols on maps represent natural (mountains, rivers, lakes) or constructed (cities, roads) details. An example of a symbol would be the star that represents a capital city. Reading a map requires a thorough understanding of these symbols. This understanding is accomplished with the aid of a key or legend.

A key or legend contains each symbol used on a map and an explanation of these symbols (see Figure 9.8). The legend is usually found at the bottom of a map. However, it can appear anywhere on the map.

### *Language*

Map language consists of names, numbers, colors, and symbols. You need to know the language to decipher a map.

Map language begins with direction. There are four basic directions: north, south, east, and west. North is the direction toward the North Pole from any other place on earth. South is the opposite of north. It faces toward the South Pole. East is toward the sunrise. West is toward the sunset.

The **equator** is the imaginary 25,000-mile line around the middle of the earth. It divides the planet into two hemispheres. The part of the earth north of the equator comprises the **northern hemisphere.** Most of

**FIGURE 9.8**
***Example of a Map Legend***

LEGEND

◉ Place of 100,000 or more inhabitants
⊙ Place of 50,000 to 100,000 inhabitants
● Place of 25,000 to 50,000 inhabitants

All political boundaries are as of January 1, 1985

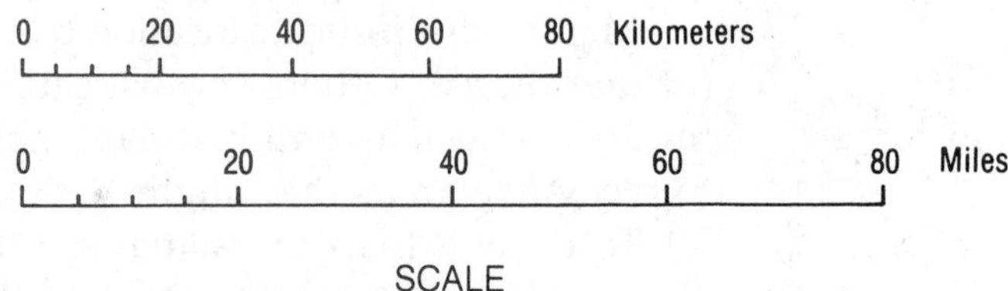


*Source:* U.S. Bureau of the Census, *County and City Data Book,* 10th ed., 1983.

the world's dry land and people reside here. The **southern hemisphere** consists of all the area south of the equator. Only two of the seven continents are in the Southern Hemisphere. They are Australia and Antarctica.

A network of imaginary lines identifies exact locations on maps. This network forms from the North and South Poles and the equator. Cartographers draw latitudes parallel to the equator. They measure **degrees** (°) north or south of it. The equator, then is located at 0° latitude. Longitudes indicate east and west directions. They run vertically from the North Pole to the South Pole. East and West are also measured in degrees. These begin at 0° longitude. This line is called the **Greenwich** or **prime meridian.**

## Types of Maps

Early maps were crude pictures. The oldest existing maps came from ancient Babylonia. Babylonians sketched these maps on tablets of damp clay. Then they let them dry in the sun. Early Chinese painted their maps on silk. But, all ancient maps of the world were incomplete. As adventurers discovered more about the world, maps became the complete, precise pictures they are today. Modern cartographers draw maps for a variety of purposes. The vast differences among these purposes make it necessary to have different types of maps.

### *Political Maps*

A **political map** (see Figure 9.9) shows the location of constructed features. The only physical features on a political map would be oceans, mountains, and/or large lakes and rivers. Political maps indicate capital

**FIGURE 9.9**
***Map of Nevada***

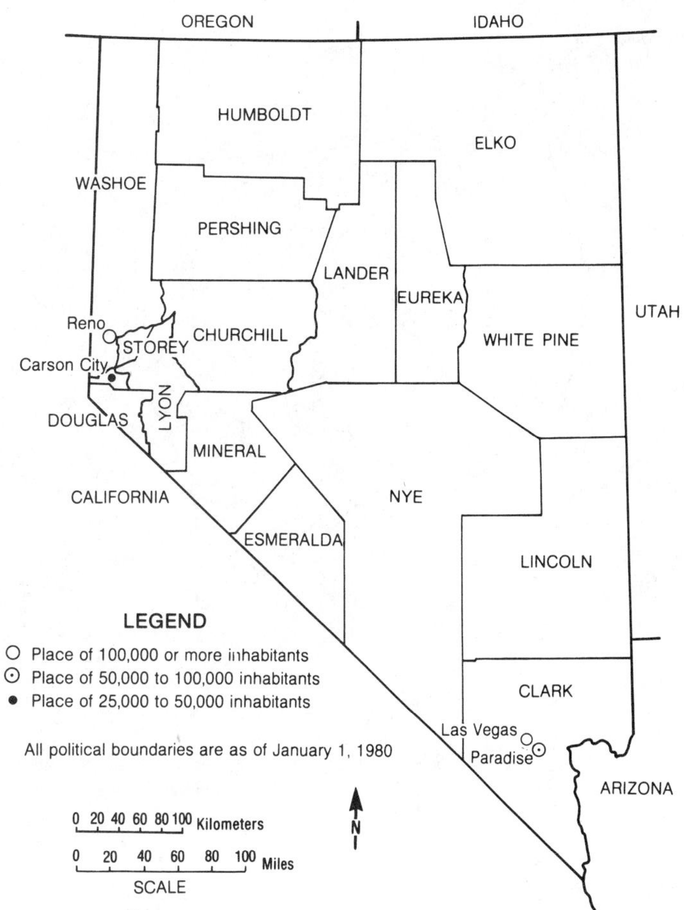


*Source:* Reprinted with permission from *Country and City Data Book,* 10th ed., 1983 by U.S. Bureau of the Census.

cities. They also show the **boundaries** or international borders between countries. These borders consist of either straight lines plotted by surveyors or wavy lines that follow natural features.

## Physical Maps

**Physical maps** (see Figure 9.10) provide information about the **topography** of an area. Topography is defined as the surface features of a place. Surface features include hills, valleys, streams, and lakes. They also provide data about vegetation. Physical maps indicate the **elevation** or **altitude** of mountains, valleys, deserts, and glaciers. Altitude is measured from **sea level,** or zero elevation. They also note depressions, areas of land below sea level. In addition, physical maps indicate the depth of the ocean. Like altitude, depth is measured from sea level.

## Special-Purpose Maps

A third kind of map is a special-purpose map (see Figure 9.11). These maps highlight some specific natural or constructed feature, such as

**FIGURE 9.10**
***The Physical Divisions In and Around the Great Plains Province***

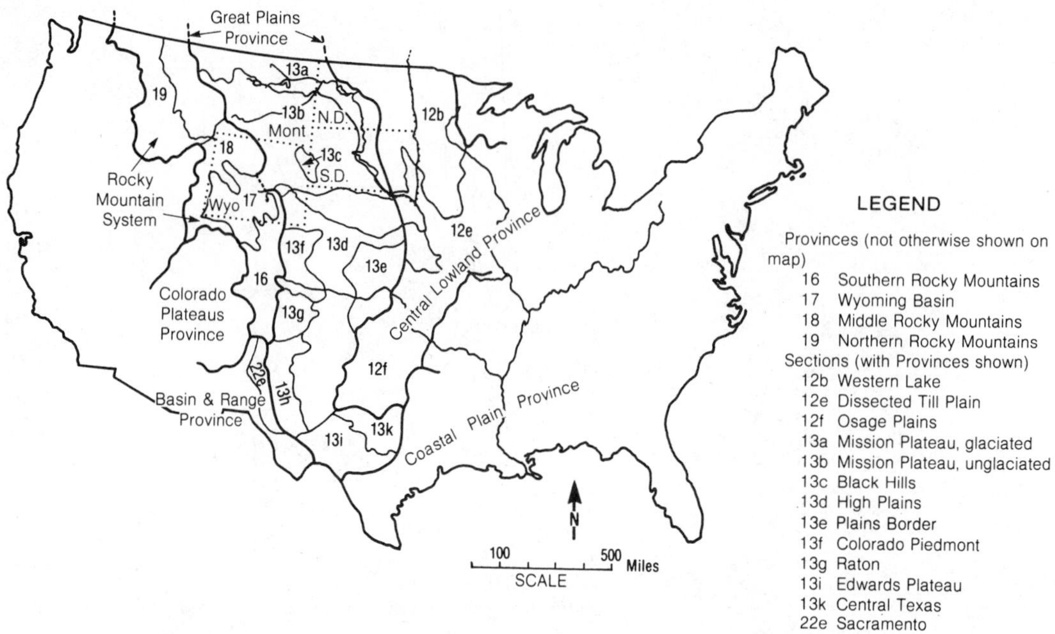


*Source:* Litton, Jr., R. B. & Tetlow, R. J. A *Landscape Inventory Framework: Scenic Analyses of the Northern Great Plains.* Res. Paper PSW-135, Pacific Southwest Forest and Range Exp. Stn., Forest Service, U.S. Department of Agriculture, Berkeley, CA, 1978.

**FIGURE 9.11**
***The Distribution of Airports in Africa as an Example of Functional Regions***

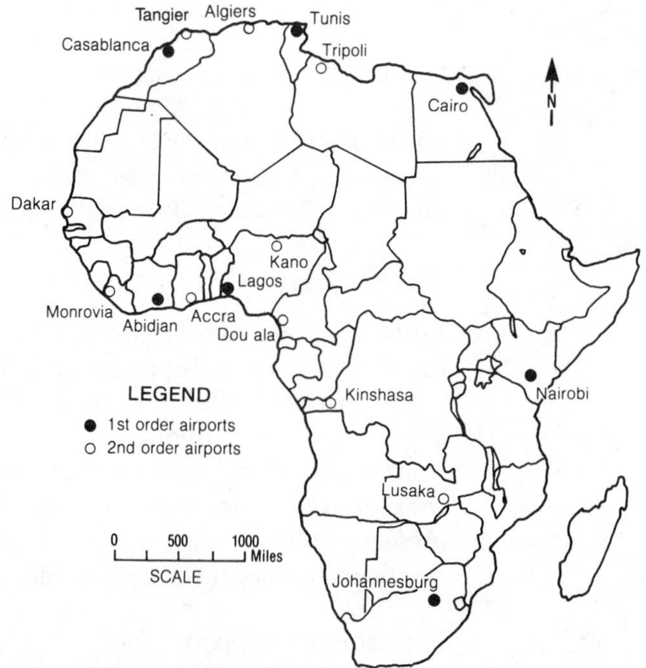


*Source:* Reprinted with permission from *The Cultural Landscape: An Introduction to Human Geography* by Rubenstein and Bacon. 

changes in a river's course or changes in population. This type of map is used by people in all sorts of occupations.

### Reading Maps

Even though maps come in various types and have differing features, you use the same steps to read them. Reading maps requires you to use context, draw conclusions, scan, and find main ideas. Maps, then, provide practice for critical reading.

STEPS FOR READING MAPS

1. *Locate and read the title to decide what geographical area is shown.* Identify the type of information that is being given about the area.
2. *Examine the map to get an idea of what it's about.* Locating direction (north, south, east, and west) may be helpful.
3. *Read the key or legend to identify symbols used on the map.* Check the scale to get an idea of how much area the map covers.
4. *If you are looking at a map as a part of the surveying step of SQ3R, stop your examination.* Continue previewing the chapter.
5. *Decide what information you need from the map.*
6. *Scan the map to find this information.* Make inferences about the material on the map.

**EXERCISE 9.10**

◆ *Examine the following physical map and caption and answer the questions below.*

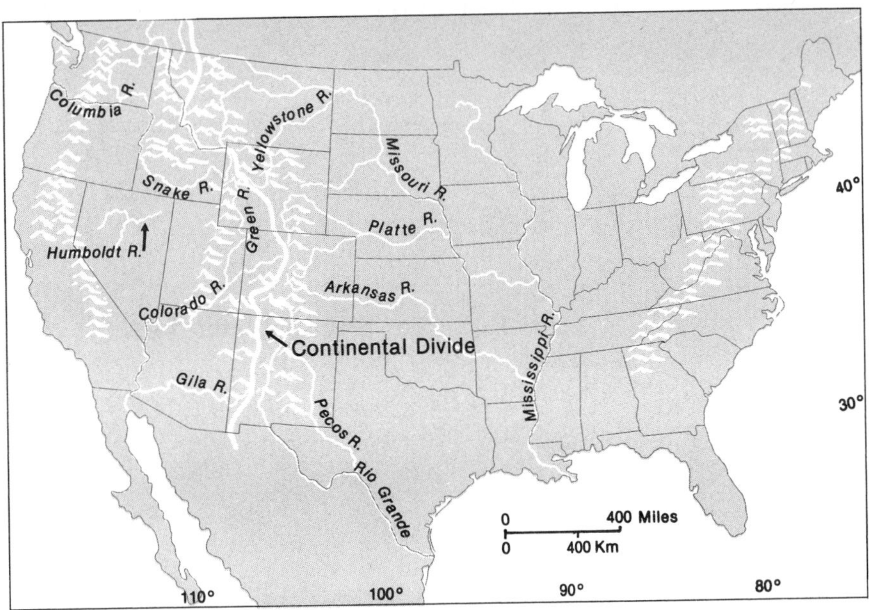


*Source:* Reprinted with permission from *Physical Geography* by Scott. Copyright © 1989 by West Publishing Company. All rights reserved.

1. Devise a title for the map.

2. What is the approximate longitudinal range of the Continental Divide?

3. What is the approximate latitude of the base of the Continental Divide?

4. Excluding the Mississippi River, into what body of water does the Platte River empty?

5. Into what body of water does the Snake River empty?

**EXERCISE 9.11**

◆ *Examine the following political map and answer the questions below.*

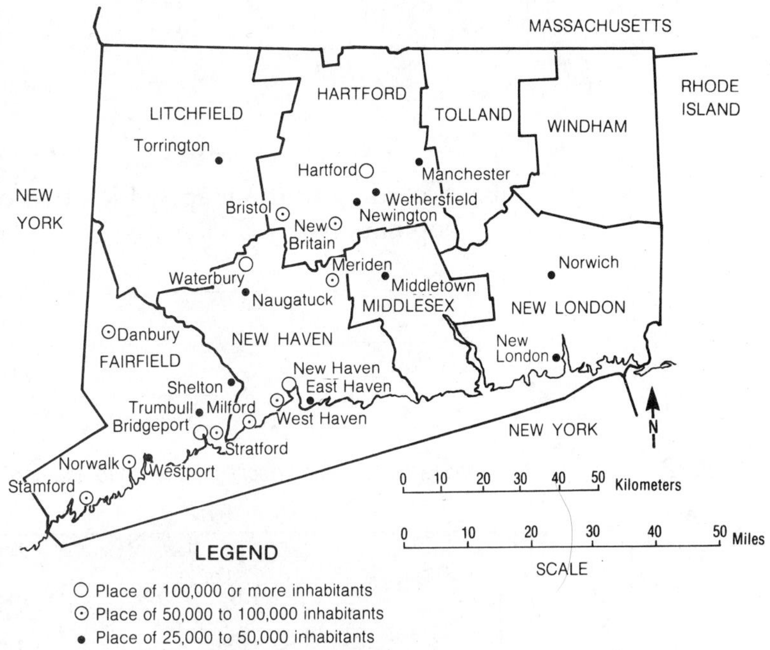


*Source:* U.S. Bureau of the Census, *County and City Data Book*, 10th ed., 1983.

**1.** What cities have populations of 100,000 or more?

**2.** What state is north of Connecticut?

**3.** Into how many counties is Connecticut divided?

4. Which counties have less than three cities with populations of at least 25,000 inhabitants?

5. According to the map, which two counties have the smallest urban populations?

**EXERCISE 9.12**

*Examine the following special-purpose map and caption and answer the questions below.*

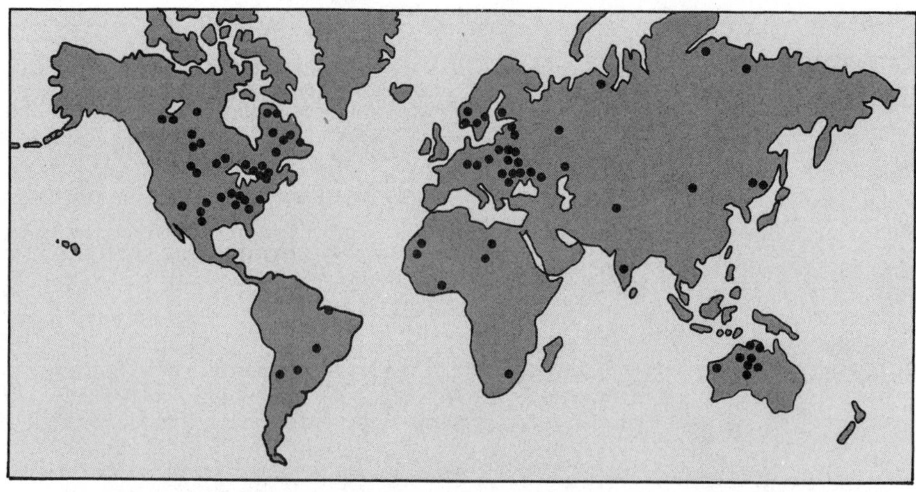

**Map showing the location of major craters thought to be the result of collisions with massive objects. It should be noted that the distribution is largely a result of our knowledge of these areas and does not purport to be a real distribution of craters.**

*Source:* Reprinted with permission from *Historical Geology* by Wicander and Monroe. 

1. What is the subject of this map?

2. According to the map, which continent has been hit the most by meteorites?

3. According to the map, which continent has the most craters?

4. According to the map, which continent has the fewest craters?

5. What fact would explain this difference?

6. Name two natural phenomena that might have caused these craters.

**WRITE TO LEARN**

*On a separate sheet of paper, construct a map depicting the route from the place you live to this class. Include the basic map features discussed in the section entitled "Characteristics of Maps." Include at least three physical features and three political features.*

**EXERCISE 9.13**

◆ *Read this excerpt and answer the following questions.*

## The Judicial Establishment: A Dual Court System

### STATE COURTS

Federal courts and state courts exist side by side in the United States. The two systems meet only on those rare occasions where state cases are heard on appeal by the U.S. Supreme Court. In one sense, the United States has fifty-one court systems. Acknowledging variations in state courts, however, the courts are commonly thought of as a dual system. At the bottom of the state court system are the minor courts, often called justices of the peace in rural areas and municipal courts in the cities. Their jurisdiction is usually limited to civil functions, traffic violations, and criminal offenses—everything from getting married to spitting in public.

Next up the ladder are county courts, which have broader jurisdiction. (They have different names in many states but are approximately equivalent in function.) Included are common pleas courts, juvenile courts, domestic relations courts, and probate courts. The main courts of original jurisdiction at the state level are trial courts, where juries hear cases. Twenty-six states have appeals courts above the county courts. In the other twenty-four states, appeals from the county-level courts go directly to the state supreme court. In the great majority of cases, the decision in the state's highest court is final. Rarely are appeals from state courts taken to the Supreme Court of the United States. The Supreme Court will take a state case on appeal only under special circumstances or if a substantial federal question is involved. A state case taken on appeal does not start over at the bottom of the federal court system but goes directly to the U.S. Supreme Court. However, state laws can be challenged in lower federal courts.

### FEDERAL COURTS

Federal courts are either legislative courts or the more familiar constitutional courts.[6] **Legislative courts** administer a particular body of law and perform legislative as well as judicial tasks. The customs court, the tax court, and the court of military justice are examples of legislative courts. Unlike constitutional courts, legislative courts may issue *advisory opinions*—that is, they may offer an opinion without having a specific case at hand.

**Constitutional courts**—federal district courts, federal appeals courts, and the U.S. Supreme Court—are the heart of the federal judiciary. Figure 16–1 shows the structure of the federal court system.

#### Federal District Courts

Like the county courts at the state level, the district courts are the trial courts of the federal judiciary. Here civil and criminal cases are tried and justice is dispensed. As courts of original jurisdiction, they first hear a case and usually make the final disposition of the case. Across the United States are 94 district courts employing 575 judges. Federal district judge is an important and exclusive job in the United States. Here is where the action is in federal courtrooms. Cases range from school desegregation to kidnapping and attempts to assassinate the president. Trials can be held without juries if all parties agree, but if a jury trial is demanded, twelve jurors must serve and their decision must be unanimous.

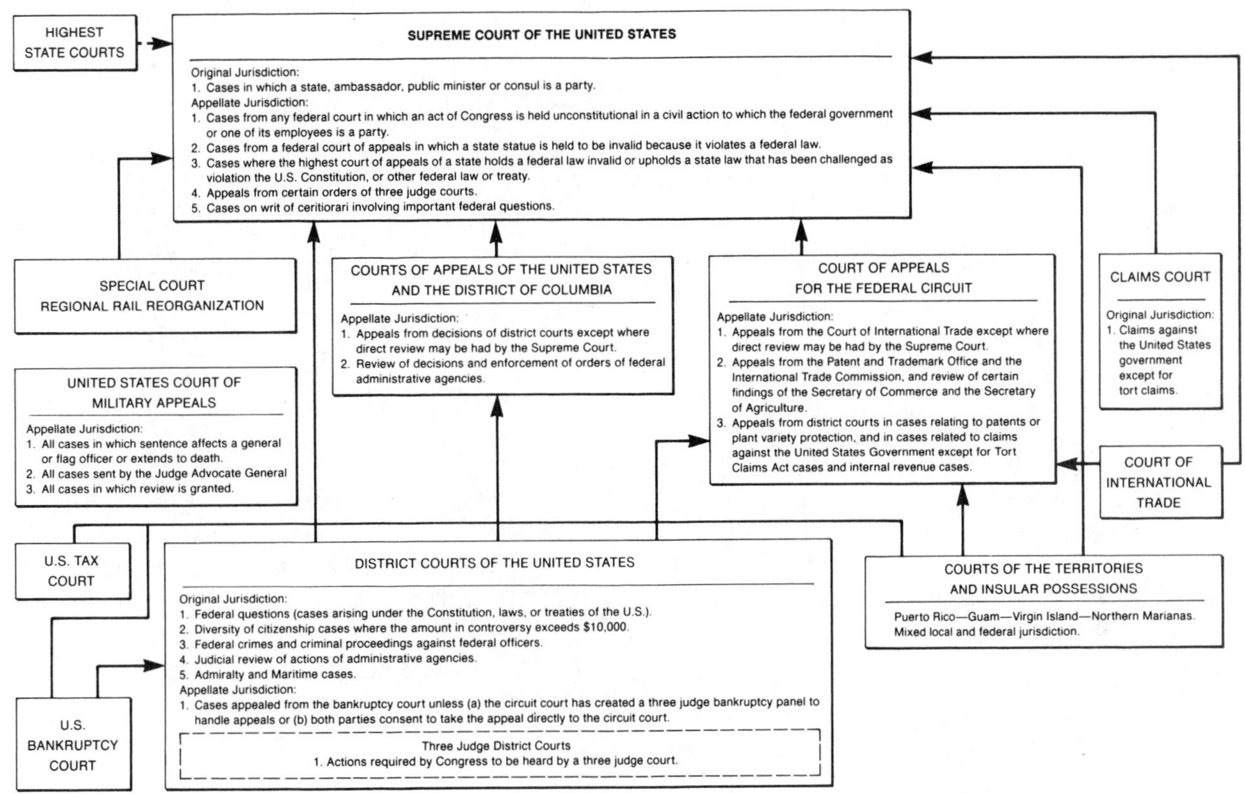


***FIGURE 16–1***
***The Federal Court System***

## U.S. Circuit Courts of Appeals

Cases heard in the federal district courts may be appealed to the federal appeals court. Unlike the lower courts, the court of appeals has only appellate jurisdiction; it considers cases that have already been tried in district court. The United States has twelve courts of appeal (called "circuit courts" from the days when judges used to ride from town to town on horseback) employing 156 judges.[7] A chief judge presides in each of the twelve circuits. Cases appealed from the district courts are not retried by juries but are usually argued in front of three-judge panels. A winnowing process results in only a small percentage of all cases being heard by the appeals courts (around seven thousand a year). Occasionally appeals from legislative courts are heard. In some districts, cases are decided strictly on the basis of written arguments. Other districts, such as the second, preserve oral argument in virtually all cases. Figure 16–2 is a map of the twelve circuits and the ninety-four districts in the United States.

## The U.S. Supreme Court

As prescribed in the Constitution, the Supreme Court is the highest court in the land. It is primarily an appeals court but, as we saw in the *Marbury* case, it has some original jurisdiction as specified in Article III. Congress may establish the number of justices on the Court. For the past century the Court has had nine justices, but it has had as few as five and as many as

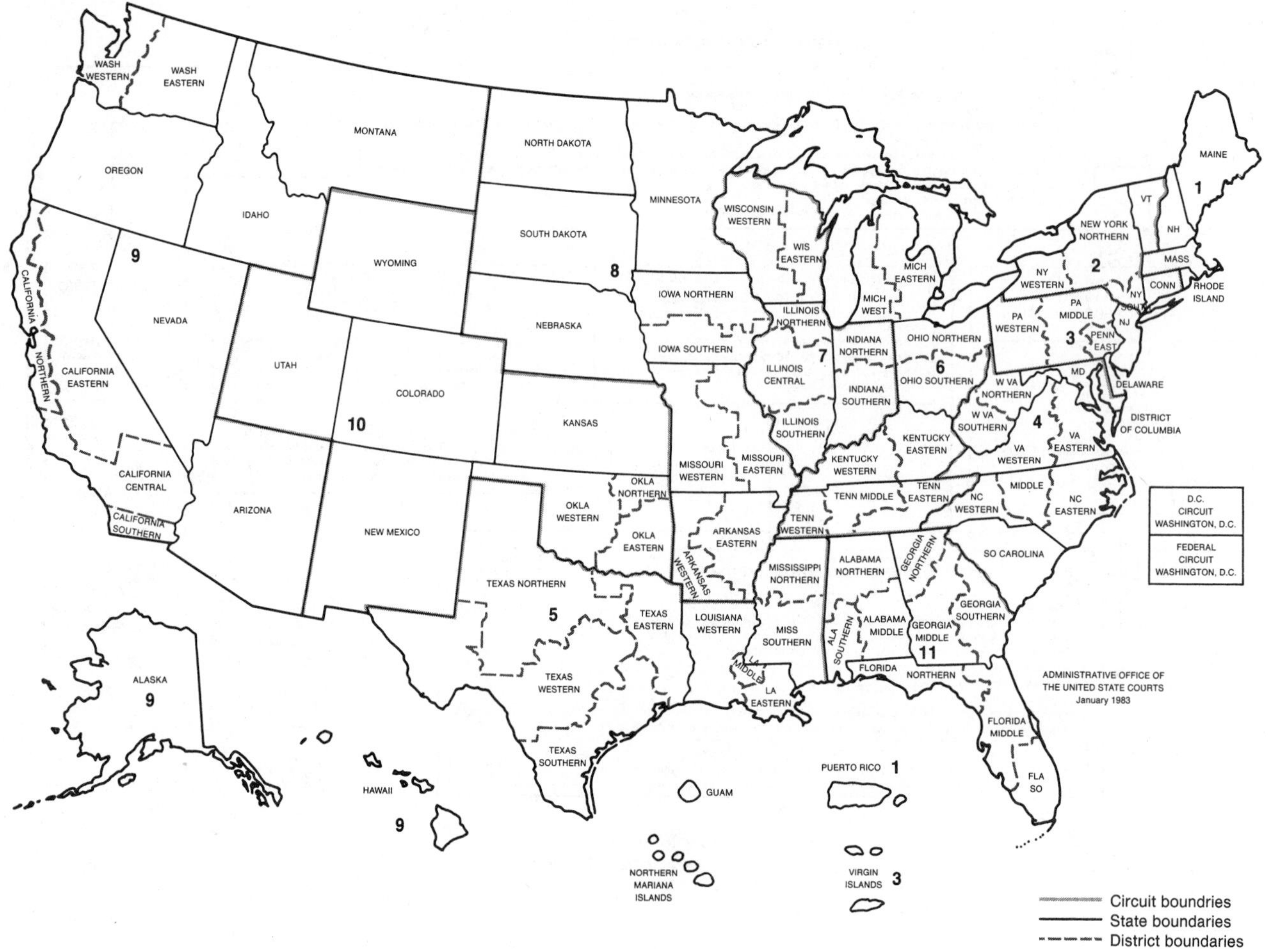


***FIGURE 16–2***
***U.S. Circuit Courts of Appeals and U.S. District Courts***

ten in its entire history. The chief justice of the United States is the first among equals and has an important impact on the direction of the Court. The key post of chief justice does not necessarily go to the associate justice with the most seniority. The president may appoint an associate justice (as in the case of Rehnquist) or someone off the Court (as in the case of Burger) to be chief justice when a vacancy occurs. The opportunity to name a chief justice is one of the most important appointments a president can make, and only thirteen of the forty U.S. presidents have had the chance. Like other federal judges, chief justices serve for life and can be removed only through impeachment. Table 16–1 lists the chief justices of the Supreme Court, one of the most elite positions in American politics. William Howard Taft, the only man to hold both the presidency and the job of chief justice, considered heading the Court to be the more desirable job of the two.

## JURISDICTION OF THE FEDERAL COURTS

Courts cannot initiate policy; they can only respond to controversies brought before them. Federal courts consider two kinds of law. *Civil law* consists of rules governing relationships between private citizens, embod-

**TABLE 16–1 Chief Justices of the United States**

| CHIEF JUSTICE | APPOINTED BY PRESIDENT | YEAR APPOINTED |
|---|---|---|
| John Jay | Washington | 1789 |
| Oliver Ellsworth | Washington* | 1796 |
| John Marshall | Adams | 1801 |
| Roger B. Taney | Jackson | 1836 |
| Salmon P. Chase | Lincoln | 1864 |
| Morrison R. Waite | Grant | 1874 |
| Melville W. Fuller | Cleveland | 1888 |
| Edward D. White | Taft | 1910 |
| William Howard Taft | Harding | 1921 |
| Charles Evans Hughes | Hoover | 1930 |
| Harlan Fiske Stone | Roosevelt | 1941 |
| Frederick M. Vinson | Truman | 1946 |
| Earl Warren | Eisenhower | 1953 |
| Warren E. Burger | Nixon | 1969 |
| William H. Rehnquist | Reagan | 1986 |

*Washington appointed John Rutledge, who served as chief justice for a few months but was never confirmed by the Senate.*

ied in statutes and established in previous court decisions (common law). *Criminal law* consists of the rules that define offenses of one person against another and that are punishable by the state.

Federal courts have jurisdiction in both civil cases and criminal cases. Figure 16–1 contains definitions of original jurisdiction and appellate jurisdiction of the courts. District courts have jurisdiction over all crimes against the United States, for civil cases of more than $10,000, and for any other category prescribed by Congress. The courts of appeal have appellate jurisdiction over almost all federal courts of original jurisdiction—constitutional and legislative courts, territorial courts, District of Columbia courts, independent regulatory commissions, and some bureaucratic agencies. The Supreme Court has original jurisdiction in only a few cases that involve the states, foreign ambassadors, or other nations. It has appellate jurisdiction over all federal courts and state courts if a federal question is involved.

## JUDGES AND JUSTICES

The judicial establishment includes the courts, court reporters, court administrators, clerks of the court, lawyers on both sides, and the public. But perhaps the most crucial participants in the judiciary are judges and justices, men and women dressed in black robes who preside over the courtrooms. Who are they? Where do they come from? How do they get their jobs?

Federal judges are a special group. Like other key national institutions, courts were long the sole province of white males from high social status backgrounds.[8] Until only recently, women and minorities were excluded. Today the Court can no longer be described as nine old (white) men. The first black Supreme Court justice, Thurgood Marshall, was appointed by President Johnson in 1967. The first woman justice, Sandra Day O'Connor, was appointed by President Reagan in 1981. Table 16–2 lists the current justices of the Supreme Court, date of appointment, and background.

**TABLE 16–2** ***The Justices of the Supreme Court of the United States (By Seniority), 1988***

| *NAME* | *HOME STATE* | *PRIOR EXPERIENCE* | *APPOINTED BY* | *YEAR OF APPOINTMENT* |
|---|---|---|---|---|
| William J. Brennan Jr. | New Jersey | State judge | Eisenhower | 1956 |
| Byron R. White | Colorado | Deputy attorney general | Kennedy | 1962 |
| Thurgood Marshall | Maryland | Counsel to NAACP, federal judge | Johnson | 1967 |
| Harry A. Blackmun | Minnesota | Federal jury | Nixon | 1970 |
| William H. Rehnquist (Chief Justice) | Arizona | Assistant attorney general, associate justice | Nixon, Reagan | 1972, 1986 |
| John Paul Stevens III | Illinois | Federal judge | Ford | 1975 |
| Sandra Day O'Connor | Arizona | State judge | Reagan | 1981 |
| Antonin Scalia | New Jersey | Federal judge | Reagan | 1986 |
| Anthony Kennedy | California | Federal judge | Reagan | 1987 |

Until recently, racial and sexual barriers were equally strong in the federal courts below the Supreme Court. President Jimmy Carter made a concerted effort to achieve greater diversity in the composition of the federal judiciary. Table 16–3 compares the number of blacks, women, and Hispanics appointed to the federal bench by the last five presidents.

### THE JUDICIAL SELECTION PROCESS

Federal judges are appointed by the president with the "advice and consent" of the Senate. It sounds simple but, behind each appointment, politics is in the swing.

On Capitol Hill the Senate Judiciary Committee conducts it own background checks and holds hearings on the nominee's record and fitness

**TABLE 16–3** ***Appointment of Minorities to the Federal Judiciary (in Percents)***

| | *U.S. COURT OF APPEALS* | | |
|---|---|---|---|
| | *Women* | *Blacks* | *Hispanics* |
| Johnson | 2.5 | 5.0 | Not available |
| Nixon | 0.0 | 0.0 | Not available |
| Ford | 0.0 | 0.0 | Not available |
| Carter | 9.6 | 16.1 | 3.6 |
| Reagan | 9.1 | 3.0 | 3.0 |
| | *U.S. DISTRICT COURT* | | |
| | *Women* | *Blacks* | *Hispanics* |
| Johnson | 1.6 | 3.3 | 2.5 |
| Nixon | 0.6 | 2.8 | 1.1 |
| Ford | 1.9 | 5.8 | 1.9 |
| Carter | 15.5 | 14.3 | 6.2 |
| Reagan | 8.4 | 1.6 | 3.8 |

*NOTE:* Reagan appointments through 1984.

*Sources:* St. Louis Post-Dispatch, January 15, 1985, based on figures compiled by Sheldon Goldman, University of Massachusetts, and the Justice Department. Updated for Carter and Reagan from Linda Greenhouse, "Policy on Black Judicial Nominees Is Debated," *New York Times*, February 3, 1988, p. 11.

for the job. The committee then recommends to the full Senate to confirm or reject the nomination. In the twentieth century, presidents have had most of their nominees confirmed by the Senate. But in a classic confrontation between Congress and the president, Ronald Reagan had a key nomination to the Supreme Court rejected by the Senate in 1987.

**Appointment to the Supreme Court.**
Only 104 individuals have served on the U.S. Supreme Court in two hundred years. Table 16–4 shows the number of appointments to the

***TABLE 16–4 President's Appointments to the U.S. Supreme Court***

| *PRESIDENT* | *NO. OF APPOINTMENTS* |
|---|---|
| George Washington | 10 |
| John Adams | 3 |
| Thomas Jefferson | 3 |
| James Madison | 2 |
| James Monroe | 1 |
| John Quincy Adams | 1 |
| Andrew Jackson | 6 |
| Martin Van Buren | 2 |
| John Tyler | 1 |
| James Polk | 2 |
| Millard Fillmore | 1 |
| Franklin Pierce | 1 |
| James Buchanan | 1 |
| Abraham Lincoln | 5 |
| Ulysses Grant | 4 |
| Rutherford Hayes | 2 |
| James Garfield | 1 |
| Chester Arthur | 2 |
| Grover Cleveland | 4 |
| Benjamin Harrison | 4 |
| William McKinley | 1 |
| Theodore Roosevelt | 3 |
| William Howard Taft | 5 |
| Herbert Hoover | 3 |
| Woodrow Wilson | 3 |
| Warren Harding | 4 |
| Calvin Coolidge | 1 |
| Franklin Roosevelt | 8 |
| Harry Truman | 4 |
| Dwight Eisenhower | 5 |
| John Kennedy | 2 |
| Lyndon Johnson | 2 |
| Richard Nixon | 4 |
| Gerald Ford | 1 |
| Ronald Reagan | 3 |

*Source:* Reprinted with permission from *Politics in America* 2/e by LeLoup. 

Supreme Court by each president. Jimmy Carter and four other presidents had no appointments during their term. The selection of a Supreme Court justice gives a president an opportunity to influence policy long after his or her term in office is over. President Adams's appointment of John Marshall is still the most dramatic example. Although he appoints a justice for life "during good behavior," a president has no guarantee of what a justice will do once on the Court. Eisenhower's appointee, Chief Justice Earl Warren, led the Court in several surprising directions in the 1960s. In most cases, however, presidents have a pretty good idea of the judicial philosophy of nominees. Based on their previous record as judges, it is usually possible to predict their general policy orientation.[9]

When a vacancy on the Court occurs through death or resignation, a complex screening process begins. Two important participants in the process are the Justice Department and the American Bar Association (ABA). Consulting with the president's advisers, the attorney general and his staff prepare a list of top candidates for the position. They look for potential nominees whose political party affiliation and political philosophy correspond with the president's. The FBI then conducts extensive background checks. A list of potential candidates is submitted to the ABA, which rates the candidates. Finally, the president selects a name and submits it to the Senate.[10]

**1.** Identify the types of graphics used in the excerpt.

Figure 16–1 ______________________________

Figure 16–2 ______________________________

Table 16–1 ______________________________

Table 16–2 ______________________________

Table 16–3 ______________________________

Table 16–4 ______________________________

**2.** Reread the excerpt and identify the page number that refers to the graphics in the excerpt.

Figure 16–1 ______________________________

Figure 16–2 ______________________________

Table 16–1 ______________________________

Table 16–2 ______________________________

Table 16–3 ______________________________

Table 16–4 ______________________________

**3.** In paragraph 1 of the section on "state courts," what constitutes the fifty-one court systems?

______________________________

______________________________

4. Reread the information found in the section on "State Courts." On a separate sheet of paper, create a flowchart using the following components: *minor courts, justices of the peace, municipal courts, county courts, common pleas courts, juvenile courts, domestic relations courts, probate courts, trial courts, appeals courts.*

5. In the subsection on "Federal Courts," what kinds of cases are heard?

   ______________________________________

6. Reread the subsection on "Federal Courts." Assuming each district has an equal number of judges, what is the average number of judges per district?

   ______________________________________

*Answer the following questions using Figure 16–1.*

7. An ambassador is involved in a court case. In which court would the case be heard?

   ______________________________________

8. A case tried in Guam is going to be appealed. Where will the appeal be heard?

   ______________________________________

9. Which court system has no level of appeal?

   ______________________________________

10. What court reviews findings of the Secretary of Commerce and the Secretary of Agriculture?

   ______________________________________

*Answer the following questions using the subsection on "U.S. Circuit Courts of Appeals" and Figure 16–2.*

11. How many courts of appeals exist? ______________ How many districts exist? ______________

12. What apparent discrepancy do you find between the third sentence in this section and Figure 16–1?

   ______________________________________

13. Examine the information in the boxes to the right of the map. How does that relate to the information in the previous question?

   ______________________________________

   ______________________________________

   ______________________________________

**14.** In which circuit district would each of the following states be found?

Nevada ______________

Hawaii______________

Minnesota______________

Ohio______________

Louisiana______________

Florida______________

*Answer the following questions using the subsection on "The U.S. Supreme Court" and Table 16–1.*

**15.** How many chief justices have been appointed?

______________________________________________

**16.** What is the average length of time that they hold the position?___

______________________________________________

**17.** Which justice held the position for the longest period of time? ______________ the shortest period of time? ______________

**18.** Which person both appointed a chief justice and served as a chief justice?______________________________________

______________________________________________

**19.** When a vacancy occurs, from what two sources do chief justices come?______________________________________

*Answer the following questions using the section on "Judges and Justices" and Table 16–2.*

**20.** Who was the first black Supreme Court justice and who appointed him?______________________________________

______________________________________________

**21.** Choosing from the West, the South, the Midwest, and the East, from what region of the country do most justices come?

______________________________________________

**22.** What president appointed the most justices?________________

**23.** On a separate piece of paper, create a bar graph depicting the appointment of justices by the following decades: 1950s, 1960s, 1970s, 1980s.

**24.** How many of the justices were federal judges prior to their appointments to the supreme court?

______________________________________________

*Answer the following questions using the section on "Judges and Justices" and Table 16–3.*

**25.** Which president has the best overall record for appointing minorities to the U.S. Court of Appeals and the U.S. District Court?

______________________________

**26.** Which president has the worst overall record for appointing minorities to the U.S. Court of Appeals and the U.S. District Court?

______________________________

**27.** What three minority groups are depicted in this table?

______________________________

**28.** Examining the totals of the percentages for each minority group, which minority group has had the highest percentage of appointments in the U.S. Court of Appeals?

______________________________

**29.** What is the difference in total percentages between the U.S. Court of Appeals and the U.S. District Court for blacks?__________ for women? __________ for Hispanics? __________

*Answer the following questions using the subsection on "Appointment to the Supreme Court" and Table 16–4.*

**30.** Why would George Washington have made more appointments to the Supreme Court than any other president?

______________________________

______________________________

______________________________

**31.** What percentage of presidents made five or more appointments?

______________________________

**32.** How many presidents made no appointments to the Supreme Court?

______________________________

**33.** List the steps in the process of selecting a justice.

______________________________

______________________________

______________________________

______________________________

______________________________

**34.** Other than the president and his staff, name two other participants in the decision-making process of appointing justices.__________

________________________________________________

## EXERCISE 9.14

*Read the following excerpt and answer the questions below.*

**An Easing of Tensions During the Gorbachev Era**

While not abandoning the doctrine of containment, President Reagan began to soften his rhetoric toward the Soviet Union following his reelection in 1984 and a major change in Soviet leadership the following year. In March 1985, Mikhail Gorbachev assumed power in the Soviet Union. Three aged and ailing Soviet leaders—Brezhnev, Andropov, and Chernenko—had died within a period of twenty-eight months. Assuming leadership at the age of fifty-four, Gorbachev provided much needed stability and a new direction in Soviet policy.

A new pragmatic approach to both foreign and domestic policy in the Soviet Union was revealed. Gorbachev launched a campaign to reform the Soviet economy called ***perestroika***—a restructuring. Hoping to overcome the entrenched inefficiency of the bureaucratized, centrally managed Soviet economy, Gorbachev wanted to decentralize and introduce some limited elements of markets into the system. A greater tolerance of free expression and a partial relaxation of the harsh treatment of dissidents was observed. ***Glasnost*** was the Soviet leader's term for this new openness. Public demonstrations against the government were tolerated. Letters to the editor disagreeing with some government policies were printed in official government media. Gorbachev demonstrated more pragmatic attitude in foreign policy. Drained by continued high levels of military spending, Gorbachev wanted to halt the still-escalating arms race in order to put more resources into the domestic economy. Troops were withdrawn from Soviet-occupied Afghanistan in 1988. President Reagan displayed a cautious but supportive attitude toward these changes.

Reagan and Gorbachev met in Geneva in 1985 for the first of their four summit conferences. Political Insight 20–1 chronicles the history of superpower summit meetings in the postwar era. Perhaps the most controversial of their meetings was the summit in Reykjavík, Iceland, in 1986. On the last day of the meetings, the two leaders discussed dramatic cuts in nuclear weapons. Discussions went far beyond the proposals that had been developed by their respective staffs. As expectations were suddenly raised, they were quickly dashed when no agreement could be reached. Reykjavík dramatized the pitfalls of summitry. Critics later claimed that President Reagan was unprepared for groundbreaking negotiations. European allies expressed concern that Reagan would offer to remove all U.S. nuclear weapons from their soil without even consulting them.

Despite this setback, the **intermediate nuclear force (INF) treaty** was negotiated and signed the next year in Washington. This represented the first progress in the postwar era of not just limiting the arms race but actually destroying existing nuclear weapons. While additional progress in eliminating long-range nuclear weapons was not made in 1988, the easing of tensions in the late 1980s was one of the most hopeful steps toward a more peaceful world since the dawn of the nuclear age in 1945.

Even with the positive developments in the late 1980s, maintaining a strong national defense remained a critical component of American public policy. We now turn to the U.S. defense establishment and some of the key issues facing policy-makers.

## DEFENSE SPENDING

### Military Budget Trends

During World War II, by far the largest portion of federal spending was for national defense. One fear of the postwar period was that demilitarization—with its reduction in military spending—would lead to a severe recession. Fears proved groundless, both because of deferred consumer demand and because, with the escalation of Cold War tensions, demilitarization never was completed. From the Korean War through the Vietnam War, defense spending fell from about 75 percent of total outlays to around 45 percent of outlays in 1968. The end of the war in Vietnam was marked by a reduction in the growth in defense spending accompanied by rapid increase in social welfare entitlements. The defense portion of the federal budget shrunk to 23 percent by 1980. The election of Ronald Reagan ushered in an era of renewed military buildup—rapid increases in defense spending to strengthen what Reagan argued was a dangerously weak military. Reagan's plan was that defense spending would compose 30 percent of the budget by the end of the 1980s.

Figure 20–1 examines U.S. defense outlays as a percentage of GNP since 1962. Observe the decline in relative spending between 1970 and 1980. Under the Reagan buildup, defense spending was slated to rise from 5

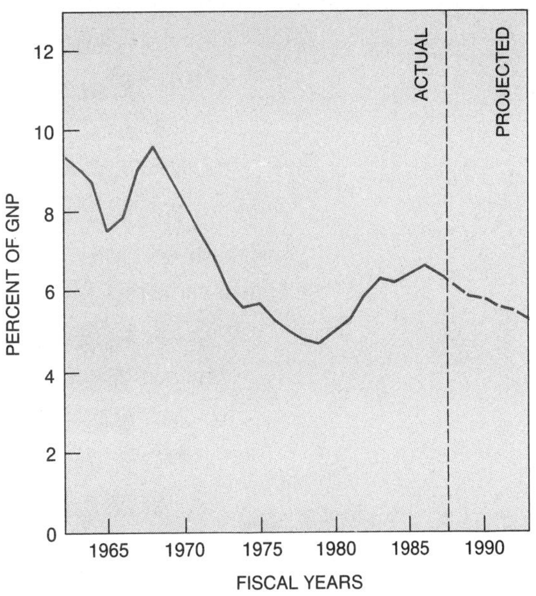


***FIGURE 20–1***
***U.S. Defense Spending as a Percentage of GNP, 1962–1993***

*Source:* Congressional Budget Office, 1988.

percent of GNP in 1980 to 8 percent of GNP by 1990. The deficits and Gramm-Rudman cut short the buildup after 1985. Defense spending amounted to 26 percent of the budget and 6 percent of GNP by the end of the Reagan administration. How does U.S. defense spending compare with that of other nations? Figure 20–2 compares defense spending as a percentage of gross domestic product for seven nations. Severe budget constraints in the United States caused the administration to pressure America's allies to increase their share of the burden in defending the Western alliance.

#### The Composition of Defense Spending

The political debate over the shape of the U.S. defense budget is conducted at two levels. The first concerns the macro-level—determining the total budget, its proportion of GNP, and the rate of real growth. The second aspect of the debate is at the micro-level, examining particular weapon systems and determining the need for and efficiency of each system.

The defense budget is broken down into its component parts in Figure 20–3. The largest components are procurement; operations and maintenance; salaries, benefits, and other personnel costs; and research and development. Almost half the defense budget goes toward salaries of military personnel and to their maintenance and support. There are two kinds of forces in the American arsenal. Conventional weapons, such as fighter planes, tanks, ships, and all the people and material that accompany them are designed to fight nonnuclear engagements. They make up

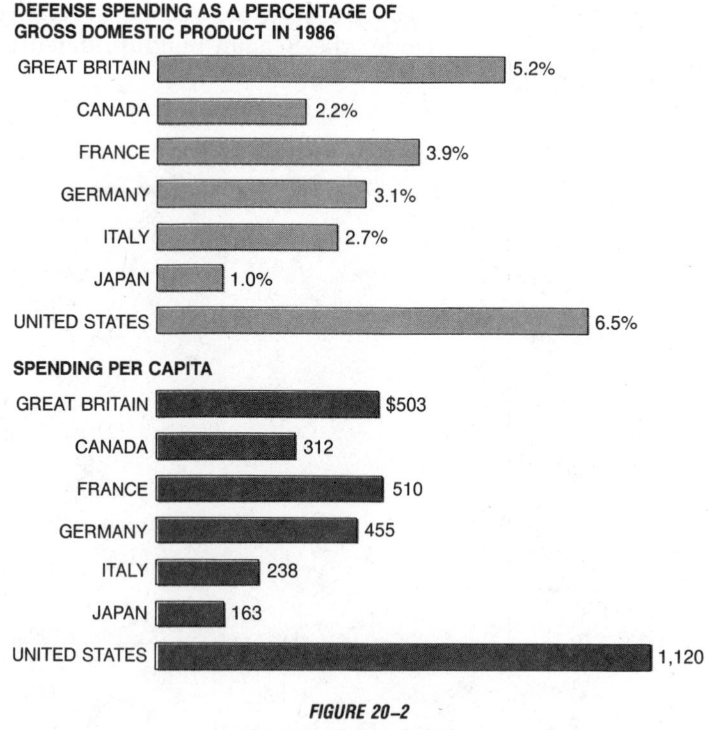


***FIGURE 20–2***
***Comparing Defense Spending***

*Source:* Defense Budget Project; Japanese Government; International Institute for Strategic Studies.

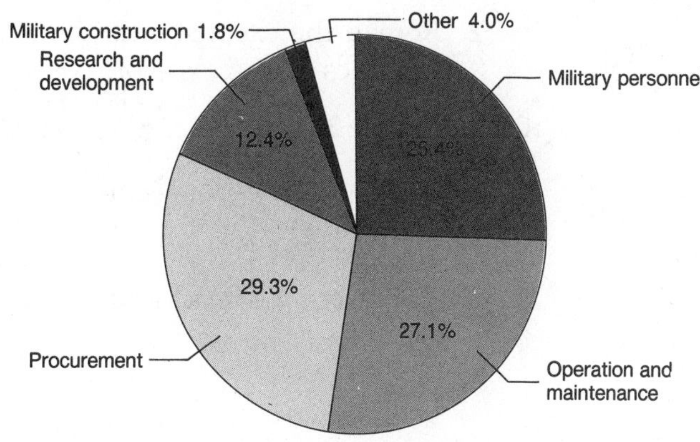


***FIGURE 20–3***
***Composition of the U.S. Defense Budget, 1987.***

*Source:* Congressional Budget Office, 1987.

the bulk of outlays. Strategic weapons—the nuclear arsenal that is designed to deter attack—make up only 10 percent of the costs of procurement, operations and maintenance, and personnel. But nuclear weapons and their delivery systems, such as the MX missile and the B-1 bomber, are among the most controversial expenditures.

**The Buildup in Conventional Weapons**

The Reagan administration reversed the relative decline in defense spending through an ambitious *procurement* program (designing, contracting for, and acquiring weapons or equipment). New procurement included a full range of military items—land forces and tanks, attack planes, fighter planes, cargo planes, submarines, battleships, and so forth. The Defense Department maintained sixteen army divisions and three marine divisions throughout the 1980s. The number of aircraft carriers was increased from thirteen to fourteen, and the number of battleships from one to four. The number of modern fighter planes (the F-15, for example) and modern attack planes was increased.

As originally projected by the Reagan administration, the total cost of the defense modernization was $1.8 trillion over five years. But huge budget deficits led even Republican allies of the president to support some reductions in the defense-spending growth rate after 1985. Even though strategic nuclear weapons make up only 10 percent of defense expenditures, perhaps the most controversial aspect of national defense involves such weapons and ways to prevent nuclear war.

*Source:* Reprinted with permission from *Politics in America* 2/e by LeLoup. 

**1.** Identify the types of graphics used in the excerpt.

Figure 20–1______________________________

Figure 20–2______________________________

Figure 20–3______________________________

2. Reread the excerpt and identify the page number that refers to the graphics in the excerpt.

   Figure 20–1____________________

   Figure 20–2____________________

   Figure 20–3____________________

3. Contrast *perestroika* and *glasnost.*

4. Where is Reykjavíc?

5. How does the INF treaty differ from prior treaties?

6. Reread the fourth sentence under the heading "Defense Spending," beginning with "From the Korean War . . .". What is ironic about this statement?

7. What has caused the decrease in defense spending since 1985?

_______________

_______________

_______________

_______________

_______________

8. In what year was the largest percentage of the GNP spent on defense? _______________ What year had the smallest percentage of spending on defense? _______________

9. Using the information in Figure 20–2, compare the spending per capita for Great Britain and France with their respective defense spending as a percentage of GDP. Summarize your findings in a sentence.

_______________

_______________

_______________

10. Using the information in Figure 20–2, compare the spending per capita for the United States and Great Britain with their respective defense spending as a percentage of GDP. Summarize your findings in a sentence.

_______________

_______________

_______________

11. What does per capita spending mean? _______________

_______________

12. Using the information in Figure 20–3 and the section on "The Composition of Defense Spending," on a separate sheet of paper create a circle graph that shows the percentage of strategic weapons costs in proportion to total costs of procurement.

13. Examine the amount of spending for military personnel and operations and management. If almost half goes for the salaries of personnel and their maintenance and support, approximately how much do you estimate goes toward operation and maintenance of equipment? _______________

_______________

## CHAPTER SUMMARY EXERCISE

*Write a chapter summary in the space provided.*

◆

## CHAPTER REVIEW

*Answer briefly but completely.*

1. How do tables differ from graphs?

2. How do circle graphs differ from other kinds of graphs?

3. Other than the examples provided in the text, name a situation that could be best explained in a flowchart.

4. Contrast map features and map language.

5. How is the equator like the prime meridian?

______________________________

______________________________

______________________________

______________________________

______________________________

6. List three features that could be indicated on a physical map.

______________________________

______________________________

______________________________

______________________________

______________________________

7. List three features that could be indicated on a political map.

______________________________

______________________________

______________________________

______________________________

______________________________

8. Complete the following analogy.
longitude : vertical :: latitude : ______________

9. Construct a timeline for the due dates of assignments and exams in this course.

______________________________

______________________________

______________________________

______________________________

______________________________

10. Contrast quality and quantity tables.

______________________________

______________________________

______________________________

______________________________

______________________________

◆

## VOCABULARY ENHANCEMENT EXERCISE

*Using the scale in Figure 3.1, rate your understanding of the following vocabulary enhancement words to the left of the number. Then write a sentence with each one.*

**1.** continuum

**2.** phenomena

**3.** clarify

**4.** suffices

**5.** discern

**6.** decipher

**7.** obsolete

**8.** mandate

**9.** vegetation

**10.** glaciers

# 10 Reading Math and Logic Word Problems

## TERMS

*Terms appear in the order in which they occur in the chapter.*

directionality
background knowledge
specialized terms
technical terms
text-based context clues
two-eight model
logic
analytical reasoning
critical thinking
premises
conclusions
arguments
deductive logic
syllogisms
inductive logic
generalizations
scientific data
analogies
causal connections
fallacy
formal fallacies
informal fallacies

## CHAPTER OUTLINE EXERCISE

*Create an outline for this chapter on the following lines.*

## OBJECTIVES

*At the end of this chapter, you should be able to do the following:*

1. Identify the relationship between reading and math.
2. Describe how to think logically.

## CHAPTER MAP

*Create a map for this chapter in the space below.*

## VOCABULARY ENHANCEMENT EXERCISE

*Rate each of the following words according to your knowledge of them.*

| | STAGE 0 | STAGE 1 | STAGE 2 | STAGE 3 |
|---|---|---|---|---|
| | *I do not recognize the word.* | *I recognize the word but am unsure of its meaning and associations.* | *I recognize the word and can make general associations with it.* | *I recognize the word and can use it in speaking and writing.* |
| **1.** fictitious | | | | |
| **2.** inspiration | | | | |
| **3.** presto | | | | |
| **4.** remote | | | | |
| **5.** erratic | | | | |
| **6.** maxim | | | | |
| **7.** deceptively | | | | |
| **8.** protocol | | | | |
| **9.** prophecies | | | | |
| **10.** manipulate | | | | |

KILROY, A FICTITIOUS American soldier, left the inscription "Kilroy was here" everywhere American soldiers were stationed in the 1940s. Even in the most unlikely spots, soldiers found Kilroy's name. Sometimes soldiers captured new territory. Certain they were the first Americans there, they were surprised to find Kilroy had been there before them. The knowledge that another American was near provided inspiration. They knew they weren't alone.

Similarly, you, as a college student enrolled in math, may feel you, too, are in battle. You fight the enemy—word problems. Perhaps you often feel isolated and fearful. You see an instructor or a classmate enter the room and presto! solve a problem that has kept you awake for hours. What you fail to realize is that the solution your instructor or peer writes on the board represents hours of work. Their initial efforts rest in a trash can somewhere. Thus, both your instructor and classmates can serve as a Kilroy for you. They either are or have been where you are now—in the remote and enemy territory of word problems.

◆

## THE RELATIONSHIP BETWEEN READING AND MATHEMATICS

College students usually take math courses such as algebra, trig, or calculus. Thus, for most students, working math problems is a common occurrence. However, math is not something everyone does with ease. Most students learn how to work math problems with some effort—

*Source:* Reprinted by permission of Phi Delta Kappan and Bo Brown.

unless the problems are word problems. Then, even the best students come unglued! You may be a student who longs for a "You are here" marker to guide you through the equations needed for solving word problems.

Word problems are difficult because they cram a maximum amount of information into a minimum amount of space. For example, where one text paragraph contains one key concept, a word problem often contains several concepts. Analyzing a math problem is much like analyzing a passage. In reading, you are looking for the main idea or conclusion. In math, you are looking for the steps needed to solve the problem.

## Reading Math Critically

Another reason students have difficulties with word problems is because they require critical reading skills (see Chapter 7). From a collection of stated facts, you determine which are relevant to the problem. You translate words into mathematical symbols. You also infer the mathematical processes required for a problem's solution. Then you form hypotheses. Finally, you judge the accuracy of your response based on information given in the problem.

### *Drawing Conclusions*

More than any other type of text reading, reading math problem requires you to draw conclusions. First, you must determine the meanings of facts and their relationships in light of their contexts. Then, you must summarize and synthesize them to condense concepts and form generalizations. Finally, you combine background knowledge with stated facts to infer the processes needed for solving problems.

In addition, Polya (1962) asserts that math problems contain unstated assumptions. While these hold true in the abstract world of a math text, such assumptions rarely exist in reality. For example, consider Polya's following word problem:

> A patrol plane flies 220 miles per hour in still air. It carries fuel for 4 hours of safe flying. If it takes off on patrol against a wind of 20 miles per hour, how far can it fly and return safely?

Polya's problem contains three unstated assumptions. First, wind speed is unchanging. Second, the plane travels in a straight line. Third, no turnaround time occurs between landing and taking off.

Such unstated assumptions exist in all types and levels of mathematics. Identifying them helps you to become a more critical reader and thinker.

### Determining Direction

One of the first rules a beginning reader learns is that of **directionality.** Directionality concerns order. You read all written text from top to bottom and from left to right. Unfortunately, this does not hold true in solving math problems. In math, you read in all different directions (see Figure 10.1). This erratic order often poses problems for students. Understanding how to use the order of operations agreement requires **background knowledge.** You need to understand how the language of math symbols relates to math processes.

### Marking Relevant Information

In mathematics, the maxim "Actions speak louder than words" often applies. Many students use the "treadmill" system of solving math problems. They read, reread, and reread, but rarely get anywhere. You need to have a destination and a map to get there.

Your destination consists of the answer to the question posed in the problem. Underlining or highlighting this question serves as a visual marker to show you where to go. Next you box or circle the facts given in the problem. These form the signposts to use along the route. Finally, you notate the processes you need for traveling. Some authors write word problems which resemble real-life. You must note only the facts and processes needed to solve the problem. If possible, you sketch or draw the situation to better visualize your situation.

### Varying Rate While Reading

Emerson once said, "In skating over thin ice our safety is in speed." Because a math text is seldom considered favorite reading, you may

**FIGURE 10.1**
***Examples of Directionality in Math Problems***

| SYMBOLS | VERBAL | DIRECTION |
|---|---|---|
| $6 + 2 = 8$ → | 6 plus 2 equals 8 | Traditional—across, left to right |
| $\frac{8}{2}$ ↓ | 8 divided by 2 | Top to bottom |
| $8 \div 2$ → | 8 divided by 2 | Across, left to right |
| $2\overline{)8}$ ← | 2 divided into 8 | Across, right to left |
| $2^3$ ↗ | 2 cubed or<br>cube of 2 | Up, left to right<br>or<br>Down, right to left |
| ↗ $5\overline{)40}$ with 8 above ← | 40 divided by 5 equals 8 | Across, right to left and up, left to right |
| ½↘·↗¼ | ½ multiplied by ¼ | Down, left to right and up, left to right |

tend to skate over its contents as fast as you can. The danger, of course, is overlooking a spot of thin ice and drowning in numbers.

Math, like any other subject, needs to be read at varying speeds. Such flexibility allows you to slow down for harder concepts, speed up for stated facts, and reread to clarify conclusions.

Your initial reading will be rather fast. Your goal is to get the big picture. Additional readings are slow and thoughtful ones. During these, you locate facts and processes. A final reading to judge the accuracy of your response will be somewhat faster. However, especially if math is hard for you, you should seldom read word problems at lightning speeds.

## Specialized Language in Mathematics

The language of mathematics often seems deceptively easy. Many words, such as *point, ray,* or *log,* are familiar ones. However, in the context of mathematics, their meanings differ. Math terms take two forms. Some are **specialized terms.** Such words have both common meanings and special ones in math. Others are **technical terms.** Their meanings are specific to the field of math.

### *Specialized and Technical Vocabulary in Math*

Whether specialized or technical terms (see Tables 10.1 and 10.2), these terms represent exact and single meanings in math. Synonyms or approximate definitions are not good enough. In addition, some terms are described by word combinations (see Table 10.3). Because precise meaning is so important, keeping a word list is especially important in mathematics. Included should be all words, their meanings, and an example in context.

**TABLE 10.1** ***Examples of Math Words with Specialized Meanings***

| | | | |
|---|---|---|---|
| base | point | square | ray |
| union | ruler | tangent | locus |
| compass | function | intercepts | coordinates |
| axis | domain | radical | even |
| value | angle | log | inequality |
| negative | slope | intervals | equilateral |
| exponent | polynomial | inverse | parallel |
| null | perpendicular | symmetrical | equation |
| infinity | finite | quadrant | paradox |
| difference | product | riprocal | variable |

**TABLE 10.2 Examples of Math Words with Technical Meanings**

| | | | |
|---|---|---|---|
| parabola | asymptotes | logarithm | pi |
| hyperbola | sine | cosine | theorem |
| topology | scalene | hypotenuse | integer |

**TABLE 10.3 Examples of Math Word Combinations**

| | | |
|---|---|---|
| real numbers | unlike terms | whole numbers |
| signed numbers | complex fractions | order of operations |
| square root | null set | imaginary numbers |
| ordered pairs | prime numbers | dependent variable |
| perfect numbers | absolute value | right angle |
| linear equation | equivalent equations | complex numbers |

### Using the Context

Context clues (see Chapter 4) comprise the best way for defining new words in math. Because math texts require exact meanings, authors use **text-based context clues.** These include punctuation, example, and definition.

Before working a problem, you need to understand the words in the problem. Sometimes the meaning of a specialized math word changes according to its context. For example, the meaning of *base* differs in geometry and algebra. Thus, when you add new words to your list, some may have more than one meaning.

### Identifying Mathematical Symbols

More than any other content area, mathematics relies on symbols to communicate meaning (see Table 10.4). Thus, math requires understanding of both words and symbols. Reading aloud, replacing symbols with words, often helps you understand confusing problems. Common symbols include decimal points, the equal sign, plus or minus signs, and the percent sign. Some symbols have more than one meaning. Other symbols are more technical in nature. Their meanings are specific to a single mathematical subject. Some texts contain a glossary of often-used symbols. If not, you need to construct your own list for easy reference.

**WRITE TO LEARN**

*On a separate sheet of paper, compare symbolism in math with symbolism in language and literature.*

**TABLE 10.4 Examples of Common Mathematical Symbols**

| SYMBOL | MEANING |
|---|---|
| . | Decimal |
| × | Multiplied by |
| + | Plus, positive |
| − | Minus, negative, the opposite of |
| % | Percent |
| < | Less than |
| > | Greater than |
| ≤ | Less than or equal to |
| ≥ | Greater than or equal to |
| ÷ | Divided by |
| $\sqrt{\ }$ | Square root |
| $\sqrt[n]{\ }$ | nth root |
| ! | Factorial |
| / | Divided by |
| ( ), [ ], { } | Treated as 1 quantity or separates a signed number from the operation symbol |
| \| \| | Absolute value |
| = | Equal to |

**EXERCISE 10.1**

◆ *Provide a general meaning and a specialized math meaning for each of the following words:*

**1.** origin

*General meaning:* ______________________________

______________________________

*Specialized meaning:* ______________________________

______________________________

**2.** set

*General meaning:* ______________________________

______________________________

*Specialized meaning:* ______________________________

______________________________

**3.** root

*General meaning:* ______________________________

______________________________

*Specialized meaning:* ______________________________

______________________________

**4.** rational

*General meaning:* ____________________

*Specialized meaning:* ____________________

**5.** intersection

*General meaning:* ____________________

*Specialized meaning:* ____________________

**6.** factor

*General meaning:* ____________________

*Specialized meaning:* ____________________

**7.** range

*General meaning:* ____________________

*Specialized meaning:* ____________________

**8.** power

*General meaning:* ____________________

*Specialized meaning:* ____________________

**9.** plane

*General meaning:* ____________________

*Specialized meaning:* ____________________

**10.** line

*General meaning:* ______

______

*Specialized meaning:* ______

______

**EXERCISE 10.2**

*Revise the following problems by replacing the symbols with words.*

**1.** $4 - (3 - 1) = ?$

______

______

**2.** $|-20| + (-4) > 10$

______

______

**3.** $\sqrt{25} + 2\,(6 + {}^{-}3) = ?$

______

______

**4.** $20\% \times .3 < 100$

______

______

**5.** $6 + 5 \geqslant 6 + |5|$

______

______

**6.** $2/3 \;/\; 1/2 = ?$

______

______

**7.** $[(5 \times 2)(6 \times 3)]4/2 = ?$

______

______

**8.** $\sqrt{4} + 7 - [3(2) - 4] = ?$

**9.** $6.2 - 3.7 \times 6\% = ?$

**10.** $[(5)(4 - 1) - 3] = ?$

# Classroom Types

BY VAL CHEATHAM

| | | | | |
|---|---|---|---|---|
| $2\times(4+3)$ | $\frac{4\times2}{3}$ | $3+(4-2)$ | $\frac{3\times2}{4}$ | $4\times(3+2)$ |
| $\frac{3\times4}{2}$ | $\frac{2\times3}{4}$ | $2-(4+3)$ | $3-(4\times2)$ | $4\times(3-2)$ |
| $3-2\times4$ | $2+2$ | $\frac{2\times2}{3+3}$ | $3+2-4$ | $3-3$ |
| $\frac{2+2}{4}$ | $3\times2+4$ | $3\times(2+4)$ | $\frac{4-3}{2}$ | $\frac{3+4}{2}$ |
| $4-2$ | $2\times3+4$ | $(2+2)=4$ | $3-2$ | $\frac{3+2}{4}$ |
| | | $\frac{3\times4}{2}$ | | |

*"Now that we all know how to set up the equation, who can tell me the correct answer?"*

## Thinking About Math Problems

Two students spent too much money on their summer vacations. Since neither one can afford to buy all they need for the semester, they plan to share. If they need three books for each of four classes, how many books does each student have to buy?

Consider the above problem:

| | |
|---|---|
| $\frac{3 \times 4}{2} =$ | Two students spent too much money on their summer vacations. Since neither one can afford to buy all they need for the semester, they plan to share. |
| $\frac{12}{2} = 6$ | If they need three books for each of four classes, how many books does each student have to buy? |

Both of these problems would be solved in exactly the same way. You only need to translate the words into symbols.

## Steps for Solving Math Problems

Most students use the maxim "If at first you don't succeed, try, try again." Unfortunately, what they try is the same method over and over. They fail to think of alternatives for working the problem. What these students, and you, need is a protocol for solving word problems. A protocol consists of a set of steps to help you use knowledge effectively. It gives you a plan for attacking, retreating, atttacking again, and finally defeating word problems.

Like many students, you may develop a "panic reflex" when you see word problems. No matter what the problem, you think you can't work it. So, the first step in solving such problems is to refrain from or cope with such feelings. Panic only results in further confusion.

Second, you read to picture the problem. You imagine the situation in which the problem takes place. This reading gives you a general idea of what you need to do. Keep in mind that most problems are unclear after only one reading.

The next three steps help you determine what is known and unknown. First, you reread to identify the stated facts and the question being asked. Still another reading helps you decide what processes you need to solve the problem. Often instructors or texts pose problems with complex numbers. This type of number makes word problems even more difficult. To cope, try the **two-eight** model (Klein, 1988) (see Figure 10.2). In this method, you replace the numerical values with

**FIGURE 10.2**
***Simplifying Equations Using Klein's (1988) Two-Eight Model.***

*Original Problem*

The union wage for a contract was \$6.55 per hour. An increase of \$1.41 was approved for next year's contract. If a worker works a 36.5-hour week, what will be the amount of the check before deductions?

*Simulated Problem*

The union wage for a contract was \$8 per hour. An increase of \$2 was approved for next year's contract. If a worker works a 10-hour week, what will be the amount of the check before deductions?
*Process:* $(8 + 2) \times 10 =$
Replace values.
*Process:* $(6.55 + 1.41) \times 36.5 =$

simpler ones like *2* and *8*. Additional simple numbers can be used if additional values are needed. Once you determine what processes you need to work the problem, you replace the original values in the equation.

Once you know what's needed to work the problem, you estimate your answer before solving it. Rounding off values often aids you in making such guesses. This gives you a "ballpark figure" and sets limits for your answer.

The next step concerns working the problem. Many students consider it to be the last step. Unfortunately, it rarely is. As Carl Sandburg said in his poem "Arithmetic," "Arithmetic is where the answer is right and everything is nice and you can look out of the window and see the blue sky—or the answer is wrong and you have to start all over and try again and see how it comes out this time." Sandburg's alternatives apply to all levels of mathematics. Once you think you have an answer, you need to reexamine the problem and judge your results.

What if you find your answer is incorrect? First, check your computations. Second, reread the problem to be sure you haven't missed any relevant information or copied the data incorrectly. Third, instead of giving up, take a break. Continued struggle often results in frustration and despair. Sometimes, getting away from the problem for a few minutes gives your mind a chance to work on it subconsciously. You may also get a fresh perspective just by getting away. Next, you get help when you are stuck. Forming study groups helps you achieve better understanding and higher grades. Single-handed attempts at problem solving are less effective. Finally, avoid self-fulfilling prophecies. If you tell yourself you're no good at math and you can't solve word problems, then you'll probably meet your expectations. Research

*"Yes, theoretically there are an infinite number of ways of checking your answers, but* please *don't test that theory on this exam!"*

shows that fear decreases when understanding increases. Most campuses have learning assistance centers or offer seminars to help you cope with math anxiety. Self-help books are also available. Math anxiety is a learned response. Learned responses can be changed.

## EXERCISE 10.3

◆ *Work each problem by following the steps below.*

### *Example*

A garden is 45 feet long and 25 feet wide. How many fence posts would be required to place one in each corner and additional fence posts every 5 feet?

**a.** *Don't panic!*

**b.** *Read to picture the problem.*
You have a garden and want to know how many fence posts are needed to enclose the garden.

**c.** *Identify the question.*
How many fence posts would be required to place one in each corner and additional fence posts every 5 feet?

**d.** *Identify the facts.*
1. Garden is 45 feet long.
2. Garden is 25 feet wide.
3. Need fence posts every 5 feet and at corners.

**e.** *Identify the processes.*
1. Figure out the perimeter (length around) the garden.
2. Divide the perimeter by 5 because fence posts are 5 feet apart.

| | |
|---|---|
| **f.** *Estimate the answer.* | **1.** Total perimeter is about 2 × (50 + 25) = 150 feet because 45 is close to 50.<br>**2.** 150 feet ÷ 5 feet per post = 30 posts approximately. |
| **g.** *Work the problem.* | **1.** 2 × (45 + 25) = 140.<br>**2.** 140 ÷ 5 = 28. |
| **h.** *Check answer against estimate.* | Is 28 less than 30? Yes. |
| **i.** *Recheck.* | No. Not necessary because answer seems correct. |

**1.** Carmen wants to buy a house that costs $55,000. The required down payment is 10% of that cost. The closing costs are also 10% of the original amount. How much money will Carmen need to buy the house?

**a.** Don't panic! ______________

**b.** Read to picture the problem. ______________

**c.** Identify the question. ______________

**d.** Identify the facts. ______________

**e.** Identify the processes. ______________

**f.** Estimate the answer. ______________

**g.** Work the problem. ______________

**h.** Check answer against estimate. ______________

**i.** Recheck. ______________

**2.** Yuan is a math tutor. He charges $100 for testing a new student. His tutoring sessions cost $25 per hour. How much would three 2-hour sessions cost, including the one-time testing fee?

**a.** Don't panic! ______________

**b.** Read to picture the problem. ______________

**c.** Identify the question. ______________

**d.** Identify the facts. ______________

**e.** Identify the processes. ______________

**f.** Estimate the answer. ______________

**g.** Work the problem. ______________

**h.** Check answer against estimate. ______________

**i.** Recheck. ______________

3. The Golden Real Estate Company sold 110 homes last year. This year the company wants to increase sales by 20%. How many homes do they hope to sell this year?

   a. Don't panic! ________________
   b. Read to picture the problem. ________________
   c. Identify the question. ________________
   d. Identify the facts. ________________
   e. Identify the processes. ________________
   f. Estimate the answer. ________________
   g. Work the problem. ________________
   h. Check answer against estimate. ________________
   i. Recheck ________________

4. Dr. Gannon is doing nutrition research with rats. She finds that rats fed with Formula A gain 1 ⅛ oz. per month. Rats fed with Formula B gain 1.19 oz. per month. Which rates gain the most weight?

   a. Don't panic! ________________
   b. Read to picture the problem. ________________
   c. Identify the question. ________________
   d. Identify the facts. ________________
   e. Identify the processes. ________________
   f. Estimate the answer. ________________
   g. Work the problem. ________________
   h. Check answer against estimate. ________________
   i. Recheck. ________________

5. Dale sent Sasha a 2 ½-pound box of candy. Sasha's little sister ate ¼ of the candy. Sasha's pet poodle ate ⅛ of the original amount. If no one else has eaten any candy, how much candy does Sasha have left?

   a. Don't panic! ________________
   b. Read to picture the problem. ________________
   c. Identify the question. ________________
   d. Identify the facts. ________________
   e. Identify the processes. ________________
   f. Estimate the answer. ________________

g. Work the problem. ____________

h. Check answer against estimate. ____________

i. Recheck. ____________

**EXERCISE 10.4**

*Solve the following math problems.*

1. Straly works math problems 40% faster than Cato. In the time it takes Cato to work ten problems, how many can Straly solve?

2. A bus started the route with only the driver. At the first stop, seven people got on. At the next stop, five people got on. At the third stop, one person got on and two got off. How many people were left on the bus?

3. Cheese costs \$1.25 per quarter pound. How much would $3\frac{1}{8}$ pounds cost?

4. Mr. Jacques teaches French. He grades assignments on the curve. (The highest 10% of the scores get A's. The lowest 10% get F's. The next 20% on each end get B's or D's. The rest get C's.) All thirty students in his class turned in the last assignment. How many got A's? How many got B's? How many got C's? How many got D's? How many got F's?

5. Two hundred and fifty students enrolled in the College of Design. Fifty are majoring in landscape architecture. Forty are majoring in interior design. The rest are majoring in architecture. What percentage are majoring in architecture? in landscape architecture? in interior design?

6. Casey answered thirty-five out of sixty questions on an exam correctly. What percentage of the questions did he answer incorrectly?

**7.** Room and board at Leeville College is $2,845 per academic year (nine months). How much is room and board per month?

**8.** Kesia earns $6.55 per hour. If she works 10 3⁄5 hours this week and 12 2⁄5 hours next week, how much will she earn for the two-week pay period?

**9.** Leotia worked 23 hours and earned $146.75. How much was she paid per hour?

**10.** Last year, 250 students completed law school. However, only 75% of them passed the bar exam. How many students did not pass the bar exam?

## THINKING LOGICALLY

*Logicians have but ill-defined*
*As rational the human kind.*
*Logic, they say, belongs to man,*
*But let them prove it if they can.*

—OLIVER GOLDSMITH

**Logic** refers to **analytical reasoning,** or **critical thinking.** Like critical reading, logic asks you to look at evidence, called **premises.** These facts lead you to make decisions or draw **conclusions.** The premises and conclusions form a set of statements called **arguments.** Logic examines the facts and conclusions that determine if conclusions are valid or not. For example, Goldsmith argues invalidly when he suggests people are not logical. He reasons as follows:

Goldsmith's acquaintances are all human.
Goldsmith's acquaintances are not logical.
Thus, all humans are illogical.

Goldsmith attempts to prove his point by using an invalid line of thinking. Nonetheless, the manner in which Goldsmith argues is correct.

Both the premises and conclusion of the following argument are valid:

All dogs are animals.
A poodle is a dog.
Therefore, a poodle is an animal.

Thus, logic involves more than simply examining facts for accuracy. It is more than examining conclusions for validity. Logic forces you to manipulate ideas, think for yourself, and read critically.

◆

## THE RELATIONSHIP BETWEEN READING AND LOGIC

Reading is not just knowing words. It is thinking. Any time you read, you use logic skills. These skills are the systematic framework within which reading takes place. Using the context requires you to analyze the sentence and choose a meaning that makes sense. When you find a main idea or draw a conclusion, you are using logic. Analytical reasoning, then, is crucial to comprehension. Learning to understand what you read is learning to think. Thinking, like reading, is a skill you improve with practice.

### Kinds of Logic

Logic tells us what conclusions would be valid if the premises are valid. A higher-level thinking skill, logic comes in two types.

#### *Deductive Logic*

Aristotle, the Greek philosopher, first introduced **deductive logic,** or **syllogisms.** His theory remains unchanged today. A syllogism consists of three statements. Two of the statements are premises, or facts. The third is a conclusion. Like logical inferences, syllogisms follow the equation "If $a = b$ and $b = c$, then $a = c$." The arguments about Goldsmith and poodles provide examples of both valid and invalid syllogisms. Table 10.5 explains the rules for a valid syllogism.

***TABLE 10.5*** ***Rules for a Valid Syllogism***

1. Three statements form a syllogism: two premises and a conclusion.
2. The two premises contain clues that support or prove the conclusion.
3. A syllogism always contains three different sets.
4. Each set must appear once in two of the three statements.
5. A term that occurs in the conclusion modified by *all* or *none* must also be modified by *all* or *none* in the premises.
6. A conclusion begins with an adverbial conjunction like *therefore* or *thus.*
7. It is not important whether or not you know if the *premises* are true. Indeed, it does not matter if the *premises* are not true. What matters is that the premises prove that the *conclusion* is valid.
8. Two negative premises yield a positive conclusion.
9. One positive and one negative premise yield a negative conclusion.

## EXERCISE 10.5

◆ *Use deductive logic to determine the validity of the conclusions* below. Justify your response.

***Example***

All flowers smell sweet.
Garlic plants have flowers.
Garlic plants smell sweet.

*Valid?* *No*

*Justification:* *Premise 1 states that all flowers smell sweet. This is a false premise. Thus, the conclusion cannot be valid.*

**1.** All doctors are wise.
All nice people are wise.
Therefore, all nice people are doctors.

*Valid?*______

*Justification:*______

**2.** Some buildings are large.
No trees are large.
Therefore, no trees are buildings.

*Valid?*______

*Justification:*______

**3.** Mammals breathe.
All whales breathe.
Thus, all whales are mammals.

*Valid?*______

*Justification:*______

**4.** All squares are rectangles.
All rectangles are quadrilateral.
Thus, all squares are quadrilateral.

*Valid?*______

*Justification:*________________________________________

____________________________________________________

____________________________________________________

**5.** All stoves are hot.
Nothing hot is cold.
Therefore, no stove is cold.

*Valid?*________

*Justification:*________________________________________

____________________________________________________

____________________________________________________

**6.** All diamonds are expensive.
Some rings have diamonds.
Therefore, some rings are expensive.

*Valid?*________

*Justification:*________________________________________

____________________________________________________

____________________________________________________

**7.** Beetlejuice is a ghost.
All ghosts are frightening.
Therefore, Beetlejuice is frightening.

*Valid?*________

*Justification:*________________________________________

____________________________________________________

____________________________________________________

**8.** No books are dull.
Some books are best-sellers.
Therefore, no dull books are best-sellers.

*Valid?*________

*Justification:*________________________________________

____________________________________________________

____________________________________________________

9. All felines have retractable claws.
No dogs have retractable claws.
Therefore, no dog is a feline.

*Valid?*______

*Justification:*______________________________

______________________________

______________________________

10. All politicians are friendly people.
All friendly people are honest.
Thus, all politicians are honest.

*Valid?*______

*Justification:*______________________________

______________________________

______________________________

### *Inductive Logic*

**Inductive logic** examines the premises of an argument. Such logic concerns whether you can believe the facts or not. For example, consider the following statement:

All women are intelligent, and intelligent women are professional.

Inductive logic requires you to ask on what grounds do you base your idea that all women are intelligent. Grounds for belief include **generalizations** (general principles) or **scientific data** (results from experiments). **Analogies** (comparison of two or more things) or **causal connections** (cause and effect) are also reasons for validity. Both premises must be true to support valid conclusions. If a premise is untrue, then the conclusion is invalid.

**EXERCISE 10.6**

Use inductive logic to determine the validity of the *premises* below. Justify your response by providing the grounds for belief. Based on this logic, determine again the validity of the *conclusions*. Justify your response inductively.

***Example***

a. All flowers smell sweet.

*Valid:* *No*

*Grounds for belief:* *General principle—I can think of a flower that doesn't smell sweet (zinnias).*

**b.** Garlic plants have flowers.

*Valid:* ___Yes___

*Grounds for belief:* *General principle—I've seen flowers on garlic plants.*

**c.** Garlic plants smell sweet.

*Valid:* ___No___

*Justification:* *Premise 1 is invalid; thus, the conclusion is invalid.*

**1.** **a.** All doctors are wise.
**b.** All nice people are wise.
**c.** Therefore, all nice people are doctors.

**a.** *Valid?*______

*Grounds for belief:*________________________________________

________________________________________

**b.** *Valid?*______

*Grounds for belief:*________________________________________

________________________________________

**c.** *Valid?*______

*Justification:*________________________________________

________________________________________

**2.** **a.** Some buildings are large.
**b.** No trees are large.
**c.** Therefore, no trees are buildings.

**a.** *Valid?*______

*Grounds for belief:*________________________________________

________________________________________

**b.** *Valid?*______

*Grounds for belief:*________________________________________

________________________________________

**c.** *Valid?*______

*Justification:*________________________________________

________________________________________

**3.** **a.** Mammals breathe.
**b.** All whales breathe.
**c.** Thus, all whales are mammals.

**a.** *Valid?*______

*Grounds for belief:*____________________

____________________

**b.** *Valid?*______

*Grounds for belief:*____________________

____________________

**c.** *Valid?*______

*Justification:*____________________

____________________

**4.** **a.** All squares are rectangles.
**b.** All rectangles are quadrilateral.
**c.** Thus, all squares are quadrilateral.

**a.** *Valid?*______

*Grounds for belief:*____________________

____________________

**b.** *Valid?*______

*Grounds for belief:*____________________

____________________

**c.** *Valid?*______

*Justification:*____________________

____________________

**5.** **a.** All stoves are hot.
**b.** Nothing hot is cold.
**c.** Therefore, no stove is cold.

**a.** *Valid?*______

*Grounds for belief:*____________________

____________________

**b.** *Valid?*______

*Grounds for belief:*____________________

____________________

**c.** *Valid?*______

*Justification:*____________________

____________________

**6. a.** All diamonds are expensive.
**b.** Some rings have diamonds.
**c.** Therefore, some rings are expensive.

**a.** *Valid?*______

*Grounds for belief:*______________________________

______________________________

**b.** *Valid?*______

*Grounds for belief:*______________________________

______________________________

**c.** *Valid?*______

*Justification:*______________________________

______________________________

**7. a.** Beetlejuice is a ghost.
**b.** All ghosts are frightening.
**c.** Therefore, Beetlejuice is frightening.

**a.** *Valid?*______

*Grounds for belief:*______________________________

______________________________

**b.** *Valid?*______

*Grounds for belief:*______________________________

______________________________

**c.** *Valid?*______

*Justification:*______________________________

______________________________

**8. a.** Some books are dull.
**b.** Some dull books are best-sellers.
**c.** Therefore, some books are best-sellers.

**a.** *Valid?*______

*Grounds for belief:*______________________________

______________________________

**b.** *Valid?*______

*Grounds for belief:*______________________________

______________________________

**c.** *Valid?*______

*Justification:*______________________________________

**9. a.** All felines have retractable claws.
**b.** No dogs have retractable claws.
**c.** Therefore, no dog is a feline.

**a.** *Valid?*______

*Grounds for belief:*______________________________________

**b.** *Valid?*______

*Grounds for belief:*______________________________________

**c.** *Valid?*______

*Justification:*______________________________________

**10. a.** All politicians are friendly people.
**b.** All friendly people are honest.
**c.** Thus, all politicians are honest.

**a.** *Valid?*______

*Grounds for belief:*______________________________________

**b.** *Valid?*______

*Grounds for belief:*______________________________________

**c.** *Valid?*______

*Justification:*______________________________________

### *WRITE TO LEARN*

*On a separate sheet of paper, explain the difference between inductive and deductive reasoning.*

## That's Illogical: Common Fallacies At Work

Consider the following question carefully before answering:

Which would you prefer—that a rabid dog bite you or a snake?

Most people would prefer that the rabid dog bite the snake. But, perhaps you thought the question asked whether it would be better for you to be bitten by a rabid dog or a snake. Such misconceptions often occur. These mistakes in reasoning are called a **fallacy.**

Fallacies refer either to an unsound method for drawing conclusions or to an unsound conclusion. Fallacies often happen because they seem logical. Sometimes they appeal to our feelings and biases. They often support conclusions we want to be valid. Two types of fallacies exist. They are formal and informal fallacies.

### *Formal Fallacies*

**Formal fallacies** occur when facts do not support a stated conclusion. For example, if some margarines contain saturated fats and saturated fats lead to heart disease, it does not necessarily follow that margarine leads to heart disease. Three of the most common formal fallacies include generalizing from a particular, overinclusive premises, and guilt by association (see Table 10.6).

### *Informal Fallacies*

Various forms of **informal fallacies** exist. Informal fallacies occur through irrelevant facts, false comparisons, wrong observations, and unclear words and definitions. Such fallacies include evading the issue, the argument ad hominem, and rabbit reasoning.

**TABLE 10.6** ***Common Formal Fallacies, Definitions, and Examples***

| TYPE | DEFINITION | EXAMPLE |
|---|---|---|
| *GENERALIZING FROM A PARTICULAR* | Overgeneralizing; conclusions based on insufficient evidence | Mary is a Catholic. Mary wears red often. Therefore, Catholics wear red often. |
| *OVERINCLUSIVE PREMISES* | Statements (possibly from a limited sample) that common sense refutes | Everybody who goes to college is a genius. Casey goes to college. Casey is a genius. |
| *GUILT OR HOLINESS BY ASSOCIATION* | Attributes based on emotion or prejudice; sterotyping | Politicians are corrupt. Abe Lincoln was a politician. Abe Lincoln was corrupt. |

**TABLE 10.7** ***Examples and Definitions of Informal Fallacies***

| TYPE | DEFINITION | EXAMPLE |
|---|---|---|
| *EVADING THE ISSUE* | Euphemism in paragraph form; diverting attention from real issue | Yes, nuclear waste is a problem, but I stand for a free America—America's freedom is the cornerstone of our nation. |
| *THE ARGUMENT AD HOMINEM* | Attacks the person, not the argument | Freud's theories are ridiculous; why, he even used cocaine. |
| *RABBIT REASONING* | Restatement of premise in conclusion; so named because rabbits, when chased, tend to return to their starting points | Rhonda is an honest person and will give Richard a good recommendation. I assure you she can be trusted to be truthful. |

**WRITE TO LEARN**

*Your instructor has divided the class into groups. Your group is to devise a presentation explaining formal and informal fallacies. On a separate sheet of paper, define and give an example (other than those in this text) of each type of fallacy within these groups.*

## EXERCISE 10.7

*Determine if the following sentences are examples of fallacious or nonfallacious reasoning. If fallacious, identify the type of fallacy and refute it.*

**1.** I think Dr. Gomez misgraded my test paper. He's rude and always late for class.

*Fallacious?* ____________________

*Type of Fallacy?* ____________________

*Explanation:* ____________________

____________________

**2.** The attorney told the judge that the defendant was insane and not capable of committing the crime of which she was accused. The attorney added that the defendant did not require psychological testing to prove her insanity, because only a crazy person would have committed such a crime.

*Fallacious?* ____________________

*Type of fallacy?* ____________________

*Explanation:* ____________________

____________________

**3.** Beautiful blonds tend to be less intelligent than beautiful brunettes, and they lack the quick temperament of redheads.

*Fallacious?* ____________________

*Type of fallacy?* ____________________

*Explanation:* ____________________

____________________

**4.** I'm glad you asked about course prerequisites for History 301. Our university has a fine history program. Many of our graduates hold positions in the legislature. This helps each year when we submit our budget to the state.

*Fallacious?* ____________________

*Type of fallacy?* ____________________

*Explanation:* ____________________

____________________

**5.** Some plants do not grow if the soil is highly acid. Therefore, soil acidity must be considered before buying plants for landscape purposes.

*Fallacious?* ____________________

*Type of fallacy?* ______________________________

*Explanation:* ______________________________

______________________________

**6.** Two students turned in similar research papers. The instructor said that he knew the poorer student had copied from the better one, because poor students cheat more often than do good students.

*Fallacious?* ______________________________

*Type of fallacy?* ______________________________

*Explanation:* ______________________________

______________________________

**7.** I've only eaten oysters once. I got sick, so I'm sure I'm allergic to oysters.

*Fallacious?* ______________________________

*Type of fallacy?* ______________________________

*Explanation:* ______________________________

______________________________

**8.** Wars involve killing, and capital punishment involves killing, so both wars and capital punishment result in death.

*Fallacious?* ______________________________

*Type of fallacy?* ______________________________

*Explanation:* ______________________________

______________________________

**9.** Americans are always impressed with the politeness of the English people. All Britons line up in the order in which they arrive at bus stops. When conversing, they never interrupt one another. And, when driving, every Briton always gives the driver in the other car first opportunity to pass.

*Fallacious?* ______________________________

*Type of fallacy?* ______________________________

*Explanation:* ______________________________

______________________________

**10.** According to the dictionary, a reliable person is dependable. Since reliability is the state of being reliable, a person who is dependable has the characteristics of being reliable.

*Fallacious?*________________________________________

*Type of fallacy?*_____________________________________

*Explanation:*________________________________________

___________________________________________________

## Steps in Solving Logic Problems

*Wise men are instructed by reason; men with less understanding, by experience; the most ignorant, by necessity; the beasts, by nature.*

—CICERO

Cicero claims that wisdom comes through logical thinking. One way you practice thinking is by working logic problems. Logic problems contain both verbal and mathematical concepts. To solve them, you manipulate both ideas and numbers. Sometimes you find more than one right answer for a logic problem.

In many ways, the steps for solving logic problems resemble the steps for solving math problems. With some changes, the same basic procedures work for both (see Table 10.8).

As in math, most logic problems are unclear after the first reading. Thus, the first step in solving logic problems consists of not panicking. Panic causes confusion. And, confusion doesn't contribute to logical solutions. Your next step is to read the problem critically to get an idea of what it says. You identify the question asked and search for fallacies in reasoning. Background knowledge and context help you infer rationally. However, you need to avoid reading more into the problem than it says. Your common sense keeps you from assuming unusual

**TABLE 10.8 Comparison of Procedures for Solving Math and Logic Problems**

| SOLVING MATH PROBLEMS | SOLVING LOGIC PROBLEMS |
|---|---|
| **1.** Don't Panic! | **1.** Don't panic! |
| **2.** Read to picture the problem. | **2.** Read to get the main idea. |
| **3.** Identify the question. | **3.** Identify the question. |
| **4.** Identify the facts. | **4.** Examine information in the problem. |
| **5.** Identify the processes. | **5.** Use background knowledge and context to infer rationally. |
| **6.** Estimate the answer. | **6.** Don't assume unusual conditions. |
| **7.** Work the problem. | **7.** Sketch the problem. |
| **8.** Check the answer against estimate. | **8.** Eliminate incorrect possibilities. |
| **9.** Recheck. | **9.** Double-check your inferences and logic. |

conditions. Once you've read the problem and drawn conclusions, try to form a picture of it. A rough sketch aids you in this effort. Such a drawing might be a straight line or a chart. A simple illustration or diagram also increases your chances of seeing the problem more effectively. The next step involves eliminating incorrect alternatives. A reexamination of your inferences and logic serves as a check for the problem.

## EXERCISE 10.8

◆ *Find the logical answer to each of the following. Sketching a line, chart, or diagram will be helpful in some of the problems.*

### Example

Tim called his friends to ask them to a party. He called Ann, Todd, Ali, and Mindy. He called Todd after Ali but before Ann. He called Mindy last. In what order did Tim call his friends?

---

Ali Todd Ann Mindy

*Explanation:* The problem states that Tim called Mindy last. So Mindy's name is put on the end of the line. The problem also says Todd was called after Ali and before Ann, so Todd's name is placed between Ali and Ann on the line.

1. Three couples (the Duttons, the Goldbergs, and the Sylvests) play cards every Wednesday night. Where does each person sit and what are their entire names?
   a. No wife sits next to her husband.
   b. Diana sits between Deborah and Charlie.
   c. John Sylvest sits between Arlene and Jed.
   d. Although Charlie sits next to Mr. Dutton, Mrs. Dutton sits next to Diana.
   e. Deborah sits left of Arlene.

   ______________________________

   ______________________________

   ______________________________

   ______________________________

   ______________________________

2. Purple canaries are live animals.
   All live animals need water.
   Assuming the above premises are valid, circle the true statement.

a. My mother's canary is purple because it needs water.
b. All purple canaries need water.
c. Certain purple canaries do not need water.
d. Some purple canaries are not live animals.

3. Find the missing number.

______, 11, 21, 13, 41, 15, 61, 17, 81

4. Sumi, Yvette, and Stephen have chosen careers as an accountant, a travel agent, and a computer programmer. Identify the career and age of each person.
a. Sumi is not an accountant.
b. Yvette is not 30 years old, but her friend is.
c. The travel agent is not 28 years old.
d. Stephen's friend is 22 years old.
e. Sumi is 28 years old and her friend, Yvette, is the one who keeps books for an insurance agency.

______________________________

______________________________

______________________________

5. Jed is older than Mara. Jacob is younger than Mara. Rachel is older than Jed. Is Mara younger or older than Rachel?

______________________________

6. You are facing east. You turn to your left, do an about-face, and turn to your right. Which direction are you facing?

______________________________

7. Eleanor, Mike, Richard, Trehan, Sharita, and Tom decide to have pizza for supper. They have difficulty ordering because everyone likes a different topping. They finally each order separately. They get six pizzas: cheese, pepperoni, hamburger, sausage, Canadian bacon, and "the Works." Who orders what?
a. Eleanor is a vegetarian.
b. Richard is allergic to pork and does not like pepperoni.
c. Tom and Mike both like pepperoni.
d. The person who ordered sausage sits across from Sharita.
e. Tom orders "the Works."

______________________________

______________________________

______________________________

8. Write the next three letters in this series:

Z Z R Y Y E X X A ______ ______ ______ V V I U U N T T G S S

**9.** Oak Street parallels Pine Street. Wooddale is perpendicular to Foster and parallels Oak. Is Pine perpendicular or parallel to Foster?

______________________________________________

**10.** Sea Cove is 100 miles west of Dallas. Rock Town is 20 miles west of Sea Cove. What follows from this? ______________________

______________________________________________

**EXERCISE 10.9**

*Read the short story below and answer the following questions.*

### A, B, and C—The Human Element in Mathematics
### Stephen Leacock

The student of arithmetic who has mastered the first four rules of his art and successfully striven with money sums and fractions finds himself confronted by an unbroken expanse of questions known as problems. These are short stories of adventure and industry with the end omitted, and though betraying a strong family resemblance, are not without a certain element of romance.

The characters in the plot of the problem are three people called A, B, and C; the form of the question is generally of this sort:

"A, B, and C do a certain piece of work. A can do as much work in one hour as B in two, or C in four. Find how long they work at it."

Or thus: "A, B, and C are employed to dig a ditch. A can dig as much in one our as B can dig in two, and B can dig twice as fast as C. Find how long, etc., etc."

Or after this wise: "A lays a wager that he can walk faster than B or C. A can walk half as fast again as B, and C is only an indifferent walker. Find how far, and so forth."

The occupations of A, B, and C are many and varied. In the older arithmetics they contented themselves with doing a "certain piece of work." This statement of the case, however, was found too sly and mysterious, or possibly lacking in romantic charm. It became the fashion to define the job more clearly and to set them at walking matches, ditch-digging, regattas, and piling cordwood. At times, they became commercial and entered into partnership, having, with their old mystery, a "certain" capital. Above all they revel in motion. When they tire of walking matches, A rides on horseback, or borrows a bicycle and competes with his weaker-minded associates on foot. Now they race on locomotives; now they row; or again they become historical and engage stagecoaches; or at times they are aquatic and swim. If their occupation is actual work, they prefer to pump water into cisterns, two of which leak through holes in the bottom and one of which is water-tight. A, of course, has the good one; he also takes the bicycle, and the best locomotive, and the right of swimming with the current. Whatever they do they put money on it, being all three sports. A always wins.

In the early chapters of the arithmetic, their identity is concealed under the names of John, William, and Henry, and they wrangle over the division of marbles. In algebra they are often called X, Y, Z. But these are only their Christian names, and they are really the same people.

Now to one who has followed the history of these men through countless pages of problems, watched them in their leisure hours, dallying with cordwood, and seen their panting sides heave in the full frenzy of filling a cistern with a leak in it, they become something more than mere symbols. They appear as creatures of flesh and blood, living men with their own passions, ambitions, and aspirations like the rest of us.

A is full-blooded, hot-headed and strong-willed. It is he who proposes everything, challenges B to work, makes the bets, and bends the others to his will. He is a man of great physical strength and phenomenal endurance. He has been known to walk forty-eight hours at a stretch, and to pump ninety-six. His life is arduous and full of peril. A mistake in the working of a sum may keep him digging a fortnight without sleep. A repeating decimal in the answer might kill him.

B is a quiet, easy-going fellow, afraid of A and bullied by him, but very gentle and brotherly to little C, the weakling. He is quite in A's power, having lost all his money in bets.

Poor C is an undersized, frail man, with a plaintiff face. Constant walking, digging, and pumping have broken his health and ruined his nervous system. His joyless life has driven him to drink and smoke more than is good for him, and his hand often shakes as he digs ditches. He has not the strength to work as the others do, in fact, as Hamlin Smith has said, "A can do more work in one hour than C in four."

The first time that ever I saw these men was one evening after a regatta. They had all been rowing in it, and it had transpired that A could row as much in one hour as B in two, or C in four. B and C had come in dead fagged and C was coughing badly. "Never mind, old fellow," I heard B say, "I'll fix you up on the sofa and get you some hot tea." Just then A came blustering in and shouted, "I say, you fellows, Hamlin Smith has shown me three cisterns in his garden and he says we can pump them until tomorrow night. I bet I can beat you both. Come on. You can pump in your rowing things, you know. Your cistern leaks a little, I think, C." I heard B growl that it was a dirty shame and that C was used up now, but they went and presently I could tell from the sound of the water that A was pumping four times as fast as C.

For years after that I used to see them constantly about the town and always busy. I never heard of any of them eating or sleeping. After that, owing to a long absence from home, I lost sight of them. On my return I was surprised to find A, B, and C no longer at their old tasks; on inquiry I heard that work in this line was now done by N, M, and O, and that some people were employing for algebraical jobs four foreigners called Alpha, Beta, Gamma, and Delta.

Now it chanced one day that I stumbled upon old D, in the little garden in front of his cottage, hoeing in the sun. D is an aged laboring man who used occasionally to be called in to help A, B, and C. "Did I know 'em, sir?" he answered. Why I knowed 'em ever since they was little fellows in brackets. Master A, he were a fine-hearted lad, sir, though I always said, give me Master B for kind-heartedness-like. Many's the job as we've been on together, sir, though I never did no racing nor aught of that, but just the plain labor, as you might say. I'm getting a bit too old and stiff for it nowadays, sir—just scratch about in the garden here and grow a bit of a logarithm, or raise a common denominator or two. But Mr. Euclid he uses me still for propositions, he do."

From the garrulous old man I learned the melancholy end of my former acquaintances. Soon after I left town, he told me, C had been ill. It seems that A and B had been rowing on the river for a wager, and C had been running on the bank and then sat in a draught. Of course the bank had refused the draught and C was taken ill. A and B came home and found C lying helpless in bed. A shook him roughly and said, "Get up, C, we're going to pile wood." C looked so worn and pitiful that B said, "Look here, A, I won't stand this, he isn't fit to pile wood tonight." C smiled feebly and said, "Perhaps I might pile a little if I sat up in bed." Then B, thoroughly alarmed, said, "See here, A, I'm going to fetch a doctor; he's dying." A flared up and answered, "You've got no money to fetch a doctor." "I'll reduce him to his lowest terms," B said firmly, "that'll fetch him." C's life might even then have been saved but they made a mistake about the medicine. It stood at the head of the bed on a bracket, and the nurse accidentally removed it from the bracket without changing the sign. After the fatal blunder C seems to have sunk rapidly. On the evening of the next day, it was clear, as the shadows deepened, that the end was near. I think that even A was affected at the last as he stood with bowed head, aimlessly offering to bet with the doctor on C's labored breathing. "A," whispered C, "I think I'm going fast." "How fast do you think you'll go, old man?" murmured A. "I don't know," said C, "but I'm going at any rate." The end came soon after that. C rallied for a moment and asked for a certain piece of work that he had left downstairs. A put it in his arms and he expired. As his soul sped heavenward, A watched its flight with melancholy admiration. B burst into a passionate flood of tears and sobbed, "Put away his little cistern and the rowing clothes he used to wear; I feel as if I could hardly ever dig again."—The funeral was plain and unostentatious. It differed in nothing from the ordinary, except that out of deference to sporting men, and mathematicians, A engaged two hearses. Both vehicles started at the same time, B driving the one which bore the sable parallelepipes containing the last remains of his ill-fated friend. A on the box of the empty hearse generously consented to a handicap of a hundred years, but arrived first at the cemetery by driving four times as fast as B. (Find the distance to the cemetery.) As the sarcophagus was lowered, the grave was surrounded by the broken figures of the first book of Euclid.

It was noticed that after the death of C, A became a changed man. He lost interest in racing with B, and dug but languidly. He finally gave up his work and settled down to live on the interest of his bets.—B never recovered from the shock of C's death; his grief preyed upon his intellect and it became deranged. He grew moody and spoke only in monosyllables. His disease became rapidly aggravated, and he presently spoke in words whose spelling was regular and which presented no difficulty to the beginner. Realizing his precarious condition he voluntarily submitted to be incarcerated in an asylum, where he abjured mathematics and devoted himself to writing the History of the Swiss Family Robinson in words of one syllable.

1. Reread the first sentence of the story. What are the first four rules of the student's art?

2. Let $x$ stand for the amount of work A does in one hour. Assuming the third paragraph correctly describes the work of B and C, translate the amount they work into math symbols.

3. Reread the seventh paragraph of the story, beginning with "In the early chapters . . .". Why are A, B, and C called *John, William,* and *Henry* in the early chapters of arithmetic?

4. Reread paragraphs nine, ten, and eleven, beginning with "A is full-blooded . . .". Identify the form of figurative language being used and explain how you recognize it.

5. Reread paragraph thirteen beginning with "For years after that . . .". Why are *Alpha, Beta, Gamma,* and *Delta* foreigners?

6. Reread paragraph fourteen beginning with "Now it chanced . . .". What is the fallacy in "raising a common denominator" or "growing a bit of a logarithm"?

7. In that same paragraph, identify Mr. Euclid. Then reread the next paragraph. Who or what are "the broken figures of the first book of Euclid." Of what type of figurative language is this an example?

8. Reread paragraph fifteen, beginning with "From the garrulous old man . . .". Identify the two meanings of *draft* used in this paragraph. How does this confusion contribute to the humor of the story?

9. In the same paragraph, explain the literal and mathematical meaning of each of the following:

**a.** "I'll reduce him to his lowest terms."

**b.** "It stood at the head of the bed on a bracket, and the nurse accidentally removed it from the bracket without changing the sign."

**10.** Identify ten math terms used in this story. Indicate whether they are specialized or technical terms.

◆

## CHAPTER SUMMARY EXERCISE

*Write a chapter summary in the space provided.*

◆

## CHAPTER REVIEW

*Answer briefly but completely.*

**1.** What is the difference between specialized and technical vocabulary?

**2.** Examine the problems in Exercise 10.3. Identify one example of what Polya calls "unstated assumptions."

**3.** Construct a protocol for marking relevant information in word problems.

4. Select any problem in Exercise 10.3 and rewrite it using Klein's two-eight model.

5. In terms of logic, what constitutes an argument?

6. Contrast deductive reasoning and inductive reasoning.

7. How is an argument like a syllogism?

8. What signal words are always found in syllogisms? What do these signal words mean?

9. Identify the grounds for believing premises.

**10.** How are formal and informal fallacies alike?

◆

## VOCABULARY ENHANCEMENT EXERCISE

*Using the scale in Figure 3.1, rate your understanding of the following vocabulary enhancement words to the left of the number. Then write a sentence with each one.*

**1.** fictitious

**2.** inspiration

**3.** presto

**4.** remote

**5.** erratic

**6.** maxim

**7.** deceptively

**8.** protocol

______________________________________________

______________________________________________

**9.** prophecies

______________________________________________

______________________________________________

**10.** manipulate

______________________________________________

______________________________________________

◆

## REFERENCES

Klein, P. A. (1988). Problem Solving: The 2–8 Model. *Research in Teaching in Developmental Education*, 5, 25–33.

Polya, G. (1962). *Mathematical Discovery: Understanding Learning and Teaching Problem Solving*, New York: John Wiley.

# 11 Adjusting Rate to Purpose: Skimming, Scanning, and Recreational Reading

## TERMS

*Terms appear in the order in which they occur in the chapter.*

scanning
skimming
critical reading
recreational reading
rate
gist
verbatim recall
framework
regression
survey
articles
conjunctions
prepositions
nouns
verbs
introductions
summaries
topic sentences
format
plot
browse
nonfiction
fiction
copyright date

## CHAPTER OUTLINE EXERCISE

*Create an outline for this chapter on the following lines.*

## OBJECTIVES

*At the end of this chapter, you should be able to do the following:*

1. Describe what is meant by flexibility in reading.
2. Identify ineffective reading habits.
3. Describe how you can vary rate by skimming and scanning.
4. Define recreational reading.

## CHAPTER MAP

*Create a map for this chapter in the space below.*

## VOCABULARY ENHANCEMENT EXERCISE

| | STAGE 0 | STAGE 1 | STAGE 2 | STAGE 3 |
|---|---|---|---|---|
| | *I do not recognize the word.* | *I recognize the word but am unsure of its meaning and associations.* | *I recognize the word and can make general associations with it.* | *I recognize the word and can use it in speaking and writing.* |
| **1.** vital | | | | |
| **2.** morsel | | | | |
| **3.** breakthroughs | | | | |
| **4.** collided | | | | |
| **5.** inset | | | | |
| **6.** reputable | | | | |
| **7.** physical | | | | |
| **8.** cast | | | | |
| **9.** documentaries | | | | |
| **10.** scenarios | | | | |

◆

## FLEXIBILITY IN READING

*Some books are to be tasted, others to be swallowed, and some few to be chewed and digested.*

—FRANCIS BACON

Have you ever wondered about speed-reading courses? How do they work? Can you really read four chapters of history, your entire chemistry text, and *Gone with the Wind* in one hour?

Would you really want to? As Bacon says, some books deserve more of your time than others. From some textbooks, you need only isolated facts. Here, "tasting" or **scanning** is sufficient. From others, you seek main ideas. Here, you need to "swallow" larger amounts of text. **Skimming** allows you to do this. Still other texts offer such complex and vital concepts that you want to "chew and digest" every morsel. This **critical reading** involves those strategies you've already learned in this text. **Recreational reading** books provide you with the chance to decide for yourself how to dine on a book. You'll find some books not worth the time it takes to skim or scan them. Others, however, you'll savor leisurely.

Speed-reading classes are popular because they help you develop faster ways to find main ideas and/or answers to specific questions. You pay your money and take the course. You become a faster reader overnight . . . or, do you?

You'll find that reputable speed-reading courses take several weeks to a few months to complete. You spend one or more hours per class learning to increase your speed and comprehension. Classes meet once a week or several times a week. You either read from special machines that automatically present text or you read from books or magazines.

All speed-reading courses have the same "magic formula":

*Practice (Effort + Time) = Speed*

The practice, time, and effort the formula requires come from you. Thus, changes in reading rate do not occur only in speed-reading classes. You can learn to do this by yourself.

But how do you know when changing reading speed is appropriate? Your **rate,** or speed, depends on the content of the material, your purpose, and your ability. Sometimes speed changes from sentence to sentence, paragraph to paragraph, and passage to passage.

For example, when you get a test back in class, you quickly look over it to see what you missed. Then you examine the test more slowly to see where you made your mistakes. Your instructor may have made some errors in grading. You wouldn't want to miss them!

Reading speed also increases when you know about a subject. When a subject is new to you, reading slows because of new terms and ideas. Reading goals, set by you or your instructor, also affect speed. You speed up when looking for details or stated information. You slow down when drawing conclusions or summarizing ideas. Finally, you speed up as you become a more skilled reader. Your reading becomes faster with practice.

**EXERCISE 11.1**

*At what rate would you read the following passages: fast, average, or slow? Why?*

***Example***

*Purpose:* to locate the correct spelling of a word in the dictionary
*Topic:* a letter to a friend

*Rate:* *fast*

*Reason:* *Need specific information quickly. Other information is not needed and should not be examined carefully.*

1. *Purpose:* to discover the main idea
   *Topic:* a description of a basketball game

   *Rate:* ______________________

   *Reason:* ______________________

   ______________________

2. *Purpose:* to review for your driver's license renewal
   *Topic:* road safety and traffic laws

   *Rate:* ______________________

   *Reason:* ______________________

   ______________________

3. *Purpose:* to decide which movie to see
   *Topic:* advertisements in the newspaper

   *Rate:* ______________________

   *Reason:* ______________________

   ______________________

4. *Purpose:* to draw conclusions
   *Topic:* a philosophy assignment

   *Rate:* ______________________

   *Reason:* ______________________

   ______________________

**5.** *Purpose:* to read magazines at the student health center
*Topic:* out-of-date sports and news magazines

*Rate:*________________________________

*Reason:*________________________________

______________________________________

**6.** *Purpose:* to read for personal enjoyment
*Topic:* a paperback copy of Erma Bombeck's *Motherhood: The Second Oldest Profession*

*Rate:*________________________________

*Reason:*________________________________

______________________________________

**7.** *Purpose:* to discover the main idea
*Topic:* the comic strip "Sally Forth"

*Rate:*________________________________

*Reason:*________________________________

______________________________________

**8.** *Purpose:* to study for a history exam
*Topic:* the causes of the American Civil War

*Rate:*________________________________

*Reason:*________________________________

______________________________________

**9.** *Purpose:* to discover the author's point of view
*Topic:* William Buckley's editorial on nuclear weapons

*Rate:*________________________________

*Reason:*________________________________

______________________________________

**10.** *Purpose:* to check information
*Topic:* a copy of your telephone bill

*Rate:*________________________________

*Reason:*________________________________

______________________________________

◆

## INEFFECTIVE READING HABITS

A student made a right turn from a left lane and collided with another car. The other driver angrily asked, "Hey, why didn't you signal?"

Without hesitation, the student replied, "Man, I always turn here!"

Some readers resemble the student driver. They read from habit. Thus, they read without thinking about how they themselves might be hindering their reading rates.

Luckily, like many other habits, reading habits can be changed for the better with thought and effort (see Table 1.1).

### Lip Movements and Finger Pointing

During World War II, the watchword was "Loose lips sink ships." In this way, government officials warned citizens that too much talk about war efforts would delay victory. Similarly, in reading, loose lips, as well as finger pointing, can sink your ship.

For example, look around the room you're in now. In a fraction of a second, your mind "sees" everything. Try naming everything in the room. Try pointing to each item in the room, one by one. Pointing and speaking are slow. You can't point to words or say them as quickly as your mind can "see" them. Thus, eliminating these physical movements increases your speed.

Habits such as lip movements and finger pointing can be hard to break. They usually have become automatic. You do them without thinking. However, you can control these ineffective habits. You stop lip movements by holding a pencil in your mouth when you read. When your lips begin to move, the pencil falls. Another way to control

**TABLE 11.1** ***Ineffective Reading Habits and Solutions***

| PROBLEM | SOLUTION |
|---|---|
| **1.** Lip movements | **a.** Hold a pencil in your mouth. |
| | **b.** Rest your chin on your hand with fingers touching your mouth. |
| **2.** Finger pointing | **a.** Hold book with both hands. |
| **3.** Lack of rate flexibility | **a.** Practice with easier texts and progress to harder material. |
| | **b.** Time yourself. |
| | **c.** Identify purposes for reading. |
| **4.** Inefficient eye movements<br>**a.** Physical causes | **a.** Have a vision exam to rule out the possibility of physical problems. |
| **b.** Regression | **b.** Read an entire sentence before looking back. |
| **5.** Disorganized information | **a.** Make a conscious effort to connect old and new information. |
| | **b.** Preview before reading. |
| | **c.** Try a simpler version. |
| | **d.** Determine structure from table of contents. |
| | **e.** Draw analogies to more common examples. |

lip movements is to read with your hand on your chin and your fingers on your mouth. You stop finger pointing by holding the book with both hands. In addition, as your reading skill and speed increase, these problems often decrease without extensive effort on your part.

## Lack of Rate Flexibility

You, like many students, may wish to read faster. Actually, the rate at which you read may be suitable for some reading materials. The problem occurs when you fail to vary that rate. Inability to vary rate often occurs because you don't know when or why you need to do so.

While you want to increase your overall speed, you need to vary your rate within reading selections. Just as road conditions dictate driving speed, reading conditions dictate reading speed. In general, you increase speed when reading easy material or information you know. You also read faster when reading for **gist,** or main ideas. You slow down when subject matter is new. In addition, you decrease rate when sentence length or word difficulty increases. You also read more slowly when you need **verbatim** (exactly as written) **recall.** Skimming and scanning also help you vary rate.

Rate inflexibility is one bad habit you can break. To learn to read faster, you need to read while timing your rate. To determine reading speed, you divide the number of words read by the time it takes you to read them. Timing yourself on various kinds of reading material—textbooks, magazines, newspapers, and so on—helps increase rate. Once you read a passage, reread it and try to break your record. As your rate increases, you need to increase the difficulty of the text. The more you practice, the more your speed increases. You need to push yourself and not let up.

## Inefficient Eye Movements

To paraphrase Omar Kahyyam's *The Rubaiyat*, "The moving eye reads and, having read, moves on." Reading speed may be affected by inefficient eye movements. Such a problem may be physical. You should have your eyes checked to detect this possibility. Vision changes usually occur slowly. It would be hard for you to notice the change. At one major university all students in reading courses have their vision checked. Twenty to 25 percent of these students each term need further testing. An eye exam tells if you see normally. If not, your eyes may become needlessly tired when you read. You need good vision for success in reading and in college.

Picture yourself walking to your math class. You know the way. You walk straight there. Now picture this scene again. This time you don't walk straight to class. You walk a block, turn around, and walk back for a half block. You go forward for another block but then go back for another half block. When you get to the end of each block you stop and stand for a few minutes.

Which method gets you to class in less time? The first one is faster. You don't waste time retreating and advancing or standing around.

When you read, your eyes move forward at a steady pace, just as you walk at a steady pace. When your eyes look back at a word you've already read, it slows your reading. It also hurts your comprehension. This habit is called **regression.** To stop regression, you make yourself read an entire sentence without looking back. Remember, a sentence expresses a complete thought. Sometimes you need to read to the end of the sentence to fully understand it.

Suppose you get to your math class and find you've forgotten your notebook. You retrace your steps and return home. Similarly, some rereading is necessary. Once you have read to the end of a sentence or thought, you may need to reread to understand. But, when you constantly reread and hesitate, you lessen your comprehension and reading rate.

## Disorganization of Information

One ineffective reading habit involves relating or storing information. Think of your brain as a giant file cabinet. That file cabinet could be disorganized and confused. Or, it could be neat and orderly. Each file in the cabinet represents a **framework.** New information is either filed in the correct framework or is stuck anywhere.

When you read, your mind pulls a file, takes and/or adds information, and returns it for future reference. By attaching new information to old, you add to your understanding. You also use the framework to predict, in general, what new information contains. In addition, the framework relates different pieces of information. It may be that you aren't using your framework effectively. You need to consciously begin to associate and relate information.

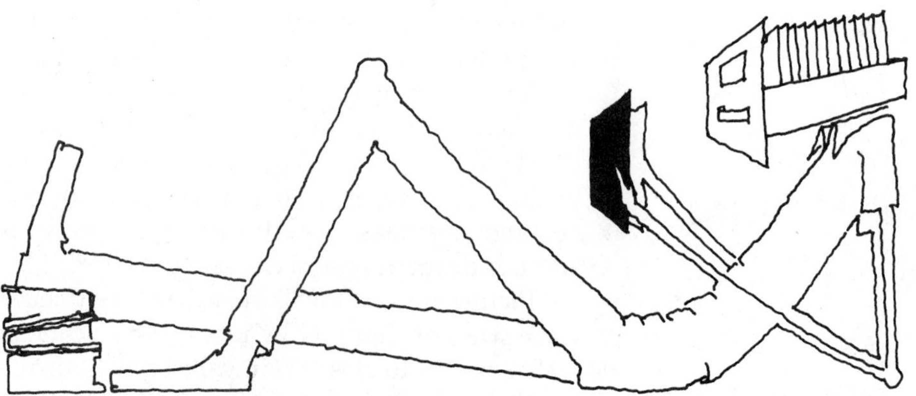

One way to do this is to preview. Previewing enables you to relate background knowledge before encountering new data. It also helps you study more effectively. You can also break this habit by reading a simpler text. Articles in popular magazines often cover topics in the social and applied sciences. Written for the public, these pieces are usually more understandable. In addition, libraries frequently have texts on a variety of subjects written at all levels of difficulty. Reading an easier text provides background information for your file. A third way you help yourself organize data concerns examining the contents of the text. This gives you a context from which to study. Similar to a map inset, this helps you see how a set of facts fits into a larger body of knowledge. Finally, making comparisons between complex concepts and simpler ideas aids your understanding. These comparisons often take the form of analogies.

**WRITE TO LEARN**

*A fellow student failed to understand the file cabinet analogy in the discussion on disorganization of information. On a separate sheet of paper, provide another illustration to clarify the concept of information storage.*

**EXERCISE 11.2**

*Time yourself as you read the following excerpt. Record your time as part of question 1. Then answer the rest of the questions below*

**Sigmund Freud: A Biographical Sketch**

Sigmund Freud was born in 1856 in the city of Freiberg, which is now in Czechoslovakia. His father, a wool merchant, moved the family to Vienna when Sigmund was four years old, in search of better markets.

Young Sigmund, the first born and favorite of his mother (the second wife of his much older father), was an outstanding student almost from the moment he learned to read. He was awarded a room of his own in the family's Vienna apartment, so that he could pursue his studies without interruption. It was the only room equipped with an oil lamp, rather than candles. At one point, the ten- or eleven-year-old Sigmund complained that his sister's piano practice disturbed his studies, though great care had been taken to locate the piano at the far end of the apartment. The piano was quickly removed from the premises.

Despite his great scholarship, or perhaps because of it, Freud did not find it easy to choose a career. In fact, he did not settle on the profession of personality theorist until sometime between the ages of thirty and thirty-five. Throughout his high school years, he seems to have had a vague intention to pursue a career in law. He got this idea from several sources: the influence of an older school friend; the effect, on him and his parents, of a fortune-teller's casual prophecy that he would grow up to be a government minister; and undoubtedly also the fact that, for the first time, there were a few Jews who had become government ministers. (As a

Jew, Freud was restricted, for all practical purposes, to a career in business, law, or medicine.)

Freud tells us that he never intended to become a doctor. Yet his growing fascination with the new and controversial theories of Charles Darwin, and the effect a public reading of Goethe's *Ode to Nature* had on him, nudged him in the direction of medical school, where he enrolled at the age of seventeen. He still had no plans to become a doctor; he considered himself more what we would nowadays call an undergraduate biology major.

Freud took seven-and-a half years to graduate, at least three years longer than the norm. At least part of this procrastination was due to uncertainty about the direction his life should take. Though he attended all the required lectures and labs in chemistry, physiology, and anatomy, he also took elective courses in philosophy and, at one point, considered taking a degree in philosophy after finishing his medical studies.

It was Ernst Brücke, the world-famous physiologist, who finally captured young Freud's attention and gave him his first sense of professional identity. Under Brücke's influence, Freud decided to become a research physiologist. Brücke, incidentally, was one of a group of physiologists who crusaded in favor of absolute **mechanistic** determinism in the biological sciences. This ideology struck a responsive chord in Freud and continued to guide his thinking, even when he constructed his theory of personality years later. Freud published a number of well-received papers on his research at the Brücke Institute, most of them having to do with the histology of the nervous system of fish and other lower animals.

Only after he had finally graduated and received his M.D. did Freud discover the sad truth that it would be unrealistic for him to aspire to a career in pure research. Such careers were the prerogative of men of independent means. Freud was poor, still dependent on his father for financial assistance. What is more, he had fallen in love with the woman who was to become his wife, and he needed to make financial provisions to marry. This was undoubtedly one of the critical moments in Freud's life.

Reluctantly, he abandoned the laboratory and began working in a hospital. Neurology was the logical choice of specialization for someone with his background. During the next three years, Freud served as house physician at the General Hospital. He kept his research interests alive by working at the Institute of Cerebral Anatomy, where he traced the tracts in the medulla oblongata. He became so proficient in this area that he could diagnose the site of a lesion in the medulla with astounding accuracy. Physicians came from as far away as America to learn his methods.

Economic reality once again directed him to specialize more narrowly in the treatment of nervous diseases. In the Vienna of that era, there were very few specialists in this branch of medicine. Of course, that also meant that there were few experts with whom Freud could study. If he were to become properly qualified as a doctor of nervous disorders, Freud would have to go to Paris and study with the famous Jean Martin Charcot. After a series of maneuvers, including obtaining an appointment as University Lecturer on Nervous Diseases in Vienna, Freud won a fellowship to study with Charcot. The year was 1885, and Freud was twenty-nine years old.

The education Freud received at Charcot's clinic was another important turning point in his life. Charcot's specialty was hysteria, a "nervous disorder'' that had no apparent neurological cause, but many intriguing psychological dimensions, as we will see very shortly. From Charcot, Freud learned many things about hysteria and its treatment, and about hypnosis. These things were unknown in Vienna.

When Freud returned to Vienna to set up his own private practice as a specialist in nervous diseases, he was one of the few doctors there who welcomed hysterical, and other neurotic, patients. Yet even in this endeavor he did not succeed immediately. At first he tried to make a living by treating cases of organic neurological pathology. Only when it became clear that there were too few cases to support all of the doctors in his specialty did Freud begin actively seeking out the more psychologically disturbed clientele that would turn his thinking in the direction of personality theory. By then he was well into his thirties; in fact, he did not entirely abandon his dream of becoming a great research neurologist until sometime in the 1890s, when he finally accepted the idea of being a mere psychologist.

That decision sparked a tremendous burst of creative activity, including book publications at the rate of almost one a year, and carried Freud into a larger, global arena. As early as 1909, he was asked to lecture at Clark University's twentieth anniversary celebration in Worcester, Massachusetts. He continued to be immensely productive for thirty more years, although he never again visited America. He left Vienna in 1938, when the Nazi storm troopers were literally on his doorstep. He fled to England, where he died on September 23, 1939.

*Source:* Reprinted with permission from *Key Ideas in Personality Theory* by Scruggs. 

**1.** Record your reading time. ______________________

**2.** Compute your reading speed by dividing each reading time by the number of words in the passage.

__________ (time)/ 1,029 (words) = __________ words per minute.

**3.** On a scale of 1 to 5, with 1 being least difficult, rate the difficulty of this excerpt. ______________________

**4.** What contributes to the degree of difficulty of this excerpt?

______________________

______________________

______________________

**5.** List five words that contribute to the difficulty of the passage.

______________________

______________________

**6.** Examine the number of sentences and the sentence lengths in the first three paragraphs. List the number of sentences and the average number of words per sentence.

7. How does background knowledge affect your understanding?

_______________________________________________

_______________________________________________

_______________________________________________

8. How do these factors (vocabulary, sentence length, background knowledge) contribute to the speed at which you read this article?

_______________________________________________

_______________________________________________

_______________________________________________

◆

## VARYING RATE: SKIMMING AND SCANNING

Imagine you are exploring an old house. You go to the attic, turn on the ceiling light, and illuminate its contents. You see a variety of items. "Hmm," you say to yourself, "this is full of old furniture" (or "clothes" or "books" or "junk" . . . or whatever else you find). You summarized your findings in a single sentence. You determined the main idea of the attic's contents.

Imagine you go to the basement. Now you are looking for something specific . . . a pair of boots, a fan, or a box. This time there is no overhead light. You have a flashlight. You quickly shine the light over the contents. You pass over items you aren't seeking. You cast the beam around until you find what you're looking for. Once you do, you pick it up and leave.

Skimming and scanning share much with these scenarios. In skimming, you have a wide focus. Your purpose is to find the main idea. Sometimes you find it stated in a sentence. Other times, you summarize it yourself. In scanning, your focus is narrow. Here you want to answer a specific question. You overlook the items you don't need. You continue searching until you find the answer you seek. Once found, you get it and take it with you. An easy way to remember the difference between the two is to think about how the words are spelled. Scanning has "an" for *an*swer. Skimming has a "mi" for *m*ain *i*dea. These letters signal the purpose of each.

### Skimming: Reading for Main Ideas

Skimming is reading at the fastest speed possible. You skim when you need to cover material quickly. When you skim, you are "racing the clock."

One way to improve your speed is by timing yourself. Begin with single pages or very short, easy-to-read passages. After reading, ask yourself what the main idea is. Reskim the same information. Try to improve your speed each time by racing yourself.

Almost like shopping during sales, in skimming, you want to get the most for the least. This means you want to find the main idea without spending lots of time.

### *Skimming as a Survey*

Skimming helps you minimize the time you spend surveying a chapter. Many readers think that reading something once is enough. They know that rereading is not very interesting. There is a way you can reread with less boredom. You skim on the first reading, the **survey.**

By skimming first, you set up your framework for the second, more careful reading. This second reading takes more time than the first. Such selective reading and rereading helps in note taking. Also, it helps you understand detailed, difficult texts.

Remember to pay close attention to the following:

| | |
|---|---|
| Title | Other boldface words and phrases |
| Introduction | First sentence of each paragraph |
| Headings and subheadings | Graphs, lists, charts, pictures |

### *Skimming Text Chapters*

When looking for the main idea, you skip parts of the passage. What to skip depends on the importance of the passage and your familiarity with the subject. The importance of a text depends on two factors. First, it depends on whether or not the information is important to you. Second, it also depends on whether or not you need the information for a specific purpose.

Many students think they must read each word in a text to understand it. This is not always true. Many words like **articles** *(a, an, the),* **conjunctions** *(and, but, or),* and **prepositions** *(of, with, to)* are not always essential. If all of these words were left out, you would find that almost half of the text had been omitted. Then you could focus on the more important **nouns** and **verbs.**

Textbooks provide additional clues as to what to skim. First, introductions, summaries, and graphics condense main ideas. Skimming them provides an overview of the chapter's key concept. Next, chapter headings and subheadings further define key information. Within these sections, **topic sentences** specify important details. These appear either at the beginning or end of a paragraph. You skim these paragraphs or sentences to find main ideas.

### *Skimming Supplementals*

Skimming an article seems difficult. Textbooks contain headings and subheadings to focus your attention. How do you know what to do when an article has no such text clues? Most articles are written in a straightforward style. As in texts, introductory and concluding sections tend to summarize information. Main ideas generally appear at the beginning of paragraphs. Thus, you read the first and last paragraphs and the first sentence in all other paragraphs to determine the main idea.

### *Steps in Skimming*

Skimming provides you with a means of getting the big picture quickly. As a review, the steps in skimming follow.

STEPS IN SKIMMING

1. *As fast as possible, read the first few sentences (or paragraphs).* This will give you an idea of what the passage is about. You can often figure out the setting and the mood from these first sentences.
2. *Next start leaving out material.* On the third or fourth sentence, let your eyes hit only key words or phrases. Key words are usually nouns or verbs.
3. *Read all of the last few sentences (or paragraphs).*
4. *Try to figure out the main idea and a few facts.* You can't pick up all the facts. You will pick up many of them.

#### *Example*

Below is an introduction to a college text called *Introduction to Child Development*. The underlined words and phrases are those you would examine when skimming.

**BEFORE SKIMMING AS A SURVEY . . .**

**How to Use the Unique Features of this Textbook**

This book is based on a method known as SQ3R. SQ3R is a five step plan that was developed by Dr. Francis P. Robinson. The SQ3R method is designed to promote effective studying, and the letters S-Q-R-R-R refer to the five steps.

**The First Step: Survey**

The S in SQ3R stands for *survey*. The first thing to do is survey the assigned

**AFTER SKIMMING AS A SURVEY . . .**

**How to Use the Unique Features of this Textbook**

This book is based on a method known as SQ3R. SQ3R is a five-step plan that was developed by Dr. Francis P. Robinson. The SQ3R method is designed to promote effective studying, and the letters S-Q-R-R-R refer to the five steps.

**The First Step: Survey**

The S in SQ3R stands for *survey*. The first thing to do is *survey* the assigned chapter. Read the titles and the headings. Glance at the captions under illustrations and pictures; read the summary at the end of the chapter. This may seem like an unusual way to begin, but it is the way the SQ3R method is designed, and it's effective. Usually you read a summary in order to review what you've covered in the chapter. But in this case the *Resources Summary* is the very first thing you should read. Although you may not understand everything, the summary will give you an overall picture of the chapter contents, and it helps to reinforce the major points when you come to them in the chapter. Once you have read the entire chapter you may, of course, reread the *Resources Summary* in order to refresh your memory.

**The Second Step: Question**

The Q stands for *question*. In the SQ3R method, every topic is introduced as a question, a means of increasing your interest in what you will be reading and helping you to focus on the material to come. In this text, the questions are already provided for you. Flip through the text for a moment and you'll notice them. You may find the interjection of questions in the text obtrusive at first, but you will quickly become used to them and find that the questions help you focus your attention. You may even find that you were about to ask many of the same questions. This shows that you are concentrating on the material and that you understand what is being presented.

**The Third Step: Read**

The first R stands for *read*. You should read the material under one heading and stop before going on to the next heading. That is, you should cover one small area within a chapter at a time. Before continuing to read, go on to step four.

chapter. Read the titles and the headings. Glance at the captions under illustrations and pictures; read the summary at the end of the chapter. This may seem like an unusual way to begin, but it is the way the SQ3R method is designed, and it's effective. Usually you read a summary in order to review what you've covered in the chapter. But in this case the *Resources Summary* is the very first thing you should read. Although you may not understand everything, the summary will give you an overall picture of the chapter contents, and it helps to reinforce the major points when you come to them in the chapter. Once you have read the entire chapter you may, of course, reread the *Resources Summary* in order to refresh your memory.

**The Second Step: Question**

The Q stands for *question*. In the SQ3R method, every topic is introduced as a question, a means of increasing your interest in what you will be reading and helping you to focus on the material to come. In this text, the questions are already provided for you. Flip through the text for a moment and you'll notice them. You may find the interjection of questions in the text obtrusive at first, but you will quickly become used to them and find that the questions help you focus your attention. You may even find that you were about to ask many of the same questions. This shows that you are concentrating on the material and that you understand what is being presented.

**The Third Step: Read**

The first R stands for *read*. You should read the material under one heading and stop before going on to the next heading. That is, you should cover one small area within a chapter at a time. Before continuing to read, go on to step four.

### The Fourth Step: Recite

The second R stands for *recite.* When you recite, ask yourself questions about the material you have just read and make sure that you are able to answer them. Your student study guide can help you in this because it contains questions with which you can test yourself. Once you know, by reciting, that you thoroughly understand what you have read, you can proceed to the next heading, reciting once again, before going on to the next heading, and so on.

Throughout the book you will find Learning Checks that help you to recite. If you can answer these Learning Checks correctly, you will know that you have read the material carefully and understand it. Remember, this is a textbook; it's a book for work. Don't feel uncomfortable about writing in it. Make notes in the margins; fill in the answers in the Learning Checks where there are blanks; circle the answers to the multiple choice questions. Recording your answers will help you to remember the material and to catch errors.

### The Fifth Step: Review

*Review* is the final R in SQ3R. When you have read an entire chapter, review your notes, check through your student study guide, and look over any questions that you have written down. If possible, have someone read through the material and ask you about it. Make sure you can answer the questions that have been posed. This is an important way of obtaining feedback.

### The Fourth Step: Recite

The second R stands for *recite.* When you recite, ask yourself questions about the material you have just read and make sure that you are able to answer them. Your student study guide can help you in this because it contains questions with which you can test yourself. Once you know, by reciting, that you thoroughly understand what you have read, you can proceed to the next heading, reciting once again, before going on to the next heading, and so on.

Throughout the book you will find Learning Checks that help you to recite. If you can answer these Learning Checks correctly, you will know that you have read the material carefully and understand it. Remember, this is a textbook; it's a book for work. Don't feel uncomfortable about writing in it. Make notes in the margins; fill in the answers in the Learning Checks where there are blanks; circle the answers to the multiple choice questions. Recording your answers will help you to remember the material and to catch errors.

### The Fifth Step: Review

*Review* is the final R in SQ3R. When you have read an entire chapter, review your notes, check through your student study guide, and look over any questions that you have written down. If possible, have someone read through the material and ask you about it. Make sure you can answer the questions that have been posed. This is an important way of obtaining feedback.

**Glossary**

Finally you will find words set in boldface throughout the text. These are terms that are defined in the running glossary on each page near the first appearance of the term. If you are uncertain about the meaning of a term at a later time, you can also look it up in the Glossary provided at the back of the book.

I hope that this text will provide you with a thorough introduction to child development, and that it will make you want to learn more.

**Glossary**

Finally, you will find words set in boldface throughout the text. These are terms that are defined in the running glossary on each page near the first appearance of the term. If you are uncertain about the meaning of a term at a later time, you can also look it up in the Glossary provided at the back of the book.

I hope that this text will provide you with a thorough introduction to child development, and that it will make you want to learn more.

## EXERCISE 11.3

♦ *Below you will find a section from a study skills text. Underline the items you should notice when skimming. What is the main idea?*

*Main Idea:* ______________________________

______________________________

______________________________

**THE HARVARD EXPERIMENT**

As an experiment, Dr. William Perry, director of a reading course at Harvard, presented 1500 freshmen with a complete chapter from a history book to read. He told them to read and study the chapter in any way they thought best to enable them to answer brief questions and write a short essay.

Twenty-two minutes later he stopped them, and to find out the methods of study they had used, he gave a multiple-choice test on the details. The entire class scored high. Then he asked them to write a short statement on what the chapter was all about. Only fifteen of "1500 of the finest freshmen readers in the country" were able to do so. These were the only ones who had "the moral courage" to pull themselves out of the details of the chapter to first skim through the pages and read the headings and sub-headings, and to read the last paragraph clearly marked "Summary." In this particular chapter, the summary was unusually clear and well-organized. Half a minute's study of this summary paragraph would have given the reader a clear overview of the entire chapter.

Dr. Perry's demonstration of "obedient purposelessness" shows the "enormous amount of wasted effort" in freshman study, especially when one considers that "a student sits with his books for nearly a thousand hours each year." Most freshmen "open the book and read from word to word," disregarding the purpose of the assignment. Dr. Perry says that an effort must be made "to shake students loose from this conscientious but meaningless approach." He urges students to use their judgment as to what to read or skip, and to "talk to themselves" while reading, constantly asking, "Is this the point I'm looking for?"

**Skimming: A Lot of Other Uses**

Some people avoid skimming because they think that skimming is reading at a superficial level, and that "anything worth reading is worth reading well." Such people fail to see that skimming may be used as a preparation for thorough reading, not as a substitute for it. For example, through skimming, the student can eliminate books or portions of books not worth reading, thus saving time for a thorough reading of material he really needs to learn.

The wise use of skimming to locate important concepts also help the student grasp the author's ideas more quickly and with a clearer view of the overall organization.

Skimming is a versatile technique since it can be used to accomplish a variety of tasks, but the speed of skimming must be adjusted to the reader's purpose. The following kinds of skimming each require a different speed and focus while you read.

1. *Browsing.* A professor of literature may place on an open shelf in the library about fifty books for unassigned, secondary reading. He may urge you "to open them, explore, and read bits here and there."
2. *The research paper.* After writing down numerous titles of books and articles gleaned from the card catalogue and from the *Reader's Guide to Periodical Literature*, the student is faced with the problem of boiling down the references to a manageable number. Books can often be eliminated from your list by skimming the preface, the table of contents, the index, and some of the summarizing paragraphs or sections.
3. *Textbooks.* Skimming the textbook as a whole before the term really gets under way, and skimming each chapter as it is assigned can set the stage for more rapid and thorough reading.
4. *Novels.* Understandably, many people say that the reader should not read the last chapter of a novel first to find out how the story ends. Nevertheless there are several practical uses of skimming a novel, especially if you are reading it for a course rather than for relaxation. If the assignment permits a choice of novels, you might skim up to the middle of the book to find out whether it interests you. Or, once you have chosen a novel, you may skim through for the story, plot, setting, characterizations, and conclusion. You may even profit from a second and third skimming: once for criticism and evaluation, and once for meditation and speculation.
5. *Newspapers.* The news items of a newspaper are organized for easy skimming: The title of the news item is the conclusion, and the first

paragraph is the summary. Each succeeding paragraph contains information in descending order of importance. A reader who wants to finish the Sunday edition of *The New York Times* can read the headline and the first paragraph of each article, then skim the balance of the paragraphs, reading more thoroughly only those that interest him.

Skimming techniques help students overcome the over-cautious approach to the printed word. We find that readers often reflect their job traits: chemists, engineers, and accountants tend to read every word of a newspaper as if it were a formula or the fine print of a contract. Using intensive reading to cope with relatively simple, straightforward material is like mooring your rowboat with a line strong enough to hold a battleship. Skimming will add versatility to your reading.

*Source: How to Study in College*, 2/e, by Walter Pauk. Copyright © 1974 by Houghton Mifflin Company. Used with permission.

**EXERCISE 11.4**

*Skim the following excerpt. Underline the items you should notice when skimming. Write the main idea on the lines below.*

*Main idea:* ______________________________________________

______________________________________________

______________________________________________

### The Direct Approach

Now that you understand the mechanics of preparing a print ad, a radio spot, and a television commercial, we are going to explore certain types of advertising that have their own special characteristics. The first of these is direct marketing, a process that sells goods directly from producer to customer without benefit of retailer or middleman. Direct marketing has long been with us in the United States but has had a tremendous boom in recent years.

***Famous Examples***

The history of U.S. advertising and selling is studded with outstanding direct marketing advertisements upon which great copywriting reputations were built. Bruce Barton wrote inspired Horatio Alger-type copy for such self-improvement enterprises as the Alexander Hamilton Extension Institute ("A Wonderful Two Years Trip at Full Pay") and Dr. Elliott's Five-Foot Shelf ("This is Marie Antoinette Riding to Her Death"). The legendary John Caples, who is virtually the patron saint of direct marketing copywriting, authored two memorable direct marketing advertisements in his first year on the job back in 1925 ("They Laughed When I Sat Down at the Piano" and "They Grinned When the Waiter Spoke to Me in French"). Both were for home study courses, as were three other famous appeals by other copywriters: "Do You Have a Grasshopper Mind?" and "Again She Ordered Chicken Salad" and, for a memory course, "Of Course I Remember You. You're Mr. Addison Sims of Seattle." Of slightly more recent vintage is the spectacularly successful Dale Carnegie book title and ad headline "How to Win Friends and Influence People."

As U.S. transportation, distribution, and retailing systems expanded and changed, direct marketing lost the preeminence it held on the advertising and selling scene in the days before supermarkets. While it never approached eclipse, direct marketing dwindled in the 1950s and 1960s to a rather modest percentage of the nation's total advertising budget. However, in very recent years, direct marketing has experienced a remarkable expansion—an explosion, some say. There are a number of reasons behind this spectacular resurgence.

#### *Reasons for Direct Marketing Boom*

Computers have revolutionized direct marketing in two ways. First, the lifeblood of direct marketing is the ability to reach highly specific prospects, and computers enable direct marketers to build, to scan, and to edit prospect lists with a speed and accuracy never known before. They give a superb measure of control over the entire direct marketing process. Second, computerized letters—through such technological processes as laser beam printing—enable advertising messages to be highly personalized, not just in the salutation but at several places throughout the message. These letters can be produced at incredible speed and in great quantities. An outstanding example is the Publisher's Clearing House sweepstakes letter.

In addition to computers, the now almost universal use of credit cards has positively affected direct marketing. The credit card makes it so very simple for the customer to complete the transaction in one sitting. And the ability in recent years to call a toll-free 800 number has made the ordering process even easier.

At the same time, the cost-per-call figures have been skyrocketing to the point that the personal salesperson is fast becoming a vanishing breed in America. Direct marketing is helping to fill this void.

One societal factor that has favored direct marketing is the increasing number of women in the nation's workforce. Between handling a career and running a home, these women have less time for in-store shopping and find shopping by way of catalog or mailing piece a great time-saving service. More and more of the country's finest firms are offering superb merchandise through direct marketing advertising. Current copywriting ace Joseph Sugarman composed a direct marketing ad selling a $2,000,000 home in Malibu, California. The ad ran in an inflight airline magazine.

All U.S. marketing is putting greater emphasis on selectivity, a selling strategy to which direct marketing lends itself beautifully. The universal, built-in advantage for skilled managers is that direct marketing advertising is scientific because it is measurable.

#### *Most Thoroughly Tested Copy*

Of all forms of advertising copy, direct marketing copy is the most thoroughly tested. In fact, every single direct marketing advertisement is a test that elicits direct feedback from its audience. Direct marketing advertising relies on no intervening variables, no go-betweens, no sales clerk. Nor can it hide or strut behind an Advertising Awards Jury gold medal or blue ribbon. If the direct marketing advertisement pulls in sales or inquiries, it passes the test. If the direct marketing advertisement does not pull in sales or inquiries, it is a flop, and unlikely to be repeated. As in the case of "Do You Make These Mistakes in English?" a winning appeal may be used time and again as long as it keeps winning in competition with newer copy appeals that are regularly being written and tested. In direct marketing advertising, the "feedback" is measurable and inescapable.

#### *Direct Marketing Media Use*

Direct marketing advertising uses a wide range of media that includes practically everything but outdoor billboards: newspapers, free-standing inserts in newspapers, magazines, direct mail, and increasingly, radio and television. It is most visible, however, in the medium of direct mail.

### DIRECT MARKETING VIA DIRECT MAIL

"Direct Mail" is a bit of a misnomer. The communication itself is delivered *direct* to the prospect—but not always through the use of the United States Postal Service. A simple printed bulletin slipped under your windshield wiper in a parking lot is direct mail advertising. A free tube of toothpaste tucked inside your screen door is a form of direct mail advertising called door-to-door sampling. A gag object, such as a bird cage delivered by messenger to an executive's office, is direct mail advertising. So while the traditional descriptive term is "direct mail," it may include nonmailed advertising. In any event, direct mail is quite accurately described as "the straight-line medium" by Hanley Norins, creative vice-president at the Young & Rubicam advertising agency.

#### *Advantage: Pinpoint Targeting*

To a direct marketer, the overwhelming advantage of direct mail lies in pinpoint targeting of specific individuals and specific markets. It flies straight as an arrow to only the best prospects. Consequently, direct mail avoids the waste circulation that accompanies use of the mass media. And no matter how elaborate each mailing piece, a direct mail campaign tends to be less costly than a campaign paying for the huge circulation of the mass media. Commercial mailing companies like Reuben H. Donnelly have the mechanics down to such a science that they can control mailings to certain neighborhoods, to one side of a particular street, to particular homes on one side of a particular street. Mailing lists can be purchased covering almost all conceivable categories, large or small, from all registered car owners to all registered nurses to all licensed pilots.

#### *Personalized Message*

Not only does direct mail go to a very select list of prospects, it has the selling advantage of being highly personalized in its presentation. It is, in effect, person-to-person communication. It can flatter a reader by generous use of that prospect's name: "Dear Mrs. White, you can be sure that no other family in Champaign will have bright spring duds like the Whites." Or it can personalize a letter by sympathetic understanding of the reader's job: "Dear Dr. White, few people in the outside world know how many hours a professor must spend in preparing lecture notes." At the time the prospect opens it, a direct mail appeal is not competing for the prospect's attention with other advertisements or editorial matter or program content.

***Tight Controls***

The marketer has the tightest control over both timing and format in direct mail. The advertiser does not have to adapt selling strategy to a magazine issue date, a television broadcast date, or the page size detailed in Standard Rate and Data.

***Creative Freedom***

Because there are no limitations on space or format with direct mail, the medium is a paradise for creative people. The direct mail piece can be a single sheet envelope stuffer or it can be a wall-filling broadside. It can be a picture postcard or a die-cut multipage book. It can be a typewritten sales letter or the corporation's annual report. It can be printed on wafer-thin paper, on wrapping paper, or on metallic paper. It can be reproduced via letterpress, offset, or silkscreen. If a writer can come up with an intriguing idea, direct mail can deliver the goods. And direct mail has no equal as a medium for introducing novelty and realism. If your product is an automobile, for example, magazine and television advertising will limit you to a picture in showing it. But in direct mail, you can send a toy-sized working model. If your product is clothing, you can send a swatch of fabric, or even construct your entire mailing out of that fabric. When plastic packaging was first coming into prominence, one imaginative processor sent a mailing of dry martinis!

*Source:* Reprinted with permission from *Advertising Writing* 3/e by Hafer and Gordon. 

## Scanning: Reading for Specific Answers

*One day Alice came to a fork in the road and saw a Cheshire cat. "Which road do I take?" she asked. He responded, "Where do you want to go?" "I don't know," Alice replied. "Then," said the cat, "it doesn't matter."*

—*LEWIS CARROLL*

Similarly, if you don't know what you're looking for when you read, it doesn't matter how you read. If, however, you want to answer a specific question, you need to scan to find that information.

Scanning is something you probably already know how to do. You just don't call it scanning. It's what you do when you look for a name on a marquee. You also use it to find numbers in the phone book or the time for a program in a television guide. The same skill can be used to find the answers to specific questions. It's a valuable and fast way to find information.

In scanning, knowing what to look for and where to look is important. That's why looking at the **format** of books helps you find information quickly. Books may be set up in many ways. These organizational formats are described in Table 11.2.

You use scanning to find answers to questions. When you scan, your eyes pass over the words and look for clues. The clues you look for

**TABLE 11.2** ***Various Formats of Books***

1. *Alphabetical.* This is one of the easiest formats. It is also the most familiar. Data is arranged from **A** to **Z.** Dictionaries, encyclopedias, indexes, and lists of names use this format.
2. *Time.* Information is listed in the order in which it occurs. TV listings, historical accounts, charts, graphs, and time lines often use this format.
3. *Rank.* In this type, information is presented on the basis of its importance. Lists, charts, and graphs may be given in rank order.
4. *Text.* Most textbooks are divided into units. The units are made up of chapters. The chapter uses titles and subheadings to show key topics.

depend on the questions you, your instructor, or your text asks. Table 11.3 shows appropriate clues for answering various questions. For example, if your question is "When did the American Revolution begin?" you look for numbers (a date). If your question is "Where is Hoover Dam?" you search the passage for capitalized nouns. In general, your searches for details consist of looking for names, numbers, and/or underlined, italicized, and boldface words.

Once you locate a possible answer, you read more slowly to check its accuracy. This reading helps you decide if you've found the correct information. Since a paragraph or passage often contains many dates, capitalized words, etc., this step is crucial to your reading. Steps in scanning are summarized below.

STEPS IN SCANNING

1. *Determine the organizational format of the information.*
2. *Estimate the type of response a purpose-setting question requires.*
3. *Search for clues which point to the answer.*
4. *Verify your answer by slowing down and reading the answer in context.*

**TABLE 11.3** ***Questioning Words and Appropriate Clues***

| *IF YOUR QUESTION BEGINS . . .* | *LOOK FOR . . .* |
|---|---|
| WHY? | words like *because, for that reason, consequently, as a result* |
| HOW? | a sequence; a list; words like *by, through, as a result of* |
| WHAT? | linking verbs; punctuation symbols (commas, dashes, parentheses); words like *involves, consists, includes* |
| WHICH? | nouns and adjectives |
| WHEN? | capitalized words like days, months, or other time periods; time of the day (written or numeric); numerical symbols for months, days, and years; words like *before, during, after, soon, later, prior* |
| WHERE? | capitalized place names (cities, states, countries); addresses; words like *behind, across* |

**EXERCISE 11.5**

*Answer the questions below by scanning the following excerpt. Do not read the entire excerpt word-for-word.*

### Group Marriage in the 19th Century

The United States in the late 19th century was remarkably tolerant. The moral code of the dominant culture stressed premarital chastity and monogamy. Nevertheless, dozens of sectarian groups with very different ideas of sexual and familial morality emerged and briefly prospered. The Mormons are the only one of them to have survived to the present day; and, as pointed out in chapter 4, one of the conditions of their survival was the adoption of the family structure of the dominant culture.

The Oneida community was one of the most successful and most daringly different of these 19th-century groups. Oneida was founded in 1847 by a Yale-trained theologian named John Humprey Noyes. It began as a group of 20 to 30 in Oneida, New York, and grew to 300 children and adults before it disbanded, in 1879.

Noyes's community was based on the principles of Christian communism. (Acts 2:32–35 offers biblical support for Christian communism.) In the Oneida community, there was no private property, and monogamy, the exclusive ownership of a spouse, was not allowed. Although Noyes recognized that the early Christians applied the communistic principle only to material goods:

"Yet we affirm that there is no intrinsic difference between property in persons and property in things. . . . The new command is, that we love one another, and that, not by pairs, as in the world, but *en masse.* We are required to love one another fervently. The fashion of the world forbids a man and woman who are otherwise appropriated to love one another fervently. But if they obey Christ they must do this." [Noyes, 1869/1961:625–627]

In the Oneida community, the practice of complex marriage meant that all men were considered married to all women. Oneida, however, was hardly the place to go if one was looking for sex without commitment. Entrance into the community required signing over all of one's worldly goods to the community as well as embracing a life of considerable physical toil, and group marriage was not simply a matter of sleeping around. Rather, the selection of sexual partners was done through a committee. At Oneida, all members lived together in a big mansionlike house. The women each had a private bedroom, whereas the men all slept together in a dormitory. When a man wished to sleep with a particular woman, he submitted a written request to the committee, which then referred it to the woman. The request could be denied by the woman on personal grounds or by the committee on the ground that too much particularism was developing in this relationship and that the brother did not show himself willing to love all his sisters. During the first two decades of the community's existence, the Oneidans avoided having children. They wished to establish both their economy and their family structure before adding the burden of children. During these 20 years they practiced a form of contraception called *coitus reservatas,* in which the man does not ejaculate. Since this technique takes a great deal of willpower and some practice, it is reported that young men were required to sleep only with women past childbearing age until they had perfected the technique. (In a parallel practice, younger women were encouraged to sleep with older men. In this case, greater spiritual growth was given as the reason.) The teaching method must have worked reasonably well, as only two children were born during this period.

Between 1869 and 1879, the Oneidans produced 59 children. The women and men who became parents were "scientifically" matched by a committee. The selection process was designed to produce children with superior mental and physical abilities. The children were nurtured by their mothers for the first 12 months and then were raised in a communal nursery. As with spouses, there was to be no exclusive attachment; adults were supposed to love all children equally. The children of Oneida apparently got exceptional care; their infant mortality rate was very low, and their educational training was excellent.

In 1879, the Oneida community disbanded. A major cause for the breakup was the erratic leadership provided by Noyes. Additional problems included the management of an increasingly large household and diversified economic enterprises. The problems were internal rather than external; the community never received a great deal of harassment from outsiders. It even advertised for visitors and sold Sunday lunches to day-trippers from New York who came up to satisfy their curiosity about these strange people. The community's hard work and economic success, as well as a strategic willingness to buy locally and help neighbors, meant that its members were generally well regarded in upstate New York in spite of their odd family system.

When the community disbanded, many members stayed on in Oneida, most of them legally marrying one of the other members. The financial enterprises of Oneida were incorporated and divided among the members. One of these enterprises, the Oneida Silver Manufacturing Company, is still a successful corporation supplying tableware for millions.



**1.** Which religious sect from the nineteenth century survives today?

______________________________

**2.** From what university did the founder of Oneida come?

______________________________

**3.** What was the name of the founder of Oneida?

______________________________

**4.** How many children and adults comprised the group before it disbanded?

______________________________

**5.** What is *coitus reservatas?*

______________________________

6. In what ten-year period did the Oneidans produce fifty-nine children?

_______________

7. For how long were children allowed to remain with their mothers?

_______________

8. In what year did the community disband?

_______________

9. In what state was the Oneida community located?

_______________

10. Which one of Oneida's financial enterprises remains in existence today?

_______________

**EXERCISE 11.6**

*Scan the excerpt in Exercise 11.4 and mark the information included in the text.*

_______ 1. Horatio Alger
_______ 2. martinis
_______ 3. English
_______ 4. Ten million dollar winner
_______ 5. Alexander Hamilton
_______ 6. propaganda
_______ 7. Japanese
_______ 8. 1925
_______ 9. 1970s
_______ 10. ethics
_______ 11. Standard Rate
_______ 12. Ed McMahon
_______ 13. Dale Carnegie
_______ 14. $2,000,000
_______ 15. *The Power of Positive Thinking*
_______ 16. die-cut

_______ **17.** Publisher's Clearing House

_______ **18.** New York

_______ **19.** gold medal

_______ **20.** Champaign

**WRITE TO LEARN**

*Your little sister needs to read a chapter in history and answer related questions. On a separate sheet of paper, explain the differences between skimming and scanning. In addition, provide for her the steps in each and tell her when each is appropriate.*

## RECREATIONAL READING

*These are not books, lumps of lifeless paper, but minds alive on the shelves. From each of them goes out its own voice . . . and just as the touch of a button on our set will fill the room with music, so by taking down one of these volumes and opening it, one can call into range the voice of a man far distant in time and space, and hear him speaking to us, mind to mind, heart to heart.*

—GILBERT HIGHET

*"I might have enjoyed this book if it hadn't been required reading."*

Recreational reading is defined as reading done for enjoyment. Reading books for fun differs from reading textbooks. Although you can learn from this type of reading, learning is not the main purpose. Recreational reading is a form of entertainment like watching TV or seeing a movie. It is a way to enjoy free time. Unlike watching a movie or TV show, you can read a book whenever or wherever you want. You schedule your own station breaks. And, the action waits for your return. If you miss something, you reread. Books are there when you want them.

## Using Recreational Reading to Increase Reading Speed

Recreational reading helps you increase speed in three ways. First, because such books are generally less difficult to read, you can read them faster. Second, the **plot** or action in the book is often such that you want to see what happens next. Third, recreational reading provides background knowledge, which increases your understanding of other subjects. As a result of this familiarity, you read other materials more quickly. Fourth, you increase speed as you learn to **browse** through recreational materials.

### *WRITE TO LEARN*

*On a separate piece of paper, provide an interpretation for Highet's quotation about books. In Highet's view, how do books contribute to background knowledge? Describe three ways in which reading has increased your background knowledge.*

## Browsing

How do you know how to choose recreational materials? Good readers often choose books in much the same way they choose movies. They use browsing or previewing techniques to help them predict if they will enjoy a certain book. They consider frameworks about themselves (interests, mood, experiences) and about books (title, subject matter, author, style) before making a choice.

Many less-skilled readers use a very different previewing technique. This technique might be described as the "length" method. They feel the shorter a book, the sooner they will finish reading it. Or they may choose a "classic" because they don't know what else is available. This method is less effective because it fails to account for what's in their frameworks.

### *Previewing: Personal Predictions*

One of the two major frameworks to consider in choosing recreational books is yourself. Your reading interests reflect you life at a specific time. Recreational reading often answers questions about career choices, relationships, new hobbies, or personal problems. Furthermore, your interest in the world around you (culture, history, politics) increases with reading. As a result of reading various subjects, you investigate issues, develop your own opinions, and share what you've learned. You read to learn more about yourself and the events that affect you. Somewhat like Thurber's Walter Mitty, you could also read to escape these.

If you seldom read recreationally, you probably haven't thought about the types of books you'd most like to read. One way to find a reading interest is to examine the television shows or movies you enjoy. Your reasons for choosing these shows relates to why you'd enjoy reading about similar subjects. For example, suppose you like to watch news shows about medicine because you know a person who has cancer. What you read could easily mirror this interest in medical breakthroughs and current treatments. While such topics are often factual (**nonfiction**), novels and short stories (**fiction**) also contain information about medicine. Exercise 11.7 will help you determine your interests. Then, Table 11.4 aids you in finding out what kinds of books

**TABLE 11.4 A Guide to Recreational Reading**

| CATEGORY | BOOK TYPE | EXAMPLE |
|---|---|---|
| NEWS/DOCUMENTARY | Nonfictional accounts of newsworthy events | *First Father, First Daughter* by Maureen Reagon<br>*Blind Faith* by Joe McGinniss |
| SITUATION COMEDY | Humorous fiction or nonfiction | *We're Still Married* by Garrison Keillor<br>*S.* by John Updike |
| WAR | Fiction or nonfiction accounts of military life or action | *A Bright Shining Lie* by Neil Sheehan<br>*The Korean War* by Max Hastings |
| HISTORY | Fiction or nonfiction based on past events | *Alaska* by James Michener<br>*The Mummy* by Anne Rice |
| WESTERN | Fiction or nonfiction set in the American West | Books by Zane Grey or Louis L'Armour<br>*The Great Plains* by Ian Frazier |
| HORROR | Fiction designed to scare the reader | *The Unwanted* by John Saul<br>*The Drawing of the Three* by Stephen King |
| SCIENCE FICTION | Fiction featuring futuristic scientific developments | *Neuromancer* by William Gibson<br>*The Handmaid's Tale* by Margaret Atwood |
| AUTOBIOGRAPHY OR BIOGRAPHY | A factual account of someone's life | *The Good Times* by Russell Baker<br>*Gracie: A Love Story* by George Burns |
| MYSTERY | A fictional or nonfictional account of some unexplained event | *Clear and Present Danger* by Tom Clancy<br>*The Negotiator* by Frederick Forsyth |
| FANTASY | A fictional account of a magical or imaginary person, place, or event | *The First Eden* by David Attenborough<br>*Mythology* by Edith Hamilton |
| ROMANCE | A love story that can be fiction or nonfiction | *Star* by Danielle Steele<br>*Love Song* by Andrew M. Greeley |

parallel those interests. It lists TV and movie categories and related book types. The table also provides examples of books or authors for each category. Once you determine what types you like, your friends or your campus librarian may suggest additional titles and authors. Browsing through a bookstore also yields other selections.

**EXERCISE 11.7**

1. List five television programs you enjoy.
   a. ______
   b. ______
   c. ______
   d. ______
   e. ______
2. Now list five movies you have enjoyed.
   a. ______
   b. ______
   c. ______
   d. ______
   e. ______
3. Classify the TV shows and movies you listed as best you can. Some may fit into more than one category.

a. News/documentary

______

______

______

______

b. Situation comedy

______

______

______

______

c. Romance

______

______

______

______

d. War

______

______

______

______

**e.** History

________________________________

________________________________

________________________________

________________________________

**f.** Western

________________________________

________________________________

________________________________

________________________________

**g.** Horror

________________________________

________________________________

________________________________

________________________________

**h.** Science fiction

________________________________

________________________________

________________________________

________________________________

**i.** Biography/autobiography

________________________________

________________________________

________________________________

________________________________

**j.** Mystery

________________________________

________________________________

________________________________

________________________________

**k.** Fantasy

________________________________

________________________________

________________________________

________________________________

**l.** Other

________________________________

________________________________

________________________________

________________________________

### *Previewing: Text Features*

The second consideration in choosing a recreational selection is the book itself. Probably the first item that comes to your attention is the title. Just as you can tell what a movie is about by its title, you can often find out what a book is about by its title. consider these titles:

*Women in Politics: ERA Comes to Washington*
*Hems: Women in Government*
*Janice Jones: America's First Woman President*

Even though each of these titles pertains to women and government, each book differs. The first two are nonfiction. That means they are based on fact. The last one would be classified as fiction, or as a story which is not true. Books for recreational reading can be fiction or nonfiction.

After you examine the title, check the author's name. Knowing who wrote the book serves you in one of two ways. If you enjoy reading it, you know an author to ask for the next time you wish to read recreationally. If you do not like the book, you know an author to avoid. Once you begin reading more, you'll develop a list of authors who appeal to you, much like certain actors appeal to you.

Once you pick a book, flip through its pages. Look at the number and length of paragraphs on each page. If there are few paragraphs per page (five or fewer), the book is probably descriptive. If there are many paragraphs per page, the book contains more action. This conclusion can sometimes be verified by looking at the **copyright date**. Books written before 1900 were written at a time when there was no TV or radio. Then books were read aloud to entertain listeners. Books from this time, then, are usually more descriptive than more modern ones.

Your next step in examining the book is reading its excerpt. An excerpt is often found on the back cover of the book. These excerpts are designed to catch your interest. If you find the excerpt boring, you probably won't enjoy the book. The excerpt should not be confused with the reviewers' comments. Only favorable reviews are quoted. Such comments may not reflect the feelings of all the reviewers. Read such comments with caution.

Finally, skim the first few paragraphs of the first chapter of the book. A good book often grabs your attention immediately. If you read these paragraphs and want to know more about the characters, setting, or plot, you've found a winner!

STEPS IN PREVIEWING RECREATIONAL BOOKS

1. *Read the title.*
2. *Check the author's name.*
3. *Check the number of paragraphs in the text.*
4. *Check the copyright date in the front of the book.*
5. *If the book has an excerpt, read it.*
6. *Skim the first few paragraphs.*
7. *Repeat these steps if you do not find a book you think you will like.*

**EXERCISE 11.8**

◆ *Using any popular fiction or nonfiction book, preview and answer the following questions.*

1. What is the title of the book?

_______________________________________________

2. Who is the author? _______________________________________________

**3.** Are you familiar with this author? ______ If so, what do you know about the author?______________________________

______________________________

______________________________

**4.** Is the book fiction or nonfiction?______________________________

How do you know?______________________________

______________________________

______________________________

**5.** Using the categories in Table 11.4, identify this book's category and explain why you believe it fits this category.

______________________________

______________________________

______________________________

______________________________

**6.** Open the book and examine the average number of paragraphs per page. Rate the number of paragraphs using the following scale:

______ fewer than 3 ______ 3–6 ______ 7–10 ______ 10 or more.

What does this tell you about the rate of action of the book?

______________________________

______________________________

**7.** What is the copyright date of the book?______________________________

What does this tell you about the book?______________________________

______________________________

______________________________

**8.** Read the excerpt, if any. Rate your level of interest in the book based on its contents from 1 (not interested) to 5 (very interested).

*Rating:*______________________________

What do you think accounts for your interest or lack of interest?

______________________________

______________________________

______________________________

______________________________

9. Skim the first few paragraphs of the book. Rate your level of interest in the book based on its contents from 1 (not interested) to 5 (very interested). *Rating:*__________

   What do you think accounts for your interest or lack of interest?

10. Would you like to read this book? Why or why not?

## CHAPTER SUMMARY EXERCISE

*Write a chapter summary in the space provided.*

_______________________________________________

_______________________________________________

_______________________________________________

_______________________________________________

_______________________________________________

_______________________________________________

_______________________________________________

_______________________________________________

_______________________________________________

_______________________________________________

_______________________________________________

_______________________________________________

◆

## CHAPTER REVIEW

*Answer briefly but completely.*

1. Complete the following analogy.
   skimming : main ideas :: scanning : ______________
2. Is *"Practice (Effort + Time) = Speed"* a magic formula, as the text suggests? Justify your answer.

   _______________________________________________

   _______________________________________________

   _______________________________________________

   _______________________________________________

   _______________________________________________

3. According to your text, reading rate should change "from sentence to sentence, paragraph to paragraph, and passage to passage." What factors affect reading rate to make this statement true?

   _______________________________________________

   _______________________________________________

   _______________________________________________

   _______________________________________________

   _______________________________________________

4. List an ineffective reading habit you have. Then design a program for ridding yourself of this habit.

5. Compare skimming to the surveying step of SQ3R, as explained in Chapter 1.

6. List and define the four types of text format. How can these help you scan texts more effectively?

7. Explain how recreational reading affects reading rate.

8. What factors affect recreational reading choice?

9. Examine the results of Exercise 11.7. Give the titles of three books you think you'd like to read.

10. Complete the following analogy.
textbooks : study :: recreational books : ______________

◆

## VOCABULARY ENHANCEMENT EXERCISE

*Using the scale in Figure 3.1, rate your understanding of the following vocabulary enhancement words to the left of the number. Then write a sentence with each one.*

1. vital

2. morsel

3. breakthroughs

4. collided

5. inset

6. reputable

7. physical

8. cast

9. documentaries

10. scenarios

# 12 Test Taking: Sailing the Seas of Exam Preparation

## TERMS

*Terms appear in the order in which they occur in the chapter.*

test anxiety
cope
stress
eustress
prime study time
synthesis
outline
mnemonics
mental imagery
physical imagery
acronyms
acrostics
location
word games
kinesthetic perception
mnemonigraphs
puns
parodies
objective
subjective
comprehensive
noncomprehensive
outline
proofread
standardized tests

## CHAPTER OUTLINE EXERCISE

*Create an outline for this chapter on the following lines.*

## OBJECTIVES

*At the end of this chapter, you should be able to do the following:*

1. Define test anxiety and methods of coping with it.
2. Describe a plan for getting organized for study.
3. Identify types of exams.

## CHAPTER MAP

*Create a map for this chapter in the space below.*

## VOCABULARY ENHANCEMENT EXERCISE

*Rate each of the following words according to your knowledge of them.*

| | *STAGE 0* | *STAGE 1* | *STAGE 2* | *STAGE 3* |
|---|---|---|---|---|
| | *I do not recognize the word.* | *I recognize the word but am unsure of its meaning and associations.* | *I recognize the word and can make general associations with it.* | *I recognize the word and can use it in speaking and writing* |
| **1.** clarity | | | | |
| **2.** ferocious | | | | |
| **3.** mettle | | | | |
| **4.** ventured | | | | |
| **5.** automated | | | | |
| **6.** occurrence | | | | |
| **7.** abstract | | | | |
| **8.** memorable | | | | |
| **9.** impending | | | | |
| **10.** reserve | | | | |

IN THE 1300s and 1400s, sailors used a type of chart called a *portolano* to navigate the coasts of the Mediterranean Sea. Drawn on sheepskin, these maps showed the outlines of coasts and harbors. As a sailor traveled, he kept a record of where he'd gone. Cartographers gradually added this information to maps. Thus, *portolanoes* identified all the areas known to sailors of that day. To show that there was more to the world than had been explored, mapmakers sketched ferocious-looking dragons on the edges of maps.

The dragons served as threats to sailors who took them literally. They thought that dragons awaited them in unexplored regions. These sailors let their fears immobilize them. They never went beyond what they knew to be safe. For them, the old saying "Nothing ventured, nothing gained" was all too true.

For other sailors, the dragons symbolized challenge. These sailors saw the dragons as almost a dare. They wanted to be the first "to go where no man has gone before." The dragons spurred them to greater adventures and new insights.

In many ways, students and tests resemble the sailors and dragons of long ago. Many students see tests as a horrible fate. They feel exams are always lurking around the corner, waiting for the right time to strike. Other students see tests as an opportunity to prove their mettle. They seek the chance to slay the dragon and win the day.

Fortunately, there exists a safety net for those students who fear the words "Close your books and take out a sheet of paper." Freedom from danger rests in coping with test anxiety and preparing for exams. For as Cornelius Vanderbilt, Jr., said, "Lack of confidence and lack of information sleep in the same bed, locked in the closest kind of embrace. . . . For confidence is the son of vision, and is sired by information."

**WRITE TO LEARN**

*On a separate sheet of paper, describe how you became or how you can become a test taking "sailor" who faces the "dragon" of tests with a smile.*

◆

## TEST ANXIETY: SEASICKNESS AT ITS WORST

*No passion so effectively robs the mind of all its powers of acting and reasoning as fear.*

—EDMUND BURKE

Taking tests bothers everyone, from new freshmen to graduate students. Feeling insecure or fearful before, during, and/or after an exam is called **test anxiety.** It is a universal experience.

The Test Anxiety Scale (TAS) was developed to identify students whose anxiety hurts their performances on tests. How anxious are you about tests? Take the TAS and find out.

## Test Anxiety Scale

*Answer the following questions as truthfully as possible. Mark T if the statement is* generally true *for you; F if the statement is* generally false. *A scoring key and explanation of your score are at the end of the chapter. Score your responses before reading the rest of this chapter.*

**1.** ______ While taking an important exam, I perspire a lot.

**2.** ______ I feel very panicky when I have to take a surprise exam.

**3.** ______ During tests, I find myself thinking of the consequences of failing.

**4.** ______ After important tests, I am frequently so tense that my stomach gets upset.

**5.** ______ While taking an important exam, I find myself thinking of how much brighter the other students are than I am.

**6.** ______ I freeze up on big tests like finals.

**7.** ______ If I were about to take a big test, I would worry a lot before taking it.

**8.** ______ During course exams, I find myself thinking of things unrelated to the course material.

**9.** ______ During course exams, I frequently get so nervous that I forget facts I really know.

**10.** ______ If I knew I was going to take a big exam, I would feel confident and relaxed beforehand.

**11.** ______ I usually get depressed after taking a test.

**12.** ______ I have an uneasy, upset feeling before taking a test.

**13.** ______ When taking a test, I find my emotions do not interfere with my performance.

**14.** ______ Getting a good grade on one test doesn't seem to increase my confidence on the second test.

**15.** ______ After taking a test, I always feel I have done better than I actually have done.

**16.** ______ I sometimes feel my heart beating very fast during important examinations.

*Source:* Sarason, I. Experimental approaches to test anxiety: Attention and the uses of information. In Spielberger, C. D., ed. *Anxiety: Current Trends,* Vol. 2. New York: Academic Press, 1972.

## Coping with Test Anxiety

*My apprehensions come in crowds;*
*I dread the rustling of the grass;*
*The very shadows of the clouds*
*Have power to shake me as they pass;*
*I question things and do not find*
*One answer to my mind.*

—WILLIAM WORDSWORTH

As Wordsworth says, when feeling test anxiety, everything worries you. You need an oasis where you can withdraw from the stress. However, there seldom exists the chance to leave school and travel to a deserted isle during test time. Since you can't run from stress, you need to learn to cope. Coping results in peace of mind.

### *Caring for Your Mental and Physical Health*

Staying mentally and physically healthy is important in coping with test anxiety, or **stress.** If your mind or body is tired, you are more likely to feel stress than if you are rested. You will feel more in control and ready to face the exam. For these reasons, it is essential that you get a full night's sleep before taking an exam. With rest, you are able to think and do more.

In the same way, it is important to eat something before going to take an exam. Even if you have an early-morning test, don't skip breakfast. Your body needs the energy food supplies. However, your body does not need to be gorged with food before a big exam. When this happens, most of your blood rushes to your digestive tract, and little is left for your brain's operations.

It really isn't surprising that you feel uneasy and even sick when you are in stress-filled situations. Anxiety is an enemy of physical and mental well-being.

### *Managing Test Anxiety*

Eleanor Roosevelt once said she thought anyone could learn to manage fear, if the person would only keep trying to do so. She thought that soon you'd acquire a backlog of successful coping experiences. In stressful times, this background would give you a reserve of coping mechanisms from which to draw.

Students with test anxiety need this reserve at three specific times. You need coping strategies before, during, and after a test. Table 12.1 provides a list of coping techniques for you to try. Once you've found the ones that work best for you, you'll have built your own reserve.

***TABLE 12.1 Coping Techniques***

IF YOU FEEL ANXIOUS *BEFORE* OR *AFTER* A TEST

1. *Try exercise.* You don't have to be a professional athlete to use exercise successfully in handling stress. Any physical activity helps, from strenuous sports to simply walking around the block.
2. *Take a class.* Many schools offer courses in relaxation techniques, time management, study skills, and/or test taking. Even if your college offers no such courses, your campus library should have books or tapes on all of these topics.
3. *Talk to others.* Stress can be controlled by discussing your feelings and fears with others. Counselors, teachers, and fellow students can react to your comments and offer suggestions and advice.
4. *Avoid cramming.* Last-minute study sessions tend to increase test anxiety and stress. Use distributed practice over an extended time period.
5. *Take a brief mental vacation.* Think of a place where you were happy and relaxed. Take yourself there by daydreaming about how you felt and what you did there. Once you've captured a feeling of ease, return to studying.

IF YOU FEEL ANXIOUS *DURING* A TEST

1. *Pause and breathe deeply.* Symptoms of panic include shortness of breath, increased heart rate, and sweaty palms. Ease the tension by taking a brief break. Stop taking the test. Turn your test paper over. Close your eyes and take several slow, deep breaths. Try to clear your mind. Once you feel calm, return to the test.
2. *Answer a question you know.* This gives you confidence in your knowledge. Such confidence reduces stress.
3. *Ask for information.* Questions that confuse you increase stress. The problem may not reside with you. Perhaps the question is ambiguous. Since what's unclear to you might be unclear to others, asking your instructor for additional information is a good idea.
4. *Use self-talk.* Self-talk is one time when talking to yourself makes sense. Sometimes you know information, but negative thoughts keep you from retrieving it. Self-talk involves your stopping negative thoughts by saying to yourself, "*Stop.* Panic accomplishes nothing." It builds confidence and positive thinking when you say, "Stay cool. You can do this."

***WRITE TO LEARN***

*On a separate sheet of paper, describe your biggest fear in test taking and how you can best cope with this anxiety.*

## Making Test Anxiety Work for You

*Stupidity is without anxiety.*

*—GOETHE*

Only people with nothing to say on a test or who truly do not care about their performance on a test feel no stress. Since some stress is unavoidable, you need to find constructive ways to use it. **Eustress** is the means

by which you do so. Eustress is the type of stress that challenges you to do your best. For example, actors and athletes use eustress to improve their performances.

Likewise, when you direct and control stress, it gives you energy to work harder. It helps you think more clearly and quickly. This motivating anxiety carries you through the situation. You turn distress into eustress by using coping skills and being prepared.

◆

## GETTING SHIPSHAPE: ORGANIZING FOR STUDY

Getting shipshape means arranging when, where, and what you study in an orderly fashion. The time, place, and subject you choose to study make a difference in how much you learn. You need to know yourself in order to know where and when to get the most from your efforts. Reading and studying, after all, require your full attention. You determine your study environment by observing three factors. These are when and where you get the most accomplished, when and where your studying results in higher grades, and when and where you feel most able to concentrate. What to study depends on your instructor, course information, and what you already know.

### Prime Study Time

**Prime study time** is the time of the day when you are at your best. This time varies from person to person. You may be at your best early in the morning. Or, you may be able to recall more if you study in the afternoon or at night.

Your best time of the day should be spent either in your hardest classes or on your most important assignments. Working on the hardest or most urgent task first means you work on that problem when you are fresh.

Threats to prime study time include any physical or mental distractions. For example, sometimes when you study you may find yourself thinking of other tasks you need to do. If so, keep a pad and pencil nearby just for this purpose and make a "worry list" of your concerns. By doing so, you literally put your problems aside until later. Being too hungry or too full also affects concentration. If this occurs, you may need to change your study or eating schedule.

Some threats to prime study time are harder to control. It may be difficult to rid yourself of friends who are concerned about your social life. Invitations to go out with the gang often come at prime study times. The solution, while simple, is a hard one to enact. It involves saying "No" in a clear, but tactful way. Sometimes it's easier to just be unavailable. Taking your phone off the hook or closing the door to your room prevents interruptions. Another way to solve this problem is to put up a "Do Not Disturb" sign. You can get one from a motel (usually free of charge), purchase one at a card store, or make your own. Remember, while you will probably never rid yourself of all distractions during prime study time, you can minimize them.

### Your Study Environment

Managing prime study time involves more than deciding the time of day at which you are at your best. You also need to manage your surroundings to maximize study time.

The place you study needs to be free of distractions. It should be conducive to work, not relaxation or fun. For instance, you may think the hallways outside class or a recreation room are good places to review. However, if recalling your notes—not talking with friends or watching TV—is your goal, you may be unhappy with what you recall later. Also, studying in bed may be comfortable, but it may also make you sleepy.

In addition, the place you choose to read or study must be environmentally right for you. It should not be too cold or too hot. You need to concentrate on what you're studying, not on the temperature. Using music or television as a background for study also affects your recall. If you find yourself singing along with a commercial, you know you aren't concentrating.

Finally, the place you choose to study should be free of clutter, while still containing all the materials you need. You need to be able to distinguish between clutter and essentials. Clutter affects your concentration. When your eyes are drawn away from your notes by the clutter around you, wasted time and stress result. Your desk needs to hold only what you are using to study. This might include pen, paper, notes, old exams, and text. All these materials should be organized and within reach to make the best use of your prime study time.

**WRITE TO LEARN**

*On a separate sheet of paper, describe the time and place you study. Is it the best time and place for you? How could you improve on this?*

## Getting Organized

Synthesizing information also helps you organize study time. It enables you to relate pieces of information from various sources (handouts, text chapters, notes, etc.). Thus, you see these pieces as part of an organized whole. **Synthesis** helps you understand the information. This contrasts with memorizing isolated facts. It is easier to remember information you synthesized because you associate it with what you already know.

The following sequence helps you organize for study.

STEPS IN SYNTHESIZING FOR STUDY

1. *Gather all materials.* This includes old tests, lecture notes, texts, handouts, and outlines. You collect everything given you in class. It should be kept together (perhaps in a notebook). If you missed any classes, get all notes from a friend who takes good notes.

2. *Synthesize information from all sources.* Identify relationships and possible associations. All course materials need to be used to develop a complete body of knowledge, or synthesis.

3. *Consider what sources were emphasized in the course.* Predict the emphasis of test questions. Some instructors place importance on in-class notes. Thus, most of their test questions probably come from these notes. Your instructor may emphasize some other source, such as the text or hand-outs.

4. *Use your synthesis and emphasized sources to make an* **outline** *of the main points.* Then add details to the outline. What you have done is started with the "bones," the main points you need to know. Then you added the "flesh," or details, which makes it easier to remember. This becomes your study guide.

5. *Outline the outline.* Be as brief as possible. Leave just enough information to jog your memory.

## Memory Techniques

*Backward, turn backward, O Time, in your flight*
*And tell me just one thing I studied last night.*
—HOBART BROWN

Memory needs training and exercise. **Mnemonics** consist of techniques for improving your memory skills. Combining methods strengthens memory because you have more ways to recall information. **Mental imagery, physical imagery, acronyms** and **acrostics, location,** and **word games** comprise mnemonics that link information.

Forming links between familiar items and the items you need to remember automates recall. For example, perhaps you relate a song with a time, event, or person. Hearing the song cues memory. Likewise, you form associations between something familiar to you and the information you need to recall. To be effective, mnemonics must be personal. Table 12.2 provides you with questions to help you choose the best technique.

### *Mental and Physical Imagery*

You experience mental imagery when you see pictures in your mind. Mental imagery is a natural occurrence since you often think in pictures rather than words. For instance, think of a car. Do you think *c-a-r,* or do you picture how a car looks, smells, feels, etc. Using other senses aids your recall of both familiar and unfamiliar items. Suggestions for making mental images appear in Table 12.3.

Mental pictures link concrete objects with their images (e.g., a picture of a car with the word *car*) or abstract concepts with their symbols (e.g., a picture of a dove with the word *peace*). They also link unrelated objects, concepts, and ideas through visualization. For in-

**TABLE 12.2 Questions for Developing Mnemonics**

1. Does the item remind you of anything?
2. Does the item sound like or rhyme with a familiar word?
3. Can you visualize something when you think of the item?
4. Can you rearrange any letters to form an acronym?
5. Do you know of any gimmicks to associate with the item?
6. Can you draw a mnemonigraph to associate with the item?
7. Can you associate it with any familiar locations?

**TABLE 12.3 Suggestions for Maximizing Mental Imagery**

1. Use common symbols, such as a heart for love or a dove for peace.
2. Use the clearest and closest image.
3. Think of outrageous or humorous images.
4. Make sexual connotations.
5. Create action-filled images.

stance, suppose you want to recall the twenty-first president, Chester Arthur. You visualize an author writing the number "21" on a wooden chest. This mental picture helps you relate chest, author, and 21. Thus, you recall Chester Arthur was the twenty-first president.

When you draw your mental image, you use another sense, your **kinesthetic perception.** Such drawings are called **mnemonigraphs.** By making mental images physical ones, you provide yourself with repetition, which strengthens memory. Drawing or diagraming information also helps. Instead of learning lists, you sketch a drawing that includes the items you need to learn. For instance, suppose you need to know the parts of a computer. Drawing and labeling the parts aid recall.

### Acronyms and Acrostics

Many courses require you to learn lists of information. Forming acronyms or acrostics helps you recall these.

When you make a word from the first letter or first few letters of the items on the list, you form an acronym. "FACE," a commonly used acronym, helps you recall spaces on a treble clef in music. "HOMES," another common acronym, cues your memory for the names of the Great Lakes (*H*uron, *O*ntario, *M*ichigan, *E*rie, and *S*uperior). Another acronym that aids your recall of the Great Lakes might be "Sho me." Acronyms, then, need not be real words. Like other mnemonics, the best ones are those you create for yourself.

Acrostics consist of phrases or sentences made from the first letter or first few letters of the items on a list. For example, "Every good boy does fine" helps you recall the lines in a treble clef. Acrostics need not be grammatically correct. They need only make sense to you.

### Location

The location method of memory dates back to a gruesome event in ancient Greece. According to Cicero (Bower, 1970), Simonides—a Greek poet—had just recited a poem when someone asked him to step outside. As he left, the roof fell. Everyone inside was killed. The bodies were crushed beyond recognition. Simonides figured out who was who by recalling where each person sat. Likewise, location memory occurs when you link a concept with a place. You might think of when you heard the concept, how it looked in your notes, which graphics were on the page with it, and so forth.

You can also make an abstract memory map. To do this, you think of a familiar place. You link what you need to know with features of that place. Then, you imagine walking around and looking at each feature. As you go, you recall the topic you've linked with it. For instance, suppose you want to learn the bones in the body. You choose a familiar route, like the route from the college bookstore to your math class. As you pass each building, you assign it a bone. Later, in class, you picture your route. As you pass each place, you think of the bone it represents.

### *Word Games*

Playing games with information also aids memory. This occurs in two ways. First, you think about the information in order to create the trick. Second, you create clues that entertain you and stimulate your recall.

Advertisers realize the value of rhymes and jingles in making their products memorable. The same principles that help you recall "Plop! Plop! Fizz! Fizz! Oh, what a relief it is!" work just as well in helping you recall academic information. A common academic rhyme/jingle is "*I* before *E* except after *C* or when sounded like *A* as in neighbor or weigh."

**Puns** and **parodies** are made by humorously copying common words or poems, stories, and songs. Puns use words or phrases to suggest more than one meaning. Parodies use humor to copy serious works or phrases. Such puns and parodies bring mental benefits. Like other mnemonics, they make learning imaginative and entertaining. For instance, suppose you want to learn the meaning of *numismatist* (a coin collector). You might parody the children's nursery rhyme "Four and Twenty Blackbirds." Instead of the king being in his counting house, counting all his money, you change the rhyme to "The numismatist was in his counting house, counting all his money." Or, you might make a pun to help you recall the definition. This could be something like "two numismatists getting together for old 'dime's' sake."

Many people use memory tricks. Sometimes people teach these tricks to help you learn common concepts. A good example of this consists of a way to remember the multiplication tables for 9 (see Figure 12.1). Others you devise for yourself. One student needed to recall what *fiction* meant. She decided to link the *f* in *fiction* with the *f* in *false.*

**FIGURE 12.1**
**Memory Trick for Multiplying by 9**

1. List the numbers 0–9 in a column.
   0
   1
   2
   3
   4
   5
   6
   7
   8
   9
2. List the numbers 0–9 in a column beginning from the *bottom* beside the numbers you've already listed. Your combined columns form the products derived from multiplying 9 times 0, 1, 2, 3 . . . 9.
   00
   09
   18
   27
   36
   45
   54
   63
   72
   81
   90
3. Note also that adding the two digits in each product equals 9 (e.g., 0 + 9 = 9; 1 + 8 = 9; 2 + 7 = 9, etc.).

**EXERCISE 12.1**

◆ *Answer briefly but completely.*

1. Reread the geography text excerpt used in Exercise 4.8 in Chapter 4, focusing on the information about adiabatic cooling and adiabatic warming. Create and describe a mental image to help you remember each one.

___

___

___

___

___

2. Referring to Table 10.7 in Chapter 10, create and describe a mental image to help you remember any one of the three kinds of informal fallacies.

3. Referring to the six types of propaganda identified on pages 248–251 of Chapter 7, create and sketch a physical image to help you remember any three of them.

4. Chapter 1, pages 39–41, identifies four review strategies. Develop and describe an acrostic for remembering them.

5. Using the text excerpt in Exercise 1.9, review the steps that lead to behavior changes identified on page 51. Develop and describe an acrostic for remembering all five steps.

6. Referring to Excerpt 1 of Exercise 6.12 in Chapter 6, identify the three components of love triangles and create an acronym for remembering them.

7. Review the types of text-based context clues identified in Table 4.2 in Chapter 4. Describe or sketch a familiar route you might use for creating a location memory map for them. Identify the places at which you would post each type of text-based context clue.

8. Using the "Helpful Hints for Copywriters" found in the advertising excerpt in Exercise 6.8 in Chapter 6, create a rhyme or jingle to help you remember the hints.

### *WRITE TO LEARN*

*A classmate missed the lecture on memory techniques. On a separate sheet of paper, briefly describe each of the mnemonic techniques discussed in this chapter and provide an example that was not given in the text.*

◆

## WALKING THE PLANK: EXAM TIME

An aged grandfather explains why he faithfully prays every day by stating, "You might say I'm cramming for my final exam." You probably recognize this feeling about an impending test. Just as you need a reserve of activities to cope with stress, you need a reserve of strategies for test taking. This reserve, useful for any type of test, helps you walk the plank of test taking and survive the dip overboard. Some suggestions for filling your reserve follow.

GENERAL SUGGESTIONS FOR TAKING TESTS

1. *Arrive on time.* If you're early, talking to others could confuse you. If you're late, you may feel rushed and panicked. Panic causes you to forget what you do know.
2. *Be alert.* Listen carefully to all verbal directions. Read all written instructions. Make sure you understand what to do. Ask questions if you are unsure of anything.
3. *Mental blocks are normal.* If you get a mental block on a question, go on. Return to that question later. You'll lose time if you delay too long on any one item.
4. *Find out if you are penalized for guessing.* If you leave an answer blank you'll get no points. If you guess at an answer and get it wrong, what have you lost? Be a gambler! Take a guess! If it won't hurt your score, never leave blanks.
5. *Don't spend too much time on any one question.*

### Types of Tests

You save yourself time, effort, and anxiety when you know what kind of test you will have. Ask your instructor what the test will cover. Find out the test's format. Knowing the type of test helps you decide how to study.

**TABLE 12.4 Types of Test Questions**

| OBJECTIVE | SUBJECTIVE |
|---|---|
| Multiple choice | Short answer |
| Matching | Essay |
| Fill-in-the-blank | Fill-in-the-blank |
| True/false | |

Tests are **objective** and/or **subjective** (see Table 12.4). Objective tests often require you to choose an answer from several choices. Subjective tests require you to write your own answers.

Tests can also be **comprehensive** or **noncomprehensive.** Comprehensive tests include everything covered thus far in the course, even if you have had prior tests. If you haven't had another test lately, much of the test probably will concern more recent topics. This part may be more detailed. Noncomprehensive tests usually consist of only the most recent material covered. They may also cover one aspect of a subject.

## Predicting Test Questions

A young sailor was being put through the paces by an old sea captain.

"What would you do if a storm sprang up on the aft?"

"Throw out an anchor, sir."

"What would you do if another storm sprang up starboard?"

"Throw out another anchor, sir."

"And if another terrific storm sprang up forward, what would you do?"

"Throw out another anchor, sir."

"Hold on," said the captain. "Where are you getting all your anchors from?"

"From the same place you're getting your storms, sir."

In test taking, it helps if you get your answers from the same source your instructor gets the questions. Since most exams are instructor-made, the instructor is the best source of information about them. Most instructors want you to do well. Thus, they will answer questions about test content and format (see Table 12.5).

Subjective and objective tests ask different skills of you. Subjective tests demand you to apply information. They require you to recall main ideas. They ask you to describe these key concepts in written form. These exams also require you to provide supporting facts in your answers. Objective tests ask you to recognize information. They focus more on recall of facts.

Because differing skills are required for each, differing procedures are needed (see Tables 12.6 and 12.7).

**TABLE 12.5 Questions for Test Preparedness**

1. How many questions will the test include?
2. What format will the questions follow (subjective, objective)?
3. Will spelling or handwriting affect scoring?
4. How much will the test contribute to the final grade?
5. How much time will be allotted for taking the test?
6. Is there a penalty for guessing?
7. Will the test be comprehensive or noncomprehensive?
8. Will any supplementary materials (calculator, dictionary, blue book, etc.) be needed or allowed?

**TABLE 12.6 Predicting Objective Test Questions**

1. Determine what the test will cover. Is the test comprehensive or noncomprehensive?
2. Answer review questions at the end of each text chapter.
3. Use old exams or question former students or the instructor to obtain clues about test item construction. Instructors are creatures of habit. The points they emphasize in class will most likely be those they test. The types of questions they ask rarely vary much from one term to another.
4. Construct possible questions based on key facts.
5. Prepare short definitions of basic terms.
6. Construct mnemonics to remember lists of information given in the text or lecture.
7. Create sample exams. Exchange with classmates and take each other's exams.

**TABLE 12.7 Predicting Subjective Test Questions**

**1–4.** Follow steps 1–4 of the preceding procedure.
**5.** Identify major principles, aims, and theories.
**6.** List pros and cons of important issues.
**7.** Look for ways to compare and contrast concepts.
**8.** Prepare definitions of basic terms. Think of examples not mentioned in the text or lecture.
**9.** Develop an outline or map of the information you wish to include in your answer (see Chapter 1). Then, create mnemonics or memory tricks to aid your recall.
**10.** Practice writing essay responses. Have someone check your answers for clarity and grammar.
**11.** Set a study schedule to review your condensed outline.

**EXERCISE 12.2**

*Use any excerpt in Chapter 1 and construct 10 objective questions (3 multiple choice, 4 matching, and 3 true/false) and 10 subjective questions (5 essay, 3 short answer, and 2 fill-in-the-blank). Identify the excerpt by title and page number.*

## Taking Objective Tests

Objective tests give you a choice of answers. They require memorizing facts. This includes such information as dates, names, lists, formulas, and other details. They demand that you know more exact information

*"I'm trying to answer these true/false questions objectively."*

than subjective tests. However, some questions may ask you to draw conclusions or identify main ideas. Objective tests consist of multiple-choice, true/false, matching, or fill-in-the-blank questions. Table 12.8 shows examples of test questions.

STEPS FOR TAKING OBJECTIVE TESTS

1. *When you get the test, look it over.* Get a feel for the test. Glance through all parts. See how much each question is worth. This helps you allot your test time.

2. *Read through the whole exam and answer the questions you know first.* This gives you confidence. Also, you get credit for the ones you know. Check or mark questions that confuse you.

**TABLE 12.8 Types of Objective Test Questions**

| TYPE | EXAMPLE | |
|---|---|---|
| Multiple choice | The author of *Romeo and Juliet* is<br>a. Agatha Christie.<br>b. Erma Bombeck.<br>c. William Shakespeare.<br>d. Alfred Hitchcock. | |
| Matching | 1. *Romeo and Juliet*<br>2. *Tom Sawyer*<br>3. *Gone with the Wind* | a. Mark Twain<br>b. Margaret Mitchell<br>c. William Shakespeare |
| Fill-in-the-blank | ______________ wrote *Romeo and Juliet.* | |
| True/false | _______ *Romeo and Juliet* was written by Agatha Christie. | |

3. *Go back to questions you didn't know.* Reread each one carefully. Try to answer the question in your own words. Then look for a matching response.

4. *If you do not know the answer, try to figure out what the answer is not.*

**Example**

The capital of Belgium is:

a. New York
b. Texas
c. London
(d.) Brussels

*Explanation:* You may not know the capital of Belgium. However, you can eliminate the following:

a. New York is in the United States.
b. Texas is a state, not a capital.
c. London is in England.

Therefore, *d* must be the correct answer.

5. *Read all choices before answering a multiple-choice question.* Don't choose the first answer that seems correct. Sometimes the choice may be between a good answer and the best answer. Or, the answer might be a combination of responses (all of the above, both *a* and *b*, etc.). Answer by eliminating obviously incorrect answers. Then select the *most correct* answer that remains.

6. *If the test contains a true/false section, read each question thoroughly.* Watch for key words such as *always, never, seldom,* and *frequently.* Statements with *always* and *never* are often false. Statements with *seldom* and *frequently* allow for more exceptions. Make sure a statement is completely true before answering true. True/false tests are known for statements that are almost true, but not quite true.

7. *If the test concerns math or science, watch your time closely.* Don't spend so much time on difficult problems that you cannot finish the test. When you're stumped, move on to the next question.

8. *Watch for double negatives.* What is $-2 \times -2$? Answer, $+4$. Negative times negative equals positive. The same rule is true in writing. Two negative terms make the idea positive.

**Example**

| | |
|---|---|
| *not un*loved | 2 negatives; means "loved" |
| *never un*clear | 2 negatives; means "clear" |
| *never in*visible | 2 negatives; means "visible" |
| *not* with*out* hope | 2 negatives; means "has hope" |
| *not* sight*less* | 2 negatives; means "has sight" |

**9.** *There are also some tricks of the trade for taking math tests.*

***Example***

12,365 × 112 =
(a.) 1,384,880
**b.** 1,236,511
**c.** 1,384,886
**d.** 5,678,920

*Explanation:* You can get the answer without working the problem. Look at the last digit of each number. They are 5 and 2. The product of those two numbers is 10. That means that the answer will *end* in zero. Thus, you eliminate answers *b* and *c*. Neither one ends in zero. Now round off each number in the problem. You get 12,000 and 100. Multiply those two together. The answer is 1,200,000. The correct answer should be higher than your estimate because you rounded each of the numbers down. This may be different for other problems depending on how you estimate. Answer *d* is, then, much too high. The correct answer is *a*.

***EXERCISE 12.3***

◆ *Complete the following test as quickly as possible. Write the letter of your answer in the blank provided.*

**1.** ______ 236,515 × 113 =
**a.** 22,726,195
**b.** 26,726,195
**c.** 16,726,190
**d.** 31,723,211

**2.** ______ 95,683 − 74,864 =
**a.** 101,329
**b.** 20,819
**c.** 20,815
**d.** 28,051

**3.** ______ The book was not incomplete. It was
**a.** only begun.
**b.** finished.
**c.** half complete.
**d.** unfinished.

**4.** ______ is the capital of Spain.
**a.** New York
**b.** France
**c.** Madrid
**d.** England

5. ______ The old man was not sightless. He could
   a. see.
   b. be classified as blind.
   c. not see.
   d. none of the above

6. ______ True or False? All mammals' offspring fully develop in the womb of the mother.

7. ______ True or False? Frequent coughing is a sure sign of lung cancer.

8. ______ The opposite of "not in" is
   a. out.
   b. in.
   c. there.
   d. missing.

9. ______ True or False? Presidents of the United States never veto bills that increase taxes.

10. ______ The people who uncovered the structure of DNA were
   a. Watson and Crick.
   b. Hall and Oates.
   c. Lewis and Clark.
   d. Reagan and Bush.

## Taking Subjective Tests

Unlike objective tests, subjective tests provide no alternatives from which to choose. Instead, you consider your knowledge of the subject and create answers of your own. There are three basic kinds of subjective tests: essay tests, short answer tests, and fill-in-the-blank tests (see Table 12.9).

The first type of subjective test is the essay test. Such tests require lengthy written answers. Your goal is to write the maximum amount of point-earning information in the shortest possible time.

Essay questions are usually graded on two factors, what you say and how you say it. Thus, your answer needs to be logical and organized. The words in the question itself can help you organize and write your answer. For them to help you, though, you must know what those words are and what they mean. Such words or phrases are listed in Table 12.10.

The second kind of subjective test is an identification test in which you must provide short, written answers. Like an essay test, you must

**TABLE 12.9** ***Examples of Subjective Tests***

*A COMBINATION OF ANALOG AND DIGITAL COMPUTERS IS CALLED A* ________________

You would answer this question by *filling in the blank* with the word *hybrid* as follows:

A combination of analog and digital computers is called a hybrid.

*CONTRAST THE TYPES OF COMPUTERS*

A typical *essay* response would be as follows:

There are two general groups of computers. First, some computers process data. These types consist of analog and digital. An analog computer measures continuing physical processes. The digital type operates by counting. A combination of these two types is called a hybrid. The second kind of computer is grouped by function. A computer of this type is either special purpose or general purpose. A special-purpose computer does a single job. However, a general-purpose computer can do many different tasks.

*BRIEFLY IDENTIFY THE KINDS OF COMPUTERS THAT PROCESS DATA.*

A typical *short answer* response would be as follows:

1. analog—measures continuous physical process
2. digital—operates by counting
3. hybrid—combination of analog and digital

**TABLE 12.10** ***Question Types for Essay Tests***

| *TYPE* | *DEFINITION* | *KEY WORDS* |
|---|---|---|
| Compare | Show how two things are alike | similarly; likewise; in like manner; equally important |
| Contrast | Show how two things are different | but; yet; however; on the other hand; nevertheless; on the contrary |
| Discuss (describe) | Give as much information as possible | that is; as has been noted |
| Enumerate (name or list) | Identify the major points | first, second, . . . ; finally; next; too; in addition; last; furthermore; and; and then |
| Explain | Give reasons | because; as a result; therefore; then; hence; thus; for this reason; for these reasons |
| Relate | Show how two things are connected | (Use words from Compare or Contrast) |
| Summarize | Briefly tell the main points | In short; in summary; in conclusion; in other words; on the whole; to sum up |

do more than recognize correct answers. Unlike an essay test, you do not have to be concerned with sentence construction and grammar.

A third kind of subjective test consists of fill-in-the-blank questions. This type differs from the first two types of subjective tests. The first two require somewhat lengthy answers. A fill-in-the-blank test focuses on specific details and short responses.

The steps for taking subjective tests follow.

STEPS FOR TAKING ESSAY TESTS

1. *Relax.* Take a minute to become calm. Read all the questions. Estimate the amount of time you can spend on each. Note the number of points each question is worth.

2. *Study the question.* Decide what you think the instructor wants. (See the list of question types in Table 12.10 for more information.) Organize your thoughts before beginning to write. Your ability to express yourself is also being tested. Thus, your answer must be written so the instructor knows you know the subject.

3. *Briefly outline your answers.* Writing an **outline** is the best way to assure you include important information.

4. *Answer the essay question you know best first.* This helps you relax and gives you confidence. It also gives you a chance to think about the other questions.

5. *Like an essay or theme in English class, writing answers to essay questions takes time and patience.* Begin with an introduction to your response. Provide supporting details in the middle to reinforce your answer. End with a summary of the important details. Include a topic and summary sentence. Think of examples as you write. Even if you don't include all of them, they'll help you clarify your thinking.

6. *Save five to ten minutes at the end of the test to review what you've written.* **Proofread** your answers. This means correcting any mistakes made when your thoughts raced faster than your pen. Check for content accuracy and careless omissions. Look carefully for spelling and punctuation mistakes. You often improve your grade by simply correcting an error or adding an omitted detail.

7. *Neatness is also important.* If your answers are difficult to read, the instructor may count them wrong. Let your test's appearance work for you, not against you.

8. *If there is a question on the test you don't know, write down any related information you do know.* Don't pretend to know the answer, but answer as best you can. You may get partial credit, especially if others had problems with the same question.

9. *Take your time on untimed tests.* Don't race to be the first one to leave. Use any extra time to check over your answers. Proofread written responses.

10. *Don't worry if others finish the test before you.* Some students always seem to turn their papers in much sooner than anyone else. However, these students may not have known many answers. They could be on their way to drop the course. Don't panic! Get back to work.

## Taking Final Exams

What do you think of when you hear the word *finals?* Often college finals have a bad reputation. But, there's really nothing to fear.

Perhaps you've been doing all the right things to make a good grade in the course. You've gone to class regularly. You've kept up with your assignments. All you have to do now is take the final.

To prepare for the final, review the suggestions for taking other kinds of exams. The same rules apply. Use them.

In addition, find out when and where the exam will be. Final exam schedules do not always follow regular class times. You will really panic if you get to your class and there is nobody there.

Many finals are more long than hard. They are almost like tests of endurance. They are usually no harder than other tests, just longer. Because they are longer, finals are often fair tests of your knowledge. They cover more information. You have a better chance because they focus on many topics.

*"This test will be a breeze. It's going to blow you away."*

**TABLE 12.11 Questions for Examining Returned Tests**

1. How many wrong answers were the result of
   a. carelessness?
   b. studying the wrong information?
   c. test foolishness (not using test-wise strategies)?
   d. misreading directions?
   e. misreading questions?
   f. poor use of time?
   g. poorly organized responses?
   h. incomplete responses?
   i. test anxiety?
2. What can I learn about the way in which my instructor constructs tests from this exam?
3. What should I do next time to improve my performance?
4. How many times did I change correct answers to incorrect ones?
5. How many times did I change incorrect answers to correct ones?

**WRITE TO LEARN**

*On a separate sheet of paper, describe the type of test you think you do your best on. Justify this opinion.*

## Examining Returned Tests

What do you do when a test is returned to you? Do you throw it away? Or, do you carefully examine it? A review of your test paper yields information about your skills. You use this to improve future test grades. Perusing your returned test helps you decide which of your learning and/or test-taking strategies were most successful. It also aids you in determining what areas need more emphasis. You make these decisions by asking the questions contained in Table 12.11.

**EXERCISE 12.4**

◆ *Using the last test you took in this class, answer the following questions.*

1. How many wrong answers were the result of carelessness?

_______________

_______________

2. How many wrong answers were the result of studying the wrong information?

_______________

_______________

3. How many wrong answers were the result of test foolishness (not using test-wise strategies)?

______________________________________________

______________________________________________

4. How many wrong answers were the result of misreading directions?

______________________________________________

______________________________________________

5. How many wrong answers were the result of poor use of time?

______________________________________________

______________________________________________

6. How many wrong answers were the result of poorly organized responses?

______________________________________________

______________________________________________

7. How many wrong answers were the result of test anxiety?

______________________________________________

______________________________________________

8. What can I learn about the way in which my instructor constructs tests from this exam?

______________________________________________

______________________________________________

9. What should I do next time to improve my performance?

______________________________________________

______________________________________________

10. How many times did I change correct answers to incorrect ones?

______________________________________________

______________________________________________

11. How many times did I change incorrect answers to correct ones?

______________________________________________

______________________________________________

## Taking Standardized Reading Exams

Taking standardized reading tests requires a few special skills. Such tests are often timed. Scoring on **standardized tests** is usually done in one of two ways. Your score may be based on the number of right answers minus a percentage of wrong answers. When scoring is done in this manner, it is most important to guess wisely. Listen carefully to the instructions for the test. Often information about scoring is part of the directions. If not, ask your instructor or the administrator of the test. If you cannot find out how the test is scored, it may be wiser not to guess. A second way to score standardized tests credits all right answers. When tests are scored this way, try to answer all questions.

TAKING THE VOCABULARY SUBTEST

1. *Skim through the test.* Answer all questions that you know. Hard and easy questions earn the same points.
2. *Go back through the test.* Make "educated guesses." Try to eliminate choices. Use context clues when possible. Watch for prefix and suffix clues. Identify the part of speech of the unknown word. Make sure your response matches it.
3. *Important: Keep track of time.* Do not spend too much time on any one question.

*Note:* Once again, if the test is scored by subtracting a percentage of wrong answers from your total of right answers, you may lower your overall score by guessing.

TAKING THE COMPREHENSION SUBTEST

1. *Preview each selection.* Get an idea of what the passage covers. Use the questions to aid your comprehension of the passage.
2. *Look at the first few questions at the end of the passage.* These questions often ask about main ideas.
3. *Go back and read the passage.* Keep the questions in mind. This makes your reading an active process. It gives you a reason for reading the passage.
4. *Some questions concern details.* The answers to these are generally stated in the passage. Try to figure out the type of response needed. Then, use scanning to locate answers.

***Example***

If the question were "Who invented the cotton gin?" the expected response would be a name. Therefore, scan the passage for names.

When you see a name, slow down. Check to see if it's the one you need. Use context clues whenever possible.

5. *Do not spend too much time on any question.*
6. *Some questions ask you to make inferences.* These answers will not be directly stated. You go beyond the facts to draw conclusions.
7. *Again, keep track of the time.*
8. *Continued effort on a confusing passage takes too much time.* If a passage is too confusing or hard, skip it. Go on to a passage you can understand.
9. *If you can't find an answer after a few seconds, skip it and go on.* Continued looking only makes you more confused and nervous. Return to that question when you have more time to look.
10. *Be sure that the answer you mark on the answer sheet is the same one as the question you are answering.*

◆

## CHAPTER SUMMARY EXERCISE

*Write a chapter summary in the space provided.*

◆

## CHAPTER REVIEW

*Answer briefly but completely.*

1. Complete the following analogy.
   noncomprehensive : part :: comprehensive : ______________

2. Describe two ways you can be mentally and physically prepared for an exam.

3. Explain *self-talk.* Provide an example (other than that given in the text) when self-talk might be appropriate.

4. Your book states that actors and athletes feel eustress. Name another profession that might also use stress positively. On what do you base this response?

________________________________________

________________________________________

________________________________________

________________________________________

________________________________________

5. Describe optimum study times and places.

________________________________________

________________________________________

________________________________________

________________________________________

________________________________________

6. Complete the following analogy.
acronym : word :: acrostic : ____________

7. Contrast subjective and objective exams.

________________________________________

________________________________________

________________________________________

________________________________________

________________________________________

8. Using information contained in this chapter, write a test question of each of the following types:
   a. multiple choice

   ________________________________________

   ________________________________________

   b. fill-in-the-blank

   ________________________________________

   ________________________________________

   c. true/false

   ________________________________________

   ________________________________________

**d.** matching (at least three sets)

**e.** essay

**9.** How are final exams different from other exams?

**10.** Describe standardized tests.

◆

## VOCABULARY ENHANCEMENT EXERCISE

*Using the scale in Figure 3.1, rate your understanding of the following vocabulary enhancement words to the left of the number. Then write a sentence with each one.*

**1.** clarity

**2.** ferocious

**3.** mettle

**4.** ventured

**5.** automated

**6.** occurrence

**7.** abstract

**8.** memorable

**9.** impending

**10.** reserve

### *TEST ANXIETY SCALE KEY*

1. T 2. T 3. T 4. T 5. T 6. T 7. T 8. T 9. T 10. F 11. T 12. T 13. F 14. T 15. T 16. T

Grade your response to the Test Anxiety Scale. If your answers match eleven or more times, then anxiety may be a problem for you.

## REFERENCES

Bower, G. H. Analysis of a mnemonic device. *American Scientist* 58:496 (1970).

# BIOGRAPHY

**Albee, Edward (American, b. 1928)** began writing plays at the age of thirty, after failing at writing novels and poetry. He is best known for his first major play, *Who's Afraid of Virginia Woolf.* It was first performed in 1962. It won almost every award a play could win. It is considered to be an American masterpiece.

**Aldrich, Thomas Bailey (American, 1836-1907)** was a poet and short story writer. He was the first well-known writer to make good use of the surprise ending. Through his use of it, the technique became respectable.

**Bacon, Roger (English, 1220-1292)** was an experimental scientist before experimental science existed. His experiments on the nature of light and the rainbow were especially well planned and interpreted. His "thought experiments" (Einstein's term) were even more notable. He was the first to suggest means of making dirigibles, airplanes, gunpowder, spectacles, and motorized ships and carriages.

**Bacon, Sir Francis (English, 1561-1626)** gained political power from 1600 onwards. He became lord chancellor in 1618. He is best remembered for inventing a scientific method and reorganizing the sciences. He was removed from power in 1621 on charges of bribery. Bacon spent his final years writing some of his most valuable works.

**Beecher, Henry Ward (American, 1813–1887)** was a liberal Protestant minister. He had a great and benign influence on the politics of his time. He was strongly opposed to slavery (abolished in 1865) and believed women should vote. Beecher also supported evolutionary theory and rational research of the Bible. Towards the end of his life he was tried for adultery with the wife of an associate. He was found innocent.

**Blake, William (English, 1757–1827)** is one of the earliest and greatest figures of the movement called Romanticism. His work was not widely understood until a hundred years after his death. During his life he was poor and obscure. He died alone. Blake illustrated his own books of poetry, some of which are thought to be among the greatest products of Western civilization. Most of his work is intensely visionary and mystical. His drawings and paintings depict heavenly scenes he saw with his eyes. His poetry is mainly concerned with religious themes.

**Bonaparte, Napoleon (Corsican, 1769–1821)** rose through the ranks of the French army to eventually rule France, beginning in 1799. Because of the instability of the government he established a military dictatorship. In 1803 he crowned himself emperor. By 1810 he was in command of most of Europe. His downfall began with his disastrous invasion of Russia in 1812. Napoleon revolutionized military organization. He sponsored the Napoleonic Code, which formed the basis of civil law codes in areas of the world once dominated by France. He also reorganized French education.

**Bowen, Elizabeth (British, 1899–1973)** wrote mostly novels and short stories. They usually had to do with the conditions of her life at the time of writing. The theme of many of her books concerns shallow and uncomfortable relationships among the upper middle class. She also wrote about the violence surrounding Irish independence as well as Nazi bombing of London.

**Brown, Mason (American, 1900–1969)** was a drama critic and lecturer. His writings were good but not so memorable as still to be thought worth reading.

**Burke, Edmund (English, 1729–1797)** was a conservative political theorist and a prominent statesman. He believed that the human spirit was a part of a cosmic plan. He felt humanity was essentially good but must keep its ideals and goals constantly in mind. In practice, he twisted these ideas into permitting abusive practices and awful judgment, as many conservatives did. For example, he believed that England's colonies should be governed according to English ideas, which he thought were the best in the world. When the governor of British India insisted that things were quite different in India and that it could only be governed according to its own ideas, Burke had him impeached. Burke was strongly opposed to the French Revolution.

**Butler, Samuel (English, 1835–1902)** was novelist whose fame rested, during his lifetime, on his novel *Erewhon*. *Erewhon* is Butler's satire of the ideas of his time, especially the idea of progress. He also satirized religion. Samuel Butler tried his hand at painting and musical composition before wholly devoting himself to writing. He said that he never wrote on any subject unless he believed the authorities on it to be hopelessly wrong.

**Carroll, Lewis (English, 1832–1892)** is best known for having written *Alice's Adventures in Wonderland* and *Through the Looking Glass*. He wrote little else of any lasting value. His expertise was in logic and mathematics, and the *Alice* books are full of delightful tricks. They are the result of a gifted mind applied purely to the amusement of children.

**Chamfort, Sébastien-Roch Nicolas (French, 1740–1794)** was a playwright and witty conversationalist. Many of the things he said became the slogans of the Reign of Terror (the bloodbath following the 1789 French Revolution). One of these slogans was "War to the châteaux, peace to the cottages." He eventually grew sick of decapitation and turned against the Revolution with such slogans as "Be my brother or I'll kill you," which made fun of the Revolutionary idea of fraternity. The Revolutionaries caught him, and he killed himself.

**Churchill, Sir Winston (British, 1874–1965)** was perhaps the greatest British statesman of modern times. From 1929 to 1939, while holding a seat in Parliament, he tried to warn his dull-witted government of the terrible danger of Hitler. It was only after the Nazis began to destroy Western Europe, in 1939, that Churchill was taken seriously. He became prime minister and eventually helped to defeat the German monsters.

**Cicero, Marcus Tullius (Roman, 106 B.C.–43 B.C.)** was perhaps the greatest orator of all time. He is certainly the most famous. Many of his works survive and continue to influence the style of modern speakers and speech-writers. Most of his speeches were directed to upholding the democratic Roman traditions during the civil wars that ended by destroying the Roman republic. He criticized Octavian, who was to become the first emperor of Rome, and Octavian had him beheaded.

**Congreve, William (English, 1670–1729)** was a writer of plays belonging to the style known as Neoclassical. This style derived its main elements from Greek and Roman models. He is best known for his comic dialogue and for his social criticism, which included satire of the rich.

**Corbusier, Le (Swiss, 1887–1965)** is the name used by one of the twentieth century's greatest architects. His buildings are functional and essentially simple, without ornamentation. They differ from the German Bauhaus school in that their shapes are bold and expressive. He was the first architect to make a considered use of rough-cast concrete, a material that appealed to him for its starkness. He was finally recognized for his genius when he was quite old, but he found the attention ridiculous.

**De la Mare, Walter (English, 1873–1956)** was an obscure poet, novelist, and writer of short stories whose work is full of mysterious presences and dreams. For him, the world of imagination was very real.

**Dekker, Thomas (English, 1572–1632)** was a relatively unimportant playwright. He may have been popular in his own day, though that is uncertain. In any case, his work was quite flawed and he was cruelly but justly satirized by Ben Jonson.

**Dickinson, Emily (American, 1830–1886)** was an extraordinarily sensitive poet. She was religious and sometimes mystical, and she refused to take her Christianity seriously. In her later years she tried to live according to the dictates of art. From forty on she wore only white and saw few visitors, never appearing in public. She was eccentric in her writing as well as in her life, and she was poorly understood. Even after her death, when her first book appeared, its editor removed the unusual dashes and punctuation in her poems, perhaps thinking them to be nervous tics. Her attention to detail is now considered extraordinary.

**Disraeli, Benjamin "Dizzy" (British, 1804–1881)** is perhaps the most well-known British prime minister besides Churchill. Serving under Queen

Victoria he helped to clear slums, prevent labor exploitation, and strengthen labor unions. He helped prevent a war with the Tsar of Russia by means of diplomacy. He also supported the Jewish settlement of Palestine. During his life he wrote several novels, all of them political. The first lampooned a man with whom he had a personal quarrel, and he was much criticized for unfairness.

**Eliot, George (English, 1819–1880)** was the first novelist to generally analyze characters psychologically, a practice that is now almost universal. Eliot was a woman; she changed her name in order to be better received in the male-dominated literary world of her day. She was intensely religious, though she doubted the truth and intelligence of most religious writings.

**Emerson, Ralph Waldo (American, 1803–1882)** is best remembered for his essays, which are some of the greatest in the English language. Because of his experiences of occult communion with nature and natural objects, he adopted Transcendentalism. This philosophy spoke of spiritual bonds between man and nature, and of an "oversoul," a moral soul shared by all mankind. He is considered to be the greatest American Transcendentalist. His ideas were quickly overshadowed by the advent of philosophical and literary Realism, which concentrates only on what can be easily perceived.

**Goldsmith, Oliver (English, 1730–1774)** was best known in his day for his two very different personalitie. On the page he was fluent and wise, even brilliant. In person, he was clumsy, vain and at a constant loss for words. He was jealous of others' achievements and always had to be the center of the party, but he often gave more to the poor than he could afford. His work is elegant and compassionately satirical.

**Hazlitt, William (English, 1778–1830)** is remembered above all for his essays, whose style is extremely simple, yet whose brilliance is undeniable. Their message is always humane.

**Herbert, George (English, 1593–1633)** wrote important poems of the metaphysical type, which means they were about God. He wrote only in Greek and Latin, and only for special occasions. He is even today considered one of the great metaphysicians. Coleridge said of his word choice that "Nothing can be more pure, manly, and unaffected."

**Highet, Gilbert Arthur (Scottish, 1906–1978)** was a classicist who spent most of his career in New York and so is considered by some to be American.

**Huxley, Aldous (English, 1894–1963)** was the author of *Brave New World,* a masterpiece which describes a world Huxley feared the world of his day might become—efficient, without misery, and totally dead. Conservative and liberal social critics have compared Huxley's vision to the reality of modern-day middle-class America, which strongly resembles it. In the 'thirties Huxley experimented with hallucinogenic drugs. He wrote about his experiences in *The Doors of Perception.*

**Jackson, Robert (American, 1892–1954)** was a justice of the U.S. Supreme court (1941–1954). He achieved nothing of lasting value. He participated in the national paranoia which banned the Communist Party. He also helped place American Japanese in concentration camps during WWII. Though he was chief U.S. prosecutor in the war crimes trials against the defeated Nazis, his work in those trials lacked vigor.

**James I, King (Scottish, 1566—1625)** was King of Scotland before he became King of England in 1603. He wrote mediocre poetry. His greatest legacy is the King James Version of the Bible—a translation from Hebrew and Greek by 54 scholars James appointed. It was a masterpiece of English prose and was the principal Bible used in England for 270 years. King James was homosexual.

**Johnson, Samuel (English, 1709–1784)** is most famous as a lexicographer, or writer of dictionaries. He wrote the first major English dictionary to use historical quotations in word definitions, an important improvement. He produced a complete edition of Shakespeare's poetry and was perhaps the first consistently good literary critic. He was also known as a great conversationalist.

**Jonson, Ben (English, 1572–1637)** is considered to be the second most important English playwright before modern times (the first being Shakespeare). His influence was great for many years after his death. The wit and spirited action of his plays reappeared in the plays of many others. He also wrote lyric poetry and literary criticism.

**Krutch (pronounced krooch), Joseph Wood (American, 1893–1970)** was a literary critic and ordinary academic until he retired to Arizona. At that time, he became interested in the natural world and published several wonderful books about the desert and its inhabitants.

**Longfellow, Henry Wadsworth (American, 1807–1882)** was the most popular American poet of the nineteenth century. He spent most of his life teaching in universities, writing textbooks and articles, and translating. His greatest work was in the tradition of Romanticism, of which William Blake was the greatest figure.

**Moore, John Bassett (American, 1860–1947)** was a scholar of law. He wrote and compiled reference works about international law. Some of them are still read today.

**Nash, Ogden (American, 1902–1971)** was a well-known American writer of humorous verse.

**Omar Khayyam (Persian, 1048–1122)** was most famous during his life for his scientific achievements. He did important work in algebra, astronomy, medicine, history, and law. Little of his writings on these matters survives. He is now known for his four-line poems, known as *roba'iyat*. These were translated by Edward FitzGerald and published in England as *The Rubaiyat of Omar Khayyam*. In them Omar finds the answer to life in appreciation of the beauties of the world.

**Parker, Dorothy (American, 1893–1967)** wrote short stories about people in big cities. These stories exposed idiocies that tended to be overlooked. She became involved in left-wing politics and reported from the Spanish Civil War, which the U.S. government preferred not to notice. Consequently, after the war she had trouble finding employment in Hollywood where she had been working as a scriptwriter.

**Phillips, Wendell (American, 1811–1884)** was a radical abolitionist, considered the most eloquent of the Northern ones in the Civil War era.

**Plato (Greek, 428 B.C.–348 B.C.)** considered his most important work to be the foundation and organization of the Academy in Athens. This was an institute for the pursuit of philosophical and scientific research. He is remembered, however, as one of the greatest philosophical writers. His thought has influenced, and even determined to a large extent, our philosophical, political, and critical ideas.

**Proverbs** is a book of the Old Testament consisting of wisdom literature, or proverbs, from about 700 B.C. to about 300 B.C. Much of the book resembles very closely an Egyptian wisdom book from much earlier. This suggests that the Bible must have derived much of its thought in this area from other Near Eastern cultures.

**Sandburg, Carl (American, 1878–1967)** was a socially conscious poet, novelist, and writer of folk songs. He admired workers and the industries but eventually lost faith in American progress.

**Schelling, Friedrich Wilhelm Joseph von (German, 1775–1854)** was a philosopher of the school known as Idealism, which developed out of the ideas of the great Immanuel Kant. Schelling was also an idealist with a small *i:* he believed it was his mission to complete philosophy, i.e. to answer once and for all every question. His work is beginning to be seen as quite important. He wrote a history of God before Creation, helped philosophy to consider the irrational (whatever cannot be dealt with by logical means), and paved the way for Existentialism.

**Shakespeare, William (English, 1564–1616)** is universally considered to be the greatest playwright ever, and by some the greatest writer. Just to read all the poems about him would take months. Almost all university English departments include at least one scholar whose life is dedicated to studying one aspect or another of Shakespeare's work.

**Shaw, George Bernard (Irish, 1856–1950)** is considered to be the greatest British playwright since the 17th century. He was known for his wit and for his comedies. He also did some excellent serious work. He was an ardent Socialist. He won the Nobel prize for Literature in 1925.

**Shelley, Percy Bysshe (English, 1792–1822)** was a great lyric poet of the English Romantic school of poetry, whose first and greatest member was William Blake. He wrote most of his poetry after he settled in Italy in 1818, only four years before his death at sea. His most famous work is *Prometheus Unbound*, an allegory for the struggle and power of humanity.

**Vergil or Virgil [Publius Vergilius Maro] (Roman, 70 B.C.–19 B.C.)** spent the last eleven years of his life working on the *Aeneid*, which is the greatest Roman epic, and perhaps the greatest work of propaganda ever. In it, the reign of the emperor Augustus is divinely ordained and equalled in glory only by the founding of Rome seven hundred years before. It is not as great a work as Homer's *Iliad* or *Odyssey*, also epic poems, but it is the greatest such poem Rome produced.

**Wilde, Oscar (Irish, 1854–1900)** was and is appreciated for his brilliant comic plays. The most famous of these is *The Importance of Being Earnest*. He also wrote novels (*The Portrait of Dorian Gray,* etc.). He is equally well remembered for his daring life as a homosexual and a wit. The barbaric laws of England put him in jail when he was forty-one. The charge was homosexuality. Upon his release he left his homeland for France but had difficulty writing, perhaps because of the trauma of prison. He died shortly after.

**Yeats, William Butler (Irish, 1865–1939)** is best remembered for his poetry. He was also a dramatist and an Irish nationalist politician. He won the Nobel Prize for Literature in 1923. He adapted Irish myths to verse and believed his work might be able to help unify Ireland.

# GLOSSARY

## A

**acronym** a word formed from the first letter or the first few letters of several words.

**active listening** conscious control of the listening act through preplanned strategies.

**active reader** one who monitors the comprehension process through preplanned reading strategies; one who reads for enjoyment as well as information.

**adjective** a word that describes persons, places, or things; a word that answers Which one? What kind? or How many? about a noun.

**adverb** a word that describes verbs, adjectives, and other adverbs; a word that answers How? When? Where? How much? or How many? about verbs, adjectives, and other adverbs.

**affix** one or more letters attached to the beginnings or endings of bases or words to alter the meaning of a base or word; prefixes or suffixes.

**allusion** an idea expressed in shortened form which refers to works of literature, history, and the arts.

**alphabetical** an arrangement of data from A to Z.

**altitude** height above sea level.

**analogy** an implied relationship between two pairs of objects.

**analytical reasoning** logic, critical reading; reasoning by looking at the relationship between, or a sequence of, facts or events.

**animate** living or lifelike.

**antonym** a word that has the opposite meaning of another word.

**Arabic numbers** one of the number symbols 0–9.

**argument** a set of statements formed from premises and conclusions.

**article** any one of the words *a, an* or *the.*

**assumption** a logical conclusion made with the use of global and language knowledge.

**B**

**background knowledge** the sum total of a person's language and global knowledge.

**bandwagoning** a form of advertising in which a person, product, or concept is made to seem attractive because it is popular with others; a "Join the Crowd!" theme.

**bar graph** a graphic in which bars indicate the frequency of data; shows quantitative comparisons; a histogram.

**base** the part of a word that provides essential meaning; a root.

**bias** prejudice or favoritism.

**boundaries** man-made (sometimes natural) dividing points between areas on a map.

**browsing** casually looking over or through a book, magazine, etc.

**C**

**capital letters** written or printed letters larger or differently shaped from other letters; upper case; used in outlines to denote significant details under a major heading.

**cartographer** one who draws maps or charts; a mapmaker.

**causal connections** cause-effect relationships.

**cause-effect pattern** in a communication, a stated or implied association between some outcome & the condition which brought it about.

**chronology** time order in which some event occurs.

**circle graph** a graphic that shows how a whole unit is divided into parts.

**cliché** overused simile or metaphor.

**column** a vertical arrangement of items.

**comparison/contrast pattern** the organization of information for placing together like or unlike ideas, situations, or characters.

**comparison text-based clues** signals that indicate that two or more things are similar or alike.

**comprehension regulation** conscious control of reading using preplanned strategies to understand text.

**comprehensive** an examination that covers all materials presented in class over the course of an entire term.

**conclusion** a decision, judgment, or an opinion reached by reasoning or inferring.

**conjunction** a word that joins sentences, clauses, phrases, or words; a combining or connecting word like *and, but, or,* etc.

**connotation** an implied or suggested meaning of a word or group of words.

**connoted** implied or suggested meaning.

**context** the surrounding words that suggest the meaning of an unknown word.

**contrast text-based clues** signals that indicate the opposite meaning (antonym) of an unknown word and that can be used to define that word.

**cope** to overcome; to meet with or encounter success.

**copyright date** the year in which a book was published.

**cramming** frantic, last minute memorization. This method lacks permanency.

**critical reading** reading in which the reader evaluates and analyzes what is read.

**critical thinking** logic, or analytical reasoning; reasoning by looking at the relationship between or sequence of facts or events.

**cross-reference** a reference from one part of a book to another.

**curve of forgetting** the relationship between recall of information without review and the time since presentation.

## D

**deductive logic** the process by which one starts with a general principle, applies it to a specific case, and makes a conclusion that is valid if the starting principle was valid.

**definition text-based clues** signals that indicate that the meaning of an unknown word directly follows.

**degree** a unit of measure; 1/360 of the circumference of a circle.

**denotation** the direct, literal meaning of a word or group of words.

**denoted** direct, specific meaning.

**descriptive** expressing quality, kind, or condition about a person, place, thing, or concept.

**details** pieces of specific information that support or communicate the main idea of a paragraph or a passage.

**directionality** the order in which a math problem must be done.

**distractions** visual, auditory, or mental occurrences that interfere with attention.

**distributed practice** a method of increasing a skill by setting time limits (practicing a certain amount of time daily) and task limits (practicing certain skills each day) rather than attempting to cram much practice into only a small amount of time.

## E

**elevation** the distance from sea level.

**enumeration/sequence pattern** placement of information in a systematic organizational pattern according to time or rank.

**estimate** to approximate an answer; to judge the size, extent, or nature of something; a guess.

**equator** the imaginary 25,000 mile line around the middle of the earth that divides the planet into two hemispheres.

**etymology** the study of the origins of words.

**euphemism** a form of figurative language that uses a word or phrase that is less expressive or direct but that is less distasteful or offensive than another.

**evaluative knowledge** the process by which one makes an objective judgment about a conclusion.

**example text-based clues** signals that indicate given example(s) of an unknown word and that can be used to define that word.

**expert opinion** the opinion of one who has knowledge and skill in a particular area about that subject.

**eye contact** two-way visual communication between speaker and listener.

## F

**fact** based on direct evidence, a statement of truth.

**factual** based on direct evidence, indicates a statement of truth.

**fallacy** a mistake in reasoning; a misconception.

**fiction** one of two types of writing; not based on fact or truth; written to entertain.

**figurative language** written or spoken words which use sensory images to create pictures in the mind's eye.

**figures of speech** expressions that use words in an unusual or nonliteral sense; used to convey meaning by comparing or identifying one thing with another that has a meaning or connotation familiar to the reader.

**flow chart** a drawing that shows the steps in a complicated process.

**formal fallacy** a mistake in reasoning which results from having a statement unsupported by facts.

**format** the general plan or arrangement of text.

**framework** a structure that holds together or supports information in your mind.

**framework-based context clues** using surrounding words to call up framework clues when predicting the meaning of unknown words.

## G

**generalizations** to infer from facts.

**general vocabulary** common, everyday words most likely found in humanities courses.

**gist** the main idea of a paragraph or passage.

**global knowledge** what a person knows about the world; information acquired through real or vicarious experiences.

**globe** a three-dimensional (spherical) representation of the earth.

**graphics** drawings or reproductions of drawings, maps, pictures, graphs, etc.

**graphs** symbolic representations of information that show quantitative comparisons between two or more kinds of information.

**Greenwich Meridian** point on a map measuring 0° longitude.

## H

**heading** in an outline, a major thought or concept; a title or classification; in a graphic, a word or phrase used to identify or label rows and columns.

**histogram** a graphic in which bars indicate the frequency of data; shows quantitative comparisons; a bar graph.

**homonym** a word that sounds like another word but that has a different meaning.

**humor** something comical or amusing.

**hyperbole** the opposite of understatement; when an author or speaker describes something as being better than it really is.

## I

**idiom** language particular to a group or region.

**image advertising** a type of advertising in which a person, product, or concept is associated with attractive types of people, places, sounds, activities, or symbols.

**imagery** the use of descriptive words to create pictures in the reader's mind as he or she reads.

**implication** a statement which requires you to form a conclusion or inference.

**implied** suggested rather than stated specifically.

**implied main idea** the central thought of a paragraph or passage that is unstated and must be inferred from given details.

**imply** to suggest rather than state specifically.

**inanimate** not living or lifelike.

**inductive logic** the process by which one collects many cases, determines what is common to all of them, and forms a rule or principle which is probably valid.

**inefficient eye movements** any visual problems that affect your reading; may be caused by a physical problem (for example, near- or farsightedness) or by habit (for example, regression or lack of speed).

**infer** to imply or suggest; not stated, must be reasoned from given information.

**inference** an indirectly suggested conclusion; an implication made by reasoning.

**inferred** suggested, not stated.

**informal fallacy** occurs through irrelevant facts, false comparisons, wrong observations, unclear words, and definitions.

**introduction** an initial, short overview or discussion.

**irony** a type of figurative language in which the speaker or writer says one thing but means the opposite.

**irrelevant** not suitable, applicable, or related to a specific subject.

## K

**key** a list of words or phrases giving an explanation of symbols and/or abbreviations used on a map; a legend.

## L

**label** a title or classification; in a graphic, word or phrase used to identify or label rows and columns; a heading.

**language knowledge** what a person knows about how language works; deals with both grammar and context.

**latitude** the distance north & south of the equator, measured in degrees.

**legend** a list of words or phrases giving an explanation of symbols and/or abbreviations used on a map; a key.

**line graph** a graphic used to show quantitative trends for one or more items over time.

**linguistics** the science of language; the study of the nature and structure of language.

**linking verb** one of several verbs that link predicate adjectives and predicate nouns to the subject of a sentence; a being verb.

**listening vocabulary** the words a person understands when he or she hears them being said.

**literal** directly and clearly stated; not inferred or suggested.

**logic** analytical thinking, critical reading; reasoning by looking at the relationship between or sequence of facts or events.

**logical inference** a conclusion that cannot be avoided; for example, if $a = b$ and $b = c$, then $a = c$.

**longitude** the distance east or west, expressed in degrees, between the meridian of a particular place and Greenwich, England.

**long-term memory** permanent memory.

## M

**main idea** the central thought or meaning of a paragraph or passage; may be either implied or stated.

**man-made** manufactured, created, or constructed by human beings (i.e., roads, cities, etc.).

**map** a two-dimensional graphic of a specific location.

**meridian** any of the lines of longitude; a circle on the earth's surface which passes through the geographical poles and any given point.

**metaphor** a form of figurative language that compares two objects without the use of *like* or *as*.

**mnemonics** devices used to improve memory and recall.

## N

**name-calling** making one person, product or concept seem more attractive by using unpopular terms to describe the competition.

**natural** occurring in nature; undeveloped, not man-made (i.e., mountains, rivers, lakes, etc.).

**network** a system of frameworks for a given topic; associated information about a given subject.

**noncomprehensive** an examination that does not cover all materials presented in class over the course of an entire term; an examination covering a set amount of material.

**nonfiction** one of two types of writing; based on fact or truth; written to entertain or inform.

**non sequitur** a conclusion or statement that makes no sense; not supported by facts or preceding information.

**Northern Hemisphere** the part of the earth north of the equator.

**noun** a naming word for persons, places, or things.

## O

**objective** a type of text question in which a student selects the answer from several choices provided by the instructor; included among these are multiple-choice, true-false, matching, and some fill-in-the-blank questions; factual, literal.

**opinion** a judgment or viewpoint.

**order** an organized system for structuring and ranking information; an arrangement or classification by rank, sequence, or quality.

**organization** plan for classifying and structuring information.

**organizational pattern** the order in which the sentences in a paragraph or paragraphs in a passage are written.

**outline** a short organizational figure that shows a pattern of ideas.

**overview** an introduction to or a survey of some chapter, subject, etc., that highlights the major points to be presented.

## P

**part of speech** one of eight grammatical categories into which words have been grouped; nouns, pronouns, verbs, adjectives, adverbs, conjunctions, prepositions, or interjections.

**personification** a type of figurative language in which inanimate objects are given traits or abilities of living things.

**physical map** a map that shows the natural features of a country or region.

**pictorial graph** a graphic that uses symbols to show quantitative amounts; a symbol graph.

**plain folks** a form of advertising in which a person, product, or concept is made to seem more common or natural by associating it with everyday people or situations.

**plot** the supporting structure of a reading selection.

**political map** a map that shows the location of man-made features.

**predict** to say or know in advance.

**prefix** one or more letters attached to the beginning of a base or word to alter the meaning of the base or word.

**premises** facts that lead you to make decisions or draw conclusions.

**preposition** a word that combines with a noun or pronoun to form a phrase that gives information about another word.

**previewing** surveying to get the main idea about something that will be read later.

**primary source** original documents or first-person accounts of an event.

**prime meridian** the point on a map measuring 0° longitude.

**prime study time** the time of day at which you are at your physical and mental best for learning.

**process** an action or operation resulting in an end product.

**proofread** to read over a paper or exam to check for spelling, grammatical, or writing errors.

**propaganda** a form of persuasion.

**punctuation text-based clues** punctuation marks (commas, brackets, parentheses, or dashes) that indicate that the meaning of an unknown word follows directly.

**Q**

**qualitative** pertaining to characteristic features.

**question** the second step of the SQ3R procedure; the act of requesting.

**R**

**rank** data arranged in order of importance.

**rate** degree of speed.

**read** the third step of the SQ3R procedure.

**reading** two-way communication between the reader and the author.

**reading vocabulary** the words a person understands when he or she sees them in written form.

**recite** the fourth step of the SQ3R procedure; to recall main points in order to answer purpose-setting question.

**recreational reading** reading for enjoyment.

**region** a broad geographical area.

**regression** a backward eye movement when reading.

**relationship** the association or kinship between two or more objects.

**relevancy** separating important from unimportant information.

**relevant** suitable, applicable, or related to a specified subject.

**review** the fifth step of SQ3R procedure; a summary or rehearsal of what has been learned.

**rhyme** words that do not begin with the same sound or letter but whose ending sounds are the same.

**Roman numerals** one of the letter symbols, C, D, I, L, M, V, and X combined to denote numbers.

**root** the part of a word that provides essential meaning; a base.

**row** a horizontal arrangement of items.

## S

**sarcasm** a form of irony used to hurt someone's feelings.

**scale of distance** a representation of size or space on maps; indicates the relationship between the distance of one place located on a map and this distance in real life.

**scanning (scan)** reading quickly to find an answer to a specific question.

**scientific data** results from experiments.

**sea level** zero elevation.

**secondary source** second-person accounts of an event.

**senses** means of perceiving outside stimuli; see, smell, taste, touch, hearing.

**sequence** systematic order.

**setting purposes** the result of the questioning stage of SQ3R; allows the active reader to develop goals for reading.

**short-term memory** immediate or brief memory.

**signal words** words which indicate the organizational pattern of a paragraph or passage.

**simile** a form of figurative languaage that compares two dissimilar objects with the use of *like* or *as*.

**skimming** reading quickly to find the main idea of a paragraph or passage.

**solution** the end product of mathematical processes; the answer to a problem.

**Southern Hemisphere** the part of the earth south of the equator.

**speaking vocabulary** the words a person uses in spoken communication.

**specialized vocabulary** words that are used in new (specialized) and unfamiliar ways.

**special-purpose map** a map that highlights some specific natural or man-made feature (i.e., changes in population).

**SQ3R** a reading/study plan developed by Francis Robinson; steps are survey, question, read, recite, and review.

**standardized tests** tests with specified tasks, normed on a reference group drawn from many schools or communities.

**stated main idea** the central thought of a paragraph or passage that is found in the topic sentence of the passage or paragraph.

**stereotypes** standardized mental pictures of someone or something.

**stress** a physical or emotional factor that causes tension; anxiety.

**structural analysis** splitting words into affixes and roots to discover meaning.

**structural irony** implies a discrepancy between what a character expects to get and gets, between what a character thinks and the reader knows, and between what a character deserves and gets.

**study plans** a systematic procedure for the study and recall of what is read.

**subheading** details that support major headings in an outline.

**subject-development pattern** placement of information in a systematic organizational pattern to introduce, summarize, or delineate a topic.

**subjective** a type of test question in which the student must provide an original written answer; a type of test question in which the instructor provides no choice of answers; included among these are essay and some fill-in-the-blank questions.

**suffix** one or more letters attached to the ending of a base or word to alter the meaning of the base or word. The suffix also can alter the part of speech of the word.

**summary** a condensed statement or paragraph that contains only the essential ideas of a longer statement, paragraph, or passage.

**survey** a preview to get the main idea about something that will be read later.

**syllabus** an outline of topics to be covered in a college course.

**syllogism** three statements; two of which are facts with the third being a conclusion.

**symbol** an idea or concept that stands for or suggests another idea or concept by means of association or relationship.

**symbol graph** a graphic that uses symbols to show quantitative amounts; a pictorial graph.

**synonym** a word which has a similar meaning to that of another word.

**synthesis** a process of forming a single body of information by associating and relating data from various sources.

## T

**table** a systematic listing of information in rows and columns.

**task limits** the completion of a specified amount of work.

**technical vocabulary** words that are specific to a content area and have no meaning outside of that area.

**term** specialized vocabulary in a specific subject.

**test anxiety** a physical or emotional factor which causes tension before, during, or after an exam; stress.

**testimonial** a form of advertising in which a famous person recommends a product or concept.

**text** a written publication; another name for textbook.

**text-based context clues** written signals that indicate the meanings of unknown words.

**time** arranged in the order in which it occurs.

**time limits** practicing a skill for a specified amount of time.

**timeline** a graphic outline of sequenced information; a chronology of important dates or events.

**tone** the style or manner of expression in speaking or writing.

**topic** the subject of a passage or paragraph; the general category to which the ideas of the paragraph or passage belong.

**topic sentence** the sentence that expresses the main idea in a paragraph or a passage.

**topography** the surface features of a location.

**trends** directions in which features change; common, contrasting, or unusual features.

**two-eight model** a method developed by Klein (1969) in which complex numerical values are replaced with simpler values to help determine the correct process.

## U

**understatement** when the author or speaker shows size, degree, or seriousness as less than it really is.

## V

**verb** a word that makes a statement about persons, places, or things (nouns); a word that asks questions or gives commands; a word that shows either action or being.

**verbatim recall** remembering a passage exactly as written.

**vicarious** experienced through imagination or indirect participation.

## W

**weasel words** a form of advertising in which a promise is implied.

**writing vocabulary** the words a person uses in written communication.

# INDEX


Acronyms, 110, 492–493
Acrostics, 492–493
Active listening
  for class lectures, 68, 86
  and notetaking, 75–76
  to increase vocabulary, 98
Affixes, 165–166
Allusions, 305
Altitude, 369
Analogy, 122–123
  in inductive logic, 420
  comparisons in reading, 451
Analytical reasoning, 416–417
Antonyms, 115, 120
Arguments, 416
Articles, 455
Assumption, 268

Background knowledge, 67–68
  and notetaking, 77
  gained from the text, 85
  making inferences, 264–265, 268
  in figurative language, 291
  and symbols, 301
  and allusions, 305
  for math word problems, 400–401
  for logic problems, 429
  and previewing, 451
Bandwagoning, 248, 250
Bar graphs, 344–348
Bases, 165
Bias, 248
Boundaries, 369
Browse, 470

Causal connections, 420
Cause-effect pattern, 202–204
  in lectures, 69
Circle graphs, 344, 347–348
Cliches, 295
Column, 342
Comparison/contrast pattern, 202
Comparison text-based clues, 143
Comprehensive, 499
Conclusions, 263–264, 268
  in map reading, 371
  to math problems, 400
  in critical thinking, 416
Conjunctions, 455
Connotations, 101–102
  and opinion, 244
Context, 98, 135
  of allusions, 305
  in maps, 371
  for solving logic problems, 429
Contrast text-based clues, 142
Cope, 487–488
Copyright date, 474
Cramming, 40
Critical reading, 241, 445
  of maps, 371
  for math word problems, 400
Critical thinking, 416
Cross-reference, 305
Curve of forgetting, 74

Deductive logic, 417
Definition text-based clues, 141
Degrees, 368

Denotations, 101–102
Depth, 369
Details, 189
  and subheadings, 13
  in summaries, 34
  and understanding main ideas, 198–199
  in subject-development patterns, 200
  in comparison/contrast patterns, 202
  answers to literal questions, 264
  in topic sentences, 455
Directionality, 401
Distractions
  external, 68
  internal, 69
Distributed practice, 39–40

Elevation, 369
Enumeration/sequence pattern, 200
Equator, 367–368
Etymology, 105
Euphemism, 323
Eustress, 488–499
Example text-based clues, 144
Expert opinions, 246

Fact, 241–243
Fallacy, 425
Fiction, 471
Figurative language, 291
Figures of speech, 291
Flowcharts, 342, 348
Formal fallacies, 425
Format, 464–465
Frameworks, 5–6
  in predicting texts, 7
  while surveying, 8
  development of, 9
  in class lectures, 67
  to derive meanings of new words, 148
  and organizational patterns, 199
  and background knowledge, 265
  and organizing information, 450
  in recreational reading, 470
Framework-based context clues, 148

General vocabulary, 153
Generalizations, 420
Gist, 449
Graphs, 342
Greenwich meridian, 368

Headings, 13, 14, 342
Histograms, 344
Homonyms, 115, 120
Hyperbole, 310

Idiom, 292–293
Image advertising, 248
Imagery, 291
Implications, 264
Implied, 264
Implied main idea, 205–206
  in passages, 215–216
Inanimate, 318
Inductive logic, 420
Inferences, 264, 268
Inferring, 241
Informal fallacies, 425
Introductions, 455
Irony, 310

Key, 346
Kinesthetic perception, 493

Labels, 342
Latitudes, 367
Legend, 346
Line graphs, 344–347
Linking verbs, 141
Literal, 101, 135
  in drawing conclusions, 264
  in figurative language, 291
Location, 492–494
Logic, 416–417
Logical inference, 268
Longitudes, 367

Main idea, 189, 192–193
  and text marking, 27
  and text labeling, 31
  in summaries, 34
  of lectures, 69
  of passages, 195, 198
  and organizational patterns, 199
  and signal words, 204
  from synthesis, 217
  of maps, 371
  and logic, 417
  from skimming, 454–456
Maps, 342, 365–371
  while surveying, 11
  in chapters, 14
  in class lectures, 86
Mental imagery, 492
Meridians, 367
Metaphors, 294–295
  and symbols, 301
Mnemonics, 492
Mnemonigraphs, 493

Name calling, 248, 251
Network, 5–6
  development of, 9
Noncomprehensive, 499
Nonfiction, 471
Non sequitur, 268–269
Northern Hemisphere, 367
Nouns, 455

Objective, 499, 501–504
Opinion, 241, 244
  and persuasive passages, 260
Organizational pattern, 189
  and implied main ideas, 215
Outline, 11–14, 491
  of lectures, 73, 86
  in essay tests, 507
Overlearning, 41
Overview, 11

Parodies, 494
Part of speech, 135–136
Personification, 318
Physical imagery, 492
Physical maps, 369
Pictorial graphs, 344
Plain folks, 248, 251
Plot, 470
Political map, 368–369
Predict, 5
  during lectures, 69
  test questions, 499–500
Prefixes, 165–166
Premises, 416
Preposition, 455
Previewing, 4
  before class lectures, 68
  for recreational reading, 473–474
Primary sources, 243
Prime meridian, 368
Prime study time, 489–490
Proofread, 507
Propaganda, 241, 248–251
Punctuation text-based clues, 141
Puns, 494

Qualitative, 244
Question, 15–16

Rate, 445
Recite, 33–34
Recreational reading, 445
  to increase reading speed, 470–472
Regression, 450
Relevancy, 252–253
Review, 39
Roots, 165
Row, 342

Sarcasm, 310
Scale of distance, 367
Scanning, 445, 449, 454, 464–465
Scientific data, 420
Sea level, 369
Secondary sources, 243
Self-talk, 69
Signal words, 200–201, 204–205
  in comparison/contrast patterns, 202
Similes, 294–295
  and symbols, 301
Skimming, 445, 449, 454–456
  other uses of, 460–461
Southern Hemisphere, 367
Spaced study, 39–40
Special purpose map, 369
Specialized terms, 402
Specialized vocabulary, 153
SQ3R, 4, 456–459
  in active reading, 26
  and summaries, 34
Standardized tests, 511
Stated main idea, 192
  of passages, 195
Stereotypes
  in frameworks, 5
Stress, 487
Structural analysis, 165
  limitations of, 178–179
Structural irony, 310
Study groups, 40
Subheading, 13–14
Subject-development pattern, 200
Subjective, 499, 505–508
Suffixes, 165–166
Summaries, 34–35, 455
Survey, 455
  before skimming, 456–457
  after skimming, 458–459
Surveying, 4
  and frameworks, 8, 10
  of supplementary materials, 15
Syllabus, 67
  for text-independent lectures, 86
Syllogisms, 417
Symbols, 301–302
  in symbol graphs, 346
  in mathematics, 403
Symbol graphs, 344, 346–347
Synonyms, 115, 120
Synthesis, 217–218, 491

Tables, 342
Technical terms, 402
Technical vocabulary, 153
Terms, 73
Test anxiety, 485–489
Testimonial, 248, 250
Text-based context clues, 140, 403
Text labeling, 30–31
  in evaluating information, 39
Text marking, 26–27
  in increasing your understanding, 39
Text structure, 69
Timelines, 342
Tone, 310
Topic, 189
  and main idea, 192
  in subject-development patterns, 200
  and implied main ideas, 206
Topic sentence, 193, 455
Topography, 369
Trends, 343
Two-eight model, 408–409

Understatement, 310

Verbatim recall, 449
Verbs, 455

Weasel words, 248, 251
Word games, 492, 494